
COUNSELING PARENTS OF EXCEPTIONAL CHILDREN

Leroy Baruth

Margaret Burggraf

Special Learning Corporation
42 Boston Post Rd. Guilford, Connecticut 06437

Special Learning Corporation

Publisher's Message:

The Special Education Series is the first comprehensive series designed for special education courses of study. It is also the first series to offer such a wide variety of high quality books. In addition, the series will be expanded and up-dated each year. No other publications in the area of special education can equal this. We stress high quality content, a superb advisory and consulting group, and special features that help in understanding the course of study. In addition we believe we must also publish in very small enrollment areas in order to establish the credibility and strength of our series. We realize the enrollments in courses of study such as Autism, Visually Handicapped Education, or Diagnosis and Placement are not large. Nevertheless, we believe there is a need for course books in these areas and books that are kept up-to-date on an annual basis! Special Learning Corporation's goal is to publish the highest quality materials for the college and university courses of study. With your comments and support we will continue to do this.

John P. Quirk

First Edition

1 2 3 4 5

ISBN No. 0-89568-081-5

SPECIAL EDUCATION SERIES

- ● Autism
- * ● Behavior Modification
- Biological Bases of Learning Disabilities
- Brain Impairments
- ● Career and Vocational Education
- Child Abuse
- Child Development
- Child Psychology
- Cognitive and Communication Skills
- * ● Counseling Parents of Exceptional Children
- Creative Arts
- Curriculum and Materials
- * ● Deaf Education
- Developmental Disabilities
- * ● Diagnosis and Placement
- Down's Syndrome
- ● Dyslexia
- Early Learning
- Educational Technology
- * ● Emotional and Behavioral Disorders
- Exceptional Parents
- * ● Gifted and Talented Education
- * ● Human Growth and Development of the Exceptional Individual
- Hyperactivity
- * ● Individualized Educational Programs
- ● Language & Writing Disorders
- * ● Learning Disabilities
- Learning Theory
- * ● Mainstreaming
- * ● Mental Retardation
- ● Motor Disorders
- Multiple Handicapped Education
- Occupational Therapy
- ● Perception and Memory Disorders
- * ● Physically Handicapped Education
- * ● Pre-School Education for the Handicapped
- * ● Psychology of Exceptional Children
- ● Reading Disorders
- Reading Skill Development
- Research and Development
- * ● Severely and Profoundly Handicapped Education
- Slow Learner Education
- Social Learning
- * ● Special Education
- * ● Speech and Hearing
- Testing and Diagnosis
- ● Three Models of Learning Disabilities
- * ● Visually Handicapped Education
- * ● Vocational Training for the Mentally Retarded

● Published Titles * Major Course Areas

Readings in
Vocational Training For The Mentally Retarded
Special Learning Corporation

CONTENTS

B. Mentally Retarded

C. Behaviorally Disabled

D. Speech, Vision, or Hearing Disabled

E. Orthopedically Disabled

GLOSSARY OF TERMS

after-image Visual impression which remains after a stimulus is removed.

amblyopia ex anopsia Amblyopia acquired through lack of use of the eye.

angular gyrus A cerebral convolution that forms the back part of the lower parietal region of the brain.

apprehensive child A child who approaches most learning tasks by being frightened of anything new, strange, or complex in nature, thus equating learning with anxiety which tends to further confuse and disorganize his thought processes.

asthenopia Dimness of vision without any apparent cause.

astigmatism Defective curvature of the refractive surfaces of the eye as a result of which light rays are not sharply focused on the retina for either near or distance.

assessment Comprehensive appraisal of strengths and weaknesses of a person's learning. Also, assessment refers to the present educational status of the child.

athetosis A form of cerebral palsy marked by slow, recurring, weaving movements of arms and legs, and by facial grimaces.

ataxia A form of cerebral palsy marked by incoordination in voluntary muscular movements.

behavior modification A set of educational procedures designed to influence and develop the occurrence of a wide range of language, social, cognitive , motor, and perceptual behavior patterns.

cataract A condition in which the crystalline lens of the eye becomes opaque for consequent loss of visual acuity.

cerebral palsy Any one of a group of conditions affecting control of the motor system due to lesions in various parts of the brain.

Childhood schizophrenia A childhood disorder characterized by onset after age 5, consisting of unusual body movements, extreme emotional abnormalities, and perceptual distortions.

congenital Present in an individual at birth.

cystic fibrosis A hereditary disease due to a generalized dysfunction of the pancreas.

diplegia Bilateral paralysis affecting like parts on both sides of the body.

Dyslexia Impairment in the ability to read generally believed to be the result of brain lesions.

dysarthria Difficulty in the articulation of words due to involvement of the central nervous system.

dysgraphia Inability to produce motor movements required for handwriting.

emotionally disturbed Characterized by inner tensions and anxiety, there is often a display of neurotic and psychotic behavior, which often interferes with the lives of others.

esophoria Latent tendency of the eye to turn inward

esotropia An observable turning in of one eye (convergent strabismus or crossed eye).

focus Point to which rays are converted after passing through a lens; focal distance is the distance rays travel after refraction before focus is reached.

glaucoma Disease of the eye marked by a mechanical increase in the intraocular pressure causing organic changes in the optic nerve and defects in the visual field.

hemiplegia Paralysis of one side of the body.

herpes simplex Cold sores on cornea.

Hyperactivity Excessive and uncontrollable movement, such as is found in persons with central nervous system damage. Also anxiety. Controllable with drugs or environmental changes.

Hyperkinetic Disorganized, disruptive, and unpredictable behavior; an overreaction to stimuli.

hypertonicity Excessive tension in the condition of a muscle not at work.

iris Colored, circular membrane suspended behind the cornea immediately in front of the lens, which regulates the amount of light entering the eye chamber by changing the size of the pupil.

inadequate immature dimension Often referred to children with characteristics such as inattentiveness, sluggishness, laziness, preoccupation, and drowziness. They often resemble children labeled autistic or prepsychotic.

kinesthesis The sense whose end organs lie in the muscles, joints and tendons and are stimulated by bodily movements and tensions.

laterality The preferential use of one side of the body, especially in tasks demanding the use of only one hand, one eye, or one foot.

Mainstreaming The placement of handicapped students into educational programs with normal functioning children.

meningitis Inflammation of the meninges (the membrane connecting the brain and spinal cord) sometimes affecting vision, hearing, and/or intelligence.

mental retardation Subnormal intellectual development beginning in childhood, resulting in deficiencies in social functioning.

Modality A way of acquiring sensation; visual, auditory, kinesthetic, olfactory, tactile are the most common.

monoplegia Paralysis of one body part.

muscular dystrophy One of the more common primary diseases of muscle. It is characterized by weakness and atrophy of the skeletal muscles with increasing disability and deformity as the disease progresses.

negative reinforcement Behavior which results in the removal or termination of events that are unpleasant in consequence.

ophthalmologist A physician who specializes in diagnosis and treatment of defects and diseases of the eye.

optician Grinds lenses, fits them into frames, and adjusts frames to the wearer.

optometrist A person who examines, measures, and treats certain eye defects by methods requiring no physician's license.

Perception Recognition of a quality without distinguishing meaning, which is the result of a complex set of reactions including sensory stimulation, organization within the nervous system, and memory.

Proximal receptors Touch, smell and taste become most important to autistic patients rather than auditory or visual receptors.

refraction The bending or deviation of rays of light in passing obliquely from one medium to another of different density; the determination of the refractive errors of the eye and their correction by prescription glasses.

sphincter muscle Muscle which contracts to make the pupil smaller.

strabismus Manifest deviation of the eyes so that they are not simultaneously directed to the same object; see heterotrophia.

stye Acute inflammation of a sabaceous gland in the margin of the eyelid due to infection.

tonometer Instrument used in measuring tension or pressure in order to check for glaucoma.

trachoma Chronic contagious conjunctivitis producing loss of vision.

vision The ability to see and interpret what is seen.

visual acuity Sharpness of vision, the ability of the eye to distinguish detail.

Visually handicapped Any degree of disability between 20/200 and average vision of 20/20 with corrective lenses.

Visual-motor The ability to relate visual stimuli to motor responses in an appropriate way.

PREFACE

Much discussion has centered around the need to counsel parents of exceptional children: however, relatively little has been written about how we, as professionals, should go about accomplishing the task. The purpose of this book is to gather into a single volume the articles that seem most relevant to counseling parents of exceptional children. These articles have been written by counselors, psychologists, doctors, professors, speech pathologists, teachers and especially parents. Some articles directly discuss counseling strategies; others provide related information that will aid in the counseling process; and some articles can be used as resources in bibliotherapy with the parents.

The book is divided into two major sections. Section 1 contains an overview of couseling parents of exceptional children and includes articles relating to techniques, model programs, parental concerns, and related research. Section 2 examines the specific exceptionalities of learning disabled; mentally retarded; behaviorally disabled; speech, vision or hearing disabled: orthopedically disabled; and the gifted and talented.

An effort has been made to compile the most appropriate articles regardless of copyright date. After all, the idea of counseling parents of exceptional children is not new; it is just presently receiving some much needed attenion. While most of the articles are very practical in nature, a few research oriented articles have been included to provide an additional dimension. Because of this diversity not every article in this book may be of special interest to each reader; however, readers should select those articles that seem most relevant for them. Also, please bear in mind that numerous articles are applicable to several exceptionalities in addition to the one under which they are listed for organizational purposes in this book.

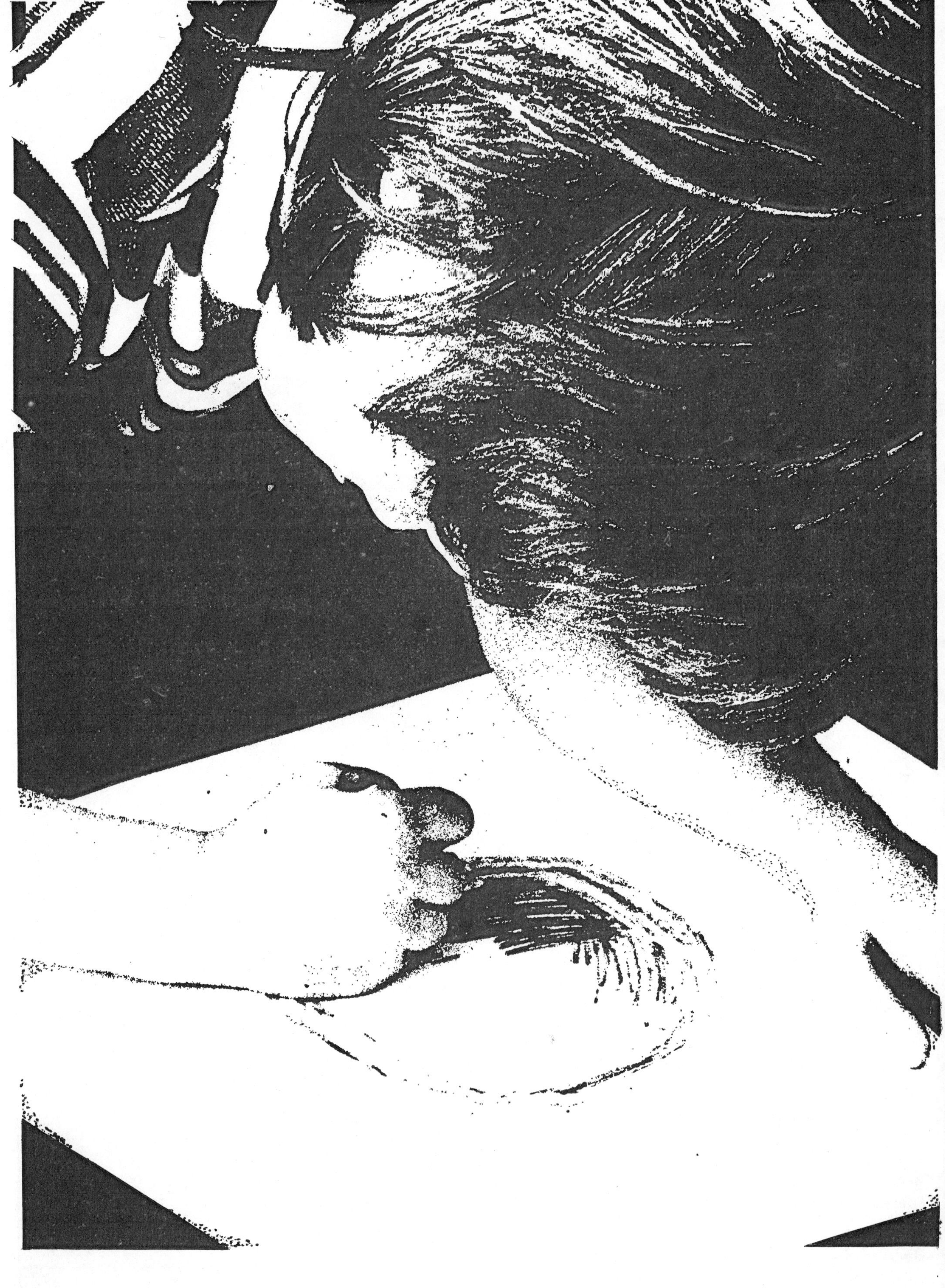

Introduction

Counseling Parents of Exceptional Children

The process that parents go through in attempting to accept their exceptional child includes grief, denial, anger, bargaining, depression, and finally, adjusting to reality. Parents must be encouraged to let others help them in the acceptance process. Other parents of exceptional children who are learning to cope may offer courage and support. Helping professionals need to become familiar with counseling procedures which facilitate the growth and change necessary for the adjustment and coping.

These parents are people and, like all of us, they have a limited tolerance for stress. The helping professional can aid these parents in acquiring relief from the frequent guilt feelings associated with having an exceptional child; they can help parents understand and adapt through extended group counseling experiences; and they can help parents secure financial assistance for education and special needs of their child.

Characteristics a helping professional must acquire are the ability to be empathic and kind, honest, truthful, and to deal with the here and now, not with what was or wasn't or might be at sometime in the future.

There are important roles for schools including working with parent groups, establishing classes and a curriculum which will have meaning to the exceptional child. School professionals must also have a willingness to incorporate the parents' knowledge about their children and how they learn best; it is, after all, the parents who have the greatest understanding and emotional commitment to an exceptional child.

Parents themselves must be open to a helping relationship. They are members of the education team helping the exceptional child grow in the least restrictive learning environment; their choice is in the nature and extent of involvement. Parents are people first and parents of an exceptional child second. Their concerns and needs are human ones. Exceptional children also have responsibilities for being; they too, must experience the struggle, pain, and joy of living. Their choices may be defined by the exceptionality, but their basic needs are human ones.

Parent-Child Relationships: Their Effect on Rehabilitation

John E. Bryant, M.A.
Commack, New York

This paper explores the three parent-child relationships most frequently observed in a clinical setting: acceptance, rejection, and compensation. An attempt is made to show how compensation, which manifests itself out of a combination of acceptance and rejection of the child and his problem, impedes habilitation and rehabilitation. Several suggestions are given regarding early counseling of parents of the handicapped.

Parent-child relationships are many and diverse. From the total spectrum of these relationships, I would like to consider the three most frequently observed in my practice with children who have congenital organic speech disorders: (1) Parents who accept their children and their disorders. (2) Parents who reject their children and their disorders. (3) Parents who compensate for their reactions to their children and their disorders.

This article is concerned mainly with the relationship between the mother and the child because the mother is usually the parent who brings the child to the clinic and there is thus a greater opportunity to observe her behavior towards the child. It would seem reasonable to assume that these observations are true not only for parent-child relationships where the child has a speech disability, but could easily apply to almost any type of disability, including children with specific learning disabilities. No attempt has been made to determine statistics regarding the number of relationships that fit into each category; rather, the information presented is based upon the observations of the writer at a speech clinic, as supported by the literature.

The first category I shall discuss is the relationship between the mother and the child where the mother accepts her child in spite of his speech disorder. This mother has gained the ability to provide for the special needs of her handicapped child while continuing to live a normal life, tending to family and home, civic and social obligations.

It is commonly agreed upon that children who are accepted by their parents generally profit more from speech therapy than do children who are rejected. It is known that "for a child to wish to speak, he must first be able to identify himself with a speaking person who loves him. The speaking person with whom identification is most frequently made is a parent" (Berry and Eisenson, p. 106). Nothing enhances a handicapped child's prognosis more than having parents who have accepted both him and his defect.

As the child progresses in therapy, he begins to seem more like the child described by May (1966) who is free of functional speech defects, who tends to come from a home in which

Parent-Child Relationships: Their effect on Rehabilitation, John E. Bryant, *Journal of Learning Disabilities,* Vol.4, No.6, June/July 1971.

parents have positive feelings towards themselves, accept their child and display emotion toward him, maintain consistent but mild discipline, avoid setting impossible standards for him, and provide ample opportunity for him to speak without being under tension. The most obvious thing about this successful relationship is that the child is treated as a child, not as a handicapped child.

• The second parent-child relationship most often encountered is that in which the mother rejects, or is unable to accept, her handicapped child. Wood (1946) states that mothers of speech defective children are more neurotic than mothers of normal children. It is not my intention to explore the area of what came first, the mother's neurosis or the child's functional defect, but it does seem a safe assumption that organically handicapped children, too, can have neurotic parents.

Hurley stated that "it seems widely accepted that rejecting or hostile parental behaviors adversely influence children's adjustment . . ." (1967, p. 199). Additionally, his study of the effects of parental attitudes on children's intelligence shows that malevolent parental behaviors are causally related to low IQ in children.

The literature supports the thesis that a good many parents do reject their handicapped children. Hurley notes that the love-hate or acceptance-rejection dimension is apparently the most prominent parental behavior variable relevant to the parent-child relationship. McCarthy (1954) indicated that children with functional language disorders have disturbed family relationships, which cause the child to experience emotional insecurity. Kinsetter (1961) reported that the mothers of the stutterers included in his study showed more covert rejection of their stuttering children than did mothers of normal dhildren. Moll and Darley (1960) detected a tendency for mothers of speech retarded children to provide less encouragement for their children to talk, but at the same time displayed higher standards and were more critical of their behavior. Berry and Eisenson stated that it is not likely that many of these parents have conscious wishes to reject their children; however, they reported that "rejection on a level which is conscious or close to conscious is not infrequently found in cases where children have physical abnormalities" (1956, p. 108). The literature also supports Blair's statement that children who are organically handicapped have problems of adjustment to face which are more complicated than those of the average child.

It would seem then, that the rejected organically handicapped child, in addition to his problems in adjusting to himself and his disability, may also have to contend with disturbed family relationships, emotional insecurity, and a depressed IQ; and while receiving less encouragement than the normal child, he will have to absorb more criticism of his behavior.

Unfortunately, the parent who rejects her child and who needs help in learning to love and accept her child, is the parent least seen by the therapist. She does not keep appointments and generally fails to follow through on recommendations made by the therapist or other members of the rehabilitative team. As a result, her attitudes are continued and the prognosis for improving the child's speech is poor.

The third most commonly observed parent-child relationship involves the parent's compensation for her true conscious or unconscious feelings toward the handicapped child. Berry and Eisenson observed in an investigation at the community speech clinic affiliated with Queens College, New York, that the parents of children with retarded speech tended to be unrealistic, rigid, and overprotective. The authors stated that "occasionally we find that parents of children with deformities set about to compensate to the children in the form of continuous instruction and training in the hope of establishing superior ability" (1956, p. 108).

Van Riper feels that "parental reaction to having a physically handicapped child is often one of resentment and guilt. The parents may feel socially stigmatized for having produced a defective child. Rejection or overprotection of the child may result" (1961, p. 513-14).

Judge Jacob Panken of the Domestic Relations Court, New York City, stated, "If parents are inadequate to their responsibilities, their children will be the victims." He went on to say, "Daily we see proof that the mere fact of parenthood does not automatically endow men and women with the knowledge and understanding mothers and fathers need."

Speaking about the mother who did not want to have a baby but had one anyway, a situation analogous in a sense to the mother who wanted a perfect baby but had a physically handicapped one instead, Blair notes that some mothers dislike and reject their babies and that this rejection arouses in them serious feelings of guilt, for mothers are not supposed to dislike their babies. These emotions of hatred toward the babies are repressed and extremely protective attitudes are substituted in their place. Some people may feel that this type of woman is a wonderful mother, but Blair feels that her overprotection makes the child feel insecure and will lead eventually to social maladjustment because the overprotected child is likely to be submissive, anxious, and lacking in self reliance.

I do not believe that a child who is overprotected will benefit from rehabilitative procedures as much as will the child who is accepted by his parents. Considering Brown's example (1936) of a child with infantile speech whose parents and older sister dominated his life by dressing, bathing, and feeding him, by walking him to and from school and by constantly watching his play to prevent him from getting hurt, it becomes apparent that if overprotection can prevent emotional growth and maturity in a normal child, it must also serve to inhibit development in a child who has an organic communication problem.

Fromm, in discussing selfishness, stated that the oversolicitious, dominating mother really has a greedy concern for her child. "While she consciously believes that she is particularly fond of her child, she has a deeply repressed hositility toward the object of her concern. She is over concerned not because she loves the child too much, but because she has to compensate for her lack of capacity to love him at all" (1947, p. 136-7). "Altogether," Fromm continues, "the effect of the 'unselfish' [compensating] mother is not too different from that of the selfish [rejecting] one; indeed, it is often worse because the mother's unselfishness prevents the children from criticizing her. They are put under the obligation not to disappoint her." Children of compensating parents do not mirror the happiness of children who know they are loved and accepted. Instead, they are anxious, tense, and afraid of the mother's disapproval.

The parent who has accepted her handicapped child usually is conscientious about keeping appointments, seeks advice regarding the raising of her child in a normal manner, and follows through on the recommendations of the team.

The rejecting parent "forgets" to keep appointments and rarely calls in advance to cancel appointments. She is not involved in the rehabilitation of the child.

The parent who is compensating for her child's disability is easily recognized. She keeps all appointments, making it clear from her emotional and physical state that she is exhausted. She is rushed, worried about the child's progress, harried about what else she must accomplish before the day's end, and most probably in a bad humor.

The parent who compensates, who attempts to accept her child over feelings of rejection, is often too involved in the rehabilitative program. She is overanxious about progress, suspicious of the quality of the program and of the qualifications of the specialists on the team.

It is interesting to note how the compensating parent will attempt to remove her rejecting attitudes and replace them with the attitudes of acceptance. The resulting attitudes often mirror both acceptance and rejection, and are manifest in behavior that is harmful to the child's emotional stability. These combinations are illustrated in Table I.

The child, if he has any sensitivity at all, senses the tension and begins to associate his mother's emotional state with his physical problem. He begins to feel uncomfortable, knowing that his disability is the root of his mother's unhappiness. The child does not want to contribute further to his mother's turmoil, and this often shows up in his inability to make progress in speech therapy. In his attempt to ease his mother's disordered life and make himself feel more comfortable, he often finds himself unable to cooperate with the therapist, who is one of the many people who keep his mother so busy.

TABLE I.

ACCEPTANCE		*REJECTION*		*COMPENSATION*
love	+	*indifference*	=	*possessiveness*
empathy	+	*selfishness*	=	*sympathy*
forgiveness	+	*fault finding*	=	*overpermissiveness*
gentleness	+	*cruelty*	=	*smothering*
caution	+	*carelessness*	=	*suspicion*
activity	+	*apathy*	=	*overactivity*

Neuhaus, in studying parental attitudes toward deaf children, discovered that as the children grow older, their parents' attitudes become less accepting as they become more aware of the children's limitations. She also stated that it is "reasonable to assume that once this parent-child relationship had been established, it would not change significantly as the child grows old" (1969, p. 725). This is so because many of these mothers are resistant to counseling and significant changes in attitude are rare.

Strickler states that "the accumulated evidence about family interactional patterns suggests that communication barriers and inappropriate role behaviors in the home may contribute to serious difficulties in the child's efforts to adapt to the social milieu of the school classroom. The consequences of such poor social adjustment may be an inhibition of normal learning" (1969, p. 31).

Wellington and Wellington reported that well over half of the underachivers admitted rebelling aginst parental pushing, while almost three fourths said their parents worry a lot about their not studying.

Research has shown that the majority of underachievers come from "good" homes, according to socioeconomic standards. But they are poor homes psychologically because the child is rebelling against his pushing parents and thus accomplishes little. "The community may step in to cure sickness and supply physical needs," states Judge Panken, "but antisocial characteristics learned in early childhood in the home are not easy to eliminate or even to modify." It is apparent, then, that the child who cowers under the wings of compensating parents may not only fail to achieve in a rehabilitative program, but faces the possibility of doing poorly in school and of developing antisocial characteristics that, when combined with his inadequately rehabilitated speech disorder, may cause him to be a handicapped person for the remainder of his life.

I feel that even in those cases where rehabilitation teams and centers have psychologists and social workers on their staffs, the clinician who has the most frequent contact over long periods of time with the parents of handicapped children must assume much of the responsibility for guiding the parents toward a healthy acceptance of their children.

Early counseling may assist the parents in understanding the following:

(1) They have a responsibility to their children, not to themselves, and that if the rehabilitation program is to be at all successful, they must allow their children the emotional freedom to profit from the program.

(2) They must realize that the program is not designed to prove that they are worthy parents, but rather to help their children in their adjustment to society.

(3) They must maintain a consistent and accepting attitude and not become discouraged or overzealous by slow or rapid progress.

(4) They must understand that their physically handicapped children have lifelong afflictions and that it is the parents' responsibility to help prepare the child for a life that is as near normal as possible.

If improved parent-child relationships can be achieved early, the result will be better emotional adjustment for both parent and child, and maximal success of the rehabilitation program. This, I believe, is the most exciting challenge in rehabilitating the handicapped child, for if this is handled well, therapy stands a better chance of providing real help for the children.

Coping With Our Children's Disabilities: Some Basic Principles

Myra R. Behmer

As I watched my ten-year-old son floundering on the floor where he had collapsed, unable to get up, I breathed an instinctive prayer. Then I went quickly about the business of getting him to the doctor and sending word to his father at work.

Only as Mark's illness (post-infectious encephalitis) progressed did we begin to realize — mercifully, in slow stages — what was involved for all of us. His disability was especially traumatic because it was sudden and its effects were utterly devastating. But we were not altogether inexperienced. The asthma suffered by our eldest son Eric had laid its iron grip over all the years of his childhood, shaping his body, limiting his activities and molding his personality to a degree that we still may not be fully aware of. Each of these illnesses was more than we could have handled without help.

In coping with our sons' disabilities, we came to rely on several basic principles. Some we discovered for ourselves; others we came to understand through the guidance of caring professionals.

> Grief for the perfect child one has lost is a genuine part of parents' feelings.

Grief

Grief for the perfect child one has lost is a genuine part of parents' feelings. A teacher who knew Mark put it into words as she watched him struggling about on crutches. "It seems twice as heartbreaking," she said, "when I remember how he used to climb everything in sight!"

And why shouldn't we have grieved? He was flesh of our flesh and, of course, we envisioned only the best for him.

But the parent who loses a child in death does not forget the one still living. So we relinquished the child who "climbed everything in sight" and turned our love to the child who now lived on crutches.

Guilt and Shame

Often more devastating even than grief, guilt is one of the most destructive feelings for parents of disabled children to contend with. It crops up everywhere. How many anguished parents have cried, "Why would God do such a thing to an innocent child?" Looking for somewhere to place the blame — perhaps even on one's spouse — is one of the ways the mind protects itself from stress greater than it can bear. But the mind can let go of this "self-preserving" shield and begin to deal with the fact of disability without the need to blame.

We would be unfit parents if we did not accept our rightful responsibility for the welfare of our children. But let's listen to the assurances of our doctor or pastor and accept the evidence of our own good sense! If we actually have been at fault in some way, counseling can help us accept that fact, learn from it — and let it go.

The initial conquest of guilt will probably not be the last. A subsequent illness or accident can revive guilty feelings.

One day my stomach turned over as a neighbor helped Mark up the steps, his knees buckling and blood dripping from cuts and scrapes all over one side of his face and forehead. We should *never* have allowed him to ride a bike after his illness, no matter how hard he begged, I thought desperately!

And yet, when I had time to think, I realized that Mark had been hurt not because I had let him ride his bike but because he had been riding it in an unsafe place *against explicit orders*. He had chosen to take a dangerous chance and, fortunately, the price had been only high enough to teach him caution.

Common sense told me that as therapy and as an instrument of independence, the value of the bike outweighed its potential for danger. My feelings about Mark's bike riding were not unlike my feelings about his older brother Carl's playing football after he had been hospitalized with an injured knee — except that Mark's disability intensified my personal sense of guilt.

Even the most loving and unself-conscious parent may sometimes feel a pang of shame when his disabled child confronts the tactless stares of strangers. Since my child was and is, in some sense, an extension of myself, I naturally felt a need for him to be admirable so that I could feel good about myself. When recognized and understood, parents' feelings of shame can be turned to empathy for our children's hurt.

Helplessness and Frustration

Frustrations create tension. When I used to notice the way Mark's brother Eric would hold his shoulders — the pounding of the pulse in his neck, the asthmatic whistling and bubbling in his chest as he struggled to breathe — a surge of anger would flow over me. I became snappish and impatient with everyone. Even Eric!

I was reacting in the most natural way to the horrible frustration I felt at my helplessness to stop his suffering. It was a long time before I understood this anger myself; how could I have explained it to him?

We became as well informed as we could about the disabilities as well as the methods and aims of treatment prescribed for our sons. We were working as an important, even central part of a professional team. Knowing that we were effective greatly helped us to overcome our feelings of helplessness.

It is also natural to feel frustrated by the extra work and the restriction of activities caused by a child's disability. And therefore angry! When my sons' care became too burdensome, I couldn't handle these feelings constructively. I had to find someone to share the work and restriction, for the boys' sakes as well as for mine. Here, their father played an important role in their care, to the benefit of all of us. A close relationship with the father is just as critical for the disabled child as it is for the healthy one. And the father needs to know that his presence, not just his paycheck, is important to his family!

Matter-of-factness

We found it helpful to "keep it clinical." We used medical terms whenever possible in speaking of our sons' disabilities, and we taught all our children to do so. This simple device tended to impersonalize the affliction, to designate it as a medical condition shared by others. It also implied that something could be done about it. We knew that there was as yet no cure for Mark's condition, but at least there was therapy and relief for some of the symptoms.

Taking another cue from medical personnel, we spoke matter-of-factly of our children's disabilities both within the family and with outsiders. Each disability was a condition to be lived with. As we learn to live with the force of gravity without self-consciousness, we can learn to do the same, for the most part, with disability.

A matter-of-fact attitude not only relieves parents and children, it does much to set others at ease. Social contacts are made easier and more rewarding for everyone.

Sense of Humor

A sense of humor does wonders for keeping things in perspective. When Eric was so ill, a grandmotherly neighbor said to me more than once, "You can either laugh or cry, but laughing is more fun!"

In the face of serious disability, a sense of humor will hardly come naturally. But it can be developed and encouraged and we, at least, have found it well worth the effort.

My pediatrician once chided me gently for my overanxiousness. "Relax" he said with a fatherly twinkle. "He'll grow up in *spite* of you, not *because* of you!"

This memory, with its note of humor, often comes back to me in times of stress. It has been comforting to know it doesn't *all* depend on us. There is a potential for development within each of our disabled children that will carry them at least part way to normal living.

A Balanced Life

I once read that a child's toy held too close to the eye will block out the view of a mountain. If held too close to the mind's eye, a child's disability can negate the life of the whole family. It is essential to develop perspective toward it.

One way we did this was to set about learning what is "normal" in family life and child development, and then simply to consider what differences our sons' disabilities might make. Most of the differences turned out to be matters of degree.

A marriage normally comes under some strain with the arrival of a child because of the new responsibility of the parents, especially the mother, to recognize and attend to the child's needs. When the child is disabled, the strain is greater but not basically different. It can be handled in basically the same ways.

Once we had begun to come to terms with such issues, we began building a balanced life for ourselves. We each joined in at least one community or church activity and got out together as a couple as regularly as possible.

As a home-bound mother, I became aware that

several aspects of my daily life were especially important to me. Time spent on personal grooming paid dividends in heightened morale. Attention to diet and physical fitness enhanced the work I could accomplish. Interests pursued at home made me a more interesting person.

My whole family benefited from my increased well-being. Because I had satisfied some of my own basic needs, I was able to do much more for my disabled children when I was with them.

> . . . my experience has convinced me that . . . a parent's first duty is to herself.

Self-acceptance

My main point may seem rank selfishness to some parents. Yet, my experience has convinced me that, beyond immediate medical care and such assurance and support as we are able to give our children, a parent's first duty is to herself.

For thousands of years we have been told "Love thy neighbor as thyself," and for thousands of years we have been putting the cart before the horse. Only as we learn to accept and love ourselves can we accept and love others. Only if we accept and love ourselves with our own imperfections can we be of help to our disabled children with theirs.

Whether in spite of us or because of us, our boys have all grown up. In some things we failed. In others we simply endured. But in many more, with God's help, we succeeded.

SUCCESS FOR CHILDREN

BEGINS AND CONTINUES AT HOME

Dorothy Rich

Mrs. Rich is the founder and director of The Home and School Institute, Washington, DC.

An old-fashioned "innovation" is beginning to sweep across education land. The educational research of the past decade, from the headline making studies of Bloom, Coleman and Jencks to the lesser known but significant early childhood studies, has confirmed what good families and teachers have known and practiced all along. The "innovation" is the home, any home, and the message is that families are the first and most important teachers of their children. The home is the critical make-or-break educational institution in children's lives, determining their future school success. And much as we might have hoped to the contrary—not even the best school can do the job alone.

Some families and probably too many teachers have been lulled in the past few years into a "let the schools do the job" attitude, forgetting about the work that needs to be done at home.

Putting across this old (but new) message and putting it into actual practice in homes and classrooms throughout the country is the work of The Home and School Institute, a nonprofit, Washington-based educational organization, offering graduate education programs in conjunction with Trinity College and Catholic University.

The action goal of all HSI programs is to raise children's abilities as learners and to build adult competencies as teachers—a new breed of teachers equipped with a wide variety of specific, easy, no cost ways that share educational accountability between home and school.

A core component of all HSI programs is the design and use of Home Learning Activities. All participants—teachers, principals, parents, teenagers—prepare recipe-style activities to help families become more effective teachers of their children at home. The big difference between HSI Home Learning and typical schoolwork is that HSI activities are designed to use the resources of the home and the community; they are not typical schoolwork, even though they concentrate on the basic 3-R skills.

Success For Children Begins and Continues at Home, Dorothy Rich, *Momentum* December 1976. ©Journal of the National Catholic Educational Association, Washington D.C.

1. INTRODUCTION

Since 1965, when the HSI parent programs began, Home Learning recipes have been prepared and tested in homes from kindergarten right through the secondary grades. It has been shown that family members don't need a license or a college background to be good home teachers; they don't need fancy equipment or even a lot of time. They have what they need: the materials available around any home and the desire to help their children achieve. HSI's role with educators in the programs at Catholic University and at Trinity College is to help the schools help families mobilize and express their abilities and resources.

H.E.L.P. Home Educational Learning Program

During the school year 1974-75, eight first grade classes—218 children—participated in an HSI Washington, DC, area study—the Home Educational Learning Program (H.E.L.P.)—designed to find out if sending home a series of Home Learning Activities would increase student achievement in reading and math over a control group of classes which did not experience this "treatment."

The treatment consisted of eight activities describing ways that the family working together at home could reinforce and supplement reading and math; they were definitely not typical schoolwork.

Each activity was written "recipe-style" on one sheet of paper. They were short, easy activities, meant to be done while the family was working at "real-world" tasks such as shopping for groceries, cooking dinner, washing the car. Materials involved included grocery lists; newspaper sports news, cardboard boxes, soup cans—ordinary items found in any home. Anyone over the age of ten—brothers, sisters, grandparents, friends—all could work with the first grader on the activity.

One in the series of activities, designed by the teachers in the HSI/Trinity School and Parent-Community Involvement program, was sent home from school (preceded only by a letter of explanation) every two weeks for a period of 16 weeks. This design was developed so that it could be completely replicable by any teacher or school system; it involved no extra monies, no extra personnel, and very little time. No additional meetings of any kind were set between parents and teachers. All participation was to be voluntary with no effect on the child's in-school grades.

The classes involved the entire Washington Archdiocese area from inner city to suburb. Two classes in the treatment group had a majority of Black children; one class in the control group was composed of all Black children. (The study did not set out to test differences between Blacks and whites in reacting to the treatment.) The teachers in the study had volunteered to be part of the project: half were randomly assigned to the treatment group, half to the control.

The treatment group of first graders using the HSI home-based activities did achieve significantly higher scores in reading (at the .05 level of significance) than the classes in the control group. They did not however achieve significantly higher scores in the area of mathematics.

Although the study did not set out to test for differences in effect between Black and white students, a look at the data made it clear that there were differences. Further examination revealed that the predominantly Black classes in the treatment group did significantly better than the predominantly Black class in the control group in both reading and mathematics. More research using larger samples of Black and white students will be needed to examine these differences.

All the families in the study did approximately the same number of activities—6.5 out of the 8 offered. Of the 89 families in the treatment group, 79 families did five or more of the activities.

The math activities were done more often than the reading ones. The data suggests that people tend to do short (under 15 minutes) math activities over longer (over 15 minutes) reading activities.

Mothers far outdistanced fathers and "others" in their involvement with the children at home. The "others" (who could be anyone in the home or community 10 years of age or older) worked substantially more with the children than did the fathers. Only mothers participated in all eight activities.

This HSI study has pointed to one possible strategy to help teachers help parents and others in their roles as teachers at home. Wider research is needed in this area, so that a smorgasbord of such strategies can be made available across the country for teachers and parents. The survey of the existing data on the parent-as-tutor model shows that something is happening to raise the achievement of children when parents work with their children at home in school-related activities. It appears that a lot of strategies within this particular model "work." They work, that, is, when they are put into action. In order to put these research models into practice, educators will want to consider incorporating into their daily programs home outreach strategies to assist parents as educators, to build a working educational partnership and thus to enhance the entire school-community relationship.

The particular contributions of the Home Learning Lab treatment to the body of research data now emerging is the delineation of one plan for practical action by the schools to help families express their valuing of education and to build the motivation and achievement of the child. When this can be effected without additional funds, staff or time, it offers the potential of being a realistic plan that can be implemented in the context of immediate schooling and family needs.*

In 1975-76, HSI began on-site training programs for educators away from its home base in Washington. Thus far, these programs have taken place in Fresno, CA, at Loyola College in Baltimore, MD, and in Benton Harbor, MI.

It is in Benton Harbor that the HSI research with the archdiocesan schools is being translated into a city-wide program for the first graders in the Title I public schools. Teachers and parents working together in Benton Harbor designed the Home Learning Activities. Results on this 1976-77 school year action research program will be available in the summer of 1977.

Parents at home don't have to wait for their schools to start sending out Home Learning Activities. The home, any home, is an incredible learning place. Here is a sampling of HSI tested activities. The learning place, as an organizing principle, is used to make it easier for the family. The use of particular rooms in the home and areas around the community provides a central reference point so that the resources already in those places can be most effectively used.

The activities that follow have been selected because they are easy, take little time, use ordinary no-to-low cost household materials. The emphasis is on basic skills—reading, writing, arithmetic, science—for children from about ages four to nine. These are approximate ages; whatever individual children are ready for and appear interested in, parents can feel free to do. And parents and teachers can feel free to adapt these ideas to make them easier or harder—whatever is needed to do the job of enhancing family learning. Older brothers and sisters, aunts and uncles, neighbors and friends are all part of the family and are encouraged to work with the children. These activities may be used along with normal household routines: the parent working in the kitchen or relaxing in the living room with the child for a few minutes can teach science or reading in an informal, at-home way as families learn together.

*Further details on this study, completed as an EdD dissertation, are available from HSI, Trinity College, Washington, DC 20017. Dr. John Olsen, NCEA, was the major advisor on this study.

The Kitchen

Reading

Hidden Letters. All around the kitchen, from the cupboard to the refrigerator, from the stove to the sink, there are LETTERS: A's, B's, F's, P's. On the soup cans, on the cat food, on the cereal box, even on the soap—there are letters. Make a game of finding these letters: ask children (without tearing up the place, of course) to find five A's or three C's or any number of letters or combinations of letters appropriate to the child's background and current skills. Start easy and build up to more difficult letters to find. Children can then write the letters on paper or just share the objects on which the letters had been "hidden." You're building reading observation skills as well as having fun toghether.

Cooking Up Directions. You don't just cook a "dish"—you have to read directions to know what comes first, second and so on. Select a simple recipe with the child, perhaps jello, instant pudding, or canned soup. On every package is a set of directions; either read them aloud to the pre-reading child or ask the young reader to do it on his own. Follow the directions step by step—enjoy the job of coming up with the product and reading at the same time.

Writing

Telephonitis. Even very young children can learn to dial a telephone. This is number and reading practice—left to right reading of numbers. Make a list of the numbers the child can read and dial on his own: weather, grandmas, friends who will listen and whose kids you're willing to hear from, too.

Day-by-Day Calendar. Personalize any calendar—be it store-bought, give-away or homemade from scratch. Have children fill in the blanks with notes on the weather, who's going where, birthdates; even write morning messages on the calendar—notes to one another in the family on what to do today, or just to say "hello."

Subject Bounce. Over a fast breakfast or a sit down dinner, play this "talk" game that prepares children for putting their thoughts into writing. Toss out a subject, starting with simple ones that children know about—summer, friends, breakfast, school. The child then comes up with a statement about it. "Summer is the best season" or "friends like the same thing you do." As children build sophistication, their subjects and statements become more sophisticated, too. These are what HSI calls "umbrella" statements for essay writing because they have to cover all of the material that comes underneath them.

Mathematics

Egg Carton Counter. Take an old egg carton and write numbers in the bottom of each section. Use anything—little pieces of paper to pennies—to match the number in the section with the right number of papers or pennies. Use for straight matching or pitching game.

Science

Ice Is Nice. Here's a freezing and melting experiment that's cool. Do this while preparing cold drinks or setting out the family meal. Put water into an ice tray and set into the freezer: How long does it take to freeze? Try this with different levels of water in different sections of tray. Set out ice cubes on the table: How long do they take to melt? Why are they melting? Put them in different places around the room: Do they melt faster in some places than in others? Ice offers lots of good scientific thinking and questions.

Living/Family Room

Reading

Find the Letters/Find the Numbers. Get those scissors out and moving. Find certain letters and combinations of letters; the ads and headlines with their big, bold print are excellent targets. Have youngsters cut out the appointed letters or words and paste them on shirt cardboards for all to see and admire.

Phonics Bingo Games. Set up cardboard grids with beginning consonants on shirt cardboards. Start with the easier ones: B, P, T, S, R, D, M, N. Keep the grids simple at first, with perhaps three or four letters. Call out the sounds for BINGO—use words, B-bat, R-rat. Ask players to cover the letters called. Make the games more complex as child's skills grow.

Writing

Scrambled Sentences. Take those newspapers and magazine paragraphs and cut up the sentences, put into jumbled order and work together to rearrange into logical order. This helps give children the feel of an orderly progression of thoughts—beginning, middle, end—and conveys the "sense" of paragraphing.

Mathematics

Catalog Shopping Spree. Let's say you have $25 (hypothetical) dollars to spend. How will you spend it? Look through a new or old mail order catalog and select your purchases, add them up, see what you have left. Have you overspent? How do other members of the family decide to spend their money? Compare and contrast purchases.

TV Watching

Cue Me In. Use the TV schedule to make selections about what and when to watch: don't be an indiscriminate viewer. Have children make their choices to fill up an hour or two of their regular viewing. Stick to a time limit and if children are spending too many passive hours in front of the TV, wean them away with a shorter and shorter time limit each week. Involving children in making choices about what they will watch cuts down on their need to watch everything.

TV and the World. Tie current events and map lore with TV watching. The daily news contains items from all over the world. By posting a world map next to the TV set, children can immediately look up references to world news spots. Keep reference books close by too—books like the world almanac and dictionaries. These offer tidbits of knowledge when children's curiosity is high.

Bathroom

Reading

Label, Label. Yes, Virginia, there is reading matter in the bathroom and it's not in magazines. Reading is all around on the medicine labels, the cleanser labels, etc. In fact, these are the very words that children have to be taught to read carefully. Spend some time with the children as they take their baths or brush their teeth to read these labels carefully. This can be a matter of life and death.

Writing

Bathroom Tasks. The child who forgets to brush his/her teeth will forget less often with a list beside the sink (written in the child's own indelible-ink hand) that says, "Brush your teeth," and lists all other needed bathroom tasks such as clean up sink after use, flush tiolet, pick up clothes.

Mathematics

Weigh Me. Bring out that bathroom scale and start weighing—anything and everything. Have the child make some guesses first about how heavy he/she thinks different things are, including his own body and parents' too. Weigh the wastebasket, weigh the clothing just taken off, weigh a full glass of water.

Bedroom

Reading

Dress Me and Body All (vocabulary builders). There are words that attach to clothing—skirt, blouse, sock, shoe—and words for body parts—foot, arm, head, knee. The bedroom is a fine place to learn these words: Say the words aloud as clothes go off parts of the body, print the words on large pieces of paper and label clothes in closets and drawers. A large sheet of brown paper with child's silhouette on it can be tacked to a bedroom wall to carry the words for parts of the body, and it's comforting for the child going to bed to see "himself."

Writing

Our Own Storybooks. "Every child an author" is the motto of this activity. Supply children with four white pages folded and stapled together with colored front and back pages. Preschool children can draw the text for adults to write. Elementary schoolers can both draw and write the stories. The child who needs some ideas to get started may be inspired by reminders of a recent trip, a person he knows, the beauties of nature, a real-life storybook known and loved. Keep these stories on a family shelf and share on special occasions. They're lovely reminders of that early learning time in a child's life.

Yard/Neighborhood

Reading

A Trip to the Supermarket. Grocery shopping can be an educational adventure, especially if it includes buying items so that the child can do some of his own cooking. Decide on a dish the child can cook—a pudding, a salad, a sandwich. Help the youngster write a list of what's needed: the child who writes can do his own list; younger ones can dictate. First check the cupboard to see what supplies are already on hand.

Reading in the World. STOP, GO, BUS, PARKING, DRINK COCA COLA—reading is all around us all the time. While riding along in a car or a bus, read the signs aloud and encourage children to sing them out as they see them. It makes time fly and improves reading skills.

Science

How Does Your Garden Grow? Every child can enjoy the adventure of growing things. From an indoor paper cup to a window box to a small plot to vast acreage, gardening is a real possibility for everyone. Start with seeds to get the real joy from the soil: green beans will almost always come through for you and carrot tops like nothing better than to show off the green growth. Measure the achievement of the plants, feed them, eat them. It's a creative experience as well as a scientific adventure.

Writing

Community Map. Large wrapping paper, a ruler, some magic markers are all that is needed for this survey of the community. The child draws his home, the school, the corner, the store and, in putting this to paper, develops a sense of local community, what is located where, the names of the streets.

Mathematics

The Gas Station/Math Quiz. How many gallons of gas did we need? What was the cost per gallon? How many miles do we get per gallon? How many pounds of air in a tire?

Scores of Chores

There are 3-R skills built into many a home chore . . . mainly because what is being learned by the child is that he/she is needed, an integral force in the home, a doer, able to achieve and to accomplish things. This is what makes the difference for school related skills as well. So, start early and keep a consistent schedule of work responsibilities around home. Brighten up drudgery with little touches that speed the work and build in enjoyment.

Treasure Hunt Cleaning. At the end of the dusting and vacuuming, hide an object to be found. This can be a reward (a movie ticket, a book, a dime or a piece of candy) or it can just be an object to find. This adds a certain excitement to the cleaning process.

Clearing the Dishwasher/Putting Away the Groceries. These may seem like chores but they're really classification skill builders: plates with the same sized plates, soups with soups. Math minded families may want to number their kitchen cabinets to be sure things are kept in order.

Talking

Talk about the heat of the stove and the cold of ice; talk about the big and little lamps; talk about the colors of the chairs, the shapes of dishes. This is the heart of the educational process. It's where it all begins with the family, in any home, using all the materials and the imagination at hand. It doesn't cost money, it doesn't take much time, and it makes all the difference in the world in the attitudes and achievements of children.

Making Contact: A Parent-Child Communication Skill Program

Care Terkelson

Care Terkelson is a counselor at Mae E. Reynolds Elementary School, Baldwinsville, New York.

A major source of family problems is ineffective communication between parents and their children. Parents and children often feel misunderstood, frustrated, and discouraged in their attempts to communicate with each other. Recently, public school counselors have attempted to educate parents in more effective methods of communication (Dinkmeyer & McKay 1974; Downing 1974; Frazier & Matthes 1975). Results of these experiences have suggested that when parents are brought together for discussions and training in communication skills more effective relationships within the family can be achieved. There have been few reports, however, describing either the programs involving the development of communication skills for both parents and their children or the results of such programs on parent-child relationships. Because communication problems within families are relational, one might expect that programs involving both parents and their children would lead to greater improvements than would programs focused only on parents. With this in mind, I decided to develop a communications skill program oriented toward both parents and their children. This article describes that program and its preliminary results on parent-child relationships.

The program consisted first of parents and children participating in six, approximately two-hour sessions that were aimed at developing communication skills. The two groups then jointly participated in an additional six sessions to practice the same skills they had learned separately. Parents were requested to participate with a child of intermediate school age (grades 4 through 6). The enrollment was limited to a parent and child from each family; six parents and six children participated in the program.

An adaptation of Brownstone and Dye's (1974) Communication Questionnaire for Parents and Adolescents was used to evaluate the effectiveness of the program. It was administered both to parents and their children before and after their participation in the program.

Parent Sessions

Session I: Introductions, overview of course, existing communication patterns. A brief overview of the sessions was presented, and parents were introduced to each other through Pfeiffer and Jones' (1972) exercise, "getting acquainted triads." After triads were formed, each member told the other two as much about himself or herself as he or she comfortably could. The other two members then reported what they had heard the member say.

Next, in order to ascertain existing communication skills, we used an exercise called "recognizing ineffective messages" (Gordon 1973). Situations were read along with messages sent by parents. For example, if the situation was read as "Child is disturbing you because he is getting attention of your guests by turning somersaults, the mother might say, 'You little show off' " (Gordon 1972, p. 311). The group was asked to explain ineffectiveness of the parents' messages, using Gordon's "Twelve Typical Roadblocks to Communication"—ordering, warning, moralizing, advising, lecturing, judging, praising, name-calling, interpreting, reassuring, probing, and withdrawing.

Finally, to amplify awareness of nonverbal messages in the communication process, parents were shown a series of photographs illustrating a variety of feelings; each photograph was discussed in terms of the feeling being expressed by the person in it.

Session II: Listening to children. Parents were introduced to active listening, an activity during which one tries to understand what another person is feeling and the message he or she is trying to get across. One communicates this understanding by sending the message back in one's own words for the sender's verification. According to Gordon (1973, p. 53), "The receiver does not send a message of his own—such as evaluation, opinion, advice, logic, analysis, or question. He feeds back only what he feels the sender's message meant—nothing more, nothing less."

At the beginning of the session, I outlined the steps for listening actively, using a tape of an actual parent-child exchange to demonstrate the steps. Parents then participated in the exercise, "listening for feelings" (Gordon 1973), which consists of the leader reading statements that a child might make and the parents identifying the feeling being communicated by the words.

Next, parents were divided into triads, with one person talking about a problem he or she had with his or her child, another actively listening, and a third observing. Roles were switched so that each person had an opportunity to practice the skill.

Session III: Sending "I-messages." This session dealt with messages the parent sends when he or she "owns the problem," which Gordon (1973) refers to as "I-messages." I-messages are non-blaming descriptions of what the other person did or is doing. They also specify the concrete, tangible effects on the person sending the message. For example, if a father wants to read the paper and the child keeps climbing on his lap, an appropriate I-message would be, "I can't read the paper and play too. I really feel irritated when I can't have a little time alone to relax and read the paper" (Gordon 1973, p. 313). After a brief theory presentation, participants were asked to respond with I-messages to situations presented by Gordon (1973).

Next, the parents role played situations proposed by the leader and the parents themselves. Two parents would volunteer to do the role play, and the other parents would communicate their observations of the role play, particularly in terms of "I-messages."

Session IV: Resolving conflicts. This session centered around the theme of resolving conflicts between parents and children. Procedures for dealing with conflict were outlined according to Gordon (1973, p. 237) as follows:

1. Identifying and defining the conflict.
2. Generating possible alternative solutions.
3. Evaluating the alternative solutions.
4. Deciding on the best acceptable solution.
5. Working out ways of implementing the solutions.
6. Following up to evaluate how it worked.

In order to clarify this procedure for dealing with conflict, each participant wrote a letter to "Ann Landers" stating a problem situation. After forming dyads, the participants applied the steps in resolving the conflict for the two letters they received. Group discussion followed.

Session V: Dealing with value collisions. This session focused on helping parents recognize their individual value systems as distinct from those of each other and of their children. The group then briefly discussed the valuing process based on Simon, Howe, and Kirschenbaum's (1972) text. The leader pointed out that when values are different from each other, conflicts could be resolved through the problem-solving techniques introduced at the previous session. Two value clarification exercises were used to help the parent clarify their own values: "changing values" (Hamlin 1975) and "values voting" (Simon, Howe & Kirschenbaum 1972).

Session VI: Review. During the final session, we reviewed the skills presented in the first five sessions.

Children's Sessions

Session I: Introduction, overview of course, existing communication patterns. Objectives of the program were outlined, and children were introduced to each other through a "getting acquainted" exercise described by Malamud and Machover (1970). In this exercise, each participant selected a meaningful, personal possession, displayed it to the others, and related its history and the feelings associated with it. Each child then interviewed three other members of the group using the form presented by Fischer (1972), which includes such items as their favorite television program, pet, and dessert. An art activity followed in which the children were asked to build something out of construction paper that reflected their personalities (Johnson 1972). After the introductions, each child took a turn at being "it," while the others reflected what they had learned about that person.

The leader outlined and gave examples of Gordon's (1973)

"Typical Twelve Roadblocks to Communication." The leader pointed out that they, too, set up roadblocks when talking to their parents. To introduce the idea that their parents might be sending nonverbal messages, photographs on moods and emotions were shown. The children then played a game of charades to see if they could determine what others were trying to communicate.

Session II: Listening to parents. Before introducing the skill of active listening, we read Berger's (1971) *I Have Feelings*, a book that emphasizes that people have deep feelings and that at times it's difficult to communicate those feelings. Next, a series of sensitivity cards (Argus Communications 1975) were presented to heighten awareness of other people's needs, feelings, and values. The cards depict interpersonal situations and ask children what they would do in the situation described. The children were then asked to identify and react to an adaptation of the "listening for feelings" exercise used with the parents. The demonstration tape on active listening was played, and the meaning of active listening was explained. The children then took turns in listening actively to the leader present problems to them, after which they took turns presenting a problem they faced, while the others actively listened.

Session III: Sending "I-messages." An explanation of I-messages and their value was outlined for the children. They were then asked to respond by role playing situations presented on the sensitivity cards (Argus Communications 1975). The children then presented their individual problems to the group, while the others sent I-messages.

Session IV: Resolving conflicts. The same procedures for resolving conflicts were outlined for this group as in the parent group. The conflict of a child being burdened with household chores was role played, and a letter tc "Salty Sam" was written. In order to clarify the steps defined earlier, the children brainstormed possible solutions to each problem and made a decision on implementing one of the solutions.

Session V: Dealing with value collisions. The children were each asked to make a values name tag, on which they were to describe themselves and draw pictures of what they enjoyed doing alone and with others. In an exercise called "value awareness" (Hamlin 1975), each child listed five personal values. Next, the children indicated in writing how they felt each value benefited them. The leader stressed that although children's values may and often do differ from those of their parents, both parties still might be able to settle problem situations.

Session VI: Review. The final session was spent reviewing the skills presented in the previous sessions.

Parent-Child Sessions

Session I: Introductions. To help each parent-child pair feel at ease with one another in the group, both were asked to draw or write something on an old T-shirt that would make the other person laugh (Scholastic Dimensions 1973). Each pair then devised three interview questions to ask another pair that would help reveal some pleasurable things about them and their family. After questions were formulated, participants interviewed each other in groups of four. All the participants then assembled into one large group and introduced each other (the parent from one family introduced the child from the other family; the child introduced the parent from the other family).

In order to clarify interests within each pair and to see what the group might have in common, an art activity was performed. Each pair received a large sheet of paper, which they divided into three sections. In section one, the parents drew a picture of something they liked to do; in another section, the children drew a picture of something they liked to do; in the third, parent and child both drew a picture of something they liked to do together. These were shared with the group.

Next, each person brought an object from home that was selected to reveal something about that person and placed it in the center of the circle. Group members focused on one object at a time, discussing what that object indicated about that person. Participants were then asked to share a favorite children's story, one that was meaningful to them, after which they began to relate to each other more intimately, expressing significant feelings.

Session II: Listening to each other. In order to become more sensitive to feelings, we played "*Feelin'*," a game developed by Argus Communications (1973). The game board consists of 16 feeling continuums, each of which depicts two opposite feelings, moving in intensity from the extreme of one emotion to the extreme of its opposite. The leader calls a Subject Card, and the players place a colored token along any of the continuums that apply to their feelings about the particular subject. After all the tokens are placed, the players discuss their reactions.

The steps to active listening were briefly reviewed, and each pair actively listened to the other's problem.

Session III: Sending I-messages. I-messages were discussed in the total group. Then each member took a turn presenting a situation, while the others practiced sending that person an I-message. The person who proposed the situation identified the group that was the most effective and explained why it was effective.

Session IV: Resolving conflicts. After the procedures for problem solving were reviewed, a situation was presented in which each pair worked independently of the group. After brainstorming and deciding on one solution, the entire group met to discuss their experiences and findings.

Session V: Dealing with value collisions. A filmstrip entitled *What Kind of Family Would Have a Pet Joke* (Scholastic Dimensions 1975) was shown as a way of dealing with the topic of family values. The filmstrip shows how children view themselves and their families and stresses the fact that every family is unique in some way; the group was then asked to complete a "family coat of arms." A group discussion followed to identify and clarify the variety of family values. Next, each pair completed a revised form of "twenty things you love to do" (Simon, Howe & Kirschenbaum 1972). This exercise further demonstrated how each family differs in its enjoyment of activities, pointing out the values of each, as well as their similarities and differences.

Session VI: Review and evaluation. The communication skills were reviewed through written and verbal evaluation. After completing the sessions, participants were sent a letter thanking them for their continued interest and enthusiasm.

Results

The results of the Communication Questionnaire administered

to the parents are reported in Table 1, which shows that the parents reported some improvement in their own behavior in terms of items 2, 3, 5, 7, 8, 9, and 10. They reported that they could stay on the subject more when talking to their children (2); they felt their children were more able to express what they feel (3); they talked down less to their children (5); they listened and valued their children's opinion more (7); they felt their children discussed personal problems with them more (8); they felt calmer when talking about a problem (9); and they explained more to their children about their objections to something the children wanted to do (10). They did not, however, see any changes in their interest toward their child's activities (1) nor in their interruptions (4). They also saw the frequency of family discussions as being the same before and after the sessions (6). As can be seen from Table 1, parents initially answered favorably on these items so that there was little room for improvement as measured by the Questionnaire itself.

The results of the Communication Questionnaire administered to the children are presented in Table 2. Here the children perceived their parent's behavior as improving in terms of items 1, 2, 4, 5, 7, 9, and 10. More specifically, they reported their parents showed more interest in the things the child did (1); their parents stayed on the topic more when discussing problems with them (2); their parents interrupted them less (4); their parents talked down to them less (5); their parents listened more to their opinions (7); their parents remained calmer when talking about a problem (9); and their parents let them know more objections to something they wanted to do (10). Additionally, the children saw improvement in being more able to say what they really felt at home (3) and were more willing to discuss their personal problems (8). An improvement was also reported in the frequency of family discussions at home (6).

In comparing Tables 1 and 2, it is apparent that the children reported a greater change in their parent's behavior toward them than the parents reported about themselves (items 1, 2, 4, 5, 7, and 10). A possible reason for the lack of differences in the parent's initial and final response could be their attempt to respond in a more socially acceptable manner, as reflected by their high initial ratings. In contrast, the children might have been more honest and less threatened by the questionnaire.

Particular attention should be drawn to item 1 (parent's level of interest in the child's activities) and item 4 (the parent's frequency of interruptions). Here the children reported a change, whereas the parents reported no change. The children also reported changes in their families' talking things over (6), whereas the parents reported no change. On the other hand, in terms of item 9, the parents indicated they were more able to remain calm when discussing a problem than their children indicated. Finally, both the children and their parents reported that the children felt more able to say what they felt at home (3) and were more willing to discuss personal problems with their parents (8).

In addition to the questionnaire, the written comments from the parents revealed an increased awareness of feelings and a willingness to express them. Parents learned more about their own and their children's behavior. The following are typical of the written comments from the parents: "It showed me how I can open up to my children and allow them the opportunity to relate their

TABLE 1

Responses to Communication Questionnaire for Parents

Item	% Never	% Almost Never	% Sometimes	% Almost Always	% Always
1. Are you interested in the things your child does and is interested in?					
Before				83	17
After				83	17
2. Do you stick to the subject when you talk to your child?					
Before			50	50	
After			17	83	
3. Is your child able to say what he or she feels around the house?					
Before			33	50	17
After			17	50	33
4. Do you interrupt your child before he or she has finished talking?					
Before		17	83		
After		17	83		
5. Do you talk to your child as if he or she were younger than he or she is?					
Before	33	33	33		
After	33	50	17		
6. Does your family talk things over with each other?					
Before			50	50	
After			50	50	
7. Do you listen to and value your child's opinion?					
Before			50	33	17
After			33	50	17
8. When your child has personal problems, does he or she discuss them with you?					
Before		33	17	33	17
After			50	33	17
9. Do you usually stay calm when you talk about a problem with your child?					
Before			67	33	
After			17	67	17
10. Do you explain your reasons for objecting to something your child wants to do?					
Before			33	50	17
After			17	67	17

feelings back to me without the fear of rejection. I feel we are beginning to let the barriers down and to trust each other." "I'm more relaxed about my feelings and opinions and have learned more about myself and my relationship with my family and friends than I was aware of before."

The children's comments indicated that they too could express their feelings more openly and that they enjoyed the sessions. The following are typical of the children's comments: "She expresses her feelings more now . . . . I always have but not her." "We can kind of communicate better . . . we could still improve though." "I can say more what I want." "She doesn't yell so much now."

Conclusions

The analysis of the results indicates that the parent's and the child's behavior can be affected by participating in a parent-child communication skill program. Both groups reported growth in

TABLE 2

Responses to Communication Questionnaire for Children

Item	% Never	% Almost Never	% Sometimes	% Almost Always	% Always
1. Does your parent show interest in the things you do?					
Before			67		33
After			33		67
2. When your parent sits down to talk to you about a problem, does he or she start talking about other things?					
Before	17	17	33	33	
After	50	17	33		
3. Are you able to say what you really feel at home?					
Before			67		33
After			33	33	33
4. Does your parent interrupt you?					
Before	33	17	50		
After	67	17	17		
5. Does your parent tend to talk to you as if you were much younger than you actually are?					
Before		67	33		
After	50	33	17		
6. Does your family talk things over with each other?					
Before	33		67		
After		17	50	17	17
7. Does your parent listen to your opinion?					
Before			67	33	
After			17	67	17
8. When you have personal problems, do you discuss them with your parent?					
Before	33		17	33	17
After			50	17	33
9. Does your parent often become upset when he or she talks to you about some problem?					
Before		33	67		
After	17	17	67		
10. Does your parent let you know his or her reasons for objecting to something you want to do?					
Before	17	17	50		
After			33	67	

themselves and the other person. It appears that they were both more willing to talk and listen to each other and share feelings with one another than they were before the program. The present results also suggest that the role of the counselor in promoting change should not be overlooked. There are, moreover, many ways for the school counselor to expand on the methods presented in this project.

An Analysis of Selected Parent-Intervention Programs for Handicapped and Disadvantaged Children

EDITH LEVITT, Ed.D.
SHIRLEY COHEN, Ph.D.
Special Education Development Center
Hunter College
City University of New York

A major effort of the Special Education Development Center of City University of New York is to develop materials for parents in the role of teachers of their young handicapped children. Towards this goal the authors have formulated a rationale (Levitt & Cohen, 1972) for parent-intervention programs with handicapped children. The present paper reviews and analyzes representative parent-intervention programs for these children.

There has been a long tradition of professionals visiting handicapped children and their parents in the home. While most of these visits were to the homes of blind, deaf, or the physically handicapped children, more recently they have also included families of children with other types of disabilities. In the main, home visits to the handicapped have emphasized the acquisition of self-help skills or the provision of physical therapy. However, current efforts with parents of handicapped children have expanded, and many now deal with cognitive skills as well. The programs selected for the present review reflect this changing orientation. Because educators of disadvantaged children have developed effective parent-intervention programs of interest to those working with handicapped children, a review of these programs is also included.

PARENT-INTERVENTION PROGRAMS FOR THE HANDICAPPED

A program for 10 blind infants who were otherwise intact was conducted by Fraiberg, Smith, and Adelson (1969) at the University of Michigan. The program focused on the first 18 months of life, the "critical period of ego formation." A worker trained either in psychoanalysis or clinical psychology made home visits twice monthly to work with mother and child. Areas emphasized in working with the mothers included interpersonal response, discovery of objects, prehension, and locomotion. Since eye to eye contact, the "matrix of a signal system" between mother and sighted infant, was obviously unavailable to these blind children, the worker had to help the parent find a "tactile–auditory" language that would permit interaction between the infant and mother. The worker demonstrated techniques that centered on holding and talking to the infant and reinforcing actions with words. Another aim, to help the child discover the objective world, was approached by the worker demonstrating the substitution of sound for vision in intentional reaching. With regard to prehension, mothers were asked to guide the child through movements so that his hands gradually became coordinated and "inquisitive." In the areas of locomotion, special incentives had to be used to get the children to respond e.g., crawling was stimulated by using a noisemaking toy just beyond the infant's reach. In a concluding statement the authors stressed the importance of promoting the "love bonds" between a blind infant and his parents. They noted that inanimate objects must be mediated through the relationship with "significant others." This then leads to the infant's investment in objects for their own sake.

Luterman (1967) reported a program for parents and their deaf preschool children initiated at the Robbins Speech and Hearing Center in Boston. Sixteen families participated over a 1-year period. The children (18 and 42 months of age) took part in an informal nursery school program which stressed language stimulation in free-play situations. Two hearing children were also enrolled in the group so that parents could learn to distinguish between normal behavior and that due to deafness. During the first half of the year, parents attended the center twice weekly. One day was spent in observing their children in the nursery and in individual tutoring sessions, while the second day was devoted to group discussion. During observation periods parents were aided by staff members, who pointed out pertinent aspects of behavior and the techniques of language stimulation being employed. During the half-hour individual tutoring lesson, the tutor first worked with the child while his mother observed; then the session was discussed, with emphasis on techniques and goals. After 2 months mothers were given an opportunity to work with a child other than their own while tutors observed and offered constructive criticism. During the second semester, each parent came to the center weekly to teach her own child under the supervision of a therapist. Parents also attended monthly group discussions, which were conducted in a nondirective manner; topics included feelings and attitudes, child management, and educational placement. Problems that arose during the program included a tendency towards overdependency by parents, staff difficulty in focusing on the parent rather than on the child, and inadequate methods of program evaluation. However, at the conclusion of the program progress was apparent, with most of the children able to do specific lip reading and to use speech in a meaningful manner.

The Home Demonstration Teaching Program for Parents of Very Young Deaf Children (Horton, 1968), modeled on one at the John Tracy Clinic, was developed at the Bill Wilkerson Center in Nashville, Tennessee. This program was federally funded over a 3-year period and served children between the ages of 6 months and 3 years. These children generally had a severe, but not profound, hearing loss. No attempt was made to assess intelligence; mean Social Quotient on the Vineland Scale of Social Maturity was 90. The primary focus of the program was parent education, while a secondary objective was to accommodate the special needs of the children. Fifty-six families have been served to date. Mother and child came to the center at intervals ranging from once a month to twice weekly. After an initial screening, the teacher became the key professional in working with the family and involved other personnel only as the need arose. The teacher planned and demonstrated some daily activity in home life that could be used for language development, and the parent then imitated her. Reception rather than expression of language was stressed. The program did not attempt to transform the parent into a teacher of the deaf but rather capitalized on the parent's natural way of stimulating and responding to the child. Training of auditory and visual attention was emphasized. While no objective evaluation of the program was made, feedback suggested that the program had distinct assets.

A home-based program for 10 deaf-blind children aged about 2 was conducted by the Industrial Home for the Blind in Brooklyn over a 1½-year period (Patt, 1969). A social worker visited parents at home and served as an initial educational counselor. A teacher was then added to the team and began to visit each family once or twice weekly. Because of the problem of communicating with Spanish-speaking parents, a bilingual paraprofessional and social worker subsequently joined the team. There were two types of children. The first were in a state of what looked like infantile autism: They disliked physical contact, and the initial effort was to help them accept such contact. The second exhibited mostly destructive "whirling dervish activity," and parents had to learn how to discipline them. An important aspect of working with these parents was to get them to use their bodies freely in relating to the child. Mothers had to learn to provide clear physical signals to their children, expressing pleasure by handling and caressing, disapproval by a firm hand or slap. Goals for the children were to help them move from the infant to the toddler stage and to master such activities as taking solid food, asking for a drink, finding a toy, and learning to walk.

Jackson, Evenson, and Elzey (1971) conducted an experimental project for preschool multiply handicapped post-rubella children over a 2-year period. The program, under the auspices of San Francisco State College, was designed to involve parents in work with their children. Criteria for admission included severe impairment of a child in both hearing and vision. The program served 15 children with an age range of 3 years–6 months to 5 years–3 months over a 2-year period. A special rating scale was used for periodic evaluation of the children, and mothers as well as teachers were asked to complete it. The program focused on self-help and gross-motor skills and on activities that stimulated visual and auditory responses. The children also received individual tutoring in language, audition, and eye-hand coordination. Parents participated in the program in a variety of ways: home visits from teachers, assisting in the classroom once a week, and working as paid aides. The children showed some degree of cognitive gain at the conclusion of the program, although the authors acknowledged that it was hard to know whether this gain was attributable to maturation or to the program.

Santostefano and Stayton (1967) directed a Massachusetts home-based program for 31 severely to moderately retarded children with mean CAs of 5 to 6, training focal attention. The researchers hypothesized that this "unique form of nurture" might make the children more amenable to instruction by others. Mothers who had volunteered for the program were trained in monthly meetings over a 4-month period. The approach to be used with the children was reviewed at an initial meeting at which mothers were given materials, a printed manual, and forms on which to keep a brief daily record. The materials, to be used for 10 to 20 minutes daily, consisted of black and white plywood cutouts of circles, squares, and triangles. These could be arranged in various combinations on a flannel board so that they provided a sequence of increasingly difficult tasks. The child was required to respond to each task by removing a specified cutout. Techniques to be used by mothers included demonstration and physical guidance, e.g., restraining the child if he was about to make the wrong response and guiding his hands through the correct one. A pre-post battery of tests (object sort, and an adaptation of the picture-discrimination task from the Stanford-Binet) was administered to evaluate the results of the program. Subjects performed significantly better than controls on four out of five of these tasks.

The Shield Institute for Retarded Children in the Bronx, New York (Hunter & Schueman, 1967) developed a program funded by NIMH for retarded infants and their mothers. It emphasized the mental health of the family and a multidisciplinary training program for mother and child. Ninety-four children under 3 years of age, with mean IQ of 41 and retardation levels ranging from profoundly to mildly retarded, participated in the program. The parent program included individual counseling and psychotherapy as well as weekly counseling groups and monthly lectures or discussion groups. The home-training program was carried out mainly by a public health nurse under the supervision of the educational director. Parents frequently received materials for their children, together with instructions for their use. They also received supervision from the language therapist, either at home or at the center. In addition, informal educational guidance was supplied by other staff members. The majority of children participated in the program for 1 year or more. Forty-five children received only home training. Of the remaining children being provided home training, 35 also received an orientation program involving part-time participation in group sessions, while 18 attended group sessions on a full-time basis. The curriculum emphasized self-care skills, social adaptation, sensory training, and communication skills. On the basis of pre-post evaluation by teachers, it was concluded that the home-training program had had a beneficial effect. However, the investigators noted that this interpretation was tempered by the absence of a control group.

A project at the West Suburban Special Education Center in Cicero, Illinois (Benson & Ross, 1972), used parents as volunteer aides in the classroom. There were 13 trainable children with an age range of 5 to 8 years. Some had orthopedic or visual handicaps. The training of parents was conducted by the teacher and had a twofold aim: to provide more individualized instruction for the children; and to promote parent involvement, so that they could work better with their children. The parents were trained in two 3-hour workshops which covered such topics as how to work on a one-to-one basis and techniques for teaching self-care, fine-motor activity, and academic skills. Reinforcement techniques designed to accelerate or refine behavior were also considered. During the second workshop, each parent was given an opportunity to work with her child. In preparation, each parent was given a behavioral-objective sheet which specified the teaching activities to be used with the child and materials relevant to these activities. While this tutoring was going on, the teacher was free to move from one mother–child pair to another and to offer guidance as needed. After the training period was completed, parents tutored their children for an hour weekly for about 8 weeks. In addition to working directly with their children, parents also attended monthly meetings at which films were shown and the progress of the children discussed. All the children gained in such areas as self-care, language, and concepts. In addition, parental enthusiasm and involvement in their children's education increased greatly.

The Home Training Program (Doernberg, Rosen, & Walker, 1968), conducted by the League School in Brooklyn, New York, was an effort to improve the functioning of young mentally ill children through work with their parents. Forty-five children and their mothers, along with 30 control families, participated in the program over a 2-year period. The children, who were drawn from the League School waiting list, were either psychotic or severely disturbed. They had an age range of 3 to 7 years and differed widely in developmental level. There were two main aspects to the work with parents: a weekly session in which the parent observed a teacher working with her child and a group meeting every other week. The teacher's interaction with the children stressed self-help skills, socialization, speech and language, and preacademic and early academic skills. At the end of the session, the teacher provided the mother with some specific guidance for working with the child at home. These sessions also gave the teacher an opportunity to review the developmental level of the child and provide the mother with a realistic baseline for working with him.

Mother and child received a warm welcome when they came for their sessions, and both were given an opportunity to interact with the training director and the teacher. Parents' views with regard to their children and their problems were given consideration by professionals and helped determine tutoring goals for each child. Parents also met every other week in small discussion groups led jointly by the social worker and the training director. They often initiated topics which elicited concrete guidance from the group leaders. The focus was not on a traditional counselling approach but rather on reinforcement of the parent's self-image as a competent person who could be effective with her child. Evaluation showed that both experimental and control children failed to make significant gains in IQ scores. However, experimental subjects showed gains in six of seven subcategories of the Vineland, as compared with gains in only two subcategories for controls.

The United Cerebral Palsy Association of San Mateo initiated a program for cerebral palsied children and their mothers (Headley & Leler, 1961) based on the nursery school cooperative model. Mothers assisted in the classroom one morning a week. Ten to 14 children aged 18 months to 5 years attended the nursery school three times weekly and received a traditional nursery school curriculum. In addition to teachers, there was an interdisciplinary team working with the children. Mothers attended weekly parent-education classes led by the nursery school director which dealt with child development and with problems related to cerebral palsy. Fathers attended monthly meetings. In addition, mothers received individual and group psychotherapy from a psychiatric social worker. The school staff observed social and emotional growth on the part of the children. The mothers reported a great decrease in their own tensions and the development of better understanding of their children's potential.

A 1-year project (Weider & Hicks, 1970) at United Cerebral Palsy of Queens evaluated the effects of an intervention program on neurologically impaired children and their families. The major focus was on parent counseling, but an early intervention program for children was also provided. Twenty-three children aged 9 to 44 months attended group sessions twice weekly. Prior to their enrollment, an educational therapist worked with the mother and child at the center to prepare the child for group participation. The focus was on behavioral control and adaptive behavior. There were two classrooms, each staffed by one teacher and several aides. A speech therapist worked with individual children and also provided guidance in speech stimulation for their parents. A home-service coordinator made periodic home visits to make suggestions concerning day-to-day management problems. Mothers met in group sessions weekly, and fathers met every other week. Individual counseling and group therapy for couples were also provided. An experimental rating scale was used for purposes of pre- and post-treatment evaluation of the children's physical, social, and intellectual growth. Although there was no planned variation between the two classes, the staff agreed that one class functioned more effectively.

A program in a New York State suburban community (Slater, 1971) focused on kindergarten children with learning disabilities and their mothers. It had three main aims: to develop an inventory for the identification of potential learning problems; to initiate a program for involving parents in working with their children; and to study the effects of intervention on later school progress. An initial readiness inventory was administered to 254 kindergarten children. The results suggested that 80 of them were potentially learning disabled. Letters were then sent to parents of these children requesting their participation in a remedial program. Thirty-five mothers agreed to participate, and the remaining 47 families were used as controls. The program consisted of three parent workshops conducted at monthly intervals. Each mother was informed of specific weaknesses in her child and then asked to work for 15 minutes daily to help remediate them. She was provided with materials and a description of how to use them. During the second workshop, the mothers' efforts to work with their children were discussed, and additional materials and activities were presented. The third workshop concentrated on outlining verbal and social-development activities to be used with the children. Mothers were also encouraged to continue working with their children for the remainder of the year. Posttest results indicated that children whose mothers were in the training group scored significantly better than controls on the Bender-Gestalt test. However, the groups did not differ in performance on the Metropolitan Readiness Test or a human-figure drawing test.

The Portage Project in Wisconsin (Yavner, 1972) used a behavior-modification approach with an unspecified number of multiply handicapped children and their mothers in rural areas of Wisconsin. The children, mostly retardates, ranged in age from newborn to age 6. During the first year of the project, an initial 3-month period was devoted to preservice training of professional home trainers; topics included orientation to the project and training in assessment techniques and precision teaching. The home trainers also attended a university extension course which focused on learning theory, child development, evaluation, and parent training. They continued to receive in-service training after the inception of the program. The curriculum was based on a set of 363 curriculum cards devised by the staff and designed to accompany a checklist of desired skills. Each card described one of these skills in behavioral terms, then outlined teaching techniques and materials needed to implement it. Home trainers visited the homes weekly to work with the child and his mother. The professionals who assumed this role the first year were supplemented by several paraprofessionals during the second year. The home trainer reviewed the results of the previous week's prescription with the mother, making revisions if necessary. She also worked with the child to demonstrate the new prescription to be carried out during the week. The parent then practiced the prescription under the guidance of the home trainer, who also guided the mother in recording and reporting procedures. At the end of the first year, the children were evaluated on the basis of unspecified tests and developmental scales. Results led the author to conclude that the average child had progressed 13 months over an 8-month period.

PARENT-INTERVENTION PROGRAMS FOR THE DISADVANTAGED

It should be noted that a number of children in programs designed for the disadvantaged could be labeled handicapped: Some have IQs below 75; some have serious emotional problems; some have learning disabilities. As special educators become involved in planning parent-education programs for the less severely handicapped population the value of examining parent-intervention programs for the disadvantaged increases.

The parent education program at the University of Florida (Gordon, 1969) was designed to stimulate cognitive growth in infants aged 3 to 24 months from indigent black and white families. The program, which emphasized warm, interpersonal relationships with the children, centered on a Piagetian approach to cognitive stimulation. It also had a language-stimulation component which was influenced by Bernstein's (1960) theory that disadvantaged adults use a restricted linguistic code hampering language development in their children. Hence mothers were encouraged to use a more elaborate code. The 216 children were divided into five groups. One experimental group received treatment from 3 months of age until their second birthdays; the second and third experimental groups were treated during the first and second years of the program, respectively. The fourth group received a control program which emphasized physical development and had a language-stimulation component. The fifth group received no treatment. A major hypothesis of the study predicted that subjects who received experimental programs would make significantly greater progress than would the controls.

Parent educators were paraprofessionals who received a 5-week training program in child development and interpersonal relationships, role playing, and practice in working both with mothers and infants. Parent educators visited the home each week, working with parents both on specific stimulation exercises and on a more general attitude related to engaging the child in play. The parent educator refrained from assuming the maternal role herself, and the parent learned primarily through imitation. The results supported the hypothesis that children who received the experimental programs would perform better than the controls. In his discussion the author commented that the children in all of the groups did not get enough opportunity to make their own mistakes because mothers were overly eager to assist them. He recommended that educators working with mothers place greater stress on encouraging curiosity and exploration in children.

As a preliminary to embarking on the Ypsilanti Carnegie Infant Education Project, Lambie and Weikart (1970) carried out a 6-month pilot project with seven disadvantaged infants aged 3 to 11 months and their mothers. The curriculum was an umbrella concept that included the development of the mother's ability to teach activities to and interact with her child. The activities were based on tasks formulated by Uzgiris and Hunt (1966) and followed the Piagetian sequence. Teachers made weekly visits to each family and focused on the following: development of an individualized program for each mother–child dyad, development of the mother's teaching and language styles, development of control techniques, and direct tutoring of the child. Important skills for the teacher were an understanding of her role as guest in the mother's home and a consequent ability to assume a position of "low power" in relation to the mother. Mothers were categorized into various types: those with a good intuitive understanding of their children's needs, those who wanted to do what was best for their children but didn't know how, and those who related to their children in a detached or detrimental manner. The teachers took these differences into account in working with mothers and used a variety of techniques with them. For example, they complimented a mother on a new insight, indicated a better approach for controlling her child's behavior, or facilitated her perception of her infant by alerting her to a specific response made by him. While pretest results from both mental and motor subtests of the Bayley Infant Scales of Development indicated that five of the seven infants were functioning below the level expected for their chronological age, five of the infants performed at or above the level expected for their chronological age on the posttest. In their concluding statement the authors commented that the process of preparing a teacher, a mother, and an infant to learn together was a critical one. They also stressed their belief that the human relationship is the essential condition for any educational growth.

A pilot study described by Weikart (1967) was carried out in connection with the Perry Preschool Project at Ypsilanti, a program for black children and their parents. Thirteen disadvantaged children with a mean IQ of 78.5 were in the group. A control group was matched for socioeconomic class and IQ. The curriculum emphasized "verbal bombardment." The teacher maintained a steady stream of questions and comments aimed at helping children attend to pertinent aspects of their environment. Children were not necessarily required to respond. The interaction between the teacher and children was similar to that between a middle-class mother and her young child. The parent-education aspect of the program was carried out through weekly home visits by teachers. They worked directly with the children and demonstrated techniques of child management while the mother was present. There were also monthly group meetings attended by both parents in which child management and other pertinent topics were discussed. The program showed significant IQ gains for experimental subjects. However, these disappeared by the end of kindergarten. The superior achievement-test scores obtained by experimental subjects lasted through grade 2.

Forrester and her colleagues (1971) initiated the DARCEE infant study at Peabody College as an extension of an earlier Peabody project geared to preschool children. It sought to facilitate growth in 10 white and 10 black infants aged 7 to 9 months by means of home visitations. A comparison group was also included in the study. The program was developed around a set of developmental landmarks in the areas of gross-motor, fine-motor, cognitive, language, and personal–social areas. It was also influenced by tasks on an infant scale formulated by Uzgiris and Hunt (1966) which dealt with such cognitive areas as schema development, development of causality, and construction of objects in space. A continuous effort was made throughout the program to translate cognitive functioning into suggestions for selection and management of play materials. Paraprofessionals served as home visitors, making up to a maximum of 24 visits over a 9-month period. The worker brought toys at each visit and left them until the next one, at which time the child's responses to them were discussed. The focus here was not simply on the use of materials as such but on how and why they were used. Mothers were encouraged to make their own materials. In addition, they received weekly assignments ranging from recording observations on a given type of behavior to making a picture book. The parent educator was viewed as a "model and reinforcer" for the mother. She took an active role in demonstrating ways of presenting materials to the child, praised helpful interactions with the infant, and made suggestions with regard to appropriate language and behavior. Results of the study indicated that experimental infants performed significantly better than the comparison group on several measures of cognitive development.

Badger (1972) outlined a parent-education program conducted by the Mount Carmel (Illinois) Parent and Child Center which was modeled on an earlier one at the University of Illinois. This program was part of a larger network based on Head Start and designed to provide services to children under the age of 3 and their mothers. While assistance was offered in such areas as health, nutrition, homemaking, and social services, the major emphasis was on education. Ten infants/toddlers, ranging in age from 1 month to nearly 3 years, attended daily group sessions at the center. Their parents participated in 2-hour weekly meetings centering on parent education. Transportation was provided to and from meetings, as was care for preschool siblings while mothers were away. A paraprofessional led discussions on child-rearing and other topics and offered demonstrations pertinent to the educational objectives under discussion. Mothers borrowed educational materials at the end of each meeting and were given assistance to insure that their selections matched their children's developmental level. They also made play materials, e.g., scrap books, lacing cards, and sorting games. The group leader made weekly follow-up home visits in which she helped evaluate the child's progress and offered other help as needed. Evidence of the success of the program included the enthusiam of the parents and the change of staff attitudes toward parents.

A preliminary report by Caldwell, Elardo, and Elardo (1972) at the University of Arkansas dealt with an intervention study with infant subjects. There were four groups, each containing 30 to 32 infants. All four groups performed similarly on Caldwell's Home Stimulation Inventory. Infants in the Level 1 group were tested in their mother's presence either with the Bayley Scales of Infant Development or with the Stanford-Binet at age 6, 12, 24, or 36 months. At Level 2, the infants were tested every month from 8 to 12 months and then every 3 months from 12 to 36 months. The purpose for including Level 1 and Level 2 groups was to control for the effect of testing on the mother's subsequent stimulation of her child. Level 3 infants were treated like those at Level 2, with the following addition: After testing was completed, their mothers were given suggestions for ways to help infants "learn new things." They were also given a bag of toys and simple suggestions for style of interaction during play sessions. In effect, these toys and suggested activities were "transfer items" for each test item at a given age range; they took into consideration specific weaknesses and strengths of individual children.

Level 4 children also received the same treatment as those in Level 3 but received home visits as well. Home visitors were research assistants and teachers who visited the home biweekly with a tutorial program. The target of the intervention programs was the parent-child unit. Children were assigned to a particular level of intervention on the basis of previous scores on Caldwell's Inventory of Home Stimulation. No data were available on the Level 1 group for the present report, but the three remaining groups showed a decline in scores on the Bayley Scales of Infant Development. The authors commented that a more intensive home-visiting program might be needed. They also noted the possibility that the intervention effect might be a cumulative one which would appear at a later date.

Radin (1968) presented a preliminary report on preschool children and their mothers at Ypsilanti. The program served 100 4-year-old children, half black and half white, along with their mothers. There were 10 children in each class, with staff consisting of one teacher and an aide. The curriculum centered on two aspects of cognitive function emphasized by Piaget: (a) the operative aspect, involving such mental operations as classification or seriation; and (b) the figurative aspect, pertaining to the type of symbolization used in these operations (e.g., concrete object vs. representation of that object). The curriculum also included the Bereiter-Englemann approach to language training. Each child was tutored at home every other week by his teacher while his mother was present. The purpose of these sessions was twofold: (a) to help the mother incorporate the role of teacher into her everyday interaction with her child and (b) to permit the teacher to give individualized attention to his special needs. The main aspect of the parent-education program was conducted in weekly meetings at which mothers met in groups of 10 with a social worker. Baby sitters and transportation were furnished for these meetings. Mothers also received weekly gifts for their children. The mothers were divided into two treatment groups, one receiving the lecture approach, while the second received a "participation approach" involving such activities as completing assignments or role playing. A third group of mothers acted as controls. The parent curriculum centered on behavior modification. The first unit reviewed management problems and dealt with such topics as reinforcement schedules and techniques of reducing undesirable behaviors; the second unit dealt with ways of fostering cognitive development; and the third unit emphasized fostering inner controls. Information on the outcome of Radin's current program is unavailable. However, a pilot project for the program had produced significant gains on the Stanford-Binet and PPVT for children whose mothers had been exposed to the parent-education program.

A program by Karnes (1968) paid parents while they were being trained to teach their young children. Fifteen children aged 3 to 4 were involved in the study, with another 15 children acting as controls. Teachers conducted the parent-education programs in weekly meetings and biweekly home visits. There were 11 weekly meetings with three teachers, each of whom worked with five mothers. Mothers were aided in making educational materials, using objects commonly found around the house. They were taught songs and fingerplays and were permitted to borrow books and toys. A major emphasis was language development, including labeling, generalization, and use of correct grammar. Teachers also visited each home at 2-week intervals to demonstrate teaching techniques and to evaluate activities the mother was using with her child. Posttests at the conclusion of the program indicated that the experimental group made significant gains on the Stanford-Binet and on three subtests of the ITPA, whereas the controls did not.

The federally funded Early Training Project at Peabody College (Klaus & Gray, 1968) attempted to counteract the progressive retardation typical of disadvantaged preschool children. The study used two experimental groups, the first participating over three summers, and the second over two summers. Home visitations were provided for both groups. There was a local control group and a second control group located at 60 miles distance, the latter included to check for a possible diffusion effect. A total of 43 experimental subjects and 45 controls were used. IQs were from 65 to 115, with MAs ranging from 27 to 60 months. All subjects were black. The program used the usual nursery school materials designed to promote growth in perceptual and conceptual areas, with the main emphasis on how and why they were used. A main focus of the program was to change the children's motivational patterns: One approach reinforced desired behavior on an interpersonal level, while a second linked appropriate responses to specific rewards. Home-visitors, who had teaching backgrounds, met weekly with mothers and wrote records of each meeting. Mothers were requested to plan training activities for their children, although some were reluctant to do so because they lacked self-confidence or because of insufficient time. The home visitor had to provide these parents with a good deal of encouragement in order to get them to participate in this aspect of the program. The home visitor frequently used role playing, with the visitor taking the teacher's role, and the mother the child's role. Parents were urged to make maximum use of books by reading them to the children, discussing pictures and concepts, and using dramatization. Posttests indicated a significant mean gain for the combined experimental groups on several measures of cognitive performance, as compared with the combined controls. Controls showed progressive retardation until they entered the first grade, when they began to make gains. All four groups showed a decline in the second year, although experimental subjects still retained their initial advantage.

The Appalachian Preschool Program (Alford, 1971), a home-oriented program carried out in four West Virginian counties over a 3-year period, involved a total of about 450 rural preschool children. It had three main components: a daily TV program, a weekly home visit by a paraprofessional, and a small group session in a mobile classroom. Four treatment groups were set up: One received all three components, a second received TV and home visits only, a third had TV alone, while the fourth was a No Treatment group. The prediction was that the group receiving all three components would do better than the remaining ones. Goals for the project—growth in the areas of language, cognitive, psychomotor, and social skills—were translated into behavioral objectives. Units of work were developed for the three treatment components of the program by a curriculum materials team. The team was responsible for a coordinated set of teaching materials which consisted of tapes, worksheets for children, parent guides, and guides for the mobile classroom. The program also contained a feedback loop that permitted actual observations of the children to be incorporated into the planning program. Paraprofessionals who acted as home visitors were provided with a 3-week intensive orientation period which concentrated on child development and teaching techniques. They brought materials to the home which were related to the upcoming TV program. They also watched the program daily with one child and reported on his reactions and the reactions of other children as described by their parents. A posttest battery failed to indicate gains for treatment groups for the first year. However, during the second year, gains were reported in language development, cognitive learning, and psychomotor and social skills for two treatment groups—the group exposed to the mobile classroom, TV, and home visits and the group receiving only the latter two components.

The aim of Levenstein's federally funded Verbal Interaction Project (Wargo, Campeau, & Tallmadge, 1971) located in Nassau County, New York, was to modify the early cognitive experience of disadvantaged young children through a home-based verbal stimulation program. Children were 2 to 3 years of age; the majority were black. One hundred and thirty such children were served in a 3-year program, most of them for 2-year periods. The program had four main aspects: a focus on the mother-child dyad; the use of trained "toy demonstrators"; a set of Verbal Interaction Stimulation Materials consisting of toys and books; and supervision of the toy demonstrators in such matters as materials selection, presentation of materials, and monitoring of home visits. Families also received counseling services. The toy demonstrators were given an initial orientation period, a handbook outlining general methodology, and a guidesheet for each visit. They kept records of their visits and received supervision during individual conferences. The first year they consisted of social workers, and in the second and third years they consisted mainly of volunteers with middle to high incomes, along with some paid low-income workers. The verbal stimulation program was built around a series of specific toys and books. One of these was presented weekly as a gift to the child, and the worker made a second visit later in the week to review progress in its use, demonstrating possible verbal interactions with the toy or book and gradually letting the mother take over. The selected toys encouraged the development of such abilities as spatial organization, problem-solving, and fine-muscle dexterity. Eight specific interaction techniques included: giving information, eliciting responses, engaging the child's interest, and describing toy manipulation. On the basis of pre- and posttests, the investigator concluded that the subjects had made a significant mean IQ gain of 17 points. The significant results held up in a follow-up test administered 30 months after the pretest.

The Waterloo Home Start II program, directed by Thompson (1972), undertook to facilitate preschool development and to help parents become more effective teachers of their preschool children. Children started at age 2 and remained in the program until they were enrolled in kindergarten. A few months prior to school entrance they were provided with a group program so that they would be better equipped for this step. The program served two groups of children. The first consisted of 55 white and 55 black children from disad-

TABLE 1
PARENT-INTERVENTION PROGRAMS FOR THE HANDICAPPED

Project director	Program/ agency	Children			Home-based			Center-based			Instructional approach
		Handicap	*N*	Mean age/ age range	Parent educator	Parent	Child	Parent group	Child group	Parent as teacher aide	
Fraiberg	The Early Ego Development of Children Blind from Birth	blind	10	newborn	social worker, psychologist	frequency not given	frequency not given				developmental
Luterman	Robbins Speech and Hearing Center	deaf	16	18–42 mos.	therapist			weekly	daily	weekly (*a*) classroom (*b*) tutored own child	language stimulation
Horton	Home Demonstration Teaching Program for Parents of Very Young Deaf Children	deaf	56	6–36 mos.	teacher					mother tutored child at varying intervals	language stimulation
Patt	Industrial Home for the Blind	deaf-blind	10	2 yrs.	caseworker, paraprofessional, teacher	once or twice weekly	once or twice weekly				developmental
Jackson	San Francisco State College	deaf-blind	15	$3\frac{1}{2}$ yrs.	teacher	frequency not given	frequency not given			weekly	developmental
Santostefano	Worcester Area Comprehensive Care Center for the Mentally Retarded	retarded	31	$5\frac{1}{2}$ yrs.	professional			4 workshops			"focal attention"

TABLE 1 (*Cont'd*)

		Children			Home-based			Center-based			
Project director	Program/ agency	Handi-cap	*N*	Mean age/ age range	Parent educator	Parent	Child	Parent group	Child group	Parent as teacher aide	Instructional approach
Hunter	Shield Institute for Retarded Children	retarded	94	under 3 yrs.	nurse, language therapist	frequency varied	frequency varied	monthly	frequency varied		developmental, language stimulation
Ross	West Suburban Special Education Center	retarded	13	5–8 yrs.	teacher			monthly meetings: 2 workshops	daily		developmental
Doernberg	Home Training Program	disturbed	45	3–7 yrs.	teacher			biweekly	child tutored weekly by teacher with mother observing		developmental
Headley	United Cerebral Palsy Association of San Mateo County	cerebral palsied	10–14	1.6–5 yrs.	teacher			weekly	3 times weekly	weekly	developmental
Hicks	United Cerebral Palsy of Queens	cerebral palsied	23	9–44 mos.	educational and speech therapist, home service coordinator	frequency not given		weekly	twice weekly		developmental, language stimulation
Slater	New York State kindergarten classes	learning disabled	35	5 yrs.	professional			3 workshops	daily		developmental
Yavner	Portage project	multiply handicapped	not given	0–6 yrs.	professional, paraprofessional	weekly	weekly				behavior modification

TABLE 2
PARENT-INTERVENTION PROGRAMS FOR THE DISADVANTAGED

Project director	Program/ agency	Children		Home-based			Center-based			Instructional approach
		N	Mean age/ age range	Parent educator	Parent	Child	Parent group	Child group	Parent as teacher aide	
Gordon	Florida Parent Program	216	3–24 mos.	paraprofessional	weekly					Piagetian
Lambie	Ypsilanti Carnegie Infant Program	7	3–11 mos.	teacher	weekly	weekly				Piagetian
Forrester	Home visiting Program	20	7–9 mos.	paraprofessional	biweekly		biweekly			developmental
Badger	Mothers Training Program, University of Illinois	10	under 3 yrs.	paraprofessional	weekly		weekly	daily		developmental
Caldwell	University of Arkansas	60–64	6–36 mos.	research assistants & teachers	biweekly	biweekly			parent was instructed periodically	developmental
Weikart	Perry Preschool Project (pilot)	13	3 yrs.	teacher	weekly	weekly	monthly	daily		"verbal bombardment"
Radin	Early Education Program	100	$4\frac{1}{2}$ yrs.	teacher		biweekly	weekly	daily		Piagetian Bereiter-Englemann language program
Karnes	University of Illinois	15	3–4 yrs.	teacher	biweekly		weekly			developmental, language stimulation
Gray	Early Training Project	43	$3\frac{3}{4}$ yrs.	teacher	weekly			daily		developmental
Alford	Appalachian Preschool Program	500	3–5 yrs.	paraprofessional	weekly			weekly		developmental TV program
Levenstein	Verbal Interaction Program	130	2–3 yrs.	paraprofessional, social worker, volunteers	twice weekly					verbal stimulation
Thompson	Home Start II	210	2 yrs.	paraprofessional	weekly			daily a few mos. at end of program		developmental

TABLE 3
SUMMARY AND COMPARISON OF PARENT-INTERVENTION PROGRAMS FOR HANDICAPPED AND DISADVANTAGED CHILDREN

	Programs for handicapped (N = 13)	Programs for disadvantaged (N = 12)
Mean number of children served	29	115
Parent educators		
Professionals	12	6
Paraprofessionals	1	5
Mixed	–	1
Primary approach to parent education		
Mother–child–teacher interaction:		
Home-based	6	12
Center-based	3	–
Workshops	3	–
Mother as teacher aide	1	–
Auxiliary approach to parent education		
Parent group	6	5
Parent as teacher aide	2	–
Instructional approaches to children		
Piagetian	–	2
Developmental	7	5
Language stimulation	2	2
Mixed	2	3
Behavioral modification	1	–
Focal attention	1	–

vantaged homes; their families received supplemental services from specialists in such areas as health, nutrition, and home economics. They were visited by paid aides as well as staff members who focused on the facilitation of parent-child interaction. The visitor and mother together would select educational materials which would help the child develop in such areas as attention span, tactile awareness, and verbal and motor expression. The families of a second group of 100 "less disadvantaged" white children received fewer services: Mothers came to the center to pick up instructional materials and received guidance from consultants. Data on the effects of the program are not yet available. However, a similar earlier program produced significant gains for scores on the Primary Mental Abilities Test compared with earlier scores on the Stanford-Binet.

SUMMARY AND COMPARISON OF PROGRAMS FOR THE HANDICAPPED AND FOR THE DISADVANTAGED

Tables 1 and 2 present an analysis of the parent-intervention programs for handicapped and disadvantaged children just reviewed, while Table 3 summarizes the analysis.

A comparison of data for the two types of program reveals that: (a) programs for the handicapped were carried out almost exclusively by professionals, whereas programs for the disadvantaged made frequent use of paraprofessionals; and (b) if we sum all the ways in which parents participated in the sample of program surveyed, we find that parents of the handicapped were more involved in school- or center-based activities than were parents of the disadvantaged (16 instances as compared with 5).

Table 4 deals with the outcomes of the parent-intervention programs under review. It can be noted that widely differing criteria were used in evaluating these programs, ranging from subjective impression to statistical tests. Seven of 13 programs for the handicapped used no evaluative measures, whereas this was true for only 2 of 12 programs for the disadvantaged. Only 2 of the 13 programs for the handicapped used standardized measures, while 10 of the 12 programs for the disadvantaged did so. The outcomes of parent-intervention programs using standardized measures are as follows: The two programs for the handicapped produced mixed results. In the case of the disadvantaged, 5 programs out of 10 using standardized measures showed clearcut gains, three had mixed results, one pilot project produced significant gains, while a second pilot project showed a decline.

CONCLUSIONS AND RECOMMENDATIONS

The foregoing overview and analysis of parent-intervention programs for the handicapped and the disadvantaged suggest the following:

1. Programs for the disadvantaged are more comprehensive and more carefully designed than those for the handicapped. For these reasons they provide valuable models for educators concerned with formulating analogous programs for the handicapped.

2. Programs for the disadvantaged are apt to use intelligence tests for evaluative purposes, whereas those for the handicapped frequently rely on subjective evaluation. Obviously, parent-intervention programs for the handicapped require a more rigorous approach to evaluation. However, the use of intelligence tests for the evaluation of educational programs has frequently been criticized because of their global character. A more promising approach to educational evaluation appears to be the use of criterion-referenced tests which relate to specific curricular goals. Such an approach deserves exploration in connection with parent-intervention programs for the handicapped.

3. Programs for the handicapped rarely use paraprofessionals, while those for the disadvantaged frequently do so. Since many handicapped children are also disadvantaged, this discrepancy warrants consideration. Specifically, the special contribution the paraprofessional can make in establishing rapport with parents of disadvantaged handicapped children requires examination.

4. It was previously noted that parents of the handicapped engage in

TABLE 4
OUTCOME OF PARENT-INTERVENTION PROGRAMS FOR HANDICAPPED AND DISADVANTAGED CHILDREN

Project director	Measures	Outcome
	Programs for the handicapped	
Fraiberg	–	–
Luterman	–	showed progress
Horton	–	showed progress
Patt	–	–
Jackson	–	showed progress
Santostefano	5 informal cognitive measures	significant gains
Hunter	rating scale	"beneficial"
Ross	–	–
Doernberg	Stanford-Binet Vineland	no gains significant gains
Headley	–	–
Hicks	rating scale	significant gains
Slater	Bender-Gestalt Metropolitan Readiness Test, human-figure drawing test	significant gains on Bender-Gestalt
Yavner	unspecified	showed progress
	Programs for the disadvantaged	
Gordon	Griffiths Mental Developmental Scale	significant gains
Lambie	Bayley Scales of Infant Development	significant gains on mental but not motor subtests
Forrester	Bayley Scales of Mental and Motor Development, Griffith Mental Development Scale, Infant Psychological Development Scale (Uzgiris-Hunt)	significant gains
Badger	–	–
Caldwell	Bayley Scales of Infant Development	decline (pilot)
Radin	Stanford-Binet, PPVT	significant gains on a previous pilot
Karnes	Stanford-Binet, ITPA	significant gains significant gains on 3 subtests
Gray	Stanford-Binet, ITPA, PPVT	significant gains
Alford	criterion-referenced test, PPVT, Frostig, ITPA	significant gains significant gains on 3 subtests
Levenstein	Stanford-Binet	significant gains
Thompson	no information	–
Weikart	Stanford-Binet	significant gains

school- or center-based activities more frequently than do parents of the disadvantaged. The implication is that parents of the handicapped may be more capable of extra personal effort and involvement in their children's education. This attitude would be a distinct asset in conducting parent-intervention programs on behalf of handicapped children.

5. The initiation of Piaget-based programs for the disadvantaged which focus on processes rather than products of cognition reflects a current emphasis in preschool education and developmental psychology. The formulation of an educational methodology for the handicapped also centering on cognitive processes would be desirable for two reasons: (a) programs for these children are now based largely on lower-level associational learning; (b) since the handicapped child is known to have deficits in higher-order processing, efforts at their amelioration would be particularly germane.

The programs reviewed were scrutinized with a view to eliciting possible common patterns among those with successful outcomes. No such patterns were discernible. Commonalities across these programs could well inhere in what Weikart (1971) called their "operational conditions," or structure. On the basis of his own and other research, he concluded that various curricular approaches used with preschool disadvantaged children produce equally effective results. However, what seemed to distinguish such programs from those that were less effective was their careful day-to-day planning, along with an ongoing inservice training and supervision of teachers to ensure that projected programs were implemented. Based on the present review, it is evident that most parent-intervention programs for handicapped children are still being conducted within the context of an informal, service-oriented tradition. There is an obvious need to explore further a more rigorous approach to these programs.

Mainstreaming Parents of the Handicapped

Merle B. Karnes

Merle B. Karnes is professor of special education at the Institute for Child Behavior and Development at the University of Illinois in Urbana.

Mainstreaming handicapped children is becoming standard educational practice. If mainstreaming programs are to succeed, teachers, both regular and special, must be convinced of the value of parent involvement. The more positive your attitude is, the more successful any parent-involvement program is likely to be.

Involving parents of the handicapped along with parents of the nonhandicapped presents a great challenge, one with far-reaching implications. Parental attitudes and values influence children. Therefore, as parents of nonhandicapped children come to understand the special needs as well as the remarkable strengths of the handicapped, so will their children. Such parental insight will be reflected in the attitudes of the nonhandicapped child toward his or her handicapped peers. It works both ways: Parents of the handicapped who observe their children in a mainstream setting with nonhandicapped children gain new understanding, which enables their children to participate more fully in the mainstream experience, and parents of normal children learn from parents of the handicapped.

Inexperience and misconception often cause parents of the nonhandicapped to resist the enrollment of handicapped children in the regular classroom. Some even conclude that handicapped children interfere with the learning of the nonhandicapped. Parents of the handicapped, on the other hand, are often anxious that their children will not "make it" or will be rejected. It is possible to dispel such fears by having parents of the nonhandicapped and the handicapped work together.

How can you make a parent-involvement program work? That rests largely on your attitudes, knowledge and skills. Here are some guidelines.

Building Attitudes

Remember that parental influence is greater than that of any teacher. If you work with parents in the following ways your efforts should pay off:

1. Plan activities that make sense to parents.

2. Provide parents with special knowledge to meet the varied needs of children. Parents will be more likely to carry out recommendations successfully if they are specific.

3. Think of parents as teaching resources who can contribute knowledge about and insight into their children, helping you enhance educational programs.

4. Involve parents in the formulation of educational policy and goals for their children.

5. Explain evaluation procedures and encourage participation in conference decisions so that parents can help decide on the educational placement of their child.

6. Encourage parents to involve themselves in classroom activities.

7. Provide parents with alternate ways of involving themselves in the educational program. Like children, they respond differently.

8. Provide opportunities for parents of handicapped and nonhandicapped children to work together productively.

9. Plan for parents to work with other parents. They sometimes can learn more from each other than from you.

10. Help parents to evaluate the educational program for their child and to assess their own contribution to that program. Parents who succeed tend to become more actively involved. Give parents adequate feedback on their successes and failures.

The more parents know about a program through active involvement, the more accurately and fairly they will interpret it. They can be potent public relations agents for interpreting educational programs to others.

New Knowledge

Until recently, there were few courses to prepare regular and special teachers for work with parents. The negative attitudes some have toward parent involvement may be the result of a lack of knowledge and experience. Indeed, some feel so inadequate and insecure in this area that they argue defensively against the development of programs for parents: "If you encourage parents to become involved, they will just make trouble," or "Parents won't take the time to get involved."

Many teachers are changing their attitudes and are beginning to seek the knowledge and experience they need to work more effectively with parents. Some of the avenues you can explore are:

1. Request universities and colleges to set up extension and inservice courses that focus on learning to work with parents and include supervised practice teaching experiences.

2. Read recent literature on parent-involvement programs and adapt this new information to your own teaching situation.

3. Visit exemplary parent-involvement programs. Even when such programs operate in an educational setting different from that of the visiting teacher (a preschool, for example, when you are employed at a junior high school), many of the principles demonstrated in the exemplary program can be transferred to other settings and age groups.

4. Invite a consultant to meet with other teachers and staff members who want to establish or improve parent-involvement programs.

5. Attend professional meetings at which parental involvement is a major topic.

6. Request help from an advisory board of parents on how they can best be involved in the educational programs of their children.

7. Urge federal and state offices of education to set up task forces to recommend ways of improving parent involvement. Such task forces should include parents among their members and could lead to ongoing, inservice training programs.

In addition to discovering how and where, you can seek out information in these areas:

• *the effect of given handicapping conditions on learning and how teaching methods and materials can be adapted.* Special teachers can help regular teachers develop useful classroom strategies as well as acquire information that will help parents understand the educational implications of their child's handicapping condition.

• *the stages of distress and reconciliation parents experience when they learn they have a handicapped child.* Parents move through these stages at different rates, and an understanding of the process enables teachers to help parents recognize when they are ready to involve themselves in their child's educational program.

• *alternate areas of parent involvement.* Interpersonal dynamics are important and home visits, large- and small-group meetings, individual conferences and classroom observation may each have appropriate uses. Other strategies for reaching parents include a newsletter, an advisory council and a parent library of magazines, books and cassettes. Some parents may be able to interpret the program to others, while other parents are comfortable teaching in the classroom or at home. Still other parents may experience satisfaction constructing instructional materials, editing a newsletter or accompanying classes on field trips.

• *the contributions of other disciplines to parent-involvement programs.*

• *serviceable record-keeping systems for parent-involvement programs.*

• *involving hard-to-reach parents and other members of the family in the educational program of the handicapped child.*

Specific Skills

To work effectively with parents, you need not only knowledge but also the skills to implement that knowledge. These skills, including those in sensitive areas of interpersonal relations, can be acquired through trial and error, particularly if trials are followed by thoughtful self-evaluation and group evaluation. Some specific skills needed to promote parent involvement include:

1. Establishing rapport in one-to-one relationships as well as with groups.

2. Interviewing to obtain accurate and complete information.

3. Helping parents assess their readiness to be involved in programs and to evaluate their progress in such programs.

4. Training parents to become better observers and to be more effective in the direct teaching of their child.

5. Helping parents acquire more effective ways of handling behavior problems.

6. Helping parents work with other parents.

7. Evaluating ourselves to determine areas where professional growth and guidance are needed.

A Chance for Leadership

You may head the professional team working with parents of the nonhandicapped and the handicapped. The special teacher usually provides supportive or consultative help as do ancillary personnel, such as psychologists, guidance counselors, speech and language therapists, physical and occupational therapists and social workers. Regardless of the team organization, you need to be willing to acquire new knowledge and skills.

Approach the parent as an individual and provide alternate forms of involvement. Parents of nonhandicapped children and parents of handicapped children can participate in direct teaching in the regular classroom and can join together in group sessions focusing on common problems.

Whether parents work together on an advisory board, in a parent library or in public relations activities, they will discover mutually advantageous benefits in mainstreaming. Handicapped and nonhandicapped youngsters are learning to understand and value each other by attending the same classroom. Their parents will also learn to appreciate commonalities as well as differences as they discover new resources by working together. You can be a leader in this breakthrough.

SUCCESSFUL INTERGRATION

Janet Kean

The Parents' Role

. . . I eagerly looked forward to the day the problem of her education could be deposited in the lap of our local school district.

When Wendy, who has a severe hearing loss, was a preschooler, I eagerly looked forward to the day the problem of her education could be deposited in the lap of our local school district. I was getting tired of my job; mothering a preschooler is demanding, and when the child has a disability the demands are even greater. In most cases, mother not only has to cope with the extra work necessitated by the disability, but also must involve herself intimately in helping her child to overcome or live with the effects of the disability.

Diagnosis of Hearing Loss

Wendy's hearing loss was diagnosed a few months after her second birthday. She began wearing her first hearing aid at about two and a half. Life with Wendy up to that time had been a hectic romp, as she did all her exploring with her hands and eyes. Wendy was a curious, active child from the beginning but, unknown to us, one avenue of satisfying her curiosity had been blocked as she could hear little in the way of meaningful sound and virtually nothing spoken in a conversational tone. Often by dinner time I was physically and emotionally exhausted from taking care of her.

Once Wendy's problem was diagnosed, my activities with her became somewhat less physical. With her hearing aid she was able to learn and explore in a more sedate manner. My job, however, was no less intense or demanding. In addition to my role as mother, I now had to function as "teacher" and as coordinator, overseer and participant in Wendy's educational experiences. Fortunately, my husband was willing and able to help by sharing these duties evenings and weekends. Specifically, our activities included working with Wendy daily on vocabulary and language skills, chauffeuring her to speech and language therapy (which meant a half-hour ride from once to four times weekly) and participating in her nursery school, a parent co-op in which I did my share of pupil transportation, classroom assistance and monthly meeting attendance. Meanwhile, Greg was born — a little over three years after Wendy.

Education: Our Permanent Responsibility

I nourished the appealing idea that when my daughter entered kindergarten — or maybe first grade — my part in overseeing her education and in actually trying to teach her myself would be finished. I was ready to relax and pursue some of my own interests. While part of my naivete may have been due to the fact that Wendy is my first child, undoubtedly I was also indulging in some rather wishful thinking. And, indeed, it rained on my parade!

Wendy started kindergarten. The school personnel knew she was coming and were aware that she would need extra help. Although most of the staff had never had contact with a hearing-disabled child before, from the outset they were genuinely interested in helping. But that was not enough, as I soon found out. My husband and I found we could not abdicate responsibility for our daughter's education.

Wendy is now a fifth grader. We are still involved in her schooling although the nature of the involvement has changed over the years. The reasons parents need to sustain their involvement in their disabled child's education may differ somewhat in each individual case, depending on the child's problem and the school's willingness and ability to respond to it. Nevertheless, our experiences have led me to three generalizations as to why it makes sense for parents to take an intelligent interest and an active part in their child's education.

Successful Intergration: The Parent's Role, Janet Kean, *The Exceptional Parent*, October 1975.©Psy-Ed Corporation.

. . . much can be accomplished if one or both parents can spend some time in their child's classroom.

Parents' Role Unique

First, parents know their child better than anyone else does. They may not be professionally trained in education, but they know his or her particular problems and needs. Parents know their child's habits and patterns of behavior and how he handles or copes with the disability. And they often know a great deal about the nature and effects of their child's specific disability, especially if it has been diagnosed well before the school years. It is possible to plan an appropriate and effective program for the child only when the parents' knowledge and experience are communicated to the professionals involved with their child at school — and taken seriously by them. For example, when Wendy was about to enter first grade, on the basis of my understanding of her situation and needs, I questioned the decision about how best to teach her reading. I was not a fully trained teacher; my reservations stemmed from my understanding *as a parent*. With the all too customary diffidence of parents when confronted with a group of well-trained professionals, I meekly questioned the decision of Wendy's teachers. Assuming that they knew more than I did, I decided to go along with it. As the people working with Wendy in first grade began to know her better, they also began to question their decision, on exactly the same basis I had. Eventually her reading program was changed to a more appropriate one. From this experience, I learned that I would have to become more self-confident and direct in communicating my understanding of Wendy's needs.

Second, not only do parents have a responsibility to provide information to the school, it is equally important for the school to provide information to the parents. When parents continue to work with their child at home, the child's teacher(s) and other school professionals can help parents be as effective as possible by offering explicit guidance as to how to work with their child and what to work on — as well as how they can best help and support their child socially and emotionally. Unfortunately, unless the child is highly disruptive in class, this kind of help is not likely to be forthcoming unless parents have demonstrably taken an active interest in their child's education.

Finally, no one can care about a child in the way that concerned parents do. The most loving, devoted and helpful professionals still have other loyalties and duties, other commitments to other children. The ultimate responsibility for a child's education remains in the hands of his or her parents. It is sometimes said that children learn in spite of school; however this may be for some children, it is certainly not the case for most disabled children. The school hours are important for our children. We parents need to make certain they are as fruitful as possible.

During the past six years we have given much time, effort and thought to Wendy's education. I would like to share some of our experiences and discoveries, in the form of advice, so that others may benefit more efficiently from procedures we groped to find.

Visit Your Child's Class

Especially in the primary grades (including kindergarten), much can be accomplished if one or both parents can spend some time in their child's classroom. This will give you an opportunity to observe for yourself your child's academic and social adjustment in the classroom. The teacher's assessment is important, of course. But if she is not familiar with the effects of your child's disability, she may misinterpret some of his behavior. For example, hearing-impaired children tend to be super bluffers. While they nod their heads yes, and look alert, they may not have the foggiest notion of what is going on. Year after year, we are told by Wendy's new teachers at the beginning of the term that she understands everything. Yet, we know full well that, given her language lags, this is impossible. Visiting and observing in the classroom, I have then been able to share with teachers the specific vocabulary and concepts that Wendy isn't actually understanding. At the same time, I help them to see the nature of her problem more clearly.

I have also found that sometimes a teacher's assessment of Wendy's "wonderful progress" is based on exaggerated or erroneous notions about the limitations caused by her disability. Sometimes expectations have been considerably lower than they ought to have been. Through classroom observation, parents can see whether the teacher's sense of what their child can and cannot handle is realistic and true, and can encourage necessary revisions.

Classroom visits give parents some ongoing idea as to whether the teacher's classroom dealings with their child reflect what she knows of him and his disability. Wendy, for instance, needs to be seated where she can lipread both the teacher and her classmates. Care needs to be taken that light is not shining in her eyes which would prevent her from comfortably watching the speaker. Whenever possible, visual aids should be used to increase her

> . . . you may discover some of your child's problems and "bad habits" are not the result of his disability but rather common to his age.

comprehension. Once, I walked into an assembly and found my child sitting where she couldn't even see the speaker — let alone read his lips!

By visiting your child's classroom, you can get a clearer idea of how to be more effective with him at home — which in turn will help generate more confidence and competence in his classroom. Teachers are usually more than willing to suggest specific things parents can do to help their child function better in class. Wendy's first grade teacher used to tape songs that were being sung at school. At home, I would write out the words for Wendy to learn, and she would then practice the tune and rhythm by singing along with the tapes. This helped her participate in a school activity that was difficult for her to manage without special assistance.

Visits to your child's classroom will give you an idea of others your child's age. This can be a reassuring and/or painful experience. Classroom observation always made me acutely aware of how much Wendy missed because she didn't hear, or sometimes couldn't understand, what was being said. These visits made me even more painfully mindful of her deficits in language and vocabulary, and the academic and social implications of this. While these comparative observations were uncomfortable, they spurred me on to find better ways to work with her in areas that could be improved and gradually persuaded me to accept what couldn't be changed. At the same time, classroom visits can also be reassuring in that you may discover some of your child's problems and "bad habits" are not the result of his disability but rather common to his age.

As your child gets older, visiting the classroom may be inadvisable if it calls attention to his difficulties or if it makes him self-conscious or uncomfortable. I stopped visiting my daughter's class when she reached fourth grade. Until then she had periodically asked me to visit. The teachers were usually pleased to have me there as I was happy to help out actively in the classroom. In some schools some teachers regularly ask for parent volunteers to help in the classroom. This provides a good opportunity for a parent to be of service while at the same time gaining useful information about his own child and building a positive relationship with the teacher and the school.

> Sometimes I don't feel like probing to find out how Wendy is progressing, or thinking about what her needs are.

Conferences Are Important

To keep in touch with your child's progress, it is important to have conferences with his teacher as well as the other professionals who work with him. I personally have not found the customary two scheduled parent-teacher conferences per school year to be sufficient. I have often requested one or two additional meetings. I did this partly out of my own need to be informed and reassured about Wendy's progress. Sometimes I found the teachers felt Wendy was making progress when this wasn't so. Often when I requested that a teacher take a closer, more deliberate look at her work, it became apparent that Wendy needed extra or a different kind of help. These additional conferences have meant that Wendy's progress has been more carefully monitored than might otherwise have been the case.

Conferences not only keep you up-to-date on your child's progress, they also provide an opportunity to share your observations and concerns with those working with your child and thus to encourage and sustain *their* interest and concern. If possible, and it usually is with a little extra effort, fathers should attend at least one conference during the school year.

In addition to having conferences with Wendy's classroom teacher, I have found it advisable to meet with all who are involved in planning and executing her educational program. These have included a learning disability consultant, a speech therapist, a supplemental teacher and a classroom teacher. Two meetings a year with this team have proved very beneficial for everyone.

The first meeting may be arranged early in the school year but only after everyone has had a chance to get to know your child. The second may take place sometime before the end of the school year but while there is still time to effect any necessary changes. At the first meeting you can ascertain the educational plan for your child and who is taking responsibility for what. You can share your view of your child's needs and make suggestions.

At the second meeting you can ask for an assessment of your child's progress. Again share your observations and concerns and discuss ways in which the program might be more effective. One of the advantages of holding these team conferences is that they ensure that all the professionals from whom your child receives "supporting services" have an opportunity to communicate with one another and share their understanding of your child's circumstances and needs.

It is the stated policy of most schools to have parent conferences. However, when the school is slow to make contact and arrange a conference, parents may need to take the initiative. Phone the responsible person, be it the teacher, principal or "specialist." It is usually tactful and efficient to start with the teacher; she will probably offer to get back in touch with you once the arrangements are made. If you don't hear from the school in a week or so, call back to see that the conference is confirmed. This may require determination, but don't be obnoxious. The goal is to develop a cooperative working relationship with school personnel around your child's interests and needs — not a courtroom or arbitration situation.

Learn Your Rights and Get Busy

How can you as a parent go about securing appropriate services for your child at school? Learn your rights. Obtain copies of laws pertaining to special education from your State Department of Education or from your local Director of Special Services. Find out the policies of your local school board with respect to special education.

Join parent groups that are organized to understand and help children with disabilities and their families. And join groups specifically concerned with the education of all children with special needs. My experience has been that such groups can provide experiences and programs that are a mine of education and information for concerned parents. Find out how other parents secured appropriate programs for their children in their school systems. You can adapt the successful strategies of others to get the right program for your child.

Be Prepared to Educate the Staff

The disabled child in an integrated school setting often requires one or more supportive services. If the coordination of your child's education with these special services is not supervised by a teacher knowledgeable about his disability, the job of "educating" teachers and tutors may fall to you, the parents. Share information with the school orally and in writing. Pass on to teachers a copy of any magazine or newspaper article that can help them to understand your child better.

Educating the school staff is a delicate matter. If you are low-key they may ignore you; if you operate in persistent high gear they may be annoyed or insulted. Sensitivity to and respect for the feelings of those working with your child are important. So is a sense of reciprocity. At the outset, when you and your child's teacher first meet, suggest that you will pass along articles related to your child's disability and ask that she do the same.

Private Help

Even if your school provides a range of supportive services, you may find it valuable to have your child seen privately for additional help. Private instruction is usually available during the summer months, whereas school programs may be restricted to the academic year.

Until recently, Wendy has worked weekly with a speech pathologist. During the past several years, the speech pathologist has not only helped Wendy greatly with her speech and language development but has been invaluable in assisting us in our evaluation of Wendy's progress in these areas, as well as in her general academic work. The speech pathologist has also shared her assessment of Wendy's progress and present and future needs with the school.

Some parents may feel that their child can best be helped through private tutoring or therapy outside the school. This may be especially advisable if a child objects to being called out of class for tutoring or extra help; if the school personnel do not have the necessary training and skill; or if the services offered at school are insufficient or inappropriate for a particular child. In such cases it is essential that the private services to the child be explicitly coordinated with his school program.

The goal is to develop a cooperative working relationship with school personnel . . . not a courtroom or arbitration situation.

It Isn't Easy

It isn't easy to be the parent of a child with a disability. It isn't easy trying to assure the sufficiency of your child's education. I personally haven't found it easy to ask school personnel for additional services, for extra conferences or for educational evaluations not recommended by the teacher.

Sometimes I don't feel like probing to find out how Wendy is progressing, or thinking about what her needs are. Sometimes I feel like taking a vacation from it all. Sometimes I do just that!

But in the end, my husband and I know that Wendy's education is our responsibility. We care the most. And the same is true of you and your child.

Educating Parents of Children with Special Needs-

Approaches and Issues

Parent intervention programs for handicapped and low-socioeconomic children have many common elements which may be utilized in program development or expansion.

Edith Levitt and Shirley Cohen

Edith Levitt, Ed.D., is a Research and Development Associate for the Special Education Development Center at Hunter College, City University of New York, New York City. Previously, she was Research Associate for the Research and Demonstration Center for the Education of Handicapped Children at Teachers College, Columbia University, New York City.

Shirley Cohen, Ph.D., is Director of the Special Education Development Center at Hunter College. Formerly, she was an Instructor in the M.A. program for training teachers of the emotionally disturbed, Brooklyn College of the City University of New York, and a resource teacher for the Junior Guidance Classes Program for the New York City Public Schools.

The assumption that parent education can make a meaningful contribution to child development is a long-standing one. Early childhood programs have traditionally included parent education meetings and individual parent-teacher conferences. Programs for handicapped children have offered similar parent education services, as well as home visitations related to child care.

In these and other interactions with professionals, parents have generally been given the role of receivers of information and advice from experts. However, within the past decade a new view of parent-child interaction has developed—one suggesting that the demarcation between experts and parents vis-à-vis the development of children is a simplistic one. This new view recognizes that parents make a unique contribution to the affective and cognitive development of their children. This contribution stems from their intimate interaction with these children in their role as informal and/or formal instructor. Professionals involved in parent intervention programs have incorporated this changed perception of parents into their work. As a result, they have been moving toward a concept of parents as partners in the educational enterprise. Most parent intervention programs cited here worked only with the mother and child. Since all persons living in the household with the target child may play significant roles in the child's development, future programs may choose to stress involvement of additional family members.

Educating Parents of Children with Special Needs-Approaches and Issues, Edith Levitt and Shirley Cohen, *Young Children,* Reprinted with Permission, Vol. 31, No.4, May 1976. ©National Association for the Education of Young People, 1834 Connecticut Avenue N.W. Washington, D.C. 20009

The newer parent intervention programs reflect this improved climate of respect for the parental role. However, participation in these programs, particularly those that are home-based, may also pose the following problems for parents: (1) The parents may have to give up an accustomed autonomy in handling their child and follow a prescribed approach—one that may be incompatible with the parent's natural style. (2) The parents are expected to acquire certain skills and may have a sense of being evaluated on their ability to master them. (3) The parents are also expected to implement these skills through interaction with their child, even when there are troublesome overtones—as is often the case with handicapped children. (4) Finally, if the program involves home visitation, the parents have to adjust to receiving an outsider into their home on a regular basis.

It would seem that parents who commit themselves to participation in an intervention program must have a high degree of motivation. Recognition that such a process is likely to enhance their children's development probably tends to outweigh initial apprehensions. In time, familiarity with personnel, increased self-confidence, and demonstrated gains by the child would make most parents feel comfortable with such a program. However, parents who continue to feel uneasy will be hampered in their interaction with their children. A study by Barbrack (1970) describes a group of mothers who conformed to this pattern.

Continued participation in a parent intervention program may also produce a new set of problems. One noted by Luterman (1967) and by Gray (1971) is the development of an overdependent attitude toward the parent educator on the part of the mother. Similarly, Levenstein (1971) has referred to the risk that a child may become overattached to the worker. Levenstein's comment points up the related problem of possible competition between parents and worker for the child's attention. An additional hazard is the possibility that the worker's expertise with the child will evoke a feeling of inadequacy in the parents.

Adjustment to the rather complex parent-worker relationship is a concern for the worker as well as the parent. Both Gordon (1969) and Gray (1971) have discussed two major difficulties that can confront the worker in such a relationship: the need to adapt to an alien life style, and the frustration inherent in coping with passive or resistant parents.

Parent intervention programs generally have had a dual focus: the first is on the mother as a person in her own right, and the second is on her role as teacher of her child. Both aspects are considered below.

The Mother as a Person in Her Own Right

Provision in parent intervention programs for the mother in her own right runs the gamut from social get-togethers to individual psychotherapy. Understandably, personal consideration is particularly in evidence for parents of the handicapped. Because of special problems in accepting and coping with their children, these parents have usually received counseling services, and, on occasion, psychotherapy as well.

Two agencies for handicapped children that have provided parent counseling programs within a formal research design exemplify this approach. The first, conducted by United Cerebral Palsy of Queens (Weider and Hicks 1970), used a group therapy format. This centered on the parents' attitudes toward their handicapped children and also dealt with more personal factors. The Shield Institute for Retarded Children (Hunter and Schucman 1967) offered a similar group therapy program. In addition, it provided individual counseling or psychotherapy which could center either on the parent or the child.

Another approach to the counseling role is provided by the home visitor who has a social work background. Such a worker is apt to be employed when the child is severely handicapped, as in programs by Fraiberg, Smith, and Adelson (1969) and Patt (1969). The visitor then provides the parent with a blend of supportive counseling and practical guidance.

Parent intervention programs for low-socioeconomic families display a broader focus in their approach to the mother as a person—one which considers her background and the problems it can produce.

Diverse approaches have been used by parent educators in attempting to help these families ameliorate their personal problems. These include providing opportunities for social interaction with other parents, inclusion of "parent-centered" topics for group discussion, help with household management, budgeting, location of health and social services, and assistance with career development. For parents involved in intervention programs, career development has often had an educational focus. For example, Klaus and Gray (1968) trained past participants in parent intervention programs to work with parents who were currently involved in them, and Karnes (1969) helped train parents in her program for work in early childhood education.

Facilitating Parents' Roles as Teachers of Their Children

Center-Based Programs

A common approach to supporting parents as teachers of their children is to invite them into the school setting. Parents are often given an opportunity to observe their children in the classroom. At times they will be accompanied by a staff member who helps them interpret what they see.

Parents may also be asked to function as teacher aides. The Pathfinder School in Bayside, Queens, New York, a school for the brain-injured, and the Preschoolers' Workshop in Garden City, Long Island, New York, a school for emotionally disturbed children, both use parents in this capacity. In at least one program, that conducted by Headley and Leler (1971), work as a teacher aide was the main method for helping the mother assume a more active teaching role with her child. One issue relating to the use of parents as teacher aides is whether this experience should be open to a selected group or to all parents. A second is whether the parent should work just with his or her own child or with others. A third concerns the question of when to involve parents in this role.

In some cases, a worker interacts with the parent and child at a center. Parent educators in the center-based programs for deaf children (Luterman 1967; Horton 1968) worked with both mother and child. Teachers in a center-based program conducted by the League School for Seriously Disturbed Children (Doernberg, Rosen, and Walker 1968) worked with the child alone while the mother observed.

In the Early Education Demonstration Project conducted by United Cerebral Palsy of New York City, a variety of staff members—the physical therapist and speech therapist, as well as the teacher—work at the center with the mother-child dyad. This agency has also developed a unique Summer Family Conference (Rafael 1972) in which handicapped children and their parents, along with other family members, are invited to spend five days in a summer camp setting. The main objective is to furnish educational and counseling services for hard-to-reach parents. The project provides both formal and informal opportunities for interaction between staff, parents, and children.

Group Programs

A few parent intervention programs have relied exclusively on workshops in preparing parents to work with their children. They are exemplified by a program for parents of retardates (Benson and Ross 1972), and one for parents of children who were potentially learning disabled (Slater 1971). Initial meetings in both these programs were devoted to orientation, demonstration of techniques and materials, and provision of take-home materials for the children. At subsequent workshops, parents were encouraged to raise questions or problems related to tutoring their children, and were given guidance for further work with them.

The parent education meetings which are common adjuncts to other intervention programs may overlap loosely with the activities of such workshops. These meetings may utilize films, lectures, or a discussion format. Content for these meetings deals most frequently with child development and with educational topics, but ranges over additional pertinent topics as well. Parent meetings may also be used for such purposes as demonstration of materials and methods for working with children, guidance in making take-home play materials, and provision of toys and books to be used at home.

The degree of stress on interpersonal interaction, and on open-ended discussion, varies at these parent meetings. Both factors tend to receive special consideration in programs for handicapped children. As an example, the atmosphere of parent meetings at the League School (Doernberg, Rosen, and Walker 1968) was described as one of "camaraderie, informal ease, and mutual interest and support." Topics for discussion often originated with parents, and group members, whether professional or parents, shared "information, observations, and insights" in a free-flowing manner.

Parent meetings conducted in a program for young children with low-socioeconomic backgrounds suggested a somewhat different atmosphere. Badger (1972) noted that in her program each parent was treated with the same respect as that accorded to professional teachers. The leader reinforced pertinent aspects of the discussion, but also relied on group members to effect attitude change through interaction with each other. The leader also occasionally confronted group members with their attitudes of withdrawal and hopelessness. Still another atmosphere is suggested by Radin's (1968) description of parent meetings which focused on behavior modification.

Home-Based Programs

Home-based programs, often a more intensive form of parent intervention, are being developed on behalf of handicapped children, as well as children from low-socioeconomic levels. As is the case in work with parent groups, parent education in the home varies in its stress on interpersonal interaction. This can pertain either to the interaction between worker and parent or to that between parent and child. Some descriptions of home-based programs place considerable emphasis on this factor, while others touch on it cursorily or omit it from discussion.

In their work with parents of blind infants, Fraiberg, Smith, and Adelson (1969) regarded the promotion of a "lovebond" between parent and child as their single most important aim. Similarly, promotion of a positive mother-child interaction was an essential aspect of programs by Lambie and Weikart (1970) and by Levenstein (1971).

In discussing the parent-worker relationship, Alford (1971) commented that it is as important to earn the parent's confidence and establish a comfortable relationship as it is to develop the child's trust and confidence. Special concern for individual differences in parents was shown in the Lambie and Weikart (1970) program. Parent behaviors were categorized into four types, ranging from those who seemed to intuitively know how to handle their child to those who related to them in a detached or detrimental manner. Workers took these differences into account in interacting with these parents.

To some extent, the feasibility of responding sensitively to parent and child is dependent on the degree of structure built into the worker's approach. As an example, in Barbrack's (1970) program the worker was asked to make a rather lengthy specified statement to the mother about the program on her first visit. The worker was also expected to conclude by reading a story to the child. These procedures seemed to leave the worker with insufficient leeway for modulation in response to either mother or child. In cases where a mother is being taught to use a behavior modification approach, it may be that her interaction with the child may be similarly restricted.

The Barbrack (1970) study also dealt with the issue of mother-centered versus child-centered intervention programs. The study included evaluations of a mother-centered program and one that focused on the child. In the latter instance, the home visitor worked only with the child and did not solicit the mother's involvement. The study produced unexpected results: The children in the child-centered program made significantly greater gains on the Metropolitan Achievement Test than did those in the mother-centered program. In interpreting his results, Barbrack noted that the mother-centered group seemed uncomfortable in the teaching role and thus tended to pressure their children during and after sessions with the home visitor. By way of contrast, while the child-centered program was formally conducted by the worker, parents got involved and withdrew as they wished. Apparently, these parents profited from their informal contact with the worker and were able to help their children in turn.

Common Dimensions of Home-Based Parent Intervention Programs

Despite their diversity, a number of common dimensions are discernible in home-based parent intervention programs. They include the following.

1. All programs make some provision for orienting and pretraining workers. Manuals are sometimes developed for this purpose, e.g., that used by Santostefano and Slayton (1967). Generally, training is an intensive effort which lasts from a few weeks to several months. It covers such topics as child development concepts, learning theory, work with parents, and curricular materials. The use of role playing is a common device in these training programs, as is observation in the field. In Gordon's (1969) program, trainees were also given direct practice with mothers and infants. After programs are initiated, parent workers usually receive ongoing supervision through individual conferences. They are generally provided with in-service group sessions as well.

2. Parent intervention programs generally make provision for the informal orientation of parents toward the program's educational goals, approaches, and materials. Preliminary group meetings or individual home visits are generally used for this purpose. Some programs also offer a more formal orientation for parents in the form of guidebooks or manuals. Example are those produced by the Far West Laboratory (1972) and by the Ontario Institute for Studies in Education (Biderman and Fowler 1973).

3. While professionals working with parents of both handicapped and low-socioeconomic level children are often drawn from the same disciplines, a contrast is evident in the use of paraprofessionals. They are frequently employed in programs for children from low-socioeconomic levels, but only rarely in programs for the handicapped (Levitt and Cohen, in press). This issue is pertinent for parent intervention programs on behalf of children who are both low-income and handicapped. Gordon (1969) has provided a convincing rationale for utilizing paraprofessionals in intervention programs designed for low-socioeconomic level parents. He noted that paraprofessionals inspire greater trust in parents, are better attuned to cultural clues, and are less likely to offend parents' sensitivities. Gordon also reviewed some special problems arising out of the employment of paraprofessionals. These sometimes included difficulty in absorbing abstract ideas and communicating them to parents, a tendency to shift from "missionary zeal" to disillusionment or boredom, and a tendency to take a rigid or pessimistic attitude toward mothers.

4. The approach most commonly used in parent intervention programs is to have the worker demonstrate ways of working with the child as the mother observes. The mother is then asked to imitate the worker. However, in Levenstein's (1971) program, this demonstration was presented on a "take it or leave it basis." Levenstein preferred this to a more direct approach which she thought might seem "patronizing" to the mother.

5. The worker also usually provides parents with more specific guidance. This may be offered on the spot or deferred to the end of the session. It may consist of specific suggestions about the parent's use of language or behavior, or ways of engaging the child in play. Other techniques employed by parent workers include role playing, positive reinforcement for the parent as well as the child, and task analysis.

6. The worker generally takes responsibility for evaluating the child's progress and formulating ongoing curricular objectives. These plans are reviewed with the parent, who is then provided with suitable materials. In the case of behavior modification programs, the determination of individual "baselines" followed by appropriate "prescriptions" is an essential aspect of the program. The worker's latitude in formulating curricular objectives for the parent varies. In some cases, materials and procedures are largely predetermined, so that the worker's decisions are principally related to pacing. In others, the worker has relative autonomy in selecting new tasks for the child.

7. Parents are sometimes consulted about the selection of materials and asked for their suggestions. Gordon (1969) has stressed the need for such consultation. He has commented that a parent has to "see sense" in the child's tasks and be able to enjoy them before the parent can use them effectively. In some programs (e.g., Gray 1971), parents have been helped to make or improvise materials from what is available around the house.

Other Techniques for Parent Intervention Programs

A variety of additional techniques have been used in parent intervention programs. Methods of encouraging parents to attend meetings include providing transportation, paying for baby-sitters, writing or calling parents in advance of meetings, and arranging small groups for those who seem uncomfortable at larger meetings. Other techniques include showing parents videotapes of their interaction with their children, paying parents for program participation, and training siblings as tutors.

Curricula in parent intervention programs for handicapped children show considerable diversity. However, they also reflect common elements in the field of special education. These include concern for presenting tasks in a clear, understandable manner and at a level geared to the child's ability. Curricular tasks may range from sensorimotor training and socialization to academic tasks for more mature children. Two curricular areas frequently stressed in parent programs for the handicapped are self-help skills and language. One ambitious curricular effort seems to be that of the Portage Project (Yavner 1972). Its curriculum was based on a set of 363 sequentially arranged curriculum goals. These covered self-help, as well as motor, cognitive, communication, and social skills. Typically, the children's curricula in parent intervention programs for the handicapped cover a number of areas. However, in some cases they have a single focus. These are exemplified by one program (Santostefano and Slayton 1967) which centered on "focal attention," and another (Slater 1971) which focused on perceptual skills.

Children's curricula in parent intervention programs for low-socioeconomic children tend to reflect major trends in early childhood programs. They present some important contracts to the curricula in parent intervention programs for the handicapped. On the whole, they are more comprehensive, more highly organized, and more apt to have been derived from a theoretical framework. Some of these programs also place more emphasis on cognitive processes, as opposed to content, whereas this is rare in programs for the handicapped.

Gordon (1969) has provided a useful commentary on curricula for parent intervention programs based on experience with his own program. He notes one basic problem: writing a task so that it is clear and usable for a paraprofessional or a mother without completely structuring its use. In Gordon's view, a task should be viewed as a point of departure for further elaboration rather than an end in itself. He believes that curriculum development should include design of the instructional phase and consideration of the interpersonal situation in which the curriculum is to be used. He also stresses the need to formulate curricula that stimulate curiosity and exploration.

Conclusions and Recommendations

- Participation in an intervention program requires adjustment by the parents to (a) the role of learner and (b) modification of their relationship with their child. Workers, in turn, may have problems in adjusting to an alien life style in parents and in coping with parental apathy and resistance. The complex mother-child-worker relationship may spark special difficulties. These include (a) an overdependent attitude toward the worker on the mother's part, (b) competition between mother and worker for the child's attention, (c) a feeling of inadequacy engendered in the mother by the worker's expertise. The success of any intervention program will hinge to some extent on its sensitive handling of these parent-worker dynamics.
- At present a wide variety of approaches is being used in intervention programs for both handicapped and low-socioeconomic level children. Systematic studies have been carried out with low-socioeconomic level children comparing some of these approaches. Similar studies are needed in the field of the handicapped.
- An important reason for using the indigenous paraprofessional with low-socioeconomic level parents is the paraprofessional's special understanding of their problems. Paraprofession-

als who would bring an analogous understanding to work with parents of the handicapped might be parents who have had the firsthand experience of rearing a handicapped child. Other family members with exposure to these children might also make good paraprofessionals.

• The categorization of mothers by Lambie and Weikart (1970) in terms of attitudes toward their children seems germane to all parent intervention programs. Variation in these attitudes would be reflected in maternal teaching style as described by Hess and Shipman (1965). One aim of parent intervention programs is the modification of this teaching style. However, if efforts at modification are too stringent, they may become counterproductive.

• The formulation of procedures for parent intervention programs on behalf of handicapped children raises an important issue concerning their degree of structure. On the one hand, certain factors argue for adaptability in teaching procedures. These include affective and interpersonal factors, along with individual differences in maternal teaching style and in the cognitive functioning of handicapped children. On the other hand, the greater the uniformity built into teaching procedures the easier it is to influence specific aspects of the program, make evaluations, and draw conclusions. It is evident that an either-or attitude is inappropriate in dealing with this issue. Rather, a logical approach for parent intervention programs would be the use of carefully designed procedures with specified alternatives that provide some latitude in their application.

• Parents have had an important share in promoting useful educational services for their handicapped children. However, work with parents in this new participatory role will also require the development of a special expertise on the part of both professionals and paraprofessionals. Training programs in special education should be expanded to include a unit designed to equip teachers and ancillary personnel for work with parents as teachers. This unit could cover observation of parents and handicapped children in the home, techniques and approaches for work with parents, and suitable children's curricula to be used in conjunction with parent intervention programs.

The Impact of the Child's Deficiency on the Father: A Study of Fathers of Mentally Retarded and of Chronically Ill Children

S. Thomas Cummings, Ph.D.
Children's Division, The Menninger Foundation, Topeka, Kansas

Psychological assessments of fathers of mentally retarded, of chronically ill, and of healthy children indicate that the first two groups undergo significant stress associated with their fathering a handicapped child. Some fathers of mentally retarded children appear subject to a pattern of neurotic-like constriction. Differences in the experiences of fathers and mothers of deficient children are discussed, and suggestions for treatment are offered.

Over the past two decades, much research has focused on families rearing a handicapped child, one who experiences some permanent limitations in adaptive capacities. Most of this research has concerned the effects on both parents as a unit or on the parent who has traditionally borne the primary child care role, the mother.[9, 11] The present report will attempt to clarify how fathers are affected psychologically by their children's handicaps. This study of fathers is a companion to an earlier study on mothers,[5] and it uses an essentially identical methodology.

There are compelling reasons, both practical and theoretical, for studying the fathers of handicapped children. For those providing mental health services, greater understanding of fathers' adaptations may aid efforts to mobilize family strengths and offset effects of long-term stress. Recent changes in American family structure and parental roles make the situation of the father increasingly pertinent. The family unit is considerably smaller than it was only a generation ago; mothers and fathers now share almost exclusive caretaking responsibility for their children, with very little assistance from surrogate caretakers (older sibs and other relatives) in the family. Other concurrent changes, notably the growing determination among many mothers to maintain careers outside the home, suggest that fathers are assuming a larger role in the care of young children. Thus there is increasing likelihood of fathers experiencing the handicaps of their children more immediately and sentiently than did fathers of only a generation ago.

Further, the study of these fathers may yield information of interest to researchers concerned with determinants of personality during middle age. The vicissitudes of parenthood are being recognized as a potent set of influences on personality during middle life.[1, 2] Changes in parental personality organization in turn influence the coping strategies adopted by parents in rearing their children during middle childhood and adolescence. Thus, while the re-

The Impact of the Child's Deficiency on the Father: A Study of Fathers of the Mentally Retarded and of Chronically Ill Children, S. Thomas Cummings, *American Journal of Orthopsychiatry*, Vol. 46, No. 2, April 1976,

search reported here is not longitudinal and does not focus on the sequential, mutual interactions between deficient children and their fathers, the results are likely to suggest a variety of applications. The major purpose, however, remains a better understanding of how a handicapped child affects the psychological life of the father, an issue with practical implications for those in clinics and child development centers concerned with fostering parental competence.

SUBJECTS

The subjects of this research are 240 fathers, 60 fathers each of mentally retarded children, chronically physically ill children, neurotic * children, and healthy children. All of the fathers have the following common demographic characteristics: intact family status; natural father of child; father of more than one living child, with half or more of his children in a healthy status; affected child in the age range 4–13; white or Negro racial status; and socioeconomic status in the upper-middle to upper-lower range. In each of the four samples of 60 fathers, equal representations are found for sex of affected child, two age groupings of affected child (4–8, 9–13) and four socioeconomic categories.

In addition to these sample characteristics shared by the entire group of fathers, certain additional qualifying conditions were imposed for inclusion of fathers in the deficiency groups to assure relative uniformity of deficiency status.

Within the mentally retarded group, the affected child was living at home with the natural parents and either had been diagnosed as retarded by a specialty clinic serving retardates, or his retardation was viewed as evident from his parents' long-term participation in a parental organization for retarded children.

Within the chronically physically ill group, several chronic illnesses of children were represented with these common characteristics: existence of the illness for at least one year; nature of the illness or its treatment such to guarantee that the parents would receive daily reminders of the child's illness status; and prognosis of the illness such that the parents faced neither the hope of imminent cure nor the threat of imminent death. Within this sample, about one-fourth were fathers of diabetic children, one-fourth fathers of children with rheumatic fever (accompanied by heart damage requiring restricted activity), one-fourth fathers of children with cystic fibrosis, and the remaining fourth were fathers of children with a variety of somatic illnesses.

Within the neurotic group, all of the children whose fathers participated in the research had been diagnosed by a community clinic as having a behavior disorder without psychosis, mental retardation, or organic brain damage.

Those in the healthy control sample, while varying in health status themselves, were fathers all of whose children enjoyed good health, as certified by a physician—they had no diagnosed deficiencies in physical health, intellect, or psychological adjustment.

METHOD

Fathers were recruited for participation in the study through cooperation of a large group of clinics, social agencies, and community physicians. Following their agreement to participate in the study, the fathers completed the battery of four self-administered tests in their own homes and returned them by mail. Most of their wives also participated in the research. Actually, cooperation from mothers was about twice the rate of that from fathers. Half the fathers in this study were husbands of women who had participated in the earlier published study of mothers.[5]

Test measures were chosen to permit assessment of four classes of personality variables: fathers' prevailing mood, especially as this was influenced by interactions with the index children; their self-esteem, both generally and in terms

* Following the design of the earlier study of mothers,[5] fathers of neurotic children were included in the present sample, but results relating to the neurotic group will not be presented in this paper.

of their evaluations of their worth as fathers; their interpersonal satisfactions in relating to family members and others; and their child rearing attitudes.

Central personality variables were assessed through three of the four tests administered: a sentence completion test, a self-acceptance inventory, and a child rearing attitudes questionnaire. The fourth test administered was the Edwards Personal Preference Schedule (EPPS),[8] a standardized personality inventory that profiles fifteen manifest psychological needs.

The 46-item Sentence Completion Test was specifically constructed for this research program to elicit the respondent's expression of feelings toward the handicapped child, other children in the family, spouse and neighbors, and feelings of paternal role adequacy. The self-acceptance inventory was the Self-Acceptance Scale of the Berger Inventory,[4] a 36-item questionnaire reflecting the respondents' expressed self-acceptance. The child rearing attitudes scale was a modification [7] of the Shoben Parental Attitudes Inventory,[13] a 30-item questionnaire on child rearing attitudes divided into subscales of Possessiveness, Dominating, and Ignoring attitudes.

The personality scales derived from the Sentence Completion Test consisted of ratings of these described variables made by two experienced clinical psychologists using six-point rating scales. The Sentence Completion Test data were divided into sets of sentence stems ranging in number from one to nine, with each set comprising the total paternal personality data available to the judge in rating subjects on that variable. All clinical judgments were made without the judges' awareness of the age, sex, or deficiency status of the child whose father's responses were being evaluated. A training session with the two judges for a particular Sentence Completion Test variable preceded their undertaking to judge that variable. Judges were instructed to distribute their ratings proportionately throughout the various categories of the rating scale for the total group of 240 fathers whose responses were being judged on any one variable. A subject's score on a Sentence Completion Test variable was the sum of the judges' ratings of a father's responses on that scale.

TABLE 1 lists the twelve central personality variables with which this research is concerned, clustered into four groups labeled: Dysphoric Affect, Self-Esteem, Interpersonal Satisfactions, and Child-Rearing Attitudes. Under the heading "Other" are listed several particularly significant scales from the EPPS which yielded important findings.

RESULTS

Findings have been determined through comparisons of the means of the two deficiency groups—the mentally retarded and chronically physically ill groups—with the means of the healthy control group fathers on the personality variables assessed. Tests of statistical significance of the differences in these group means have been carried out. Analysis of variance procedures have also been used to evaluate the effects of age and sex of child on the paternal personality variables.

TABLE 1 presents the means of the three groups of fathers on each of the central personality variables studied, plus the contrasts (t-values) indicating the sizes and levels of significance of the differences between these group means. At the bottom of the table are listed three EPPS test variables which distinguish the fathers in the mentally retarded group from the fathers in the healthy control group. While none of our original study hypotheses related to expected variations in these EPPS variables, the findings on three of them provide a basis for inference about the personality differentiating effects on these mentally retarded group fathers of experiencing their children's chronic adaptive limitations.

Comparison of findings from the mothers' study [5] with the results from the present study will be noted where pertinent, even though only half the mothers reported on are the wives of these fathers.

Fathers of the Mentally Retarded. The fathers of mentally retarded children evaluated in this research are clearly different from the healthy control group

Table 1

DIFFERENCES BETWEEN HEALTHY AND DEFICIENCY GROUPS ON PATERNAL PERSONALITY VARIABLES

CLUSTERS AND TRAITS	MEANS			CONTRASTS (t-values)		
	HC	MR	CI	MR–HC	CI–HC	MR–CI
Dysphoric Affect						
Depressive Feeling	5.5	7.5	7.1	5.20[c]	2.72[c]	2.42[b]
Preoccupation with Child	6.4	8.3	6.4	2.88[c]	—	2.88[b]
Difficulty in Handling Anger at Child	6.3	6.8	6.4	1.24	.34	.93
Self-Esteem						
Expressed Self-Acceptance	152.0	147.4	149.8	−1.33[a]	−.74	−.71
Sense of Paternal Competence	7.6	6.5	6.6	−2.78[c]	−2.50[c]	−.28
Interpersonal Satisfactions						
Enjoyment of Child	8.6	5.4	7.1	−8.64[c]	−4.14[c]	−4.76[c]
Evaluation of Other Children	9.0	8.4	8.3	−1.77[b]	−2.21[b]	.42
Evaluation of Wife	9.1	8.4	9.1	−1.68[b]	—	−1.74
Evaluation of Neighbors	8.4	8.0	7.4	−.81	−2.20[b]	1.44
Child Rearing Attitudes						
Possessiveness	23.8	25.0	24.0	1.24	.21	1.10
Dominating	34.4	35.4	35.1	.92	.67	.30
Ignoring (rejection)	26.4	27.3	25.7	1.30[a]	−1.03	2.33[a]
Other (EPPS)						
Order	36.9	56.0	32.8	3.95[c]	−.83	4.67[c]
Dominance	68.6	58.4	68.1	−1.97[b]	−.11	−2.07[b]
Heterosexuality	67.4	57.7	64.5	−2.10[b]	−.65	−1.40

HC = Healthy Control, MR = Mentally Retarded, CI = Chronically Ill.
One-tailed tests of significance are used for contrasts of deficiency groups with the healthy control group; two-tailed tests are used for contrasts among deficiency groups, augmented for multiple comparisons.
[a] Significant at .10 level; [b] significant at .05 level; [c] significant at .01 level.

fathers on the personality variables studied. On three of the four main trait clusters, they show marked differences. In the Dysphoric Affect cluster, both Depressive Feeling and Preoccupation with Child indices are clearly involved. In the Self-Esteem cluster, the component of these fathers' esteem derived from their fathering experiences seems to leave them with a sense of their relative inferiority as fathers. There is a suggestion that this carries over into their overall general esteem for themselves as men, as indicated in the lower Expressed Self-Acceptance score, but this result should be interpreted cautiously in light of the minimal confidence level attached to the statistical test.

In the Interpersonal Satisfactions cluster, these fathers show a relative lack of relationship gratifications in three of the four areas measured. The single most emphatic finding in the research emerges in the trait, Enjoyment of Child (referring to the index child), where the satisfactions are markedly lower, as indicated in the largest t-value found in TABLE 1. (This finding duplicates the results in the mothers' study.[5]) Two other scales in this cluster, Evaluation of Other Children and Evaluation of Wife, are also lower in these fathers, implying some negative backwash on their overall gratification from family relationships.

An unforeseen outcome among the fathers of the mentally retarded is the appearance of three EPPS variables with significant differences from the healthy controls, specifically in the need-variables: Order, Dominance, and Heterosexuality. The Order variable depicts a person's emphasis on neatness, orderliness, organization, and routine in the conduct of daily affairs; high Dominance characterizes those people who value strong assertiveness in group situations; the Heterosexuality variable measures a person's degree of ready expression of sexual interests in members of the opposite sex. Compared to the healthy control group fathers, needs of the mentally retarded group fathers were rated higher on the Order and lower on the Dominance and Heterosexuality variables. This triad of effects, taken in combination, is strongly suggestive of a constricted male accentuating his compulsive tendencies in order to suppress his aggressive and sexual drives. It will be discussed further below.

Fathers of the Chronically Ill. The fathers of the chronically ill children also reveal significant negative effects from the experience of fathering a health-deficient child, although these are not as great as among fathers of the retarded children.

In the Dysphoric Affect trait cluster, only the trait, Depressive Feeling, is significantly different from the healthy control group. In the Self-Esteem pair of traits, only Sense of Paternal Competence is adversely affected.

However, in the Interpersonal Satisfactions cluster, three of four components demonstrate significantly lower levels of gratification in relationships—Evaluation of Child, Evaluation of Other Children, and Evaluation of Neighbors.

Father Groups Compared. Although the findings on these two groups of fathers are similar, there is statistical evidence to support the conclusion that fathers of the mentally retarded experience a greater negative impact from fathering their children than do fathers of chronically ill children. Inspection of the number and magnitude of each of these group's differences with the healthy control group (TABLE 1) indicates this, as does comparison of the groups with each other. This latter comparison (TABLE 1, MR-CI) reveals that Depressive Feeling, Preoccupation with Child, and Enjoyment of Child all stand at psychologically more stressful levels for the fathers of the mentally retarded.

Mothers and Fathers Compared. As mentioned above, the sample compositions of the mothers' and fathers' studies completed thus far do not allow a comparison of parents within the same family. However, some information on the comparative effects on fathers and mothers of experiencing their child's deficiency can be offered.

Among parents of the mentally retarded, both mothers and fathers are deeply affected by the psychologically stressful experience of rearing a retarded child. Mothers expressed a slightly lower level of Dysphoric Affect in the Difficulty in Handling Anger at Child component, but a greater spread of negative effects within the other two major clusters, Self-Esteem and Interpersonal Satisfactions. The extent to which differences in repressive tendencies associated with gender identity affects the results of these self-administered tests is unknown. Also unaccounted for is the undoubtedly greater burden on mothers who do not have the adaptive advantage of spending most of the day outside the home at work, which interrupts the continuity of stressful contact with the child, and which provides an area for the application of one's energies, capacities, and talents wherein approximating one's ego-ideals is largely under personal control. But while ambiguities remain in interpreting the comparative levels of psychological stress experienced by mothers and fathers of mentally retarded children, these data leave no doubt that fathers experience significant stress as parents of retarded children, even when they have also experienced the pleasures of having one or more healthy children.

Comparison of fathers and mothers of the chronically ill yields a result similar to that found for parents of the retarded, only more so. Fathers of the ill children seem to acknowledge their psychic pain more readily than do the mothers, as indicated by the larger number of personality variables indicative of stressful experience which reach statistical significance. Especially noteworthy is the clearly diminished sense of competence as a parent among these fathers, compared to mothers of the chronically ill. In the mothers' study,[5] a relatively small number of psychological stress indicators appeared; several factors contributing to this finding were discussed, including a strong repressive orientation, and a reduction in the sense of impotence, futility, and guilt achieved through daily health maintenance practices which might directly aid the child's recovery. The fathers do not appear to have the same repressive orientation, nor have they similar opportunities for helpful caretaking of the ill child; thus, they may be somewhat more vulnerable to psychological stress associated with the child's chronic limitations.

Response to Child's Age and Sex. We began this study with the belief that the stress felt by fathers of handicapped children would be more responsive to the age and sex of the child than was true for mothers in our earlier study. However, analysis of variance procedures for the combined deficiency groups do not indicate any significant differences related to sex. Age differences do appear on three of these paternal personality variables. The fathers of older index children (9–13), compared to fathers of younger children (4–8), show slightly lower psychological stress levels; they are rated lower on Depressive Feeling and higher on both Enjoyment of Child and Evaluation of Wife. While these data do not explain the disparity, a longer period of gratifications from interacting with their healthy children, as well as reassurance regarding their handicapped child's longevity and relative durability, seem likely ingredients of the difference between fathers of these age groups.

DISCUSSION

The finding that fathers of retarded and chronically ill children experience psychological stress thereby is not a surprising one. What is surprising and demands some further attempt at understanding are two related issues: 1) the degree of potency of the negative effects on fathers of fathering a limited child, relative to the traditional child rearing roles and responsibilities of fathers; 2) the indication that many fathers of mentally retarded children undergo long-term personality changes which resemble a pattern of neurotic-like constriction.

In accounting for the seeming stressfulness of fathering a handicapped child, which in our study appears to be greater for the fathers of mentally retarded than for the fathers of chronically ill children, several factors need to be considered: the father's confrontation in his daily living patterns of the child's deficiency condition; the ameliorative child care-taking opportunities available to the father; the opportunities for stress modulation through sharing experiences with other fathers who bear a similar burden of loss-stress. Even though most fathers of handicapped children spend much of their time away from their children during working hours, they experience ample reminders of the child's deficiency condition from direct observation when present and from maternal and sibling reports of their interactions with and worries about the limited child. But fathers' parental roles only infrequently include such rehabilitative or health-maintenance tasks as trips to the doctor, the drug store, the physical therapist, the special school, or other special health services. Fathers, relative to mothers, thus characteristically have fewer opportunities to do something directly helpful for their handicapped child, something which provides concrete evidence of their loving, caring, and benevolent concern. Relatively few opportunities for counterbalancing the sense of loss, frustration, and attendant anger are thus included in the father's role.

At the same time, organizations for parents of handicapped children seem to offer fewer services to fathers and to obtain less participation from them, resulting in less social sharing of the burdens of parenthood of a limited child than is typically available to mothers of these children. The personal experience of having conducted some group therapy series specifically structured for mothers of retarded children,[6] and finding that during such series a few fathers would always insist on attending and sharing their views, has led the senior author to believe that fathers are being less adequately provided for than are mothers in the development of supportive mental health services to the parents of the handicapped. It seems likely that the combination of these factors characterizing the life of a father of a handicapped child makes it somewhat more difficult for him to reduce his stress load, relative to the opportunities which mothers have to do so. In turn, as indicated by our research, these factors would seem to contribute to the fathers clearly and definitely reflecting their psychological stress, even while the overall stress load they bear is characteristically lighter than that borne by their wives.

Of special interest is the pattern of neurotic-like constriction in the fathers of mentally retarded children. Benedek [2, 3] described how parents, in the process of rearing a child, reexperience some of their own earlier struggles with drive control efforts and conscience strictures. She pointed out that parents have the opportunity in this process to modify some of the superego rigidity they have learned, reassured by their accumulated experiences since childhood of the groundlessness of the threats of the immature superego. In contrast, this opportunity for rendering the superego more benign is relatively less available to many parents of handicapped children because:

> Unsuccessful experience of the parent with unsuccessful children undermines the parent's self-esteem and enhances the strictness of his superego, thus rendering it pathogenic for the parent and consequently for the child. Incorporated into the psychic system of the parent, the child may mitigate or intensify the strictness of the parent's superego.[2]

Our study of fathers of mentally retarded children offers some direct confirmation of this unfortunate developmental trend toward neurotic constriction, which appears in our sample even among those who have fathered normal as well as deficient children. There can be little doubt that the pattern of many of these fathers —with lowered self-esteem, depressive feelings, little sense of themselves as competent fathers, few satisfactions from family relationships, a need for compulsive ordering of their experience and tight control of social and sexual interests—indicates a mid-life augmentation of earlier neurotic tendencies. When results of our earlier study [5] are inspected and reinterpreted, many of these also suggest an analogous trend associated with being the mother of a retarded child.

CLINICAL IMPLICATIONS

There are several ways in which those who work with fathers of deficient children can make use of these findings. First, by recognizing that fathers, as well as mothers, need opportunities for mourning the partial loss of their ideals for their children that confronting a child's permanent handicap entails. Implied here is the professional helper's ability to reexperience his own loss experiences in order that blockages to the fathers' expressions of loss and helplessness are not unwittingly set in place. Implied also is the worker's willingness to allow the father to express fully his grief, frustration, and anger, rather than expecting the father to serve primarily as the controlled suppressor for the feelings of the mother and other family members.

Finally, those helping families of handicapped children must recognize that their mourning is a long process involving varied expressions of loss on the part of each parent, and that no brief or standardized mode of dealing with the situation will serve all parents equally well.[10, 12, 14] Especially in working with fathers of handicapped children, where the occupational role and gender role components of being a father may interfere with their integrating their loss and grief experiences, we may miss opportunities to forestall neurotic trends with lifelong crippling effects. Rather than simply accept their defenses as their essence, we must recognize and deal with these fathers' efforts to avoid painful contact with inner feelings of loss and lowered self-esteem associated with this significant segment of their total experience of themselves as procreators.

REFERENCES

1. ANTHONY, E. AND BENEDEK, T. eds. 1970. Parenthood: Its Psychology and Psychopathology. Little, Brown, Boston.
2. BENEDEK, T. 1959. Parenthood as a developmental phase. J. Amer. Psychoanal. Assoc. 7:389–417.
3. BENEDEK, T. 1970. The family as a psychologic field. *In* Parenthood: Its Psychology and Psychopathology. Little, Brown, Boston.
4. BERGER, E. 1952. The relation between expressed acceptance of self and expressed acceptance of others. J. Abnorm. Soc. Psychol. 47:778–782.
5. CUMMINGS, S., BAYLEY, H. AND RIE, H. 1966. Effects of the child's deficiency on the mother: a study of mothers of mentally retarded, chronically ill and neurotic children. Amer. J. Orthopsychiat. 36:595–608.
6. CUMMINGS, S. AND STOCK, D. 1962. Brief group therapy of mothers of retarded children outside of the specialty clinic setting. Amer. J. Ment. Defic. 66:739–748.
7. DREWS, E. AND TEAHAN, J. 1957. Parental attitudes and academic achievement. J. Clin. Psychol. 13:328–332.
8. EDWARDS, A. 1959. Edwards Personal Preference Schedule, Revised. Psychological Corp., New York.
9. FARBER, B. 1960. Family organization and crisis: maintenance of integration in families with a severely retarded child. Monogr. Soc. Res. Child Devlpm. 25(1).
10. HIRSCHBERG, C. AND BRYANT, K. 1961. Helping the parents of a retarded child. Amer. J. Dis. Children 102:52–66.
11. JORDAN, T. 1962. Research on the handicapped child and the family. Merrill-Palmer Quart. 8:243–260.
12. MANDELBAUM, A. AND WHEELER, M. 1960. The meaning of a defective child to the parents. Soc. Casewk 41:360–367.
13. SHOBEN, E. 1949. The assessment of parental attitudes in relation to child adjustment. Genet. Psychol. Monogr. 39:101–148.
14. SOLNIT, A. AND STARK, M. 1961. Mourning and the birth of a defective child. Psychoanal. Study of the Child 16:523–537.

Rearing the Disabled Child: A Framework for Further Research

Jean O. Britton
The Pennsylvania State University
Kenneth R. Thomas
University of Wisconsin

Summary: This paper presents a framework which could be used by researchers to obtain descriptive and experimental data about the child-rearing practices of parents of disabled children. In addition, the authors suggest specific areas of research which might prove useful in assisting school psychologists to develop programs of counseling for the parents of such children.

Despite the plethoric number of theories which hypothesize a relationship between the ways a person is reared in childhood and his adult personality characteristics, little research has been conducted to measure the effects various modes of child-rearing have upon the disabled. While later learnings from peers, teachers, and employers may modify the effects of earlier experiences, it is the family, with its social and emotional intimacy, which is the first and perhaps most influential socializing agent in a child's environment. Indeed, for the disabled child, the family may assume an even greater importance as a socializing agent because of the child's somewhat limited access to other sources of influence. For example, recent studies suggest that the attitudes disabled adults hold toward various types of dependence have antecedents in the ways the culture and especially the family have taught them to handle their disability (Thomas, 1969; Thomas & Britton, 1970; 1970-71; 1972).

Several authors have commented on the attitudes of the family, particularly the mother, toward the disabled child (Kaplan, 1971; Kennedy, 1970; Olshansky, 1962). Negative feelings, such as hostility and chronic sorrow, as well as feelings of being cheated for having produced a defective child, are reported. Moreover, it is often implied that these feelings are expressed in various covert and overt behaviors toward the child, and that they can be detrimental to the child's development.

In recognition of these potential difficulties, parental counseling has been recommended as offering direction and support during the years in which the disabled child is growing up (Kaplan, 1971; Schiller, 1961). Unfortunately, however, little empirical data exist upon which to base such counseling since most of our understanding of child-rearing practices has been derived from research conducted on the "normal" child's rearing (e.g., Sears, Maccoby, & Levin, 1957; Yarrow, Campbell, & Burton, 1968). The purpose of this paper is twofold: (1) to present a framework which could be used by researchers to obtain descriptive and experimental data about the child-rearing practices of parents of disabled children, and (2) to suggest areas of research which might prove useful to school psychologists in developing counseling programs for the parents of such children.

THE PROCESS OF BECOMING SOCIALIZED

A child, whether normal or disabled, begins life with a fairly small number of behavior patterns. At first these patterns are related most directly to the child's biological needs and do not require formalized training for him to

Rearing the Disabled Child: A Framework for Further Research, Jean O. Britton and Kenneth R. Thomas, *Journal of School Psychology*, Vol. 1, No. 2,

become proficient. For the disabled child, however, even this basic biological functioning may be extremely difficult and the demands upon the parents for assistance can be quite heavy. Research is needed to determine how the parents of disabled children perceive and adapt to these demands and, in turn, how the parents' reactions to these demands affect the parent-child relationship.

As the child develops physically, his behavior repertoire expands considerably and he learns that he can do certain things for himself, such as reach for the rattle attached to his crib or squeeze the rubber toy in his playpen. However, although it is obvious that the range of behaviors for some disabled children may be significantly less than for "normals," the social meaning of these restrictions to the parents has not been studied systematically.

Simple physical maturation does not, of course, account for all of a child's development. To learn to become a *person,* both the normal and disabled child must receive training; they must learn through social interaction with others in their environments. While variations exist, there are usually certain common standards of conduct and behavior which any given culture expects from its members. Undoubtedly, notions are also held concerning the behaviors expected of disabled persons. For example, it might be expected that a child with a congenitally amputated leg would eventually attempt to master the use of a prosthetic device.

Usually persons are evaluated regarding whether their behavior conforms to the standards expected of them at various points in time. Throughout the life cycle certain early acceptable patterns have to change to provide for new behaviors that are deemed more appropriate by the culture. For example, sucking behavior must change to drinking and eating solid foods. Rage and direct agression in an infant must be replaced by culturally approved modes of expression. Childhood and adolescent dependence on parents for financial support must eventually be replaced by economic independence and self-sufficiency.

Parents play an essential role in this social learning process, not only because they are the persons most intimately associated with their child's development, but also because it is they who in many instances must decide what behaviors need to be changed. To make these decisions, parents must determine which new and presumably more mature behaviors need to be added to the child's existing behavior repertoire and which behaviors need to be extinguished. Further, parents must decide which training methods will be most effective in facilitating these behavior changes.

HOW DO PARENTS DEFINE BEHAVIORAL GOALS FOR THEIR DISABLED CHILD?

Basic to an understanding of the socialization process would be a description of the ways parents define behavioral goals for their disabled child at various stages in his development. What, for example, do they use as guidelines for appropriate behaviors in the child? What values do they attempt to establish? How high are the goals which they set? What demands do they make of the child and what privileges do they grant him? What risks, if any, which are related to a person's becoming more mature is the disabled child encouraged or even permitted to take? The list of potentially useful research questions in this area is extensive.

HOW DO PARENTS DISCIPLINE THEIR DISABLED CHILD?

Another aspect of the child-rearing process that offers potential for useful research concerns the manner in which parents discipline their disabled child in helping him to change his behavior. They can use both reinforcing or punishing methods with variations according to the sex and age of the child, sex of the parent, and the specific behaviors involved. It is not known, for example, how parents behave toward the disabled child who is aggressive toward them. Do they typically spank him, reason with him, ignore him, or verbally empathize with him? Presumably the training methods parents choose could influence not only their child's rate of behavior change but also his later values and expectations.

HOW DO PARENTS' ATTITUDES TOWARD THE DISABLED CHILD AFFECT THEIR CHILD-REARING PRACTICES?

Still another area of research deserving attention concerns the attitudes parents have toward their child and his disability, as well as their perceptions of themselves as parents, which tend to influence them in selecting one method of child-rearing over another. It is unlikely that the training practices of parents occur in a haphazard way. Rather, such practices are probably selected largely as a function of the parents' own personality characteristics, values, and beliefs. Moreover, it seems reasonable to hypothesize that factors such as the parents' religious and ethnic backgrounds, socioeconomic status, the family size, the child's age at disability onset, type and extent of disability, and sex also relate to the types of training practices selected. Many specific research questions might be delineated: Do differences among parents' beliefs concerning the reasons for their child's disability result in different training practices? Do the personality patterns of the parents themselves relate to their attitudes toward their child's disability? Do the types of training practices selected vary as a function of the parents' socioeconomic status?

WHAT EFFECTS DO PARENTAL TRAINING PRACTICES HAVE UPON THE CHILD'S LATER DEVELOPMENT?

Finally, and perhaps most important insofar as the objectives of this paper are concerned, research is needed to determine the effects of various parental training practices on the subsequent behaviors and development of the child. For example, is there a relationship between an insistence that the disabled child assume responsibility at home and his later independence at school and at work? Does permitting the disabled child latitude in the expression of his aggression facilitate or impede his later interpersonal relations with others? What specific antecedent training practices of parents are most typically related to the child's developing positive attitudes toward himself and his disability, work, and school? These questions are admittedly somewhat more difficult to answer than those suggested in earlier sections of this paper. However, if school psychologists are to assume an active role in assisting the parents of disabled children, they should be able to provide empirically derived suggestions for improved child-rearing practices.

Obviously, not all meaningful interactions between parents and children are rationally designed training exercises. A great deal of what parents do with and for their children is simply a result of the parents' enjoyment of, or annoyance with, their children as persons. Also, it can certainly not be assumed that all forms of parent-child interaction are particularly important in influencing the child's later behavior. However, to the extent that various modes of child-rearing do influence the later development and behavior of the disabled, research questions such as those outlined in this paper deserve investigation. Both school psychologists and parents need more extensive, more empirically based data than our research efforts to date have been able to provide.

The Rights of Children and Their Parents

State and federal courts have played an active role in the field of education in the past few years. The result has been a reshaping of the rules that teachers and administrators must live by as they make decisions on the educational future of children. Basically, the many court cases have defined further who is entitled to an education, and the due process to which every child and parent is entitled. Currently, the influence of the judiciary is seen in the modification of state and federal laws and procedures in education.

Basic Rights of Children and Their Parents

- All children are entitled to an appropriate education and an education in the least restrictive environment possible.
- Parents have the right to appeal a decision made to alter their child's educational program.
- Parents have the right to review and use in their appeal all information used by the school to make the decision.
- Parents have the right to have a neutral party decide on the most appropriate program for their child.
- Parents have the right to have the benefits of a special program specified and evaluated.

Implications for Educators

- Educational services must be available to all children regardless of severity of handicap.
- A variety of special education services must be available if children are to receive an education that is appropriate and as close to a program of normalization as possible.
- To promote understanding, parents should be informed early of difficulties experienced by their children. They should be involved in the planning and evaluation of the special services provided.
- Educational decision making must be based on the efforts of an educational team that collects and uses all appropriate information, not on a single test.
- Measurable objectives must be set for children receiving special services. The progress of these children must be reported to their parents.

The demands of courts and school laws should not frighten us. They are only saying that every child has the right to "fair play" and an appropriate education in the schools. This is no more than what we would wish for our children.

The Rights of Children and Their Parents, *Exceptional Children,* Vol. 42, No. 2, October 1975.

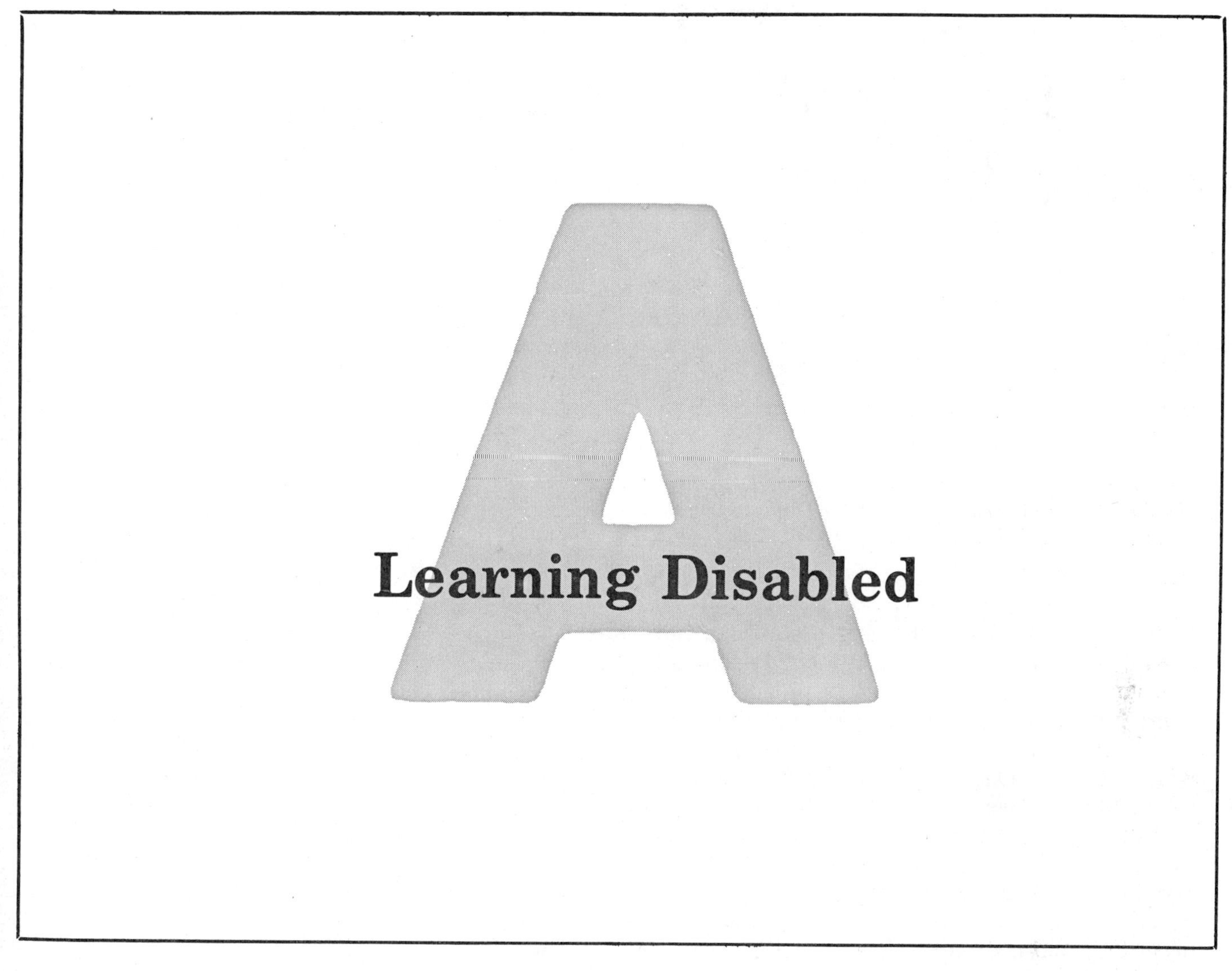

A Learning Disabled

In the past, parents did not play much of a part in the treatment of children with learning disabilities. Doctors treated the problem as neurological or physiological, analysists searched for fixations in early development, and teachers often used parents as scapegoats for classroom failures; and, indeed, it has long been recognized that poor family relationships contribute to learning disabilities. Children caught in the no-win situation of trying to please their frequently unpleaseable parents or finding themselves as the link between dissatisfied parents, may cease learning, thus precipitating a cycle of parental resentment, guilt, and overprotectivness. A child, who, for example, is lacking in concentration, patience, attention, cooperation, and stimulation presents a difficult challenge to parents. Members of the helping professions often felt that the parents were entirely to blame, lacked training and insight, and sometimes preferred to keep their children sick.

More recent developments indicate a clear relationship exists between a child's achievement and parental love and attention; that learning disabled children are usually angry children who are afraid of their anger, that perceptual difficulties have an emotional basis; and that helping professionals gradually came to understand the need to concentrate on ways in the parent-child relationship to improve the child's self-esteem. Fruitful communication between parents and teachers became a possibility. Parents, although initially upset by terms like mental handicap, brain damage, and learning disability, were capable of moving beyond anger, guilt, and the desire to blame someone, could be taught to provide a home environment which was structured, regular, with reinforcement, could learn to understand their child's behavior in terms of underlying emotional feelings, could perform at-home exercises to help correct deficiencies, and could monitor and help adjust medical dosages when the child needed them. Further studies showed that when the parent received counseling, the child improved at school, and when parents met in groups, positive results often ensued. Members of the helping professions now understand the importance of treating the learning disability as a family problem, of helping parents to learn how to build the child's self-confidence, to discipline without ego damage, and to express love and support without being overprotective.

Counseling Parents of Children With Learning Disabilities

Patricia M. Bricklin

Patricia Bricklin is Clinical Associate in the Department of Psychiatry and Parent Counselor at the Parkway Day School, Hahnemann Medical College and Hospital, Philadelphia, Pa.

MANY MEMBERS OF the helping professions have mixed feelings toward parents and their aid in a child's remedial program. There are a number of forces at work in producing the negative feelings many professionals harbor toward parents of patients.

First, all are heir to the legacies of the environmental school, which seeks to explain people largely in terms of parental influences. Most professionals realize the negative things parents can do to their children. Yet few have worked out the relationship between causal, deterministic explanations on the one hand, and notions of "accountability" or "blame" on the other. Hence, consistency is rare in these matters, and while one "explains" behavior among those toward whom one feels positively inclined, the tendency is to "blame" and "condemn" these same behaviors among those toward whom one lacks positive regard.

Second, professionals often project their own self-anger at parents. It is not unusual for a professional to blame himself or herself for not helping the patient to a greater degree than has been possible. This all-too-human anger often ends up directed at the parents, who are seen as the "real" reason the patient is not making more progress.

Third, all professionals and non-professionals harbor ambivalent feelings toward their own parents. These feelings are often confused with feelings toward other peoples' parents, including those of patients.

Fourth, many professionals believe that since it took them so long to master their helping skills, it is unlikely that others less trained than ourselves could contribute anything of importance to a helping process. Stated bluntly, many professionals are unwilling to believe a lay person can be therapeutic and/or helpful.

Fifth, likewise, those impressed with the role of the unconscious in human behavior are sometimes unwilling to acknowledge that help can be had from the uninsightful. Professionals of this persuasion seem to believe that because a good bit of behavior

Counseling Parents of Children with Learning Disabilities, Patricia M. Bricklin, *The Reading Teacher,* Vol. 23, No. 4, January 1970. Reprinted with Permission of the Author and The International Reading Association.

occurs outside, so to speak, the purview of conscious intention, that therefore *all* significant behavior is outside the influence of conscious will.

Lastly, many professionals seem to believe that *since* some parents are motivated *in part* by a desire to *sustain* their childrens' problems, this desire constitutes the major force in *all* parent-child relationships.

Thus while it is true that parents *are* in fact responsible for some of their childrens' problems, and while it is true most parents lack insight into the why's and wherefore's of their childrens' problems, and may even desire, at least in part, that their children stay sick, it does not follow that these negative forces define the whole of parent-child relations. Nor does it follow that all or even most parents cannot be depended upon for active help in a remediation program.

Thus professionals such as Barsch (1961), Ginott (1961), and Rappaport (1969) have emphasized the utilization of parents in remedial programs. Prior to this emphasis (or in its absence) parents felt even more guilty than was necessary, left out, impotent, and decidedly angry, consciously and unconsciously, at the professionals who stood between them and their troubled youngsters.

The parents of a child with a learning disability have usually lived through several years of doubt and confusion in relation to their child. They have probably been given much conflicting advice. They have tried many things—pushing, not pushing; yelling, not yelling; helping with homework, not helping. Nothing has worked —at least not for long. It is no wonder that they approach the interviews of a diagnostic study with fear and doubt.

When a special school is recommended, some parents breathe a sigh of relief: "Now someone else will do the job." Then they withdraw. Others, although willing to follow the recommendation, continue to hover anxiously. For all, there are unasked questions, unresolved feelings and much doubt about the future.

When a child enters Parkway Day School his parents also enter a parent conseling group composed of about six couples who meet weekly with a group leader. The Counselor also meets weekly with the teachers. The philosophy underlying these sessions is that parents have very important and specific roles to play in the helping process, that remediation is a twenty-four-hour-a-day affair (not just a matter of a schoolday or a therapeutic hour), and that parents as well as their children have both the capacity and underlying desire for positive change.

PURPOSES AND CONTENT OF THE SESSIONS

The most obvious purpose is to provide the parents with information concerning learning disabilities, to define the entity, not only in a broad general way but specifically for each family. This is a prelude to helping a parent-pair face the problem, its true implications, and their feelings about it. Much anxiety grows from a lack of knowledge. Too long some professionals have felt information should be kept from parents or else have couched the information in complicated terminology. This was done either because the professional doubted the parents would or could do anything positive with the information, or because of some other irrationality on the professional's part.

2A. LEARNING DISABLED

The first time a parent has his child's problem explained to him he usually misses a great deal. The information is perceived too emotionally. His own hopes and fears get mixed in with what is told him. There is no time to assimilate the information. He does not want to hear. This same parent comes to the (later) counseling sessions with three important questions on his mind:

1. *What is* this learning disability my child has?
2. What caused it? (He really means: Who is to blame?)
3. How long will it take to overcome it?

Initially sessions are spent discussing the varying types of learning disabilities, identifying the problems of particular children, showing similarities and differences among different children and categories, spelling out and defining characteristics, and listing things that can be expected with the passage of time. The question of causality is handled honestly in terms of current professional knowledge.

Parental anger and guilt emerge rapidly. Almost at once parents begin blaming themselves (or others) for their childrens' problems. They are helped to see the utter futility (but understandableness) of this approach—that not only is it unlikely any one person or thing caused the difficulty, but that "blaming" solves nothing anyway. The focus then becomes: what can we do to help?

The matter of the time necessary for remediation is handled concurrently; however this is impossible to answer directly, but it does make sense to talk of sequences children go through as they improve. It is via observed movement through these stages that improvement is gauged. How long a particular child will remain at a particular level is difficult to predict in advance.

The second purpose of the sessions is to provide a liason between home and school. What are the child's reactions when he arrives home? What has the teacher seen? Has the child seemed especially tired, unhappy, out of control? Such matters can be explored with the parents. Information about the child's reactions at home and school can be pooled, to better plan a coordinated program. Within this context it is important that the need for both honesty and confidentiality be stressed. It is important for the counselor to be able to assess accurately how a parent will use information about a child's behavior in school. It is important, also, that the children do not see the parent sessions as "tattling" or "blaming" meetings, but rather as one more essential part of the remedial program.

Parents have many questions about a special school program and many feelings to express. "Why does my child have no homework?" "My child *has* homework, but why is it so easy?" "Why do you tolerate bad behavior?" "Why is my child allowed to talk in class?" "Were you punishing him when he had to work alone today?"

In other instances it is easier for parents to express their negative feelings about certain aspects of a school program to some one whom they see neither as their child's teacher or as a member of the school administration. (This should be established at the outset, along with the groundrules.)

It is essential that both school and home be aware of the importance of a twenty-four-hour-a-day coordinated approach. It helps parents and teachers not to feel so frustrated or impotent. Neither feels alone. The importance of knowing someone else understands how you feel can never be overestimated, for parent or professional.

The third purpose of the meetings is to help parents understand the behavior of their children and to understand the feelings in the child which generate certain kinds of behavior. Along with this, parents work on understanding their own reactions and feelings to the child's behavior. The aim here is to realize that a child's total behavior is important in the remediation of his difficulty. The way in which limits are set or the way in which independence is encouraged or subtly not encouraged may have a great bearing on how the child learns in school. In the course of the school program the child's behavior may change markedly. A formerly inhibited, tightly controlled child may suddenly begin acting out. A parent needs to be prepared for these changes and offered suggestions on how to cope with them.

Some parents approach any discussion of their child's behavior with "We're sending him to school to learn to read. Other than that, leave us alone." Some come looking for gimmicks. "What magic words can I use to get him to do his homework, clean up, come in for dinner?" Occasionally this kind of parent will attempt to parrot the counselor's words in response to a child's behavior. Sometimes it works and the child responds appropriately. But it may not work the second time, and the parent becomes disillusioned.

The aim then is to get away from gimmicks or the "What do I do when?" question and *develop a total approach* to the child's behavior. In order to do this, it is necessary to discuss behavior both in the context of typical child development and within the context of a particular child's specific problems. Several things are important here. The parent needs to learn to really listen to the child and become an accurate observer, so that he can find out what the child is trying to communicate through his behavior. Parents begin to understand that before the child can change they must accept him as he is with all his problems. This is a very hard step. They also begin to understand that children with learning disabilities are usually angry children who are very much afraid of this anger. They begin to accept too that they are angry parents. Again these are very hard steps. They start to learn to accept themselves as they are, to be honest with themselves and gradually to reduce their anger both at themselves and their children. They work on effective ways of setting limits and encouraging independence.

The sessions by their very nature are child centered. Feelings and actions have been discussed in relation to the children and the total family. The final purpose of the sessions applies to some but not all parents. Occasionally as the sessions develop and the child progresses in school, a parent will realize that a readiness has been developed for deeper personal exploration. Such parents may seek psychotherapy for themselves.

ORGANIZATION AND IMPLEMENTATION OF THE SESSIONS

In setting up groups of parents an effort is made to group parents of children with similar problems and age. Thus parents of "acting out" children, "tightly controlled" or "overly dependent" children might be in different groups although the children themselves might be in the same classroom. Grouping is flexible and may be changed during the school term. Parents of children new to the school are usually seen individually, then as a group, and only then gradually worked into an existing group.

The degree of structure the leader gives to the session and the amount of leader participation varies considerably. In the beginning when basic ground work is being developed and the importance of conveying accurate concepts is considerable, the sessions are well structured. Leader participation is great. As the sessions progress to areas involving feelings and reactions to children's behavior, leader participation diminishes. During this phase the leader accepts and acknowledges feelings, keeps the discussion child-centered and problem oriented and serves as a sounding board against which various solutions to problems can be tested. The group and the leader together summarize each session.

Mrs. S., the mother of eight year old Billy whose learning disability involved number concepts, arrived at one of the sessions very upset. Her younger son Johnny, six, had just begun first grade. Johnny had always seemed happy and self-confident. Since the beginning of school Billy, the eight year old, had followed first-grader Johnny around after school asking him, "How much is 300 plus 400? 600 plus 200? 25 plus 50?" Johnny seemed increasingly less and less happy. He ran to his mother for answers. Even after the boys were in bed at night, she could hear the quizzing continue. She was upset because she was unsure how to respond to Billy. Billy had had great difficulty with number concepts, and now, although he knew and understood the answers to the questions he was asking, still lacked confidence in himself. Billy sought to bolster his own confidence at Johnny's expense. How much of this should you tolerate? Is it fair to allow Billy to build his confidence at Johnny's expense.

The group's initial and uncensored response to Mrs. S's problem was: "Tell Billy to keep quiet." But they rapidly decided this would be unwise. They agreed this was a difficult thing for Mrs. S., and began to discuss the possible negative outcomes if Mrs. S. lost her temper with Billy, her immediate impulse. Should this happen the group decided: 1] both children would learn that this was a good way to upset Mommy, 2] Johnny, the little one, might define himself right into a helpless dependent role, and 3] Billy, the eight-year-old learning disability child, might confuse his mother's condemnation of his testing his younger brother, with condemnation of him for knowing something his brother didn't. The group then decided that the real problem was how to respond to both children so as to help both.

Further discussion revealed that all the parents had observed this behavior in second and third graders toward first graders and agreed that it was typical of children this age. They also agreed that in Billy's case it was occurring in excess. This served to place the behavior in appropriate perspective.

After further discussion it was decided that responding positively to Billy's new-found skill in adding and not responding at all to his questioning of his brother might be helpful to him. Mrs. S. decided that she wanted Billy to know she was pleased at how well he could add, that she knew it took a lot of hard work and that he must be very proud of himself. These were the things that she and the group felt were important in what Billy was saying.

To the younger child, Johnny, who had always seemed self confident and happy, they decided that when he came to his mother for the answer she should tell him the answer and add: "This is something that you are not supposed to know now. You will learn it later in the year." From this they thought Johnny would learn 1] "I'm not supposed to know it now so I'm not dumb if I don't," 2] "Mommy will help me when I need it," and 3] "I'll soon be able to do it myself."

Summarizing, it was pointed out how what seemed like such a simple piece of behavior turned out to be quite complex—that it was extremely important to find out what the child was really saying to you through his behavior. Even more important, however, each parent had to decide what he wanted the child to learn *before* he responded. Too many times one responds to a child thoughtlessly and the child learns an unintended message—a message one would never want conveyed. Many parents, at the outset, worried about the exact words they would use in communicating with their child. The more practice they had in thinking through just what they wanted to communicate, the more easily the words came.

REACTIONS OF PARENTS AND TEACHERS

A recent discussion with a group of parents who had attended sessions for two school years, and a separate discussion with the teachers, revealed some striking similarities.

1. Members of both groups felt their ability to see the child from different perspectives was very helpful. A given child may have been provoking at home, but not at school, and vice-versa.
2. Parents and teachers both thought it helpful to know everyone was struggling for the same things—that there were no easy magic answers, known to others but not a particular person.
3. Everyone found it helpful to know more about sources of daily stress.
4. The teachers felt greater empathy for the parents, and no longer saw them as "critical" outsiders.
5. A greater understanding was gained by all that each adult was not totally responsible for a child's actions. "When a child has a difficult day, it may not be my fault, or anybody's for that matter."
6. Both parents and teachers were better able to evaluate the truth of the child's utterances. In the beginning, parents and teachers accepted as gospel the childrens' tales: "My mom won't give me breakfast." "All we do is play all day in school." Now much needless anger was avoided.
7. Parents and teachers were both able to set more effective limits. Parents and teachers appreciated the consistency of an approach that attends better communication.
8. One parent summarized the feeling of being better able to ask the right questions: "Remember when I used to ask you every week when he'd be ready to go back to public school and he couldn't even read a pre-primer? It might be more useful

for us to talk about all the bragging he's been doing lately. It's so unrealistic." That particular session then moved to a discussion of ways children have of coping with their fear of failure. Each parent had examples and they exchanged ideas on the best ways to respond.

CONCLUSION

In a school for children with learning disabilities parent counseling sessions serve a number of functions:

1. They provide information concerning learning disabilities and help parents understand and cope with their feelings about their own child's problems.
2. They coordinate home and school activities so that the approach to the child is relatively consistent.
3. The sessions help parents understand their child's behavior as it relates to typical child development and to sort out those behaviors growing out of his learning disability. They learn to recognize and accept their own feelings as well as those of the child.
4. The sessions help parents set more effective limits, accept and acknowledge feelings and develop appropriate independence in the child.

Much that is asked of parents during the counseling sessions is difficult. It is hard to look at things differently, to explore feelings and to change ways of responding to children. Parents, however, just as their children, have the capacity to change. To the degree that parents are already basically healthy from an emotional standpoint have they been able to profit from the sessions. Some, however, have realized that many of their problems with their children stemmed from deeper personal needs and have sought individual psychotherapy.

HELPING PARENTS OF CHILDREN WITH LEARNING DISABILITIES

William C. Adamson, M.D.

This article attempts to spell out a three dimensional approach to helping parents of children with learning disabilities: (1) educative counseling, (2) interpretive counseling, and (3) habilitative involvement of parents. Such an approach has been effective with parents regardless of the nature and degree of their neurotic problems, or their level of psychological sophistication. The method is adaptable to individual casework or group parent counseling. Family therapy counselors can also use much of the content as elaborated on in the article.

Parents of children with learning disabilities carry an important key to helping their children achieve social, emotional, and educational mastery of their disabilities. No one approach to helping parents is a panacea. There is, however, a growing body of knowledge and counseling skill being developed concerning the process for affecting growth and change in parents' attitudes and effectiveness in helping their children achieve a greater sense of self-mastery.

It has been our experience that to work with parents more from a conceptual base which underlines individual habilitation is more helpful than focusing too heavily on the global concept of "working up to your potential" as a catch phrase to prod children. Often we become so preoccupied with measuring and talking about "growth potentials" that it is hard to see the child as he or she really is through the fog of the "potential" issue. Individual habilitation, on the other hand, includes prescribed educational curriculum to alter or influence the developmental learning imbalances of each student, along with an educational-clinical support system which may free the growing student from emotional conflicts which have dampened complex learning processes.

THREE DIMENSIONAL APPROACH

Parents are able to respond to a three dimensional approach which contains educative, interpretive, and habilitative experiences. In the first dimension emphasis is placed on *educative counseling:* educating parents in the 3 Rs of routine, regularity, and repetition. By *routine* we are referring to "structure" in the home environment as it applies to time, space, and movement for the child. We are not thinking of routine in the rote sense but rather as a state of mind which helps parents find confidence and strength to help their child grow and develop.

In defining *regularity*, parents are encouraged to plan the child's life at home "in the same way every day" as much as possible within the family style of living. Here the clock is thought of as an external control; planned activities allow for a tapering off and slowing down at the end of the day prior to the bedtime ritual.

Along with the importance of routine and regularity, the need for *repetition* of positive learning experiences is emphasized. This has been called the "rub-in" technique. Behaviorists would refer to it as positive conditioning. What it represents is an attempt to reinforce successful experiences while trying to alter or eliminate negative experiences.

In establishing such a 3R-program between parents and child, we are stressing the psycho-

Helping Parents of Children with Learning Disabilities, William C. Adamson, *Journal of Learning Disabilities,* Vol. 5 No. 6, June/July 1972.

logical principle of applying control from the outside for the dysfunctioned child by parents or other adults until the child is able to build up "controls from within." We recognize that there is a biological and psychological need for self-organization within the child. However, because of the lack of intactness in the child's central nervous system, he or she often is not able to achieve this degree of self-organization without external controls. Another important psychological principle is the reduction of decision-making on the part of the child. By planning a structured environment where things are done the same way every day, fewer decisions have to be made by the child and this, in turn, reduces tensions, frustrations, and anxiety experienced by the child as well as struggles of will which might be set up between parent and child.

BREAKING THE INADEQUACY CYCLE

As parents are helped through this educative counseling to meet the child's needs in a planned way along the lines suggested in this first dimension, we often see the breaking up of the *inadequacy cycle* between the troubled child and his puzzled parents. In this cycle the child attempts an activity and fails, thereby increasing his feelings of inadequacy. The frustration in the attempt and the feelings of inadequacy often lead the child toward an effort to control his parents; to avoid the failure situation by manipulation; or to act out the anger of his failure on the rest of the family. Parents at this point in the cycle are trying to help. The signals may be mixed or unclear until the time that educative counseling is begun. Perhaps the parents are trying to get the child to yield, obey, or succeed, or they may have become angry at the child for his behavior.

What usually happens is that the parent unwittingly increases the demands on the child which results in one of several possibilities. The child may comply to the parent demand but in a dependent fashion, thereby becoming excessively dependent on the parent, or the child may comply but suppress feelings of resentment and anger to the degree that these suppressed feelings cause a dampening off of much of his emotionality as well as a dampening off in learning where he won't take risks but takes on a passive-resistant pattern. Another possibility is that the youngster may try the task again and may succeed, or he may have tried and failed which only caused a repetition of the inadequacy cycle described above. Breaking up this inadequacy cycle by active educative counseling before the total family system becomes loaded with despair, anger, overprotectiveness or martyrdom becomes an *imperative* first step in working with parents of children with learning disabilities or dysfunctions.

INTERPRETIVE COUNSELING: THE SECOND DIMENSION

In the second dimension our focus with parents is on *interpretive counseling.* We encourage, train, and educate the parents to "read" or "decode" their child's behavior in terms of the underlying emotional feelings which are the mainspring of the behavior. We ask parents to develop a "stop! look! listen!" attitude. Stop to look at what the child is doing. Stop to listen to what the child is saying before moving too quickly to ask questions of the child. We suggest to parents that one of the child's major problems is difficulty in his impulse-to-action behavior. He cannot delay the impulse long enough to think of the consequences. By stopping to look and to listen, parents become the model of a "listening person" for the child. For the parent to stop to listen not only serves to demonstrate to the child that parents can delay their immediate impulse to react, but it also gives the child the opportunity to sound off about school. This sounding off we refer to as "blowing out his system" which then frees him to talk more openly about the situation on the bus, in the classroom, or with the teacher.

In addition, we counsel parents not to put the child on the spot with such questions as "What did you do today?" or "How was school today?," but to ask more specifically, "How did you feel about math class?" "about Jimmy Jones?" or "about Mr. Smith?" This invites the "blowing off and blowing out" of feelings that have accumulated during the day. The child can then talk about the more positive experiences after the negative ones have been recounted. It is also in line with the new move in curriculum planning for the classroom related to the development of awareness of feelings which we have about ourselves and others, in line with Human Development Laboratory material or the Science Research Associates' social science material focused on human relationships. We encourage parents not to defend the school and the teachers at these moments when children are blowing off and blowing out. The child's feelings need to be accepted and the parent can then suggest that the child ask himself or herself what part each had in the problem. That is, was the child part of the problem or part of the solution to the problem which later developed in the classroom? We want the student to become increasingly aware of both his feelings and the behavior which is used to express the feelings. Out of such a healthy verbal expression by the child and open acceptance of strong feelings by the parent, a deeper sense of mutual appreciation and trust for one another will emerge between the parents, the child, and the school staff. Such an interaction creates a positive learning climate at school and in the home.

An equally important part of the second dimension of interpretive counseling for parents is helping them to work through their own feelings about being the parents of a child with a learning disability.

Invariably the first feeling is one of self-pity and a sense of bereavement at the discovery that the child they have cannot immediately fulfill their dreams and aspirations. It is as though part of themselves has been lost – at least for the moment. This kind of initial reaction often leads to feelings of sadness, depression, and occasional guilt. Parents may ask, "What did I do to deserve this?"

Gradually the sense of self-pity and bereavement gives way to hurt and anger. Often these feelings are directed toward seeking the cause of the problem while pressing the medical, neurological, and educative authorities for a prediction as to what the child will be like at 17 or 18 years of age. Here the parents may be seeking an answer to the question, "Why did this happen to me or to us?

AVOID LONG-RANGE PREDICTIONS

The parents' anxiety is a genuine concern impelling them to seek assurance that their child will outgrow the problem or will be made nearly normal again. We respect and admire parents for this drive for normalcy. We know, however, that it will be difficult for parents to take one year at a time. Yet we have found this to be a *second imperative!* We cannot and should not make long-range predictions as to the child's functioning in the future in response to the demands for parents. But we can prescribe for today and measure the results tomorrow, next week, and next year, to see where the strength and weaknesses in the child really are and to follow his progress. Holding steady in face of parental pressure to know a prediction for the future actually keeps parents looking at the present and helps them to deal more realistically with the child's situation in the present. In this way, we begin to break up the mechanism of denial in the parents which often leads them to say there is nothing wrong with their child that time will not cure. Children of these parents will mirror their parents' denial mechanism by saying there is nothing wrong with them, it is just in their eyes. By staying with the situation as it is revealed in the diagnostic teaching and psychodiagnostic studies, we are able to uncover the nature of the learning disability in the child and to discuss it with the child and his parents. We shift from a state of confusion to one of clarity which allows for a shift from denial to partial or more total acceptance in both parents and child.

As a result of increasing acceptance of the child as he or she may be, parents are freed to move toward constructive programming for their child. They are able to seek out help which allows the child to deal with and accept his differences from other children. At the same time, the action-oriented parent begins to work with other parents in setting up realistic programs for these children, much as the members of A.C.L.D. have done in the last decade. It is this total constructive effort which then leads to a more widespread change in attitudes in the community toward children with learning disabilities and to the organization and legislative funding for constructive community programs for children with minimal learning disabilities.

HABILITATIVE INPUT BY PARENTS: THE THIRD DIMENSION

The third dimension of our work with parents is called the *habilitative dimension.* By this we mean that parents are included as part of the helping team from the time of their very first contact with the school. They prepare the child for coming, working with him on the reasons and the needs for coming. They set the tone for readiness of their child to use the school. They help the child in the separation process should the child need to move into residence. They participate in planning visits and arranging phone calls and carry on an active correspondence to help the child with feelings of separation anxiety. We encourage parents to increase their contact with the school through parents' nights and group meetings. We counsel parents to help their child "to tell it as it is" when he or she comes home from school. As part of the habilitation team parents encourage the child to express his mixed feelings about the school, rather than attempting to take the feelings away from the child by saying "you shouldn't feel that way, they are such nice people."

At this time, also, we counsel the parents to be supportive of the school effort and the school program rather than to be manipulative to achieve their selfish ends. We know that parents who care will be parents who share a high level of expectation with their child. They want to see results. They become impatient about school programs and homework. They may be critical of the teaching methods and unwittingly put the child in the middle between the teacher and their own aspirations. We hope parents see the importance of backing off and reducing the nature of their overinvestment in their child's learning. In this way the parents can become more objective and at the same time more supportive of both the child and the school. As the parent frees himself from excessive worry and preoccupation with immediate progress, the child is also freed to learn.

In every school and every learning situation the struggling child will attempt to gain sympathy from parents through denying his part in the problem and attempting to project the fault or blame on other children, teachers, or perhaps on siblings at home. We encourage parents, as members of the habilitative team, to patiently stay with the child and begin to peel back the child's needs to deny or avoid facing his own sense of failure, his hurt pride, or his own problem during that particular day. As parents are able to help the child in this way, there is a gradual reduction in the need for such a projection system and the child will begin to see his own responsibility for the feelings which led him into the difficulty, as well as admitting to the behavior which resulted when he attempted to express these feelings. This is an important first step! It is a step toward awareness of feelings within himself. It is an individual attempt toward the healthy expression of strong feelings in socially acceptable ways. It is a greater step toward admitting that the problem is within himself rather than being put upon him by others.

Perhaps the most significant goal in working with parents as part of the habilitative team is to help parents build "a bridge of mutual trust" between the home and school. Once this bridge is firmly established, parents, their learning disabled child, the total family, and the school staff can all walk over the bridge together. They can walk together from the side of doubt and despair to the side of self-confidence and hope.

A Parent's Perspective of Learning Disabilities

Richard M. Gargiulo
Judith Warniment

Richard M. Gargiulo, PhD, is an assistant professor of special education, and Judith Warniment, MEd, is a clinical supervisor for the Department of Special Education, at Bowling Green University, Bowling Green, Ohio 43403.

ONE OF THE MOST DIFFICULT things for parents to admit is that their son or daughter may have a learning disability. Many times parents hear their child being called brain damaged, lazy, an underachiever, or emotionally disturbed. Such inappropriate labels and accompanying misconceptions often leave parents in a state of confusion with feelings of hopelessness and utter despair. All too often parents feel ashamed and embarrassed because their child has a learning handicap. Some parents feel as though they are alone, the only parents with such a problem. To combat these negative feelings, the following discussion was prepared by parents who, themselves, have often asked, "Why me?"

Question 1

"As a parent, what does the term *learning disability* mean to you?"

Parent 1: I think it is a very confusing and frightening term. When my husband and I were told by our family doctor that our son had a learning disability, or hearts sank. Immediately, we thought our boy was retarded, but he's not retarded. In fact, he is a very bright child in his own way. The doctor said that James has minimal brain damage, but he never explained what minimal brain damage was, nor could he tell us how our son got it.

Parent 2: It's a very troublesome term. I hate to use that term even now because I don't feel it really explains the situation. Right now, when I think of learning disabilities, I think of a child who has a handicap—a mental handicap—but, somehow, comparing my child to a child with a physical handicap really makes me feel sad. I guess it's something that we're going to have to live with and learn to live around.

Parent 3: Even though I've been living with this term for a good number of years, I still cannot appreciate it, nor do I fully understand it. To me, a learning-disabled child is an intelligent child, but one who, for one reason or another, has difficulty learning like other children do. Personally, it's hard for me to accept that label. I look at my son and say, "No, I'm imagining

A Parent's Perspective of Learning Disabilities, Richard M. Garguilo and Judith Warniment, *Academic Therapy*, Vol. 11, No. 4.

this. It can't be my child." I can tell myself that my child has a learning disability but not others. It is still too much of an emotional term. I keep trying to rationalize the problem, but it just doesn't work.

Question 2

"When did you realize your child was having learning problems?"

Parent 1: I first became aware of the problem after reading an article in *Life* magazine. When I read the article, I just knew that they were writing about our son and not somebody else. When my husband came home from work, I said, "They wrote an article about James today. The only thing is that they changed his name, but he fits all the descriptions." This was the first time we were made aware that other parents had similar problems, and that there was a place to go for help.

Parent 2: I first realized that Susan was having problems in school when she was in kindergarten and her teacher wanted to hold her back. My husband and I pushed her on but, after she had so much difficulty with first grade, we realized that something was wrong. It was very difficult to understand what the problem was because Susan's teachers kept telling us she was just not mature enough to continue. They gave no suggestions for psychological testing nor any hints that Susan even had a learning disability.

Parent 3. I think I first came across my child's learning disability when Bruce was in the first grade. The teacher called me in for a parent conference and told me that Bruce had a learning disability. She equated learning disabilities with mental retardation and also told me that my son was brain damaged. I was really floored, imagine a teacher telling me that my son was retarded and brain damaged!

Question 3

"How did you handle this information emotionally?"

Parent 1: It was like a slap in the face. James is adopted. My husband and I were going to raise the perfect child, but I guess the perfect child hasn't been born yet. At first I cried a lot. I choked out words. It was very upsetting to try and talk to anybody. Your friends want to listen to you because you've got to talk to somebody. First you feel like, "Gee, I'm really the only one who's got this problem," and really you're not. Yet, when you're first told, you feel you're all alone, that everybody's against you. I really have to say I cried an awful lot, and prayed a lot.

Parent 2: I had mixed emotions. I was relieved to find out that there was something wrong with Susan other than being immature, something that my husband and I could help her overcome. I also felt very sad in a way because Susan couldn't be normal and enjoy school like all the other kids. I often asked myself, "Why me?"

Parent 3: It upset me tremendously. I shut my mind to it, said it couldn't happen to me, it couldn't be true. I ignored it. I really did.

Question 4

"Did your child's problem affect your marital situation?"

Parent 1: I would have to answer no. I think it brought us closer together. It was harder for my husband to realize that there was a problem. I think he knew it was there, but he just didn't want to admit that something was wrong with his son. I think it made us come closer to each other, if that is possible. It made a stronger marriage because we both knew that we had to work with this child in order to get him through life so that some day he could marry and have a family of his own.

Parent 2: At first, Susan's problem did affect my marriage. My husband acted as though he was ashamed of her, and I became overly protective. As we became more aware of her problem and what we could do to help, we began pulling together, realizing that our daughter needed both of us. In the long run, it has strengthened our marriage.

Parent 3: My marriage was, and still is, very much affected by Bruce's problem. My husband does not want to accept the responsibility associated with our son's learning disability. He very much ignores it. His solution is to be very, very firm with Bruce. I'm too easy. This has led to terrific disagreements about our son. At times, the situation is so desperate that I have often thought of taking Bruce and leaving my husband. My marriage is better if we both pretend that Bruce doesn't have a learning disability or that he doesn't even exist.

Question 5

"What was the grandparents reaction to your child's problem?"

Parent 1: In our particular situation, at first the grandparents were a hinderance. It was never the child. They believed that the problem was with my husband and me. We were at fault. They just couldn't admit that something could be wrong with their grandchild. It's only been within the last six months, after they witnessed one of James' temper tantrums, that they finally realized that a problem exists. They now realize that we were not to blame and are helping us with James.

Parent 2: I don't have to worry about the grandparents. They just don't seem to care. In fact, they never say anything about Susan's problems.

Parent 3: Our grandparents feel that Bruce can do nothing wrong. He could break every window in their house, and they would still not find fault with him. This belief has caused a great many problems for my husband and me, as both grandparents blame us for Bruce's learning and behavior problems.

Question 6

"Where did you go to seek help?"

Parent 1: At first, we were uncertain as to where to seek help. Our family doctor referred us to a pediatrician who was trained in learning disabilities. We also had James tested by a psychologist at our own expense.

Parent 2: We took Susan to the mental health clinic. They directed us to the appropriate professionals within the community.

Parent 3: My husband and I sought help in two places. We went to a nearby university that had a learning disabilities center, and we also contacted our local Association for Children with Learning Disabilities (ACLD).

Question 7

"Was the information gained from these sources of use to you?"

Parent 1: The information obtained from the pediatrician and the psychologist was of some use. They both confirmed that James had learning problems, but neither one of them told us exactly what the problems were or how we could help our son. My husband and I were very frustrated. We knew James had problems, but we didn't know how to help him.

Parent 2: My husband and I were somewhat confused by the pediatrician's findings. The tests confirmed that Susan had a learning disability, but the doctor could not find any medical reason for her learning problems. As parents, we wanted to help but didn't know what to do. We did receive a great deal of useful information from a learning disabilities teacher. This particular teacher provided us with learning tasks that we could do at home with Susan to help remediate some of her learning deficiencies.

Parent 3: Bruce had a complete diagnostic evaluation at the university. When all of the information was gathered, the psychologist told my husband and I what areas Bruce needed help in, and how we could go about remediating some of his deficiencies. I would have to say that the information was extremely useful.

The information we got from the ACLD was invaluable. They gave us so much help and were so understanding. I don't know what we would have done without the support of these other parents.

Question 8

"How did your child's teachers react to his or her learning problem?"

Parent 1: All of the teachers that I've come into contact with either don't seem to have the time to help James, or they aren't sure how to help him. It seems as though teachers have a mold, and they want every child to fit into this mold. It's been our experience that, if James can't read, he's failed. If he has trouble with arithmetic, he fails that also, to the point where he is continually asking, "Hey, what can I do? I'm no good at anything." James brought home an arithmetic paper last week and very lightly written across the top was, "I failed again, I failed again, I failed again." When I questioned him about the paper, he told me, "Don't look at it, I probably didn't pass, so I just gave myself an *F*. I get an *F* on everything."

There have been many nights when I cried myself to sleep because of the problems that James has in school. My husband and I have talked with his teachers and explained James' problems, but it doesn't seem to do any good. We also spoke with principals and superintendents. All we hear about is the lack of funding and qualified teachers. It really hurts to see your son daily fighting a losing battle in school. You have to wonder when it will all end.

Parent 2: Even though Susan is in a different school district, we experienced similar problems before she was placed in a learning-disabilities classroom. Susan's teachers catered to her every whim. If she couldn't do the work, they just let her sit and do nothing. After a while, Susan stopped trying completely and didn't even want to go to school. My husband and I were so upset with the situation that we were ready to send her to a private school. It wasn't until she was placed in the learning-disabilities unit and received individualized help that she started working again and enjoying school.

Parent 3: It's been our experience that Bruce's teachers don't understand the nature of his problem, nor do they have the time to give him the individual help that he needs. My son has not been fortunate enough to be placed in a learning-disabilities unit and, therefore, must struggle through school in a regular classroom. Every report I get from the school states that he is lazy, won't cooperate, and doesn't care. I know how difficult it is for Bruce, being taught subjects he cannot grasp, and the frustration of repeated failure. I don't want to blame the school for his problems, but I don't believe that he is getting the best education possible. It's very frustrating for my husband and me and also very expensive, as we had to hire private tutors to help with his school work.

Question 9

"What is your main concern as a parent of a learning-disabled child?"

Parent 1: Our main concern is that our son receives an adequate education. A great deal of emphasis seems to be placed on the young learning-disabled child, which is very good, but everyone seems to forget the 11 to 16 year-old learning-disabled child. It is as though these children don't exist. Our son is 13 years old, and there isn't a learning-disabilities classroom for him. I'm sure that my son is not the only adolescent who needs special education. This age is difficult enough without the added problems of a learning disability compounded by an inappropriate educational environment.

Parent 2: Our main concern is that our daughter will become aware of her learning problems and be able to accept them. Most of all, our wish is that she will accept herself for what she can do. I want her to have pride in herself and to be confident in herself. Finally, then, as a mature woman, she will be a self-reliant, dependable, and productive citizen.

Parent 3: I actually have two major concerns. First, I hope that, somehow, my marriage will survive and, secondly, I have grave concerns regarding my son's low self-esteem. Bruce's self-concept is very, very low. He views himself as a worthless child and a poor son. I only wish I knew of some way to build up his confidence. It is extremely difficult when both the school and your own husband work against you. There are times when I don't know what to do or to whom to turn. I feel as though I'm a poor excuse for a parent and a mother.

Question 10

"In summary, what advice can you offer to parents who have a learning-disabled youngster?"

Parent 1: The first thing would be to contact your local ACLD. Learning disabilities are a parents' problem too. Parents with learning-disabled children will find out that they are not alone, and that their problems are not unique. Many times I locked myself in my bedroom and got down on my knees and prayed, "Dear God, don't let me go near him, because I'm going to kill him if I do." Afterwards I think, "Gee, I'm a terrible parent. I shouldn't be feeling this way towards my son." After you meet other parents in these ACLD groups, you discover that you're not the only one. One wonders how many thousands of us have had similar experiences.

By meeting with these other parents, you not only help yourself and them, but you also are able to help your child. By banding together with other parents, you have *parent power*, a voice as to who gets elected and how money is spent in the school systems. An active parents' organization, like the ACLD or similar groups, is really a big asset.

Parent 2: I think it is most important that parents stand behind their child and never lose faith in him or ever stop loving him. Your child will always be a part of you, regardless of what he can or can't do. Don't ever forget the child or make him think he is alone. Make sure he knows you will always be there.

It is very difficult for us, as parents, to understand the hidden handicaps that our children have acquired in one way or another. Yet, it is most important that we understand our children before we can break the barrier which holds them back from an equal education and a fair chance in life.

Parent 3: Don't put your head in the sand. Don't ignore the problem. When you ignore it, you're not helping your family, certainly not yourself, and, most important, you aren't helping your child.

Conclusion

While the foregoing discussion will not make the job of being a parent of a learning-disabled youngster any easier, it is our wish that some insight may have been gained as to how these parents faced their problems. It is absolutely crucial that all parents remember that they need not stand alone, nor should they!*

---

* Additional information on how to start a local ACLD chapter can be obtained by contacting your state ACLD office or the national ACLD, 5225 Grace Street, Pittsburgh, Pennsylvania 15236.

What Do You Say When A Parent asks, "How Can I Help My Child?"

Jennie Jennings DeGenaro, M.S.

Parents are seeking ways to help their learning disabled children develop reading skills. An obligation of professionals is to give meaningful suggestions which parents can employ with a minimum of orientation. This article describes practical techniques for strengthening the child's visual modality. No special equipment is required and the cost is minimal. Methods are suggested to increase visual discrimination and memory, left-to-right orientation, eye-hand co-ordination, visual imagery and phonetic awareness.

Parents of learning disabled children often ask clinicians and teachers to suggest ways for them to help their children at home. Many parents leave a conference frustrated and as devoid of ideas as when they arrived.

Materials used in schools and clinics are often expensive and too specialized to share with parents. It is often impossible to purchase the same material locally and many teachers are reluctant to recommend an extensive home-study program.

The following suggestions utilize materials usually found around the home. The only requirements are old newspapers or magazines, scissors, paste and magic markers or crayons. The teacher should keep a supply of old newspapers and out-of-date magazines in the event the parent does not have these readily available. A brief demonstration of the following suggestions should be given to the parent and the child.

Ideas or suggestions are categorized to reflect the major skill to be developed, however these are not discrete and may well fit into several categories.

(1) To increase visual discrimination and a left-to-right progression across the page:

(a) Ask the child to circle the letters of the alphabet in sequential order. Commence with "a" and end with "z." Any magazine or newspaper article will suffice. Letters which do not appear after three lines of print may be written in by the child or parent. Letters appearing infrequently are q, v, x and z. A copy of the alphabet should be available to the child who does not know the alphabet in sequential order.

(b) Ask the child to draw an arrow pointing to the right under the first letter in every word in a specified number of paragraphs.

(c) Ask the child to locate and underline a designated word. Select words from the Dolch Basic Sight List or words he finds difficult. The parent should determine if the specific word is present in the article before asking the child to look for it.

(d) Ask the child to underline the first word in every sentence.

(e) The child circles every "b", both capital and small, in an article or paragraph. (This is especially helpful for the child who cannot distinguish "b" from "d"). Next, give him a red lead pencil, preferably, and ask him to make the small "b's" into capital "b's".

(f) Ask the child to cut out all of the "B's" in the headlines. These may be pasted on a sheet of paper to compare different types of print used to make the same letter.

(2) To increase visual memory:

(a) Point to a three-letter word in a magazine and ask the child to write the word from memory. Display the word to him to determine the correctness of his response. To vary the activity, ask him to repeat the letters rather than writing them. Occasionally, have him walk around his chair before writing the letters or giving them verbally.

(b) Select a word from an article and write it in manuscript on a card or a sheet of paper. Then ask the child to locate the word in the magazine and underline it from left-to-right.

(c) Display a picture in the magazine. The child studies the picture for a minute or so.

What Do You Say When a Parent Asks, "How Can I help My Child?" Jeannie Jennings De Genaro, *Journal of Learning Disabilities,* Vol. 6, No. 2, February 1973, © Professional Press, Inc.

Remove the picture from view and ask the child to name everything he can remember. Display the picture again. He names the items he did not remember initially. Then cover a segment of the picture. Ask the child to name the part that is missing.

(d) Cut out three or four pictures. (Example: a boy, a tree and a dog.) Arrange these in front of the child. The child studies the pictures for a few seconds and closes his eyes. Remove or change the position of one picture. The child tells which picture is missing or has been rearranged. Increase the number of pictures and the number of manipulations as the child's skills improve.

(e) Arrange pictures in front of the child. Let him study them for a few seconds. Remove the pictures and ask him to name them in order as they appeared from left to right.

(3) To improve fine-motor skills (eye-hand coordination):

(a) Provide various colored magic markers (for high interest) and a pair of scissors. Paste should also be available. The child selects a picture and outlines it with one of the markers. Next, he cuts around the line he drew.

The child should keep a scrapbook of pictures dependent upon his interests. For the child who has not developed interests, encourage him to organize his pictures when he pastes them in the scrapbook. Have him label each picture, either by hand or by cutting out the headline or title.

(b) Use the classified advertisement section of the newspaper. Turn the page lengthwise in front of the child and ask him to draw lines between the columns from left to right. (If the child is right-handed, tell him to stop drawing the line when his "little" finger falls off the page.) This will help the child to develop the habit of leaving margins. The left-handed child may need a crease, or fold, to indicate the margin. Lines drawn should be used to write words or letters.

(c) To make a jigsaw puzzle, the child selects a picture, cuts it out, and pastes it on cardboard. Next, he makes "wavy" lines in the shape of an "X" across the back of the cardboard and then cuts over the lines. This will give the child a four-piece jigsaw puzzle. Puzzles may be stored in old envelopes for future use.

(4) To encourage the child's interest in words and reading:

(a) Ask the child to look through the magazine and cut out all of the words in headlines that he recognizes. He should paste the words on a sheet of paper for reading to his parents. He may also cut out large individual letters, arrange them into a word, and paste these words on paper for reading to his parents.

(b) Have the child locate all the happy words, scary words or action words in an article. If the child cannot read, the parent can read sentences and have the child indicate when he hears a word from the designated category. The child can keep running lists of words by categories.

(c) The child can cut out squares of the various colors he sees in a magazine and paste the color swatches on a sheet of paper. On a separate card, write the names of the colors for him to match with the correct color swatch. To make this a self-checking activity, small squares of the color can be pasted on the backs of the cards bearing the color words.

(d) Encourage the child to write his own "Rebus" book. The child writes a few words and completes the sentence with small pictures from the magazine.

(e) When the child asks the parent to read to him from the magazine, the parent can read orally and run his finger under the print while reading. The child can learn to recognize many new words in this manner as well as learn to direct his eyes from left to right.

(5) To build a phonetic awareness:

(a) Use an empty egg carton for this activity. Paste a letter for each consonant sound in each egg indentation in an egg carton. Ask the child to find pictures starting with each sound and to cut the pictures out. He places each picture in the indentation labeled with the correct initial sound. (Example: Place a picture of a boy in the indentation labeled "b"). Or, conversely, pictures may be pasted in each indentation and the child directed to cut out letters and place in the correct picture indentation.

(b) When looking through the magazine with the child, play "I see something you don't see and it begins the same as the word ______" (select a word that begins the same as some object in the picture). When the child guesses the correct object, it is his turn to be "IT" and the parent's turn to guess the correct object.

(c) Assist the child to start his own book of sounds. You will need a notebook or a stenographer's note pad, or twenty-six sheets of paper stapled with a construction paper cover. The child writes a capital and a small letter at the top of each page for every letter in the alphabet. He looks for a picture, or pictures, to represent each initial sound. He should cut out the pictures and paste these on the page with the letter indicating the correct beginning sound. This activity may be extended to include consonant blends, digraphs and so forth.

(6) Developing visual imagery:

(a) Show the child a picture in the magazine. Ask him to describe what is happening now, what happened before and what will happen next. Let him describe the mood of the picture, whether it is night or day and so forth.

(b) Ask the child to tell a story about the picture. Encourage a beginning, a middle and an ending. The parent may wish to write the child's story as he tells it. Cut out the picture to accompany the story. When several stories have been written, let the child decide which story goes with which picture. It may be necessary for the parent to read the story to the child.

(c) Cut out three or four pictures. Describe one of the pictures and have the child identify which picture is being described.

(d) Ask the child to cut out pictures and headlines. The headlines should be arranged in one group with the pictures in another. The child is to match the headline to the correct picture. For the nonreader, the parent can read the headline while the child locates the correct picture from among several.

* * *

The preceding suggestions are for the parents who are interested in ways to help their children develop reading skills. The parents of many learning disabled children are most anxious to help and will do so effectively when they are properly guided. Parents should be cautioned to keep the sessions short, fun and to stop while interest is high.

When given some of the above suggestions, one mother said, "I had no idea you could do all this with just an OLD magazine," – and she was confident and eager to begin helping her learning disabled child to become a more productive, achieving student. – *3 Berkshire Rd., Richmond, Va. 23221*

Family Systems and the Learning Disabled Child: Intervention and Treatment

Jules C. Abrams, Ph.D.
Florence Kaslow, Ph.D.

Types of learning disorders are manifold, and each may require different modes of intervention. In children whose learning difficulties stem from psychological causes, family dynamics can play a significant role. Different family constellations provide clues as to the best possible intervention for the individual child. Presented here is a continuum of the varying types of treatment that might be employed, dependent upon the child's problem and the family dynamics. Factors which are important in ultimate choice of treatment are detailed.

It is axiomatic that there is no one single cause for all learning disabilities. Rather, learning problems are usually the result of a variety of factors, all of which may be highly interrelated. Unfortunately, the child is frequently approached with a unitary orientation so that vitally important aspects of his idiosyncratic disorder may well be ignored. The tendency for each professional discipline to perceive the entire problem "through its own window of specialization" often obscures critical factors which may contribute to, or at least intensify, the basic difficulty. To conceive of only one cure, or one approach, as a panacea for all types of learning disabilities is to be myopic.

In treating a learning disability, it is essential to first establish a working diagnosis. Attention here is focused primarily upon those factors that are related to the dynamic interactions that occur in families of children with severe learning handicaps. In some cases, the very nature of the family relations becomes the most important etiological factor in the child's learning disorder. In other instances, it is the child's own defensive and manipulative behavior in reaction to his learning disability that is extremely disruptive to the family. Most often a vicious cycle is perpetuated, with cause and effect closely interwoven.

In this paper, we shall examine the problems of LD children in whom emotional problems figure prominently. After a brief discussion of some common family dynamics that contribute to learning disabilities, we shall place special emphasis upon the specific family constellations that provide clues to the best possible mode of intervention for the individual child. For those parents, teachers, and other professionals who must cope with the aberrant behavior of so many of these children, a knowledge of some of the factors important to consider in the ultimate choice of treatment can be very helpful. All too often one may recognize that a child needs some specialized professional help but one may be puzzled as to the appropriate referral.

FAMILY DYNAMICS: A POTENTIAL CONTRIBUTOR TO LEARNING PROBLEMS

Most often, the term, "learning disability," is used to denote a specific learning disorder that appears to exist relatively independent of environmental influences. However, our formulation of what constitutes a learning problem is considerably broader than this very circumscribed definition. We recognize that one must always take into consideration the total functioning of the individual, including psychophysiological, psychological, and familial factors which may effect a learning problem. For instance, there may be tensions and conflicts in the child's current home situation that could have a disastrous effect upon his learning ability.

For example, in order for a child to learn, he must be able to attend to and absorb what is to be learned. If a child is preoccupied with his home situation, with the possibility of parental separation or divorce, with alcoholism, with intrafamilial conflict, exposure to threatened seduction, or incest, it is improbable that he

Family Systems and the Learning Disabled Child: Intervention and Treatment, Jules C. Abrams and Florence Kaslow, *Jouranl of Learning Disabilities,* Vol. 10, No. 2, Febuary 1977. ©Professional Press, Inc.

will be able to concentrate on learning activities in a meaningful way.

The values and attitudes of the parental figures toward the child play an extremely influential role in shaping his receptivity to the learning process. In some families, excessive stress is placed upon the necessity for school achievement. Very early in life the child in this family type realizes that it is essential for him to achieve in school in order to maintain an adequate relationship with his mother-figure. When he begins to despair of ever gaining total parental approval, he may withdraw from the struggle. It is as if he senses that his parents are simply too difficult to please and that no matter what he does, he will only meet with their criticism.

Further complications may arise from the fact that monetary and emotional stresses are usually much greater in families of learning disabled children than those with normal children. Examinations by neurologists, psychologists, audiologists, optometrists, etc. are costly and often burdensome. Conflicting diagnoses and vagueness of physicians compound the confusion, self-castigation, denial and/or wish to escape felt by many parents. In responding to the ambiguity, they may fluctuate between being overprotective and rejecting, between clinging together on behalf of the child or detesting one another for having created a handicapped child. All parents need some time apart from their children and when a child is hyperactive and demanding, the parents' need for separate periods may well be intensified. Yet they may be unable to find a baby-sitter willing to cope with the more difficult behavior presented by their child. Or, to compensate for their perceived annoyance, one or the other may refuse to go out and "abandon" the child — thus becoming a resentful prisoner. The rage builds up and periodically explodes, and the painful cycle of resentment, guilt, overprotectiveness, and often too much permissiveness becomes repetitive — to the disadvantage of everyone involved. A child trapped in such a morass has little energy free to invest in the task of learning.

The learning disabled child may become the recipient of much family criticism and antagonism and may acquire the role of family scapegoat (Vogel & Bell 1968). He is viewed as the source and cause of all family problems and bears the burden of helping his parents avoid confronting other deep-rooted problems. The child may become the negative bond welding his parents together — he is the tangible symbol of a joint production for which each is responsible and equally guilty, and from which neither can lightheartedly escape. No matter how unhappy the marriage, it must be preserved for the sake of the child and because leaving one's spouse under such circumstances is socially and morally untenable. So, added to the child's learning chores may be the weighty task of being the link between two dissatisfied parents.

DIFFERENTIAL TREATMENT APPROACHES: A CONTINUUM

In this initial effort, we have identified seven possible intervention strategies any of which might be the "treatment of choice," contingent upon a myriad of factors. In the elaboration of each treatment approach, the rationale for its selection and the values inherent in utilizing it will be presented. Although we speak of a continuum, no one intervention is superior to any other — rather, each may be preferred for a different set of circumstances.

(1) *Educational Intervention Only.* Tutoring and/or special education in areas of greatest deficit or difficulty are recommended to provide a better foundation, improve basic skills, and develop better ego functioning through mastery when the child seems to be hampered only by a learning disability. To arrive at such a conclusion, the person making the evaluation would have to discern a stable, reasonably happy home situation and a relative absence of emotional problems in the child.

(2) *Individual Therapy Only.* Occasionally, one is confronted by parents who seem inaccessible. They may be drug addicts, alcoholics, severely retarded, psychotic, or so thoroughly rejecting of their offspring as to be deemed unreachable. The child cannot be left to flounder completely alone and therapy should not be contingent upon parent involvement. Rather, contact with the parents should take the form of written, formal reports to keep them informed of the child's progress and needs.

Such a child will require a great deal of acceptance, understanding, and ego support from his therapist. He may also need protection from hostile, abusive, or negligent parents and an opportunity to learn to cope better with his home life situation. He can benefit from the chance to recognize his existing capacities and to learn to his full potential. The therapist can encourage and assist him in formulating his own goals and future direction. The therapist can enable the child to build a better self-image and develop greater self-confidence by helping him work through his guilt, confusion, and self-loathing, and by cooperating with his teachers in helping him acquire real skills.

There are other sets of factors which also converge to make a decision for individual child therapy the most favorable one. When the child's difficulties are largely internalized and personality restructuring seems to be advisable, child analysis or intensive child therapy stands out as the treatment of choice. This is especially so when there is no strong indication that the parents should be in therapy. Periodic contact with the parents should be maintained so they can give the therapist data about the child and he can offer them better ways for coping with and enjoying the child.

(3) *Parent Group Counseling.* When the parents of a learning disabled child get along well together and therapy with the parents is not warranted, parent group sessions frequently prove valuable if the parents desire some involvement with the child's school and can benefit from educative and interpretive counseling. Parents can learn to incorporate the 3 Rs of routine, regularity, and repetition in their child's daily life. They can be aided in intercepting the failure-inadequacy-dependency-martyrdom cycle that they may have been perpetuating, and they can learn how to "read or decode their child's behavior in terms of the underlying emotional feelings which are the mainspring of the behavior" (Adamson 1972).

The group affords a forum in which to consider and thrash out concerns common to all. Members can receive support and encouragement from each other, and those who have successfully dealt with certain problems can share their experience and add their recommendations to those of the therapist and teacher. Group meetings offer a respite, a time when parents do not have to hide concerns or pretend that all is well if it isn't. They serve to lessen the sense of aloneness with one's burden. The value of such groups is underscored by the fact that many parents on their own have banded together in organizations like ACLD.

(4) *Individual Therapy Plus Tutoring.* When the parents are considered "unreachable" or when it is not essential for them to be in treatment for reasons such as those elucidated in No. 2 above, and when normal classroom instruction needs supplementing, the child may require individual psychotherapy *and* tutoring. The merits of this combination include those cited above. In addition, the tutor, who most likely will be seeing the child often, becomes another pivotal adult in the child's life space. This person affords a supportive, positive relationship, augmenting what is happening in the individual treatment sessions and tending to offset the child's impression that adults are depriving, nonnurturing persons to be feared and avoided.

It is crucial to point out that providing both modes of intervention concurrently is not necessarily the optimal approach. The relationship of the child to another key adult in the person of the tutor may possibly dilute the therapy, just as the alliance with the therapist may dilute the intensity of the tutor's relationship and value, so a careful differential diagnosis is essential to determine the preferable course and in what sequence.

(5) *Concurrent Therapy of Child and Parents with Different Therapists.* There are several criteria for choosing concurrent therapy with different therapists. At times the parents are much too angry or disturbed to be seen together with the child. In some instances the child is so emotionally depressed that he is unable to share the therapist's time and attention even with his parents. In others, the child needs to be protected from the onslaught he would receive in joint sessions. Also, if any of the parties involved are highly suspicious, they are unable to accept the avowal of confidentiality, and this makes being assigned to different therapists almost imperative.

Such a pattern and process make it possible for parents and child each to have a chance to work separately on their reactions to the learning disability, the many complexities that accompany it, and on their feelings toward each other – and for each to acquire more productive attitudes and interactive behaviors. In their sessions separate from the child, parents can deal with the frustrations, disappointments, hurts, guilt, and recriminations which emanate from the child's impairment. They can be assisted profitably in sorting out what really stems from the child's condition and what is the expression of marital discord. Where the latter becomes apparent, marriage counseling might have as much efficacy as counseling the parents on understanding and dealing with the child's behavior and the responses it evokes in them.

(6) *Concurrent Therapy of Child and Parents with the Same Therapist.* When parents and child each appear to need their own time with the therapist but are not so enmeshed in a battle for power or are not so competitive that they are unable to share the same therapist, this

approach can be most advantageous. There is no danger that the two therapists in the picture (as in option No. 5) might be working at cross purposes or that the family members can play them off against one another. A single therapist may acquire a better view of the entire situation and integrate the progress in therapy of his several clients.

Besides having all of the benefits mentioned in relation to option No. 5, this strategy has the further advantage that parents and child sense that they are all working together to improve the situation. Since the therapist is seeing their child directly, the parents assume he knows what they are confronted with and are more apt to accept his suggestions on how to aid their child to achieve greater self-sufficiency, mastery of skills, and independence.

(7) *Conjoint Family Therapy of Child, Parents, and Siblings.* Conjoint family therapy (Satir 1964) provides an atmosphere in which all family members can gain a better understanding of themselves, each other, and how they interact. It affords an ongoing opportunity for them to engage in joint problem solving, to confront each other's troublesome attitudes and behaviors candidly and face-to-face while simultaneously enabling them to be mutually supportive. Because all of the family are involved, the possibilities of "undercutting" that exist in individual psychotherapy are minimized. In seeing everyone together, the therapist has an actual laboratory in which to diagnose the real nature of feelings and interactions. Distortions based on faulty memories or subjective misperceptions are the *data* under consideration; what is transpiring in the therapy hour itself becomes much of the content (Ferber, Mandelsohn, & Napier 1972). Transfer of feelings to the therapist is reduced since real family members are present and can be dealt with in vivo.

Because the lives of the child, his parents, and siblings are so closely intertwined, the needs and actions of each influence all other members of the family. A systems view of the family expands the therapist's comprehension of the family dynamics as well as the intrapsychic dynamics of each family member (Kaslow 1973). Each has reactions to the learning disabled child who in this context is the identified patient (Satir 1964), and perhaps the family scapegoat (Vogel & Bell 1968). Maximum therapeutic benefit can be derived when the family can function as a unit to try to improve a situation which involves the self-concept of all members and affects their relationships with their extended family, neighbors, friends, school chums, and colleagues at work.

Other reasons for selecting family therapy are that outside the treatment hour, members can reinforce each other's gains since they are attuned to one another's efforts and goals. They can help each other guard against backsliding. By opening up the communication network, working through family secrets and myths, and facilitating greater honesty (Satir 1964), the therapist enables the entire family to achieve a higher, more satisfying level of functioning.

SUMMARY

We have emphasized in this presentation that learning disabilities have multiple determinants. The concept of a circumscribed area of learning disability is highly questionable. In actuality, there are many kinds of learning disorders, and each may require different types of intervention. A continuum was presented to suggest the varying types of intervention that might be employed dependent upon the nature of a child's problems and the family's dynamics. It is extremely important that the techniques of identification and diagnosis be further refined in order to make the selection of the specific type of intervention more scientific and justifiable. — *Parkway Day School, 130 W. Schoolhouse Lane, Philadelphia, Pa. 19144.*

A Parents Guide To Amphetamine Tretment of Hyperkinesis

By a parent, Barbara Fowlie

This article suggests specific ways in which the parents of a child requiring treatment with stimulant drugs can most effectively administer the prescribed medications – ways in which they can bridge what is often a communication gap between their child's doctor and teacher. A parent's insights, gained from first-hand experience, attempt to support and reassure other parents involved with such a treatment program.

If your pediatrician has recommended a program of medication for your child that includes an amphetamine-like drug such as Ritalin or Dexedrine, there are probably many questions you will be asking the doctor. Some of the questions that will occur to you will be difficult, maybe impossible, for the doctor to answer. That is because, although he knows generally what to expect from the drugs, he also knows that each child reacts somewhat differently to them. He most likely has never lived with a child who needs this kind of treatment and he doesn't know, unlike you, what it is like to live with *your* child. So it will be up to you to know what to look for. You will be the liaison between child, teacher, and doctor.

As a parent with a hyperactive child who has been taking a combination of Ritalin and Benedryl (an antihistamine) for over five years, I have acquired some answers to some of those hard-to-answer questions. I'd like to share my findings with you in order that it may help you more easily live with a possibly long-term treatment for your child.

When the pediatrician first prescribes medication for his patient, he may suggest a tentative dose, usually small, to be given once or twice a day. Then he may add, as mine did, "... play it by ear." Playing it by ear isn't always that easy to do. It is a matter of your being able to observe behavioral changes in your child's ability to control himself. It also means talking to the teacher frequently and telling her what to look for. She will have to be able to communicate to you the needs of your child in a school setting. After a while you will be able to relate the dosage (amount and frequency) of medication to the child's actions and abilities. I had some reservations at first when it occurred to me that perhaps the drugs were making my boy into someone that he wasn't. The psychologist who first diagnosed my child as being hyperkinetic, Dr. James Benjamines, reassured me by saying, "This medicine does not control the child. It just helps him to control himself. It enables him to be the kind of boy he wants to be!" Apparently the amphetamines stimulate the control centers of the central nervous system thereby allowing the hyperkinetic child to function more normally.

As you and the doctor work toward developing proper dosage for your child, consider the following variations. Some children need and tolerate well a relatively high daily dose; some may benefit by a small amount. Still others, who at first do well on a light dose, need to have the dose increased as the body adjusts to the medicine. Timing is another factor in determining medication. There are children who do best on one dose in the morning before school and a second one at noon. The medication for them is effective for about four-and-a-half hours. There are other children who need to have medication every three hours, but perhaps in a smaller amount each time. When there is homework to be done at night, an extra dose may be needed, but not until the end of the day or about a half hour before the work session begins. It is possible that this could be smaller than usual amount for two reasons: in the home situation there are

A Parent's Guide to Amphetamine Treatment of Hyperkinesis, Barbara Fowlie, *Journal of Learning Disabilities*, Vol. 6, No. 6, June/July 1973.

fewer distractions, and also there is somewhat of a cumulative effect, a residual build-up from the medication given earlier in the day that may lessen the need for a full dose. The two side-effect from these amphetamine-like drugs listed by the pharmaceutical companies that manufacture them are "insomnia" and "appetite suppression." In the case of my son we found that he had more difficulty falling asleep when *off* the regimen of drug therapy – because of his hyperactivity and inability to "slow down." Any loss of appetite experienced by a child taking these drugs can be controlled somewhat by timing meals and snacks so that the medicine is dispensed at mealtimes or shortly after. In four hours or so, when the drug wears off, the appetite returns (as any dieter taking amphetamines will testify). Bedtime is a good time for a rich and nutritious snack to make up for any reduced caloric intake earlier in the day. Don't forget, though, that there are plenty of average children who do not take medication but yet have eating lags, who are thin or small, who have small appetites, and who need little sleep. So within a range of your own child's regular eating and sleeping pattern you can make a judgment as to how much these side-effects actually are involved in his individual development.

There are questions for you to ask yourself, or the teacher, to help you decide whether your child is functioning properly in a certain setting with a given medication dosage. In a school situation where ability to conform and perform is most important, these are some of the things to ask a teacher in her observations of your child:

(1) Does the child work slowly or in spurts, often not finishing the assigned work?
(2) Is his handwriting illegible and messy?
(3) Does the student get involved in (or initiate) most of the classroom incidents, such as throwing paper wads, fighting, etc.?
(4) Do the little noises and movements of the other pupils disturb and distract him?
(5) Does he seem to have a poor or fluctuating memory – remembering things one day and not the next but maybe the day after?
(6) Does he have a loud voice that seems to speak out at inappropriate times?
(7) Is he impulsive in his work, not seeming to think things through or plan ahead in answering, writing, or asking?

All of these things, if extreme and continuous, would indicate attention problems, poor concentration, distractibility, and an inability to focus on one thing at a time. These characteristics can cause real behavior problems. No matter how intelligent a child is or how great his potential they can create low academic performance. If a teacher can note progress in these areas of a student's classroom activities after medication is prescribed, then you can assume that the medication is effective. If there is room for a lot more improvement, then perhaps a higher dosage would be indicated. A teacher can also help determine the possibility of overdosage. Ask her if the child under observation has become too quiet – reserved to the point of near shyness, not typical for this child. Ask if the youngster has developed nervous habits like picking at his hands or face excessively. Check as to whether he has become unusually overcritical of himself. Attitudes and mannerisms that reflect anxiety might demonstrate the need for a smaller amount of medication or maybe medication given less often.

At home you can make the same kind of observations to see how effective the amphetamines are for your child. When my son received his first half-tablet, the first thing he did was to get a rather complex jigsaw puzzle out of his toy closet. It was a puzzle that he had never been able to complete and that had particularly frustrated him. It had always angered him that his sister could do it without much difficulty. he worked at it for a whole hour, methodically fitting each piece or discarding it without evidence of temper or frustration. His concentration was deep, his patience, unusual (for him); the ordinary distractions that always had interfered with his completing a task did not appear to disturb him. The change was extremely noticeable. It surprised me because never before had he been able to devote more than ten minutes to one activity. The repeated failures that he experienced every day had taken a toll on his self-esteem. We were both elated by the boost he got from his new success with the puzzle. Shortly after he finished the puzzle we held our first sensible two-way conversation. At five years old his interest in the sounds of words had seemed to distract him almost to the point of his ignoring their meaning. Our communication had been very poor, with his attention constantly drawn to rhyming, onomatopoeia, and alliteration. Watch your child, and ask yourself:

(1) Does he finish what he starts – be it chores, games, projects, etc.?

(2) Does he play with other children cooperatively?
(3) Is he flexible about sudden changes in plans and in new situations?
(4) Is he impulsive and does he take risks without thinking?
(5) Does he dawdle and procrastinate a lot?
(6) Does he "fool around" and do most everything at mealtime except eat?
(7) Does he get overstimulated, "high as a kite," or lose control when angered or excited?

For a hyperkinetic child proper medication should bring about marked improvement in all of these areas of family life. Life at home, like life at school, needs to be better for children who have spent most of their lives being scolded, punished, corrected, and reminded. Because of this they have a very poor self-image. Their egos are damaged and, like that of my son, their self-esteem is low. Once behavior and performance improve at home and at school, the chain of events leads from one success to another. Successes build confidence and provide a basis for further motivation. Parents are pleased; their children are pleasing to them. Self-image improves, self-esteem grows to the point where the need for medication at home is lessened. Eventually the medication can be used strictly as a tool for aiding school work. The natural maturing process is taking place and is working along with the medicine. Developmental lags catch up with the passage of time; as the nervous system matures the inner controls can take over and the need for medication diminishes.

Medication won't solve all the problems that come with correct management and treatment of a hyperkinetic child. It can't be used as a crutch by parents who won't face the fact that their child may have some emotional problems that need additional treatment. Many hyperkinetic youngsters have anxieties that are directly due to the low regard they have for themselves. Dr. John Dorsey, our pediatrician, feels that these anxieties may inhibit the effectiveness of the drugs being used in treating some young patients. Parents would do well to get a professional opinion as to the exact state of their child's emotional health. They would all benefit to learn how best to: (1) build self-confidence in their children; (2) discover ways to manage and discipline their children that would avoid ego damage; and (3) express love and support in a way that is not overprotective but that does encourage growth of responsibility and maturity. Not all behavior problems (acting out, compulsive behavior, anxiety, depression, frequent temper outbursts, etc.) are necessarily attributed directly to hyperkinesis. Therefore medication of the type I'm discussing here will not help correct them. Counseling, to discover the cause and treatment of additional emotional difficulties, could at least make medical treatment for a hyperkinetic child more successful. At most it would work hand in hand with the medications in building self-esteem and self control at home and at school.

The child's newly found self-confidence thereby gives the parents a feeling that they too are a success! Understandably they feel like "good parents" when they see their offspring begin to do well in school, become more accepted by friends and relatives, and cooperate more fully within the family. They see that they must have been doing something right (after all the criticism they probably received) when their child suddenly seems to shape up after perhaps years of all kinds of difficulties. And it is largely due to their efforts to understand and help him – with plenty of love, concern, and acceptance thrown in.

Because of their desire to help their child, parents must realize that it is necessary for him to eventually depend on internal controls without the help of any medication. Past successes and an improved self-image, plus the added control that develops with a more mature nervous system, will enable an older child to make the extra effort to concentrate without as much medication. Dosage can be reduced gradually over a period of time; each individual has his own time-table. One can cut down on quantity of medication first on week-ends, then in the summer, and then eliminate it at those times entirely. "Home-work doses" can be reduced. A program of gradual reduction to fit the individual's needs and schedules is the end goal. Take advantage of the preadolescent attitude of not wanting to be "different." Often at this age the child will drag his feet at having his peers think his need for pills "different," so he will be extra motivated to make the effort to take less medication less often. Encourage this attitude but with some reservations. You don't want to have him experience a serious setback. Close observation will indicate very soon after the amphetamines are reduced whether there are new problems or old ones returning. It should be clear to the student as well as the teacher, through the quality of the schoolwork during a trial period, if some medication is still needed. Emphasize to the youngster that he is using this medication for concentration while doing exacting work. It is not a "personality changer" and it is not a "behavior controller."

Current concern with drug abuse leads me to a reassuring quotation from Dr. Leon Oettinger who said in an article entitled "Amphetamines, Hyperkinesis and Learning": "Amphetamines and similar drugs, as well as other drugs affecting the brain, are useful tools which are the most valuable yet found medically to aid in stabilizing the brain of children with learning disorders and hyperactivity. They are unusually safe, much more so than aspirin or penicillin, and when used properly do not lead to habituation, addiction or abuse, but rather help control the underlying psychological and physiological problems which lead to such abuse."* — *378 S. Cranbrook Road, Birmingham, Mich. 48009.*

**Leon Oettinger, "Amphetamines, Hyperkinesis and Learning." Calif. Assoc. for Neurologically Handicapped Children, August, 1970.*

The Effectiveness of Parental Counseling with Other Modalities in the Treatment of Children with Learning Disabilities

Unpublished Ed. D Dissertation by
Dr. Bruce E. Baker

Reviewed by John V. Gilmore

For some years educators, parents, and some members of the medical profession have been interested in a certain visual malfunction that seems to appear more frequently in children who are having difficulty with their school subjects, particularly reading. The condition, first called "dyslexia," is now referred to as "perceptual difficulties" and in some cases simply "learning difficulties." Since the condition is not clearly described nor defined even in medical books, the tests for its diagnosis are consequently lacking in validity and reliability. Its frequency is therefore difficult to determine but it is conservatively estimated to be present in approximately 10% of the school and adult population.

The validity of the concept that perceptual difficulties are a causative factor in learning disabilities has never been adequately established. It is an obvious assumption that since reading is a visual process, difficulties in reading could be functions of visual impairment, but for some fifty years psychologists and educators have attempted with little success to associate the causes of inability to learn with visual malfunctions. The latest attempt began with the use of the term "dyslexia" which was applied to apparent visual and auditory handicaps that were observed in the children having difficulty in learning. In addition to perceptual difficulties, many of these students who have been so diagnosed have been found to have physical conditions that could be classified as psychosomatic. Many of them also have behavioral and acting out problems.

Many theorists have viewed the cause of perceptual difficulties as a dysfunction of the neurological system—a point of view largely supported by the medical profession. A number of articles attempt a possible

The Effectivness of Parental Counseling with Other Modulaties in the treatment of Children with Learning Disabilities, Bruce E. Barker, *Journal of Education,* Vol. 23, No. 4.

explanation of the neurological and physiological foundations for this condition. Money (1966) was unable, however, to find substantial evidence supporting the specific neurological dysfunctioning in brain pathology and has cautioned his associates to disregard what he calls a theory of "quasi-neurological" interference as a basis for learning difficulty. He claims that in the majority of cases no brain damage can be demonstrated by current diagnostic techniques.

Psychoanalytic theory attempts to explain the etiology of a child's learning difficulties by the fixations which may have occurred in his early development, among which may have been his unconscious association at the oral stage between the difficulty of intake of food and the intake of knowledge, both of which the child rejects. Developmental problems at the oral and anal stage may be associated with low self esteem; hence an excessive amount of doubt, an inability to do written assignments, and the refusal to participate orally in classes may be caused by fear of criticism dating to early stages of development. Other personality theories tend to cluster around the emotional and various intrapsychic factors that center on the family process. Validity of this later approach is found in the observation of the disturbed social behavior and the psychosomatic ailments of these children.

Support for the influence of the environment as a causative factor among the emotional factors associated with perceptual difficulties is found in many studies of the underachieving child. A vast amount of well conducted research has found that affective and nurturance variables discriminate high and low academic achievers. For an example, Winterbottom has substantiated the link between the mother-father relationship and the achievement of elementary boys ages six to ten. High achieving boys had more demands placed on them by their mothers and also received supportive types of affection from them. McClelland (1953,61) has also found a relationship of physical expressions of caring (such as hugging and kissing) to high achievement in boys and has determined the mother's particular importance in fulfilling this affective need. Roth (1960) found that the boy's perception of maternal regard was significantly differentiated in achieving and underachieving boys. Hilliard and Roth (1969) and Roth and Meyersburg (1963) stated that the lack of affection and general support was an etiological factor in underachievement and proved to be a fertile area for research. Gilmore has found that methods of counseling parents that follow the directive consultation model emphasizing the importance of affective nurturance result in improvement in the children's social behavior as well as their academic achievement. Since a positive emotional interaction with the mother is associated with high achievement it would seem essential that in any study of underachievement maternal counseling be incorporated as part of the treatment process.

Baker has found in the literature that most of the neuro-educational remedial techniques used in the treatment of perceptual difficulties are based on a hypothesis of a possible brain dysfunctioning and inadequate neurological framework. The teaching methods involve the training of the visual and auditory perceptual processes and memory integration. One study using a tutoring method found improvement on the Gilmore Oral Reading and the California Achievement Test Scores, but too few studies have pointed to the effectiveness of this approach in the remediation of children with neurological problems. The failure of current teaching methods which are attempting remediation of a supposed neurological deficit casts serious doubt on the validity of the neurological causation hypothesis. Several methodological limitations of the studies on perceptual difficulties are noted by Baker. The selection of students with symptoms of learning disabilities often includes variables other than visual difficulties such as a general underachievement syndrome. Affect, for example, is mentioned in a few studies, but has not been adequately diagnosed or treated in many. The effectiveness of the counseling or tutoring relationship in the improvement of children with perceptual handicaps has been neglected in many studies.

In the light of conflicting theories as to the causes of perceptual handicaps (related to underachievement in children) and the lack of well controlled studies on the effectiveness of the treatment programs, it appears that a well designed, multidimensional study of dyslexia would be a marked contribution to the fields of teaching and counseling. Such a study would give some clarification to the factors which are causing confusion and misdirected discussion among teachers, parents, psychologists, and other professional people working with students.

Baker has provided an excellent method of solving the problem of measuring some of the factors that may interfere with the child's functioning in the classroom. He has also provided an evaluative technique for measuring three different kinds of instructional treatment for children so diagnosed. In his study he includes a separate class type of approach, the purpose of which is to aid children with their reading difficulties through group instruction. Another teaching approach included in his study is the individual tutoring on a one-to-one basis. The third method of treatment is the counseling of the mother and the child in separate interviews.

Inasmuch as the literature emphasizes the family as a factor in learning difficulties, one of the goals of Baker's study is to assess the effectiveness of maternal counseling as it influences the relationships between the mother and the child. The counseling model provided is one characterized by high levels of accurate empathy, unconditional positive regard, genuineness, and a depth of self exploration in the mother's role in dynamic family conditions. Theoretically, some self exploration in the mother's role will help the mother to supply more adequately the essentials required for the emotional and cognitive growth of her children.

Experimental Procedures

The students selected for this project were in grades one through five. Learning difficulty in children had first been identified through the administration in 1968 of the Stanford Achievement Test. Various combinations of scores on this 1968 Stanford Achievement Test with former language scores from previous Stanford Achievement Tests in grades one through five constituted an indication of language or reading difficulty. One hundred seventy-five students were chosen at random to be individually tested by the Wechsler Intelligence Scale. The students who had a full-scale score of less than 90 were disqualified from this particular study on the assumption that their learning difficulties could be influenced by a lower general ability as measured by the Wechsler. The Bender Visual Motor Gestalt Test was used as evidence of visual motor retardation.

The resulting population of 104, from which the final 48 students were selected, was split into two groups: children from grades two and three formed a pool from which placement was made in the lower level groups, while children entering grades four and five formed another pool. The measures of change and improvement in the children were conducted along cognitive, affective, environmental and psychomotor dimensions. The cognitive aspects of the children were measured by the Wechsler Intelligence Scale for children and the Stanford Achievement Test. The affective variable was measured by the Thematic Apperception Test, the Draw a Person Test, the Bender Visual Motor Gestalt Test, and the California Test of Personality (personal section only). The environmental variables were measured by the Maryland Parental Attitudes Scale and the California Test of Personality. The psychomotor variables were measured also by the Bender Visual Motor Gestalt Test.

Teacher effectiveness was determined on the basis of an "Observational Rating Form," for which there were three trained rating observers. All the teachers met the State Certification requirements of Massachusetts and had taught elementary school for at least three years. Counseling and therapeutic skill was determined by the Accurate Empathy Scale. Empathy, unconditional positive regard, the therapist's congruence, the depth of self exploration role were measured by the Truax Carkhuff Measuring Self Congruence Scale.

Methods of Treatment Appertaining to the Experiment

Baker then divided the 48 students into two groups of 24 each. For one group of 24 students, there were two special classes of 12 each which involved group instruction in reading and various forms of learning exercises. The other group of students was tutored on a one-to-one basis. The instruction and tutoring in these two groups were called "primary intervention."

To determine the effectiveness of counseling on the academic and other performances of the students, Baker further divided each of these two groups of 24 in another manner. In an experimental group, 12 students came from the special class group and 12 from those receiving tutoring. These 24 students were further divided into three groups. Eight students (in each primary intervention group) received play therapy, eight mothers received counseling, and in the remaining eight a combined method was employed in which mothers received counseling and the child received play therapy (a form of counseling). The counseling sessions with the mother were of one hour duration and involved seven to ten sessions. The play therapy was conducted in a one-to-one relationship for 17 to 22 sessions of 40 minutes each. The other 24 students were used as a control for the counselled group.[1]

Results

The various hypotheses formulated by Baker were tested for statistical significance. He found that the class teaching method is more effective in bringing about improvement in academic achievement and on test performance than is the tutoring approach. He also found in the group approach that the parents' attitudes are changed toward the child and there is an improvement in the child's attitude toward the parent.

The effect of the teacher on the child's improvement could not be verified. It would appear from observation that the special class teachers and their aides were highly skilled in teaching children. The tutoring groups on the other hand were exposed to numerous qualities of teaching. The teaching qualities as such of both groups, were not incorporated in this study as a control. Baker did, nevertheless, compare the teachers who scored above the mean on the Observer's Rating Form with those who scored below. (Since there was not in this rating form an observable cut-off score which would differentiate "good" teaching from poor, he employed this technique as a method of comparison.) Baker found that the teacher effectiveness, at least as measured by this rating form, could

1. The counseling of the child was conducted by Dr. Claire Siegel and the counseling of the mother by Dr. Baker.

not explain the differences in the improvement of students in the group class as compared with those who were tutored. One observation not tabulated was the symbiotic relationship between the tutor and the child which appeared to develop as the tutoring program progressed. The interpersonal difficulties of this nature which might accrue from such a relationship may have prevented the tutor from being effective in the teaching situation.

For those in the group teaching class the parental counseling and the play therapy did significantly contribute to improve class performance at the 5% level of significance. A significant improvement in the test scores of the psychomotor intelligence measure was also found in this particular group. The conclusion is that high quality counseling, when added to the group class instruction, adds significantly to the improvement in parent-child relations and hence to the general performance of the class.

For those in the tutoring group, play therapy only with the child, or counseling only with the mother, or a combination of play therapy and parental counseling brought about a greater improvement in achievement and test performance than when only tutoring was employed. Baker also found that if any one of the three types of counseling is added to the tutoring method there is a significant improvement in the parent attitude toward the child, the child's achievement factors, and the adjustment pattern between parent and child. There is also some indication that when neither the mother nor the child has been counseled, there is a deterioration in the parent-child adjustment score. In the tutoring group, scores on psychomotor intelligence decreased when the treatment program was terminated.

Conclusions

Baker concluded that when parents are given a high quality counseling or when parent counseling and play therapy are combined each or both become an effective method of treating learning disabilities in children. He goes on to say that one of these treatments may be more effective than another or than both in combination, but the results are not differentiated in his study. They therefore cannot be substantiated at this time. An analysis of variance between the three therapeutic treatments—counseling with the mother, play therapy with the child, and a combination of the two (play therapy and maternal counseling)—did not indicate any significant differences in the child's improvement. When one or both, however, is added to either the group teaching or the tutoring situation counseling (provided it is of high quality) for either the mother or the child, will be effective in the improvement of the child's academic and test performance. The high level therapy, then, was instrumental in causing a change in the parent-child relationship to a greater extent than was either the tutoring or the special class situation singly. The counseling of the parent or play therapy with the child proved to be a valuable treatment as an adjunct to the services of either the special class or the tutoring situation.

The tutoring treatment alone is the least effective remedial method. Baker claims that in the remediation of any learning disability either form of counseling (with the parent or with the child in the form of play therapy) may be considered as effective as any other psychotherapeutic treatment. There was some indication that when the mother was overprotective (a form of rejection) there was a lower correlation with the child's achievement.

It would also appear from his study that the teachers are an insignificant factor in the remediation of the child. Perhaps the Observer's Rating

Form is not sufficiently sensitive to the differences in teaching methods of either the special class or the tutoring method. If one has to choose either the special class or the tutoring method, it would appear that the special group method of teaching is more effective in the remediation of learning difficulties than is tutoring alone.

Additional Comments

Baker has observed other variables in the parent-child relationship which were not included in this study. When, as noted above, the mother was overprotective, and her child was consequently more dependent, he found that lower achievement was more likely to occur in the child. He also found that as the parent counseling situations continued, the enuresis which was present in some children diminished or was practically eliminated (a similar experience has occurred with many clinicians working with parents of enuretic children). Moreover, when the child's enuresis diminished the parent reported improvement in his general behavior.

Another interesting unpredicted observation was made of the children who were on some form of constant medical prescription. The counselors observed that as the counseling proceeded, there was less need for medical treatment and fewer prescriptions were filled. It was also observed that when the parents felt that the child was getting better (as in the case of the enuresis) their self esteem improved and they were consequently better able to relate to the child. This observation gives additional validation to Coopersmith's findings of the relationship between parents' ability to give esteem to the children and their own self esteem.

A child's poor physical condition often is the cause of guilt feelings and lowered self esteem. In these children there are difficulties with vision, enuresis, and other physical conditions—psychosomatic or organic in origin—which cause guilt and concern to parents and diminish their self esteem. The alleviation or improvement of the child's physical condition lessens the parents' guilt and hence enhances their self confidence.

The lack of difference between the effectiveness of play therapy and parental counseling in the improvement in the child requires some explanation. One possible suggestion deals with the play therapy situation, which is a one-to-one counseling relationship. Since the therapist in this study is a woman and the children as a group are theoretically dependent, the therapist may function as a mother substitute. Observation of these children's behavior indicates limited coping skills which are related to an emotionally deprived environment. They are not esteemed in their own home and their behavioral, intellectual, learning and health problems are symptoms of this lack of esteem. The attention, therefore, afforded by the play therapist, might be just as effective as the change in attitude of the mother.

In any event, the foregoing observations are important contributions to this study. The elimination of enuresis, the diminishing need for medical treatment, the increase in the parents' self-esteem, all would give some credence to the fact that perceptual difficulties do have an emotional basis. The fact that the tutoring situation was ineffective may also point to a possible symbiotic involvement of the child with any form of mother or nurturing person. The vulnerability of these children to this kind of relationship in the tutoring situation presents a doubt as to whether it should be continued. By contrast, in the group some esteem may be gained by associating with peers who have similar problems and to whom the child can relate.

The research findings and the additional observations in Baker's study raise some very important questions as far as the treatment of perceptual difficulties is concerned. His research suggests that the current methods of teaching the so-called perceptually handicapped child which are employed by the schools with either the group or the tutoring approach are not successfully treating the child's difficulty. These methods are based on an unfounded assumption that all perceptual difficulties have a neurological cause. It would appear that except in a medical case of a thoroughly diagnosed neurological impairment, the current treatment method is dealing with symptoms and not with causes. Research in experimental psychology has found repeatedly that emotional conflicts can interfere with the visual process. Any improvement secured in the child under the current teaching methods will be of doubtful permanency since it is not eliminating the conflict caused by an emptiness and an emotional deficit that these children apparently experience. Until the advocates who claim that perceptual dysfunctioning in itself is a direct cause of learning difficulties can present well documented research based on matched experimental and control groups, pre- and post-testing procedures, and adequate follow-up studies, we have to doubt the validity of their assumption.

Dr. Baker's findings can be validated with individual cases of perceptual difficulties with which we have worked during the past five years in parental counseling. Our approach is to persuade parents of dyslexic children to ignore the perceptual difficulties and concentrate on methods and techniques in the parent-child relationship that will improve the child's self esteem. When parents follow these recommendations the child's reading, school work, and social behavior improve – in some cases almost miraculously. Baker has made a marked contribution to this controversial subject and has paved the way for further research. It is hoped other such studies can be conducted at the junior and senior high school levels.

Baker's study has important implications for the training of counselors. Since the counseling of the mother and child secured an improvement in the child's behavior and school performance, it can be inferred that the causes of learning difficulties lie in the parent-child relationship. Counseling parents on techniques of relating to and with their children is apparently treating at least one of the causes of learning difficulties if not the most important one. Universities should therefore provide training in parental counseling in their graduate programs for this and other forms of malfunctioning in students of all ages.

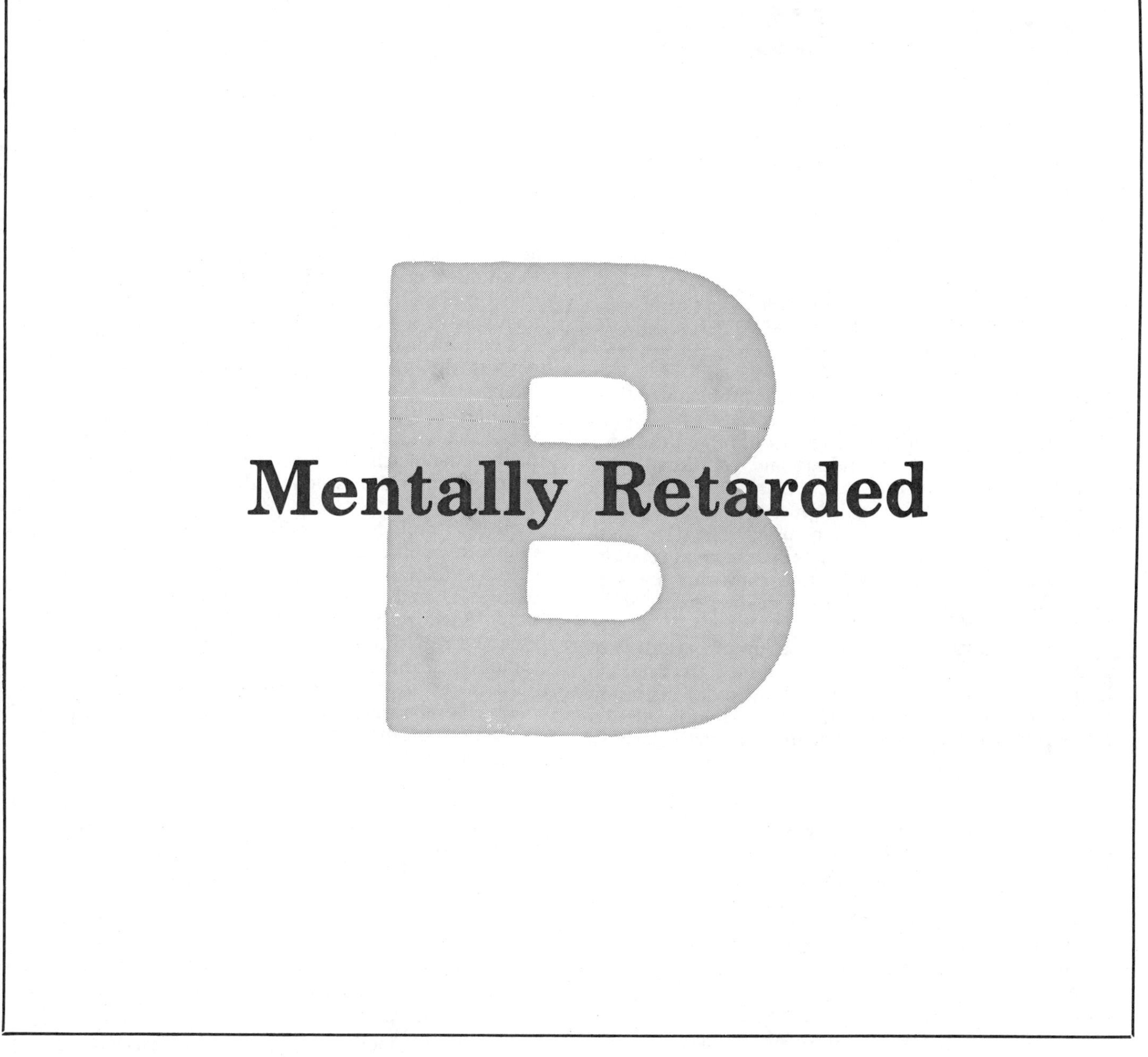

Of all disabilities, mental retardation may be the hardest for parents to accept, particularly it seems, for fathers. Even when the difficult initial stage of understanding and acceptance is accomplished, the family encounters problems of placing blame, sibling favoritism, despair and guilt, not to mention the decisions concerning finances, life-style adjustments, and lifetime care. The fact that the child cannot share the "blame" places a greater burden of guilt on many parents. In some cases, the mentally retarded child seems to catalyze marital conflicts. The child's inability to develop is frustrating to parents, which in turn often creates a vicious pendulum of hostility and over-indulgence. Hostility may be directed outward or may be self-directed and lead to depression or a "martyr" complex.

These problems present the helping professional with the challenge of working to establish family stability. They emphasize that basic needs--for love, for being loved, for security, for being understood and accepted as a person--of the mentally retarded child are the same as for any other child, that the mentally retarded child is more like normal children than different from them. The counselor needs to be honest, attentive, accepting, dignified, capable of eliciting emotions without placing value judgments, able to allow parents to make decisions, and resourceful in emphasizing areas and degrees of possible success. The helping professional needs to recognize the variance of parental reactions and the state of readiness of the parents to move from information seeking through emotion sharing to mature decision-making. Finally, the counselor needs to evaluate the coping mechanisms of all members' rights to have needs satisfied, and work toward livable family interaction.

Counseling the Parents of Retarded Children

Kishwar Ishtiaq

The author is a doctoral student at Lucknow University, Lucknow (U.P.) India. She is doing research under Shri Chandra, head of the Department of Psychology at Lucknow.

MENTALLY RETARDED CHILDREN present problems to their parents, families, community and society as a whole. Current prevalent approaches consist of residential care, special classes, parent counseling, and vocational rehabilitation. Some aspects of parent counseling that could be significantly effective in improving the lot of mentally retarded children will be discussed. The term counseling is used here to describe the interpersonal relationship which takes place when the counselor seeks to influence the behavior and attitude of the parents of the mentally retarded children.

Active cooperation and participation of parents is of prime importance in rehabilitation of mentally retarded children, as training for basic life attitudes begins in the home. To accept the fact that one's child is intellectually retarded is indeed a difficult task, particularly in our society where a great premium is set on educational achievement and intellectual attainment. The hard fact itself causes various emotional problems, worries, anxieties, and annoying symptoms among the parents; therefore, the primary object of parent counseling is to free them from such symptoms. Counseling and therapy in some cases, frequently becomes essential for such parents of mentally retarded children. Some parents present symptoms of neurotic behavior, excessive guilt and emotional disorganization. Under the circumstances, the counselor's consideration must be directed towards the attitudes and emotions of the parents. The counselor, beyond conveying factual information, must help the parents to learn to work with the child as he is. At the same time they must be assured that they have the support and assistance of those individuals, agencies and programs whose goal is to try to bring the child to a level of functioning commensurate with his abilities. It can be explained that hope lies in the direction of developing all of the mental capacities the child has and in fostering self-confidence which will permit him to use his capacities to the greatest advantage. Thus, one of the main goals in counseling parents is to secure improved functional efficiency in the mentally retarded children through parental understanding and acceptance.

Parents often display guilt feelings about the child; this presents major difficulties for the counselor. The fear of hereditary influence plays an important role in some parental attitudes and exaggerates emotional reactions. Parents may internalize these fears and begin to question origins and family strains. In addition, they sometimes fail to face the prejudices of less informed members of the communities in which they live.

The counselor or the therapist, while counseling the parents should pay special attention to the mode of interpretation of the problem. Efforts should be made to interpret the problem in a convincing and realistic manner, taking care, at the same time, that the desire of the parents to achieve something from training and education of the child is not shattered. A desired outcome of counseling is that the parents achieve insight into their own problems, for which, of course, establishment of parent-counselor rapport is a must. It can be difficult to maintain rapport throughout the entire counseling session because of various types of parent reactions. Such reactions can be categorized as follows: accepted reality, circumstantial excuses, and total unacceptance of the reality.

In order to establish rapport for therapeutic purposes, the counselor should first assure the parents of his understanding and sympathy. Secondly, information about the diagnosis and expectations about the child should be elicited. The third step would be to counsel the parents towards an emotional reconciliation of the problem. At this stage there should be sufficient agreement between the subjective feelings and objective facts (reality situation), which helps in wise handling and planning for the child and encourages realistic orientation. In order to impart insight into the possible causes of mental retardation, various factors contributing to the condition could be discussed. This can help make the parents feel guilt-free and emotionally ready to accept the condition.

An effective method of relieving the anxieties of the parents is group therapy, which can stimulate parents to discuss their mutual problems and methods of training. The idea of sharing problems and feelings can relieve emotional stresses, fears, and worries. Various local chapters of associations or organizations of parent groups, such as National Association for Retarded Children, as well as the American Association on Mental Deficiency offer services and information to keep citizens abreast of the latest developments in mental retardation. In this way, parents learn to cope with the problem of rearing a handicapped child.

It is apparent that parents of mentally retarded children need to be heard and properly understood. Effective counseling services should be provided for them so that they can face the problem objectively and without feelings of guilt or inferiority.

Counseling Parents of the Mentally Retarded Child, Francis H. Norton, *The School Counselor*, Vol. 23, No. 3.

Psychological Counseling With Parents of Retarded Children

by Philip Roos

ABSTRACT. Counseling with parents of retarded children presents psychologists with difficult and unique problems. A therapeutic interview technique is recommended since recognition of retardation in one's child tends to precipitate severe emotional reactions. Typical parental reactions to retardation are described in this article, and specific suggestions for counseling with parents are considered. Special attention is given to the use of evaluative techniques as part of the counseling process.

In their painful search for answers to their dilemma, parents of retarded children frequently turn to the psychologist for counseling and guidance. Fruitful interaction between parents and psychologists requires special skill and sensitivity on the part of the psychologist. This presentation is an attempt to clarify important ingredients in the successful counseling situation.

The psychologist working with parents of retarded children should remember that he is probably dealing with highly distressed people. Reactions to the very real trauma of recognizing retardation in one's own child are, of course, infinitely varied, but certain general patterns recur with enough frequency to be considered more or less typical. Understanding of these patterns by the psychologist is helpful in dealing with the parents.

Parental Reactions to Retardation

Many parents suffer a severe loss of self-esteem when they recognize retardation in their child. In our culture children are often considered by parents as ego-extensions; that is, the parent closely identifies with his child, taking pride in his accomplishments and basking in his reflected glory. A serious defect in the child tends to be experienced by the parent as his own defect. Hence, the parent may feel responsible for disappointing his mate, his own parents, and other family members by "presenting" them with a defective child. The possibility of genetic etiology leads some parents to renounce plans for having other children. Self-esteem may be further lowered by threat to the fantasy of immortality through one's children—the individual is suddenly faced with the prospect that he will leave no descendents after him. Life goals and basic approaches to the world may be abruptly and radically altered.

Closely allied to loss of self-esteem is the feeling of shame experienced by many parents. They may anticipate social rejection, pity, or ridicule, and related loss of prestige. It is not uncommon to find parents withdrawing from social participation and altering plans which might expose them to social rebuff. They tend to view their child's school years with particular apprehension, since during this time his defect will become most apparent.

Parents' feelings toward their retarded child are typically extremely ambivalent. Not only are they constantly frustrated by the child's lack of achievement, but the child's inadequate control often leads to extremely irritating behavior. Resentment and hostility generated by repeated frustrations may be expressed in death wishes toward the child and feelings of rejection. Typically such feelings arouse considerable guilt in the parent, who then tries to atone for his hostility by developing overprotective and overindulgent attitudes toward the child. The inconsistent reactions by the parent of demandingness, hostility and rejection, alternating with overprotection and overindulgence, are likely to disturb the child and thereby further reduce his efficiency, in turn increasing parental frustration. Such a self-perpetuating "vicious cycle" may further reduce the child's intellectual efficiency.

Hostility generated by frustration experienced in their interaction with the retarded child is often displaced by the parent onto other relation-

Psychological Counseling with Parents of Retarded Children, Philip Roos, *Mental Retardation*, December 1963.

ships. Parents may present a "chip-on-the-shoulder" attitude. Their irritable, resentful demeanor tends to alienate others and leads to rejection and avoidance by friends and relatives, further frustrating the parents and thereby increasing their resentment. The counselor should be alerted to the possibility that his clients may be in the grips of such a vicious cycle. Inappropriate attacks against the counselor are more easily accepted if recognized as manifestations of displaced hostility stemming from serious frustrations.

Feelings of depression are to be expected. The absence of such feelings, particularly when realization of the child's retardation is recent, is unusual enough to raise suspicions regarding the possibility of atypical techniques of handling emotions (e.g., repression and isolation of affect). Some parents react to the retarded child as if he had died and manifest the typical grief reactions associated with the loss of a loved one. Such extreme reactions tend to be most prevalent in highly intelligent parents who tend to equate being human with the possession of intelligence. Disappointment in the child and concern for his future are appropriate reactions typically accompanied by some degree of unhappiness. Parents' ambivalence toward the child may contribute to depression, inasmuch as the hostility toward the child may be redirected toward the self.

Feelings of guilt and self-reproach may accompany depression and usually reflect internalization of hostility toward the child. It is not uncommon for parents to indicate that they feel responsible for the retardation, which may be described as a form of punishment for sins or as the outcome of transgressions. Cause of the retardation is sometimes erroneously attributed to guilt-ridden sexual activities.

Some parents adopt a masochistic position, almost welcoming the suffering they anticipate will accompany rearing the defective child. They may think of themselves as "martyrs" who will devote all their energies and sacrifice all pleasures for the child. The retardate may become the focus of a lifelong pattern of self-sacrifice and lamentation. It almost seems as if such parents "love to be miserable." They may dwell in detail on the tragic and sordid aspects of their situation and often share their unhappiness with all who will listen. Such parents are typically reluctant to institutionalize their child—no matter how severely incapacitated he might be—and may neglect siblings, relatives, careers, etc., for the "welfare" of the child. In counseling with such parents, it usually becomes apparent that the retardate plays a very significant role in the parents' adjustment patterns.

Realization that a child is retarded often has disruptive effects not only on the parents but on the entire family unit, and possibly on friends, acquaintances, and neighbors as well. Siblings and grandparents are very obviously involved, and increased tensions typically develop within the family. Marital conflicts may be aggravated, and the retarded child may become the focus of mutual blame and criticism by the parents. It is as if the child were a catalyst activating long-dormant conflicts into overt explosion.

Ambivalence toward the child may lead to defensiveness as well as to overprotection. Parents may become acutely sensitive to implied criticisms of the child and may react with resentment and belligerence. It may be difficult in such cases to present factual information which may be interpreted as depreciating the child.

A more extreme position is found in those parents who have attempted to protect themselves against the pain of recognizing retardation in their child by failing to become aware of its existence. Human beings can become highly skilled at remaining unaware of a certain aspect of reality, even when it is thrust upon them with some force. Mechanisms of denial, repression, and selective inattention have been described in detail as techniques whereby people are able to exercise control over the extent of their awareness. It is not unusual, therefore, to find parents who claim that "there is really nothing wrong" with an obviously severely retarded child. They may attribute the child's complete failure in school to a vindictive teacher, for example, or to bouts of tonsillitis. Parents may be helped in this self-deception by relatives, friends, and at times even professionals, who have reassured them of the child's "normality." Reluctance to face a painful and irrevocable situation is not limited to parents, and it is not surprising to find, therefore, that others have likewise failed to recognize the situation.

The trauma of experiencing retardation in one's child may precipitate serious existential conflicts. Concern with religion, the meaning of life, the tragedy of death, the inescapability of aloneness, and the relative insignificance and helplessness of man may preoccupy the parents. Although these concerns are usually less obvious than the other reactions described above, their significance should not be underestimated.

The Therapeutic Interview

Since parents of retardates typically approach the psychologist with several of the reactions just described, it is important to furnish them with the opportunity for a therapeutic interview. In its simplest form, parents should be given the opportunity to express their feelings in a nonthreatening interpersonal interaction. The basic ingredients of such an interview include the following:

(1) The counselee should be treated with acceptance and respect. By treating his client with dignity, the counselor helps decrease the feelings of worthlessness, self-blame and shame which plague many parents of retardates. Feelings of loss of self-confidence and helplessness are decreased when the parents feel accepted, understood and respected.

(2) The psychologist should resist the temptation to assume an authoritarian role. Although the assumption of a godlike role may enhance the counselor's feeling of self-esteem, it tends to have the reverse effect on his clients. Furthermore, the authoritarian role tends to discourage parents from expressing their views and feelings; they tend instead to await expectantly the words of wisdom which the psychologist will bestow upon them.

Few competent psychologists regard themselves as authorities in the area of mental retardation, for, if one is at all in contact with the field, one cannot but be impressed with the vastness of our current ignorance. Therefore, assuming an omniscient role is a bit of a fraud, and most parents soon grow painfully aware of the counselor's real limitations.

(3) Perhaps the essence of the therapeutic interview is that it is an interpersonal transaction wherein the interviewer allows the interviewee free emotional expression. In this respect, it differs rather markedly from the great majority of interpersonal interactions, since typically one is constantly reminded that many emotional reactions are rejected, condemned, censored, etc. As a result, of course, it becomes increasingly difficult to tolerate these "condemned" feelings within one's self, and one develops any number of ingenious mechanisms for disguising, disowning, and otherwise rejecting one's own feelings. The parent's statement that "sometimes this child makes me so mad!" may have repeatedly been countered with statements that he "shouldn't feel that way," that the child "can't help" how he acts, and so on. After these reactions, the parent has never even allowed himself the much more "reprehensible" thought: "I wish this child were dead!"

By encouraging emotional expression without passing value judgments on the expressed feelings, the counselor helps the parent to tolerate his feelings with less guilt and anxiety and, consequently, to deal with the feelings more effectively.

(4) Since the parents, and not the psychologist, will have to share life with the retarded child, decisions should be reached by the parents rather than the psychologist. By encouraging the parents to make their own decisions, the counselor enhances their feeling of self-confidence and helps them to assume responsibility for their actions. The counselor's goal should be to help the parents reach their decisions with as full an awareness as possible of their own feelings and of the reality of the situation.

(5) An important principle in conducting interviews with such parents is to let the parents determine the direction of the interview. That is, counseling seems most helpful when it is parent-centered rather than counselor-centered. The psychologist may have preconceived notions regarding the content and course which the interview should follow, and he may indeed experience feelings of accomplishment and satisfaction upon completing an interview successfully directed into these directions. The parents, on the other hand, may have quite different expectations regarding the interview and may, consequently, leave disappointed, frustrated, or confused. After all, the goal of the interview is generally assumed to be to help the parents—not the counselor—and a parent-centered interview seems most successful in reaching this goal.

(6) The last important ingredient of a therapeutic interview is perhaps the simplest and most difficult; namely, honesty. Although most psychologists do not plan to deceive their clients, their own needs and tensions may tempt them to distort, minimize, evade, ignore, and otherwise tamper with reality.

Not infrequently, the psychologist's need for approval and for maintaining the myth of his own omniscience leads him to deceive his clients by disguising his own ignorance and by bombarding them with assorted bits of impressive information. To a parent's question regarding the etiology of his child's defect, for example, the counselor may vaguely indicate that the etiology of many forms of retardation is not yet fully understood, and he may then embark upon a truly engrossing review of chromosome studies in Mongolism. Such a discourse may impress as well as confuse the parents, especially if their child is not a Mongol. In an attempt to "protect" parents against anxiety and depression, some counselors distort reality by minimizing the degree of retardation or by focusing upon unrealistic possibilities of eventual treatment or "cure."

Importance of Listening

Perhaps the most difficult skill for the psychologist to acquire is the ability to listen to his client. Listening not only implies attentiveness, interest, and sensitivity, but it also involves the capacity to remain silent. Many people find it difficult to refrain from speaking. Psychologists and other professionals often act as though their mission in life is to pass to the less informed the great wisdom which they possess.

Careful listening by the counselor has numerous beneficial results. The client's statements, for example, can be a valuable clue to the appropriateness of the counselor's comments. One does not respond in exactly the same way to an uneducated laborer as one does to a university professor. Detailed accounts of the latest studies of the reticular formation may be a bit inappropriate when directed to a truck driver, just as basic explanations of the meaning of electroencephalography are inappropriately condescending when directed to a physician.

By attentive listening, the counselor should succeed in reaching more or less valid conclusions as to the parents' current needs. If the counselor listens to the parents with the question, "Why are they seeing me here and now?" constantly in mind, he may frequently find that the initially stated reason for the interview is indeed far removed from the real reason which brings the parents to him. Having ascertained the parents' real needs, the counselor is better prepared to supply them with information which will be meaningful to them, and he can more intelligently make recommendations with regard to further evaluation and planning.

The psychologist who succeeds in controlling his need to speak is more likely to encourage his clients to express their own feelings, concerns and opinions. The parents' observations of the retarded child are frequently of considerable value, and their estimates of functioning level are often quite accurate. It is not unusual to discover that parents come to the psychologist having already made important decisions and searching for support or a chance for catharsis rather than for information or evaluation. On occasion, encouraging parents to voice their opinions reveals surprising distortions and erroneous beliefs, indicating areas in which information is most needed.

Use of Evaluative Findings

Since psychologists are frequently requested to determine the presence of mental retardation, psychological evaluation often becomes the subject of the interview with the parents. If the parents and the psychologist agree that formal evaluation of the child may be desirable, the parents should be informed of the nature and purpose of the evaluation. It is important to acquaint parents with the answers they may expect from the evaluation. If the results may prove to be relatively meaningless, the parents should be so advised. Parents' resentment at being told of uninterpretable results of complex and often expensive procedures is not entirely inappropriate, particularly if they were not forewarned of this possible outcome.

The psychologist should endeavor to expedite evaluative procedures. Allowing parents to linger in the agony of doubt is cruel and destructive. The period of evaluation is usually experienced as highly stressful and distressing by parents, and it should be kept as short as possible. As soon as the evaluation has been completed, the parents should be informed of the results.

Evaluative findings should be presented in terms that will be meaningful to the parents. Operational formulations and concrete examples are to be preferred to abstract and theoretical constructs. Presenting the child's level of functioning in mental age equivalents is usually considerably more meaningful than references to the intelligence quotients or social quotients. As a matter of fact, parents are often surprisingly accurate in estimating the child's level of functioning in terms of developmental level.

Description of probable accomplishments in terms of illustrative behavior is usually extremely helpful. Emphasis on those activities which the child may be able to perform is more helpful than dwelling on areas of limitations and expected failure. A statement such as, "Your child will probably be able to master fifth or sixth grade work," is much less likely to cause pain than saying, "Of course, your child will never complete junior high school," and it is equally factual.

Parents should be acquainted with the limitations of the evaluative findings. Parents usually have questions regarding etiology, diagnosis, and prognosis, and the counselor will, in many cases, of course, have to indicate that in one or more of these areas he is making an "educated guess." Although the majority of parents are blissfully ignorant of such concepts as validity and reliability, it is meaningful to indicate the relative probability that the present findings are accurate and, particularly, the likelihood that predictions will prove to be correct.

Although it is neither realistic nor appropriate to present exact probability figures, the counselor can indicate that his predictions regarding a severely retarded, ten-year-old microcephalic are made with considerable confidence, whereas his predictions regarding a two-year-old, mildly retarded child with no apparent neuropathology are made with less assurance. Comments regarding the possible value of future evaluations can be helpful, and they may include acquainting parents with suitable referral sources.

Concluding the Interview

Even if further referrals are not indicated, the psychologist should encourage parents to formulate tentative plans. Some parents are so overwhelmed with their tragedy that they seem to flounder in the present and to recoil from the future. With tactful encouragement and support the counselor can help such parents to think constructively about the future. In attempting to plan for the child, the parents can be helped by presentation of factual information regarding community resources, referral agencies, institutions, psychotherapists, and so forth.

In concluding the interview—or series of interviews, as the case might be—the psychologist can be supportive by informing parents that he will remain available for further contacts should the need arise. The parents then leave the counselor with the feeling that they have been understood and that they are not completely alone in their misery.

The Family Behavior Profile: An Initial Report

Keith F. Kennett

ABSTRACT. Aware that much of what each individual learns is the product of observing the behavior of others, especially those of the immediate family, the AAMD Adaptive Behavior Scale was extended by the development of the Family Behavior Profile. The Family Behavior Profile provides behavior patterns of related individuals and a family constellation as an aid in identifying deficiencies in the home environment, in developing appropriate training programs to increase awareness of the importance of the home environment, to provide behavioral information relevant to cultural and familial aspects of etiology, to aid in developing realistic goals and to aid in devising modelling techniques in a real situation.

Since at least the early 30's researchers have sought to develop techniques for investigating, defining and evolving a mode of measuring adaptive behaviors in mentally retarded individuals. By 1970, the AAMD published scales (Nihira, Foster, Shellhaas, & Leland, 1970) were described by Leland (1972) as " . . . prototype scales for the purpose of measuring adaptive behavior in institutional populations and enhancing and furthering research with retarded populations within community-based agencies (p. 72)."

The Adaptive Behavior Scale (ABS), attempts to ascertain one's level of behavioral efficiency in terms of one's social awareness and subsequent social competence. Social competence skills usually originate in the home. Most individuals living at home have been exposed to situations involving cleanliness, care of clothes, use of telephone, assistance in the kitchen, preparation of meals, and the acceptance of age appropriate responsibility. In such areas the ABS examines coping strategies that are essential for the development of basic independent functioning, personal and social responsibility.

For meaningful assessment, the evaluation of behavioral patterns in the mentally retarded person rests on the assumption that norms of acceptable social behavior exist and are essential to the survival of the community as well as its individual members. Thus, the ABS is designed to measure behaviors that are considered to be normal or usual ways of doing things (Kennett, 1976).

Part I ABS items cover personal care habits, eating skills, cleanliness, appearance, travel experiences, money handling, and shopping skills. Such skills are essential for independent socially acceptable functioning in a community. Part II of the ABS concentrates on maladaptive behaviors, (e.g., violence, destructiveness or antisocial tendencies), that may result in rejection by others in the environment.

These assessments reflect value judgments about behavior that are an integral part of the socio-economic status group, the community group and society as a whole. There is need to examine further not only the behavior patterns as they reflect or approximate a set of behaviors deemed appropriate by society, but also those behavioral patterns that are unique to the home environment, which may deviate from the accepted modes of social conduct of the society in which the family lives (Kennett, 1975). This may mean the recognition that it is all right to be different.

As the ABS gains wider use for evaluating adaptive behavior in retarded individuals living in the community, the significance of the home environment directly influencing the learning of social competence increases. Various reports suggest that the home environment is an important determinant of human behavior (Kennett, 1974; Kennett & Cropley, 1970; Kennett & Grant, 1975). Baumrind and Black (1967) reported that pertaining competent behaviors in relation to parents' rearing practices is as applicable to parents of a mentally retarded child as they are to parents of normal children.

Aware that much of what each individual learns is the product of observing the behavior of others, especially those members of the immediate family, the Adaptive Behavior Scale was extended by the development of the Family Behavior Profile (Kennett, 1973) as an attempt to show in diagrams the behavioral patterns of related individuals and family constellations that are directly and specifically related to the mentally retarded individual rated on the ABS. The Family Behavior Profile (FBP) is designed to provide comparative data on the family including the mentally retarded person.

The ABS assesses the level of social awareness and social competence demonstrated; the FBP assesses the behavioral tendencies of all members of the family to show the ongoing daily experiences within the home. This assessment involves a rating

---

[1] This profile was developed while a visiting Professor, Nisonger Center, Ohio State University, Columbus, and research into its use was funded, in part, by the University Research Council Grant CCB 1006.

Name ....

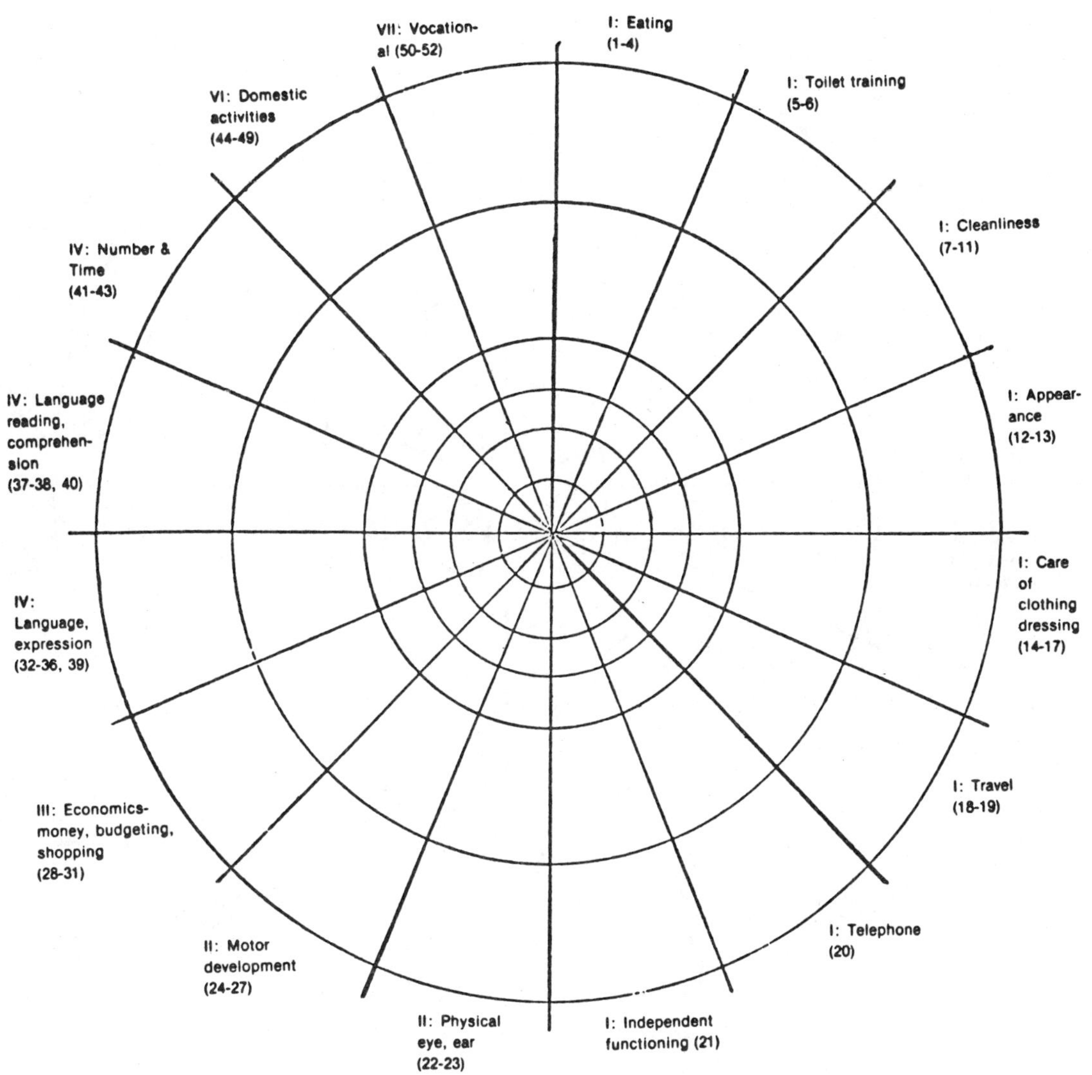

COMMENTS:

Name ....

FAMILY BEHAVIOR PROFILE

(Score in a clock-wise direction)

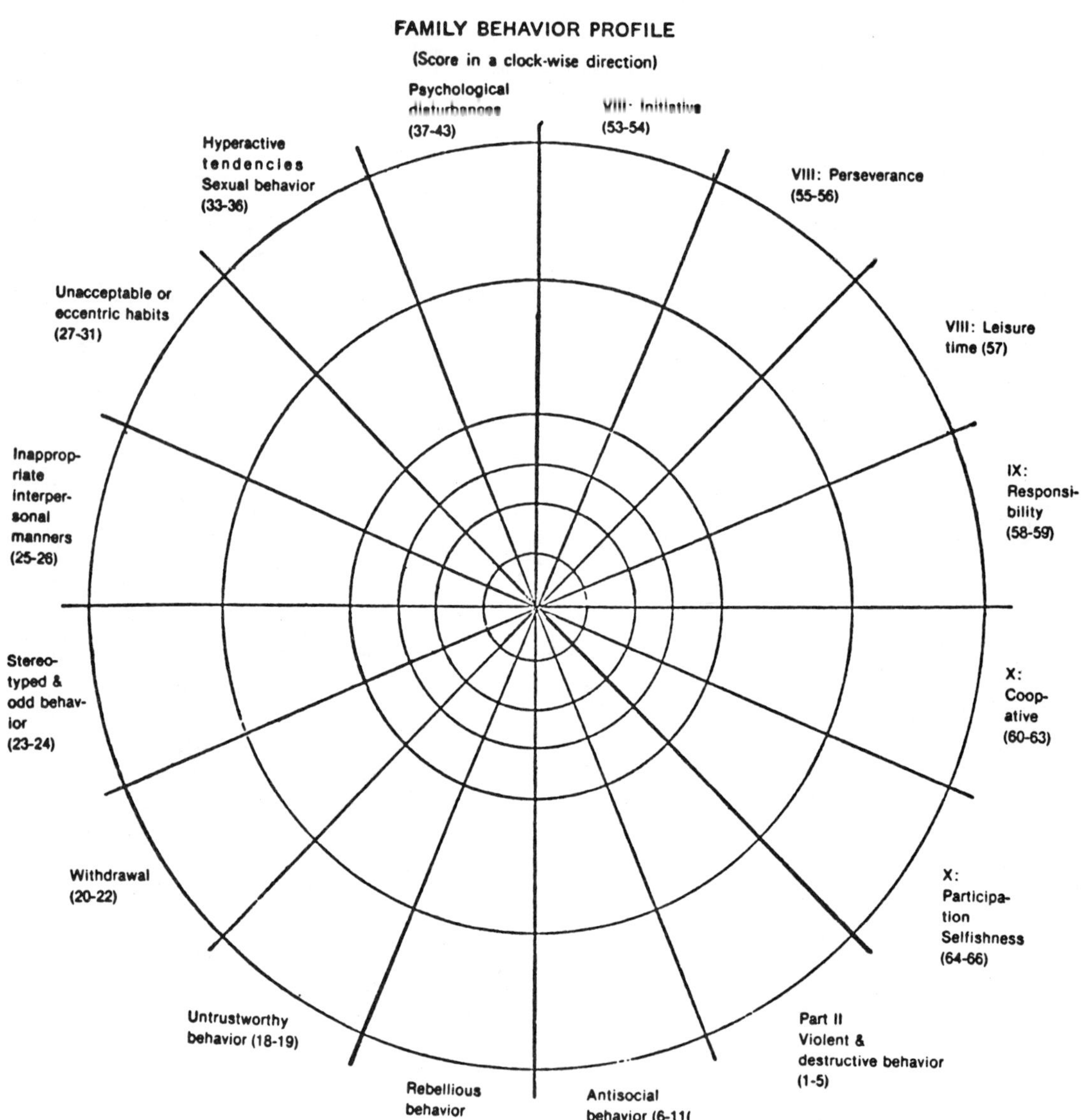

COMMENTS:

General Instructions for Administration of FBP

Description of Profile form. The FBP consists of two graphs of pie-shape with each sector representing a sub-domain of the Adaptive Behavior Scale. Each of these sub-domains is shown on the circumference of the graphs (see illustration). Each sector is divided into three areas by concentric circles; these areas represent retarded, normal, and exceptional conforming coping behaviors.

The inner circle area of each sector has been numbered from 0 at the center of the total graph to 4 on the circumference of the inner circle. The 0 indicates noncoping behavior and 4 represents a minimal level of social competence as compared to normal behavior. The middle area allows for scoring responses that are generally acceptable in society. The area allows for general differentiation but involves no scaling as did the inner circle area. The outer area is reserved for exceptional conformity to social norms and may indicate tendencies to be so exacting that normal flexibility is eliminated for the sake of conformity to social norms.

Immediate Scoring. The FBP is used after administration and scoring of the ABS. It is necessary that the interviewer has had previous contact with the family and knows the general content listed under each ABS sub-domain. The FBP scoring can be done directly onto the Profile Sheet. The whole family may be scored as a composite, if they all seem to cope in a normal way, or individual scoring may be done if needed.

Comparative Data. The technique provides a pictorial representation of coping behaviors for all members of the immediate family in terms of independent functioning, personal and social responsibility. Additional information can be written down in support of the score placement whenever necessary.

Conclusion. It is anticipated that the FBP will assist in planning for retarded persons and their families by providing information on family interaction that appears important to the development of essential coping strategies.

A Stimulation Program for Young Sensory-Impaired, Multihandicapped Children

Philip L. Safford
Laura A. Gregg
Glenda Schneider
Janice M. Sewell

Abstract: Some of the multiply-handicapped, 18 to 36 month old children enrolled in a parent-child early intervention program, exhibited severe impairment such that those program activities normally implemented were inappropriate. Consequently, the interdisciplinary team–teachers, physical therapist, occupational therapist, speech pathologist, psychologist, and social worker--developed an individualized program of sensory stimulation. Of central importance was the careful monitoring of sensory input and programming of the child's encounters with his environment. The responses of individual children and of the group as a whole are summarized and described, following a description of the methods employed and their rationale.

During the first year of Project HEED (Safford & Arbitman, 1975) a special group program for physically handicapped children between the ages of eighteen months and three years, those children who were functioning at very low developmental levels seemed to require a different approach than that used for less impaired children. Toys and activities were not appropriate to their level, and for the most part their behavior in the program was similar to what they did every day, all day, at home; that is, wandering aimlessly or further withdrawing into their own world–their bodies and self-stimulation. These children appeared over-stimulated or irritated by the room, the activities, and the many people and objects in the environment. Some acted out in response while others withdrew.

Rationale For A Sensory-Oriented Program

It was determined that input for these children must be both primarily sensory in nature and carefully monitored if it is to be meaningfully processed. The main goal in establishing a "sensory group" was to provide for each child appropriate experiences with minimal failure or frustration, for both child and parent.

These sensory impaired children did not react to stimuli in a "normal" or expected manner. For the most part, they were irritable children with poor sleeping and eating habits. They rejected body contact–especially facial stimulation. It was also noted that they seemed to dislike cuddling unless it was initiated by them. In keeping with the pattern of tactile defensiveness described by Ayres (1972) and others, hypersensitivity of palms, feet, and oral area was observed. Some were self-stimulating–rocking, arm-waving, masturbating, and engaging in tongue and lip play–while other were self-abusive, with patterns of self-biting, hair pulling, eye scratching and pressing, and head banging. In addition many were fixed eaters, sustaining on a one-meal diet of baby cereal and the bottle, rejecting any new food or texture, gagging and/or refusing to eat for days afterward when new foods were presented.

It was determined to present for these children a meaningful program with attainable goals which would make a difference in their lives and to their parents. The primary objective was to make the child less irritable, more content within himself, and easier for the parent to manage. With an increase in tolerance, isolated stimuli could be presented, leading gradually to an increased awareness of and, ultimately, interaction with the environment. Related objectives were to

A Stimulation Program for Young Sensory-Impaired, Multihandicapped Children, Philip L. Safford, Laura A. Gregg, Glenda Schneider and Janice M. Sewell, *Education and Training of the Mentally Retarded,* Vol. 11, No. 1.

increase verbal reactions, eye contact, and attending, in order to help the child move from self-stimulation to interaction with the external world. It was necessary to remember that only if the interaction was meaningful to the child would it be pleasurable and thus likely to be pursued in preference to self-stimulation.

Feeding as a social, sensual, and developmental stage was an area of prime concern to parents, but also one toward which they could work and experience success. Moreover, it was something that the child could enjoy if desensitized. However, before accepting new foods, the sensory impaired child must be able to tolerate varied smells, tastes, and textures (tactually as well as orally). The oral region must be desensitized prior to feeding and a consistent program must be followed at home.

The level of functioning of children in this group was so low that many were not able to use their own bodies as a tool in problem solving. This is illustrated by the child who, although he could crawl, would not move toward a desired object. Another child was physically capable of walking but seldom engaged in purposeful interaction with his environment. Consequently, he had not learned to walk but seemed instead content to stimulate himself forever. Beyond the obvious similarities of impaired motor functioning or limited intelligence, these sensory damaged children evidenced differences both from most mentally retarded and most physically handicapped youngsters. Consequently, an approach uniquely suited to their unusual needs had to be developed.

The Sensory Program

Each child as he was enrolled in the Sensory Group was assigned to a staff member with whom he maintained a one-to-one relationship throughout the session. For the first activity introduced each day, a relaxation exercise, the child was placed in a supine position and rocked rhythmically for a period of ten minutes. The adult attempted to get the child to attend to her face by gently calling the child's name. The atmosphere was quiet and the lights dimmed. All toys and furniture were removed, and the children were placed in different parts of the room to limit distractions. The children were then held and rocked gently in a total withdrawal posture so that no parts of their bodies were in contact with the floor. This was done to provide a sense of motion, to relax, to inhibit spasticity, and to build up a tolerance of being held.

A routine of activities was followed in the following sequence: (1) Relaxation; (2) Sensory; (3) Relaxation; (4) Feeding; (5) Exploration of equipment and environment.

Relaxation

The purpose of relaxation activities was to control the environment, limit the input to the children, and to keep their muscles relaxed. They included the following:

Sitting in a tub of warm water with or without inflatable toys

Slow swinging in sheets

Rolling on a large beach ball or air pillow

Stroking and brushing with a vibrating brush on sensitive parts of their bodies, i.e., soles of feet, forehead, forearms, under chin

Holding close and touching (Cuddling)

Wrapping tightly in a sheet (Cocoon Wrap)

Sensory

These activities were carried out with a staff member and a child on a one-to-one basis with only one of the child's senses, tactile, olfactory, or auditory, being given the stimulation. These varied activities give training and exercise for senses which might otherwise remain defective or dormant.

A variety of sensory materials were employed, including:

Rice mixture (rice, macaroni alphabets and split peas)

Shaving cream

Play dough

Water (cold)

Carpet and tile floor alternation

Rubbing with wet and dry terry cloth towels

Textured materials (sponges, velvet, sandpaper, burlap)

Auditory stimuli (bells, tambourine, xylophone, maracas, wood blocks)

Feeding

The feeding period was introduced by desensitization of the child's mouth. This was facilitated by applying pressure and stroking around the lip area or rubbing with ice. Stroking for desensitization is done three times all around the mouth. This causes the lip and the area directly inside the mouth to become less sensitive to textures. The ice is applied to the lips, and under the jaw. This not only desensitizes the oral area, but also facilitates swallowing. At times, vinegar and granulated sugar were placed into the children's mouths in an alternating pattern to help with swallowing.

When the feeding component of the program was initiated, each child was seated in a chair facing away from the table and toward the feeder. For the first two weeks, four sessions, the children were given cooked oatmeal, which was slightly more textured than the strained baby food to which they were accustomed. Then gradually, more textured foods were introduced. These included soggy cold cereal, small pieces of fruit in gradually decreasing amounts of liquid, cottage cheese, jello with small pieces of fruit, and applesauce with small chunks of apple. With follow-through at home, the children became accustomed to a variety of textures, and began to chew. They were then introduced to toast with jelly. When the children could tolerate all the textures that had been introduced, and could eat them without difficulty, they were turned so they faced the table and encouraged to begin finger feeding. They were given small pieces of cheese, banana, apple, cantaloupe, crackers with peanut butter, and toast.

The feeding portion of the program was included because most of the children in this group presented serious feeding problems at home. The mothers, who viewed their children as babies, had either fed them baby foods exclusively or, if they had presented regular table food, had withdrawn it because the child had gagged. Staff members, by showing the parents how to introduce other foods to their children, were attempting to help the parents with one of the main problems children such as these experience.

To facilitate carry-over, staff offered several specific suggestions:

1. Three daily meals should be attempted, with snacks eliminated.
2. All infantile food should be eliminated, as well as the bottle and distracting bib.
3. The child should be positioned in a chair so that he is faced directly.
4. Breakfast may be decreased and amount and timing of meals geared to the child's manifestations of hunger.
5. Milk should not be forced, since it tends to fill the child up.
6. If the child refuses to eat, the meal should be ended rather than rewarding refusal with wanted baby or strained food.
7. The child should be allowed to experience different types of food, varying texture, temperature, tastes and color.
8. The child is most comfortable with a consistent program and will be happy when he knows what to expect, in feeding as in other areas.
9. Desensitization of the oral area prior to each feeding is accomplished by rubbing gums firmly in circular stroke, three times over each area around the mouth.

Exploration of Environment

For the last fifteen minutes of the session, the children were encouraged to explore the physical environment and selected equipment. One toy was chosen for each child, taking into consideration the child's functional level. The child was free to explore the toy in any way in which he might receive feedback. This included touching, mouthing, banging, and pushing. Movement was also encouraged to provide stimulation and feedback from the variety of textures to be found in the room, such as the smoothness of the linoleum floor, the roughness of the rug, and the coolness of the window glass.

Effectiveness of the Approach

After approximately six months of participation in the sensory program, the children's progress was assessed by means of observational procedures, standardized measures, and parent interviews. At the time of this assessment, these children ranged in chronological age from two years, two months through four years, three months. Their I.Q.'s on the Cattell Infant Intelligence Scale were found to be 24, 28, 35, 40, 47 and 70. Two had been diagnosed as having cerebral palsy (spastic quadriplegia), two with "mental-motor retardation," one with neurofibromatosis, and one with left hemiparesis as a result of CVA.

These children presented a wide range of individual differences in virtually all areas of functioning and all seemed to respond uniquely to the program which had been implemented. Individual descriptive summaries of each child's progress are therefore provided.

Chuck

When Chuck entered HEED he was totally withdrawn from the people in the class and was often found behind the curtain at the window. He showed no awareness of the environment with the exception of the chairs, which he pushed around aimlessly. He spent a great deal of time in self-stimulating activities, such as licking the cool window and masturbating. Chuck gave no discernible response to voice, including that of his mother, or sound. His mother reported that he would become very irritated and unmanageable when he accompanied her to a social gathering or on a necessary errand. Chuck displayed hypersensitivity in his palms, oral region and feet, being unwilling to put his bare feet on the floor. He recoiled from any tactile stimulation. However, Chuck did not respond negatively to pain. His mother reported that he had been severely burned and did not make any attempt to get away, and it was observed that when his fingers were stepped on by another child he did not respond. Chuck ate only bottled junior foods and would not chew.

After six months he seemed not nearly as withdrawn and now sought out staff and other children. To some degree he replaced chair pushing and masturbation with physical contact with people in the room. He began to "explore" by touching and by climbing on staff and peers. He would now occasionally maintain eye contact, although this remained minimal and, although he would chew a variety of foods, finger feeding was sporadic.

Auditory awareness appeared to increase slightly. Chuck responded to more sounds than previously when his hearing acuity was doubted by staff, turning now when he heard certain pull-toys or voices. He remained hypersensitive in palms and feet and hyposensitive on his trunk area. Chuck now pulled to standing on furniture and cruised and could both stand alone and take a few steps. Chuck's mother reported that he had become more tolerant of people around him, did not withdraw or fuss, and that his eating and sleeping habits had improved. She also described him as more affectionate and seeking to be near her. Now aware of another child for whom she was caring, Chuck appeared jealous of this child's presence.

Bobby

When Bobby entered HEED he seemed overwhelmed by the staff and the physical environment. During the relaxation segment of the program Bobby scratched and pressed his eyes. He avoided physical contact, especially with the facial area, and was irritable when he was handled. A fixed eater, he would not tolerate sitting in a chair, nor would he allow textured food to be put into his mouth. Bobby had had some experience with a cup, but it had been abandoned at home. Thus, he was bottle fed all liquids and some meals. Bobby spent a great deal of time shaking, banging his head and waving his arms.

After six months Bobby remained a feeding problem, although showing slight progress in tolerating the feeding routine. Now able to sit facing the feeder with less irritability, he would accept some textured food and occasionally drink from a cup. He continued to bang his head, but no longer scratched or pressed his eyes as frequently. Bobby showed greater awareness of sound. Upon hearing his mother's voice he now turned toward it and attempted to seek her out. He now laughed and squealed aloud, showing his enjoyment of an activity such as water play, and began to explore his peers by reaching out and touching them.

David

When first introduced to HEED, David would spend most of the session sitting and whining. Other vocalizations were rarely heard. He was fed like an infant, held in his mother's arms. His mother questioned hearing and sight and seemed uncomfortable handling him.

After six months in the sensory program, David showed less irritibility. He would now sit and manipulate selected toys, but was as yet not motivated to crawl for a desired toy. He would now tolerate sitting in a chair for feeding and would finger feed and drink from a cup independently. David began to attend and to maintain eye contact with staff for simple imitations, such as playing patty cake and tongue clicking. He would make some non-specific vocalizations. David's mother reported that he was beginning to be aware of her absence and that she could no longer leave the room unnoticed by him. She also related that David enjoyed being near her. However, the mother continued to have difficulty in following through on suggestions from staff.

Karl

Karl had already been enrolled in HEED for one year before the special sensory program was introduced. He was a fixed eater, eating only pureed baby foods and rejecting any textures. He was fed liquids from a bottle. His mother reported that he slept fitfully and went many nights without sleep. Karl crawled aimlessly around the room, seemingly overwhelmed by the environment. He was abusive to himself and others by biting and hairpulling. He would not respond to his name when staff members called, but did when his mother called. His mother seemed to be unrealistic about her expectations for his progress, and therefore found if difficult to cope at home. Although she was ambivalent about staff suggestions, and expressed discomfort with them, she carried them out.

Karl showed excellent progress in the feeding area, now eating all types of food. His mother, who was very conscientious about following through at home, was elated over his progress in this area. Karl appeared more responsive to sound, attending to it and tracking it. He drooled less and emitted more vocalizations. Karl would now interact with a toy on an infantile level by banging, batting and throwing. He seemed now to respond to his name and began to maintain eye contact.

Karl became able to get himself from a prone position to a sitting position unaided, and his mother reported he was beginning to pull himself up to a standing position in his bed. He continued to be abusive to himself and others by biting, however.

Patty

Patty entered HEED soon after arriving in the United States. Both Patty and her mother seemed very uncomfortable and somewhat suspicious of staff and the setting. Patty was not permitted by her mother to explore or to mouth toys. Because of cultural beliefs she had been prohibited from lying on her stomach, with resultant further delays in motor development. Very spastic and dominated by extensor tone, she could not sit without support and the staff suspected that she was rarely placed in a sitting position by her mother, spending most of the time supine. Lip closure was not observed and, when any stimulus was presented to the oral area, withdrawal reaction was seen.

Patty continued to have separation problems, but seemed less suspicious of staff and became able to separate for short periods. Substitute mothering by staff was replaced, in part, by the gradual introduction of independence. Patty now participated in some staff-initiated activities, such as rolling a ball, bursting bubbles, and looking at picture books. She also began to do simple imitations and to reach for desired toys. At the staff's suggestion, Patty's mother gave her more freedom to explore. She was now permitted to explore toys by mouthing them and was occasionally placed on her stomach by her mother.

Kenny

Kenny is a hemiplegic with decreased sensation and increased irritability to manipulation and touch. Hyperactive, he required a one-to-one relationship to prevent him from hurting himself or others. Kenny was a good eater but his mother used food as a reward for negative behavior, giving food to keep him quiet when he acted out. He spent a great deal of time in oral stimulation.

Assessing Kenny's progress was difficult due to his poor attendance. However, he did show an increased attention span and less hyperactivity in a one-to-one relationship.

Results

Measured gains in assessed functional age equivalent of gross motor functioning increased for all children during this six month period at a greater rate than would have been predicted on the basis of initial assessments. The recorded gains were .5, 1.0, 1.0, 2.5, 3.0 and 3.5 months for an average of 1.9 months. The average gain in language age as indicated by the Houston Test of Language Development was 1.8 months. In the measures of perceptual and fine motor performance, patterns of gain were idiosyncratic, with three children gaining markedly in unilateral skills (3, 5 and 6 months), one child gaining 9 months in bilateral skills and two children gaining 3 months in activities of daily living.

The results attained to date suggest that the sensory program, with its individualized focus and care which is given to the monitoring and sequencing of sensory experience, has demonstrated promise as an approach to working with young children who manifest severe sensory impairment.

Behaviorally Disabled

Parents of a behaviorally disabled child must be taught how to cope with and change unacceptable behaviors of their child. Discipline is necessary and parents must understand the goals of that discipline. Parents help their child develop a sense of security when they have consistent expectations and behavioral standards.

Characteristics which help parents work with their behaviorally disabled child include: persistence, firmness, fairness, consistency and a sense of joy in the child's successes. A parent's awareness and willingness to work with a disabled child are key ingredients to early intervention programs that can remedy behavior disorders.

Residential re-education centers, including those in North Carolina and Tennessee, exist for the behaviorally disabled child with the average period of stay for a child being six months. Such centers work to establish trust with the child, offer experiences which assure success, develop confidence, self-respect, acceptance, and competence in work and study skills. The importance of each child knowing joy in each day is emphasized.

Parent programs and parent training models are important in the treatment of the behaviorally disabled child. Direct parent involvement, in many cases, must be over the child's life span.

Learning to Live Happily With Jimmy

Malinda S. Tomaro

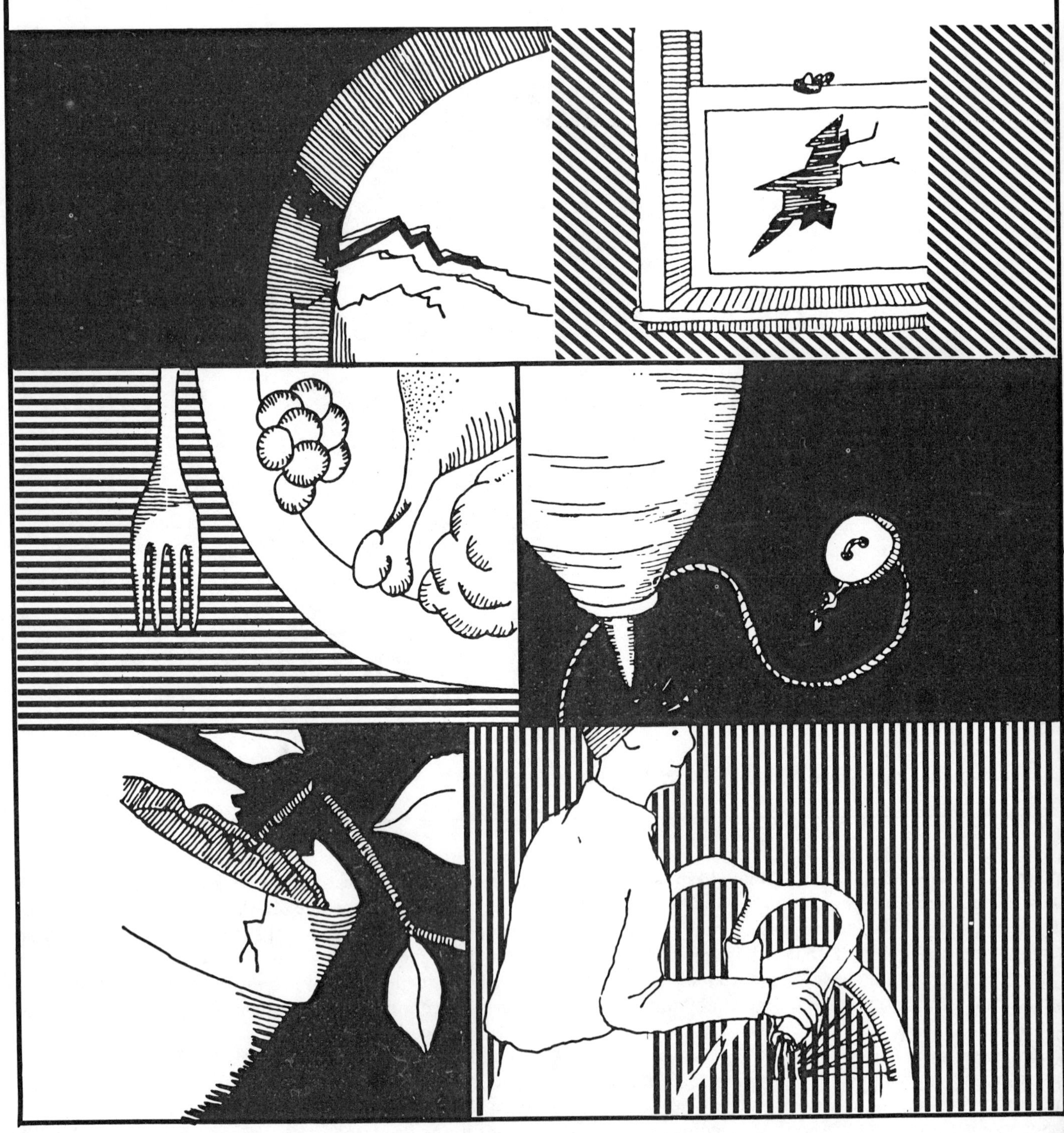

Learning to Live Happily with Jimmy, Milinda S. Tomaro, *The Exceptional Parent,* Vol. 1, No. 6, 1976, © 1972 Psy-Ed Corporation.

Learning to Live Happily With Jimmy

Fall is not far away and in our yard we are watching the children enjoying the last few days of summer vacation. Maria, our daughter, is sharing confidences with friends. Her twin brother, Jimmy, is delighted with the squeals from the girls when he swerves toward them on his bike, then veers off into the driveway. It is a time of contentment, a time six years ago we never dreamed possible.

The children are now eight years old. Maria attends the third grade and Jimmy is developing into a happy, responsive boy. The first four years of his life he was a withdrawn and frustrated child. Screaming tantrums, which continued sometimes hour after hour, broke his otherwise total silence. Other nerve-wracking acts such as: broken windows, shattered by thrown objects; the constant clatter of spinning pot lids; the banging bed throughout the night; dirty diapers; formula bottles (he would not be weaned); objects whizzing past our heads; and the tension of trying to live with that wild, unreachable, well-loved child formed the patterns of his early life, and ours with him.

How did we ever arrive at this happy, peaceful afternoon? In retrospect, what we learned about coping with and changing Jimmy's unacceptable behavior seems to be the major factor.

Proper behavior

Ideally, proper behavior is the result of the appropriate choice of action made by the person involved in a given situation. We choose to behave "properly," not always in order to get what we want, but because we consider the possible results of our actions. Jimmy could not understand these concepts. He knew only his desires and attempted to fulfill them any way he could, preferably immediately. The manner in which we disciplined him had to be carefully thought out and enforced. As an undisciplined child, Jimmy was hard to live with. Also, his sense of security was threatened by not knowing what to expect. Our disturbed child could make no choices because he had not been taught behavior which reflected social awareness. "I want what I want when I want it" describes Jimmy's behavior before we started to work with him.

Teaching Jimmy and Learning Ourselves

In helping our disturbed child to acceptable behavior, we found the most necessary characteristics that we, as parents, had to possess and show to Jimmy were persistence, firmness, and joy (joy in his improvement, joy in *our* growth with him). Patience did not come simply with our understanding of the problem. We had to learn patience through the menial, never-ending, repetitious tasks that had to be done.

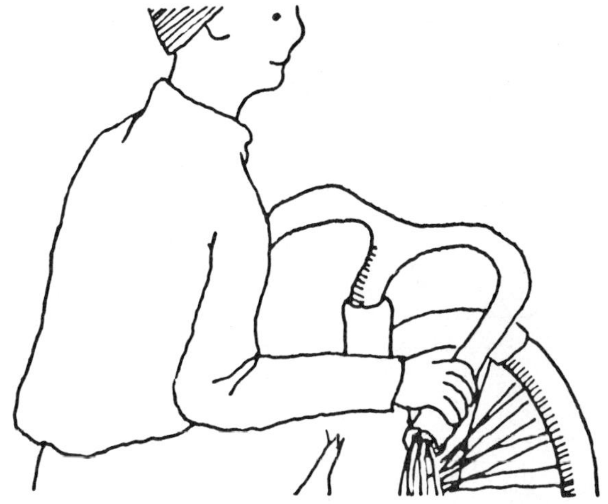

Patience

Jim always got out of bed several times during the night and attempted to roam around. Night after night, year after year, we got up and put him back to bed saying, "Now Jim goes to bed." It took patience to repeat this every night for years, but finally Jim responded to the command and now sleeps through the night. Jim constantly jumped up and down on the beds. Hundreds of times we removed him saying, "Beds are for sleeping." In time, the words had meaning for him. We found our patience became thinner and thinner with every repeated word and action, but Jim's resistance became weaker and weaker, also. We strived *not* for unlimited patience, but just enough to outlast Jim's resistance.

Persistence

Persistence, that is, our commitment to Jimmy's "education," was necessary so he would learn to know what was expected of him. There were times when illness, fatigue or simple self-pity tempted us. It would have been so easy to let him roam the house or jump on the beds. It took less time just to pick up the clothes he pulled from the drawers than to grasp his hands and make them move through the motions of, "Put it back." However, we soon realized that when we failed to always respond the same way to his misbehavior, our next attempt at controlling his behavior was met with renewed resistance.

Firmness

Jim needed firmness from us. We filled his need by responding with either praise or corrective action. We were very indecisive with him in the early years when we were bombarded by advice from well-meaning relatives and friends. When he screamed for hours, we were advised to spank him, quit spoiling him, or ignore him. When we spanked him we felt guilty. When we refused to be gently responsive to him, we felt sick at

heart. When we ignored him, we felt we were not helping him to learn. Very quickly we decided to look squarely at the behavior that bothered us, decide on a fair and possible solution, then, with a commitment to firmness that resisted contradictory advice, we learned to do our utmost to react with persistence and patience.

Setting Limits

Because of the inability of our disturbed child to make choices, we had to guide Jimmy in choosing. For example, one of his compulsive habits was spinning anything he got in his hands. When guiding him to appropriate choices we did the following. We said, "The plate is for eating, the top is for spinning," and with these directions the plate was taken away and a top placed in his hands. This routine had to be performed repeatedly until he was able to learn the appropriate function of various objects.

We learned to build on this limiting type of discipline by including specific locations where certain things might be done. Jimmy went through a spitting period and a definite place was specified where this habit was allowed. Locations would be the bathroom sink, outdoors, toilet, or various other appropriate places. Anytime the spitting started, Jimmy was moved to the designated area with the words, "Do not spit on people, you may spit in the sink." Throwing objects was a problem, another phase we survived. We designated a spot where throwing things was safe, never forgetting to verbalize our actions as we did them, "No throwing in the house, Jimmy may throw in the basement."

We learned that nothing was ever gained by the use of extreme physical punishment. Because of Jimmy's withdrawn state, incidents were isolated from each other so that he did not see the spanking as a direct result of his act. He knew only that it was a painful experience at the hands of another human being. The only time a spanking was effective was after Jimmy was disciplined in other ways for a long period of time and had become aware of cause and effect. Until this awareness occurred, mild physical punishment was of no effect, except to drive him deeper into his withdrawn state. When we had to release the anger *we* felt, we kicked a pillow, slammed a door or punched a pillow, but we never used extreme physical force on that child whom we deeply loved!

Child-Proofing the Environment

In the initial stage of helping Jimmy choose acceptable behavior we had to be willing to live in a child-proofed house. When Jimmy constantly pulled down drapes, it was far better to remove them for a few weeks until his impulse subsided and a new activity held his interest. Jimmy constantly pulled books from the bookcase. We turned the case around for about three weeks. When we righted it, Jimmy completely ignored it. In spite of the discomfort of living in an undecorated home, it seemed far better and easier than having something of value permanently destroyed. We learned that Jimmy, in his slow progress to more acceptable behavior, passed through most of these stages in a few weeks.

Anticipating trouble

We also learned that we encountered fewer discipline problems by anticipating trouble spots and trying to avoid them. For example, Jim became very upset when he had to leave the car. Because he always had to leave at some point, we would repeatedly have this running commentary: "Now we are riding. Later, Jim gets out of the car." This observation was made at each corner near our destination. Upon arrival we would say, "Now Jim gets out of the car." It took four months for the crying to stop. When he no longer had tantrums, he would get out of the car, spit on it, and go happily along. Now he gets in and out of the family cars, school busses, and off bikes, slides or swings without reactions.

Jimmy's own place

We had an ideal situation in that our disturbed child had his own room. Where this is not possible for your child, he should have some area in the house which is his alone. This sort of area can be employed in disciplining the child. There were times when Jimmy did something that was not dangerous, nor destructive, but did irritate or embarrass us, such as loud crying, yelling, nose picking, masturbating, etc. In this way he could continue such actions and we felt better not being directly involved in it. We tried to remember, and eventually *learned* that each human being belongs to himself first; a person's mind and body are always his own.

A major problem we encountered in moving Jimmy to his area for a certain activity was keeping him there. We realized that locked doors, tying a child down, and similar restraining techniques are usually futile and harmful to the child. We had to be prepared to repeatedly return Jimmy to the area with the same words time and time again.

A very effective means for keeping him in selected

areas was to set up barriers. Not locked and confining barriers, but physical limits. Cape Cod doors are quite good for this purpose. The top half can be left open but the bottom shut. Expansion gates, used for toddlers, are very good. Room dividers, pieces of furniture, and sometimes just a piece of twine tying off an area will work.

Masters at Avoiding Trouble

Jim disliked houses where he was cramped by small spaces and many people hovering over him, telling him "No, no, don't touch." These were the places we visited when the children did not have to accompany us. We did not isolate him, for in isolation he never could learn to make any adjustments or cope with given situations. By practice at home or at the home of a friend who accepted and understood, Jimmy learned the niceties of visiting.

When waiting was intolerable for him, we chose a restaurant where he could walk around while waiting to be served. When yelling was a problem, we chose a noisy place. We felt the informal atmosphere of family style restaurants would be best. There was always a lot of noise and many children at drive-in fast food places. These were the first places we tried in warm weather, when there were tables outdoors.

Later we were able to stop in ordinary restaurants on turnpikes and parkways. Jimmy became very frustrated when required to walk around in stores so, when he had to accompany us, we chose a store with a grocery cart so Jimmy could ride while we shopped.

Trial and error

Generally, we never demanded that Jimmy behave just to win our point or concede to our wish. He has never attended church because it is not a place where he is free to walk around and make sounds. He has *had* a private baptism where he could express his displeasure at being anointed with cold water. At home, he is not required to remain at the table after he has finished his meal. Learning to avoid trouble spots was a talent which we had to develop. Only through trial and error and being "tuned-in" to Jimmy's reactions, did we become masters at avoiding trouble. Sometimes we misjudged a situation, but the times we succeeded in a smooth outing out-numbered the times of temper tantrums and frustrations.

Talk, Talk, Talk

Parents are asked again and again to talk to their non-verbal children. This was difficult to do and to carry through because Jimmy did not respond. The content of the talking is very important. Not only did we use a running commentary, but we tried, in simple sentences, to describe what Jimmy was doing and what he apparently felt.

We saw Jimmy drop a book on his toes, then immediately pick up the book and hurl it across the

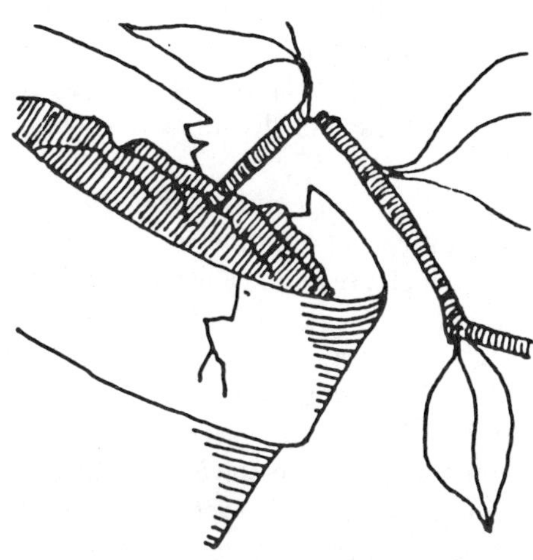

room. We responded to this situation by saying, "Jimmy dropped the book on his toes. His toes hurt. Jimmy is angry at the book. Jimmy wants to hurt the book. Jimmy throws the book because Jimmy is angry." In this way Jimmy had his feelings and actions put into words. After many incidents of this type he began to understand the pain and anger that suddenly burst upon him.

We also used this procedure in discipline. Jimmy would get angry because he could not perform a desired action. His anger grew until it completely engulfed him. This engulfment was a frightening experience. His fear began to blot out all reality. Words, used properly over a period of time, helped him understand this torrent of emotion. "Jimmy is angry at the toy." "Jimmy is mad at Mommy." "Jimmy is angry with Daddy." "Mommy is angry with Daddy." "Daddy is angry with Mommy."

Reassurance needed, reassurance given

We found that Jimmy needed the reassurance that feeling anger is all right. We told him! We verbalized every chance we got. Sometimes it was difficult. To state the situation as we saw it sometimes meant diplomacy had to be dropped. It was hard for me to say, "Daddy is angry at Jimmy because Daddy is tired," or, "Daddy does not understand." We made mistakes, and this too we tried to explain to Jimmy. "Mommy stepped on Jimmy's foot. Mommy is sorry. Jimmy is angry at Mommy. Mommy is sorry she made Jimmy's foot hurt."

Storms used to frighten Jim. We helped him through them by watching for the flash of lightning and then announcing, "Now it will thunder."

Consistent Words and Deeds

In teaching discipline to Jimmy we tried to remember that words can and must be used as the tool. For our non-disabled child, adult actions without words were *sometimes* hard to interpret. For Jimmy, *all* actions had to be accompanied by words and all words had to be accompanied by consistent actions until he had developed an understanding of the words alone. In our process of discipline, to say "No" and then to allow the action to continue only weakened the power of the spoken word. Jimmy needed the reinforcement of action to prove that the spoken word had value and was a meaningful means of discipline and communication in itself.

Jimmy had no conception of what was harmful to himself or others. Many times our command was the only thing which prevented a terrible accident. This is a hard lesson to teach a disturbed child and the use of the two words, "Do not!," must be often reinforced by actions for a long, long time before they are understood.

Helping Jimmy solve his own problems

The child should help solve the problem he creates. When Jimmy upset the flower pot, we took his hands and moved them through the motions of cleaning up the mess, talking about the action as it was performed. We told him he had upset the flowers and that he now must help clean up. This carried the action to a conclusion. Over a period of time Jimmy learned the process of cause and effect. He began to learn what part he had in the action and in the creation of a problem situation and the consequences of such a situation.

Jimmy taught *us* how to give him joy. We wanted to discover some means of rewarding him for good behavior. This was extremely difficult because he was totally disinterested in toys, he ate nothing but peanut butter sandwiches, and drank only milk or juice from his bottle. Because his eating problem was so severe, we did not want to withhold his food or drink as a means of changing behavior. From the time he was a toddler he had loved a finger-play game that ended with tickling under his chin. It is very hard not to laugh with a hilarious child so we would all begin laughing together. This became our reward to him, and we still have chin-tickling sessions every night. Laughing together has been great therapy for all of us. It seems that Jim has reached harder for reality since it became a happy place!

In summary, the important questions we asked, and ask, ourselves about the goals of discipline are:

1. How important is this behavior I am demanding of my child?
2. What purpose will compliance to my demands serve?
3. Is this demand serving appearances, my own ego satisfaction, or the safety of my child?
4. Can this rule be enforced *all* the time?
5. Does this rule help my child grow and develop?
6. Does this rule satisfy the entire family, the child particularly?

We often wondered whether we had enough patience to outlast our child. But, we found it somehow when we set specific goals.

Influencing the Child: A Program for Parents

J. Jeffries McWhirter, Carolyn Cabanski

J. Jeffries McWhirter, Assistant Professor, Department of Counselor Education, Arizona State University, Tempe, serves as a consultant to Devereux Day School. Carolyn Cabanski, also a consultant to Devereux Day School, is a graduate student, Arizona State University. *The authors would like to express their appreciation to Frank Dale and Bette Hammer of Devereux Day School and to Garth Blackham and Douglas Gross of Arizona State University for their involvement in the Parent Program.*

An innovative, psychoeducational-social program at the Devereux Day School in Scottsdale, Arizona, has included a parent program under its comprehensive approach to the treatment of children with learning disabilities and emotional disorders. The school, operating under the auspices of the Devereux Foundation, Devon, Pennsylvania, began its operations in 1967; at present there are 110 children enrolled. School personnel use the most creative techniques available in the education and treatment of each child. Individual programming is directed toward the following areas: cognitive/intellectual, language/speech, emotional/social, and psycho-motor.

Because Devereux is a private day school and because of the influence the family has on the development of the child, an attempt has been made to involve the parents more directly in the educational milieu of the child. Recent writers (French, 1963; Fullmer & Bernard, 1968; McWhirter, 1966) have suggested that parental education, counseling, and consultation is an appropriate extension of the school's function. This description of the various aspects of the Devereux Parent Program is intended for use as a possible model for public and other private schools.

The Parent Program, developed during the last two years, consisted of a four-pronged approach to working with the parents. The underlying premise was that the family is a primary influence in maintaining or changing a child's attitudes and behaviors about himself and his environment. Learning does not cease when the child leaves the school at the end of the day. It is a continual process, greatly affected by familial relationships which can be detrimental or facilitating in the development of the child's natural curiosity—a primary factor motivating him to learn.

It is important for school personnel to concern themselves with the ideas, attitudes, and interrelationships existing in the child's home. It is equally important that parents understand the school's educational philosophy and processes so they can carry out the behavioral directives recommended for their child. It was for this reason that when their child was enrolled, parents were assessed a required, compulsory fee of ten dollars per month for the Parent Program. At that time the expected involvement in parent groups and the reasons for this expectation were explained. Parents were assigned to their particular groups on the basis of how long their child had been enrolled, his individual problem, and the preferred type of group as indicated by the parent. If parents did not attend these groups, a telephone followup was conducted to find out why and to encourage attendance. Parents were also allowed to change groups, if they so wished, at any time throughout the year.

The four aspects of the Parent Program were: (a) individual contact, (b) Parents' Aid Program (PAP), (c) educational groups, and (d) counseling groups. Individual contact with parents was provided by the school psychologists as needed. These therapy sessions aided in modifying feelings, attitudes, and approaches which could have been harmful to the child's optimal development. The individual sessions also provided the parents with an understanding of the educational, psychological, and social processes involved in their child's individually prescribed program.

The Parents' Aid Program (PAP) involved parents directly in the school program by having them visit the school and observe educational processes in operation. When parents expressed interest in learning more about the way the school functioned, what kinds of educational and behavior modification techniques were used, and the type of social experiences provided by the school, they (parents) were invited to spend an entire day at the school. They were assigned to observe a child who had similar learning problems and behavioral characteristics as their own child. For an entire day they would follow the child from class to class. The parents were not encouraged to observe their own child, as it was felt that their presence would bias his normal school reactions, and that the parents and teachers would experience less threat in a more objective, observational situation. Parents were encouraged to question anything they did not understand, to express honest reactions to staff members, and to offer suggestions they felt would be of a constructive nature to the school. In this manner, there was a give and take relationship between the staff and parents which benefited both sides and in the long run benefited the child. Through the PAP the school hoped to serve these three functions:

1. The parents would gain greater insight into the problems, interactions, and behavior of their own child.
2. They would be exposed to a wide variety of educational, social, and behavioral models which would hopefully open new alternatives for their own behavior.
3. The parents would have a better understanding of the educational philosophy and operations of the school.

Educational groups

The parent educational groups met twice a month with a group facilitator for one-and-a-half hour sessions. There were four groups which provided for didactic input and group discussion on a wide variety of basic issues. The groups were divided into those which had *new* parents (whose child had just enrolled at the school) and those which were comprised of *regulars* (whose child had been at the school for at least one year). Educational materials used in these groups were geared to the members' level of exposure and sophistication regarding pertinent specific topics. First year parents were given a basic course in understanding the principles of child development, cognitive and emotional aspects in learning, basic styles of adjustment and defenses, learning disabilities, and other factors which might influence intellectual achievement, academic performance, and behavior. The parents were also provided with basic principles of behavior modification using such texts as Patterson and Gullhan's *Living with Children* (1967). They were instructed in possible applications of these contingency management principles which were in accordance with the school's assessment of what the child may need.

First year parents also focused on any feelings they may have regarding placement of their child in a special school for learning disabled and emotionally handicapped. They touched on their feelings of the stigma attached to this type of placement, their own feelings of guilt in having been a possible influencing factor affecting the child's need for this type of school setting, their fears regarding the child's intellectual and emotional adjustment, and the ability of the entire family to cope with the uncertainty of this new school setting.

As members became more familiar with basic concepts of personality functioning, learning, behavior, learning disabilities, emotional needs, and styles of coping, facilitators provided more specific technological information. This was especially true for groups with parents whose children had been in the school the previous year or longer. Facilitators provided didactic sessions on behavioral disorders, emotional dysfunctioning, and learning disabilities. For instance, one of the educational groups used Johnson and Myklebust's text, *Learning Disabilities* (1967) to provide the basis for lecture material. The following topics were discussed: psychodynamic factors in learning, peripheral and central nervous system functioning, various terminologies used in describing minimal brain dysfunction, and types of learning disabilities (agnosias, aprazias, dyslexias, aphasias, and nonverbal learning disorders). Discussions also focused on general personality characteristics often found in learning disabled and emotionally handicapped children. A source used for these discussions was Hewett's *The Emotionally Disturbed Child in the Classroom* (1968). This information generally was shared on an intellectual/cognitive level. Occasionally, an emotionally toned manner was used to reach the parents at the gut level. Through these discussions parents gained more insight and feeling into their own child and the child's experiences in terms of a poor self-concept, a low frustration tolerance, and the ability or inability to handle stressful day-to-day situations, (distractibility, inattentiveness, impulsiveness, unpredictability, and hyperactivity).

After these particular concepts were thoroughly discussed, the explanation and application of general and more specific behavioral modification principles were presented. Parents were taught principles of contingency management for the home and given specific suggestions related to their new understanding of their child's particular behavioral problems. Often the discussion of learning disabilities and the parents' new knowledge provided the impetus for parents to change goals, expectations, or demands which had been previously set up for the child. The response most often heard from parents was that the lecture materials provided them with more realistic appraisals of their children's capabilities, a new understanding and empathy for what their child had experienced, and a reevaluation of themselves in relationship to the child.

Counseling groups

The fourth area of the parent program was the counseling groups which met twice a month for two-hour sessions. In these groups parents were encouraged to take part in open dialogue aimed at discussing specific problems or concerns with emphasis upon emotional catharsis and the development of more effective communication patterns. The groups provided parents with an opportunity to talk over their feelings of anxiety, hopelessness, responsibility, guilt, or anger related to their own child's learning disability or behavior difficulties. One of the primary advantages of the groups was that they provided the parents with a mutual source of emotional support. Parents could relate the group experience to their own, realizing they were not alone in their fears, helplessness, and discouragement.

It was felt that one of the most important contributions to the group counseling was the creation of an environment that enabled parents to discuss freely their intimate feelings in many areas. The groups also provided an opportunity for the parents to develop their communication skills, enabling them to better understand and communicate with their child, each other, and significant others.

There were a number of recurring themes in the parent counseling groups.

School-home communication. Topics in this area seemed to occur more often when a group was beginning or when the members seemed to need an escape from more emotionally charged areas. Parents were given an opportunity to vent negative feelings about specific school situations and administrative decisions. Whenever possible, immediate attempts were made by the staff to rectify legitimate parent complaints. Details of the child's educational program, behavior, and progress in school seemed to help the parents to understand the school's overall approach. The group was also an excellent vehicle for exchange of information about the discrepancies in the child's home/school behavior.

Behavior problems. Parents were often anxious to discuss their child's behavior which caused them the most distress. When appropriate, parents were supplied with specific information related to their own child's emotional and behavioral disorders or learning disability. Considerable attention was given to parents to help them understand the dynamics of misbehavior and to understand and modify their own feelings, attitudes, and behavior, which often perpetuate their child's misbehavior.

Interpersonal relationships. Parents talked mostly of their own child, but they did not limit conversation to him alone. Anxiety producing relationships with significant others were often areas brought up for discussion. The facilitator used many therapeutic techniques to enable members to better understand their own contributions toward the unsatisfactory conditions in the particular relationships. Suggestions were offered for more appropriate behavior in the future.

Recurring emotional experiences. Certain categories of feelings appeared often. In the initial stages of the meetings, denial or inadequate resolution of these feelings seemed to be a frequent impediment to positive change. However, as the groups continued to meet and as mutual respect and trust evolved, there was less resistance toward admitting and realistically facing the negative aspects of one's own attitudes or emotions.

Many parents exhibited considerable anxiety over such future concerns as: Will my child fit in when he returns to public school? Will he be able to go on to college? Will he be employable? Their future concerns were realistic. However, it was felt that excessive concern and rumination about the future was a defense mechanism used by the parents to avoid or resist a threatening discussion of present problems or failures in family relationships. When this happened, the facilitator identified and clarified the dynamics of resistance. This aided the parents in understanding what the more immediate causes of their anxiety or hopelessness were.

Another category was the feeling of guilt which seemed fairly common in many parents. Usually this was connected with a sense of responsibility for the child's learning disability or emotional handicap. Often feelings of guilt about the past served to impede the parents in adopting newer, more flexible behavior patterns. At times it seemed that guilt over the past was so overwhelming that parents were threatened by any insights or possible changes, because these were perceived as threats of experiencing even more guilt in the future. The facilitator dealt with this on a comfortable, nonpressuring level which enabled parents to change without experiencing severe emotional upheavals.

A third category was the ambivalence parents felt toward the child. Anger, blame, and even hatred directed against the child for having made a hardship out of the parents' lives were often not dealt with, because they were not always consciously experienced. Denial of these unacceptable feelings often precipated regressive, immature behavior toward the child which increased the parent's sense of guilt. The psychologist carefully evaluated the parents' strengths and abilities to face their ambivalence before he attempted to clarify it to them. If the parent was judged to have sufficient strengths to face the ambivalence, a nonthreatening approach was utilized in facilitating insight and attitudinal changes.

While negative aspects of feelings and group interactions were not avoided, they were not emphasized. Basically the parent counseling groups were of a positive nature and focused on assets rather than liabilities. Emphasis was placed upon positive interactions, behaviors, situations, and attitudes. Parents were also encouraged to develop a worthwhile sense of identification apart from their child in order to fulfill some of their own needs. The staff felt that if parents could develop a better sense of self-esteem and independence from their child, they would give more to him.

Results

Over three-fourths of the parents were included in some aspect of the Parent Program. A fairly large number of the families availed themselves of more than one part of the program. Out of 110 families, parents of 74 children participated in the groups. Informal feedback obtained from parents suggested that they found the experience informative and beneficial, not only in new ideas, understanding basic concepts, and ways of interacting with their children, but also in their own assessment of the school and its efficiency in operations. In other words, the groups served as good public relations between the school and parents. Parents have expressed the desire to have the program continued.

Teachers have also indicated to the group facilitators that the Parent Programhas been helpful to them in two areas. They have noticed positive behavioral changes more from those children whose parents were regularly attending the groups than from those children whose parents avoided attending groups. The teachers also felt that the program lightened their load. Facilitators were able to sort out complaints and fears so that teachers were not apt to be approached by parents with anxiety-ridden misconceptions of certian school situations. Rather than being barraged by unnecessary complaints and questions, the teachers' time was more constructively spent in solving problems with those parents who had a realistic need of contact with teachers.

References

French, E. L. Residential treatment for emotionally disturbed young people. *Mental Hospitals,* July, 1963.

Fullmer, D. W., & Bernard, H. W. *Family consultation.* Boston: Houghton Mifflin, 1968.

Hewett, F. M. *Emotionally disturbed child in the classroom.* Boston: Allyn & Bacon, 1968.

Johnson, D. J., & Myklebust, H. R. *Learning disabilities.* New York: Grunne & Stratton, 1967.

McWhirter, J. J. Family group consultation and the secondary schools. *Family Life Coordinator,* 1966, *15,* 183–184.

Patterson, G., & Gullhan, M. E. *Living with children.* Champaign, Ill.: Research Press, 1967.

Parental Treatment, Children's Treatment, and the Risk of Childhood Behavioral Problems

James R. Cameron, Ph.D.

2. Initial Temperament, Parental Attitudes, and the Incidence and Form of Behavioral Problems.

Childhood behavioral problems are found to be related to both early temperament and parental behavior, in that first-year temperament scores predicted mild (but not more severe) problems. A parental pathology scale discriminated more severe cases among girls only; more severe cases among boys were accompanied by negative temperament changes. For both sexes, the form of subsequent behavioral problems was associated with first-year temperament patterns.

Clinicians have long suspected that childhood psychopathology in its various forms arose somehow from the interaction of childhood temperament and parental attitudes or behaviors. Previous researchers[1, 2, 4–7, 11] have described some of the possible forms of this interaction, and a companion article[3] has described the relationship between various clusters of parental characteristics and variations or changes in their offsprings' temperament. These results, drawn from the New York Longitudinal Study's data,[9] suggested strongly that parental responses to the child's initial temperament mediated between that temperament and the possibility of the development of eventual behavioral disturbances.

This article is intended to complete the preceding analysis[3] of the impact of initial temperament and parental characteristics on children's emotional risk by reanalyzing the degree to which each domain (or both domains combined) is related to the risk for the various forms of behavioral disturbance. It will also provide a "retrospective analysis," by examining the extent to which different forms of symptomatology (such as excessive withdrawal, negativism, or demanding behavior) are related to different temperament styles revealed in the children's initial year of life.

Previous publications[8, 9] based on the NYLS data reported successful discrimination between "nonclinical" and clinical cases, using nine scales of tem-

Parental Treatment, Children's Temperament, and the Risk of Childhood Behavioral Problems: 2 Initial Temperment, Parental Attitudes, and the Incidents and Form of Behavioral Problems, *American Journal of Orthopsychiatry*, Vol. 48, No. 1,

perament. Most of these significant discriminations employed temperament data gathered during the children's fourth and fifth years, and since behavior problems began to emerge among these children as early as the second year, the issue of predictability was never directly raised. In addition, the "clinical" group was divided into "active" and "passive" subgroups, and no results were presented that separated mild from moderate-through-severe cases, nor boys from girls. Since the first part of the present investigation found these separations to be of value,[3] it was decided to examine the risk issue with these finer discriminations in mind.

SAMPLE AND DATA COLLECTION

The extensive publications of the NYLS team have described in detail both the nature of their sample (children and parents) and the data collection methods.[8, 9] To recap briefly, 69 boys and 67 girls were followed longitudinally from birth into adolescence, with particular emphasis during each of their first five years on their standing on nine scales of temperament. In addition, data on parenting behavior and attitudes were gathered through a structured interview administered to each set of parents simultaneously but separately around the time of the sample child's third birthday.

For the purpose of the present analysis, the nine temperament scales were reduced to four by means of a pivot variable cluster analysis.[10] Pivot variables were selected mainly on theoretical grounds, which suggested they would provide the most logical "predictors" of eventual behavioral problems. The four pivot variables, along with the temperament scales most closely associated with each pivot variable, are described in TABLE 1.

To compute each child's "temperament risk" scores for each year (one through five), each year's four cluster scores per child were transformed into deviation scores. For a yearly "summary risk score" per child, the four deviation scores were summed, so that high summary risk represented high persistence, withdrawal, low adaptability, and negative mood.*

Based on these global risk temperament scores, all children were assigned a risk ranking for each of the five initial years. In turn these rankings were divided into quintiles, the frequency with which children in following years developed behavior problems was computed per quintile, and chi-square analyses were employed to determine whether a significantly greater number of clinical cases emerged among high-risk quintiles.

TABLE 2 presents the quintile data for these temperament risk rankings. Only in the fourth year did the temperament risk data significantly *predict* future clinical cases, although across all four years the lowest risk children (Quintile 1) produced consistently the fewest clinical cases. These findings parallel the results reported in earlier NYLS publications, where temperament data from the fourth and the fifth years provided the best basis for discrimination between nonclinical cases and children who had been or were to become clinical cases.

For the purpose of comparing the relative effectiveness of temperament data against parental data in predicting which children will develop behavioral problems, a "parental pathology" scale was computed for each child's parents by summing the cluster scores on the three parental dimensions (*parental conflict in child rearing, maternal rejection,* and *inconsistent parental discipline*) that provided the highest correlations with negative changes in children's temperament across the first five years.[3] Only when the four lower-risk intervals were compared with the highest interval on these parental rankings was the chi-square difference significant at better than the .05 level.

The two columns on the far right in TABLE 2 report the results of combining parental pathology rankings and children's temperament risk scores. Note that in each year except the fifth, the predictability is enhanced over the children's temperament score alone; by the

* This "summary risk score" corresponds in general to Chess and Thomas's "difficult child pattern," plus high persistence.

Table 1

DEFINING TEMPERAMENT SCALES FOR FOUR PIVOT VARIABLE CLUSTER DIMENSIONS AND RELATED SCALES CONTRIBUTING TO EACH CLUSTER

VARIABLE	RELATED SCALES [a]
1. PERSISTENCE: The degree to which a child maintains an activity in the face of obstacles.	1. Intensity (.24) [b] 2. Threshold (–.12)
2. APPROACH-WITHDRAWAL: How the child reacts to any new situation, such as new foods, people, toys, or procedures.	1. Intensity (.17) 2. Activity (–.12) 3. Threshold (–.12)
3. ADAPTABILITY: The degree to which the child's initial response can be easily modified in a desired direction.	1. Rhythmicity (.27) 2. Threshold (.22) 3. Intensity (.–36)
4. MOOD: The amount of joyful, pleasant behavior to crying, unpleasant, unfriendly behavior.	1. Intensity (.29) 2. Distractibility (–.14)

[a] Definitions of these contributing temperament scales can be found in the initial article[3] or in any of the NYLS publications.[8, 9]
[b] Scale weights are given in parentheses.

fourth year, it has improved over the parental pathology scale alone.

SEX DIFFERENCES

When the boys and girls in the sample are considered separately, girls' clinical cases appear slightly more predictable. For boys, neither parental pathology nor temperament data produced a p value better than .50, but for girls there was a trend ($p<.10$) at the first year for temperament scores to discriminate clinical and nonclinical cases. Although this trend seemed to wash out in the second through fifth years, there was also a significant discrimination ($p<.01$) between clinical and nonclinical girls' cases based on parental pathology scores. Such a finding is consistent with the results presented in the introductory article,[3] where individual parental factors provided consistently higher correlations with girls' temperament change scores than they did with boys' scores.

DIFFERENCES IN SEVERITY

It seemed worth asking whether both global temperament risk scores and global parental pathology scores might be more effective predictors of moderate-to-severe clinical cases than of mild cases. In fact, as TABLE 3 indicates, global temperament risk scores were generally stronger predictors of mild than of moderate-to-severe clinical cases. Oddly, the significant discrimination between moderate-to-severe males and nonclinical males, based on first-year temperament data, reflects the unexpected finding that moderate-to-severe boys fell consistently in the lower three risk quintiles. When the moderate-to-severe boys are separated in this fashion and this "reverse prediction" phenomenon teased out, predictability from temperament data returns to boys' mild cases, particularly from first-year temperament data.

Table 2

NUMBER OF SUBSEQUENT CLINICAL CASES FALLING IN EACH RISK INTERVAL (QUINTILE) BASED ON FIVE-YEAR SUMMARY TEMPERAMENT RISK SCORES

	TEMPERAMENT SCORE ANALYSIS							DYAD ANALYSIS	
	QUINTILE								
YEAR	1	2	3	4	5	Q1–3 vs. Q4–5	p	χ^2	p
1	4	7	11	8	11	.68	<.50	3.75	<.05
2	7	10	5	9	8	.21	<.70	1.90	<.20
3	5	5	11	4	9	.89	<.50	3.66	<.10
4	3	1	3	6	7	5.20	<.05	7.50	<.01
5	1	2	2	1	4	2.50	<.20	2.50	<.20

Table 3

PREDICTABILITY OF MILD AND OF MODERATE-TO-SEVERE CLINICAL CASES BASED ON TEMPERAMENT DATA AND ON PARENTAL DATA

	MILD CASES ONLY				MODERATE-TO-SEVERE CASES ONLY			
	BOYS		GIRLS		BOYS		GIRLS	
YEAR	χ^2	P	χ^2	P	χ^2	P	χ^2	P
1	5.51	<.02	4.08	<.05	6.00	<.02	.33	<.70
2	1.76	<.20	.09	<.80	3.13	<.10	.09	<.80
3	.17	<.95	2.88	<.10	.87	<.50	.00	1.00
4	2.88	<.10	.83	<.50	.11	<.80	.08	<.80
5	4.00	<.05	.34	<.70	.00	1.00	4.00	<.05
PPS [a]	.20	<.90	.08	<.80	.004	<.98	8.23	<.01

[a] Parental Pathology Scale.

ORIGINS OF PREDICTABILITY OF MILD CLINICAL CASES

To carry this analysis one further step, it was asked whether all four pivot variable clusters contributed equally in the first year to the predictability of mild clinical cases, or whether one or two clusters stood out. In fact, boys who subsequently became mild clinical cases, and who ranked in the top two quintiles of temperament risk scores in their first year, average over half a standard deviation (.60) above the mean on the *negative mood* cluster, nearly half a standard deviation (.43) above the mean on the *persistence* cluster, and below the mean (—.41) on the *adaptability* cluster.

In contrast, girls who became mild clinical cases and who in their first year had been ranked in the fourth or fifth quintile were below the mean (—.27) on the *persistence* cluster, consistently above on *withdrawal* (.73), and positioned similar to mild male cases on *adaptability* (—.65) and *mood* (.93).

TEMPERAMENT ESCALATION IN MODERATE-TO-SEVERE CASES

The lack of predictability from temperament data of moderate-to-severe clinical cases raises the issue of the importance of temperament to the origins of such pathology. To examine this issue, the "progress" of the two groups of moderate-to-severe clinical cases was charted across each of the first five years, on the basis of their average scores on the four pivot variable dimensions. The results (TABLE 4) indicate that, although temperament scores do not *predict* subsequent moderate-to-severe clinical cases, they do *reflect* what appears to be escalation into pathology.

Although the number of cases in each group represented in TABLE 4 is too small to allow tests of statistical significance, the trend seems clear for both groups to increase in *persistence* and decrease in *adaptability,* particularly in the third and fourth years. Thus in moderate-to-severe clinical cases, if first-year temperament scores do not predict later behavioral problems, temperament scores at later years may mirror changes occurring in the child as these behavioral problems approach.

SYMPTOM FORM AND EARLY TEMPERAMENT

Another way of establishing the significance of temperament in the etiology of childhood behavioral problems is to demonstrate a link between the *form* taken by a child's behavioral problems and his or her initial temperament. Prior publications from the NYLS project indicated that "active" or "passive" clinical cases would be differentiated from nonclinical cases on the basis of temperament data, particularly data from the children's fourth and fifth years. A more substantial indication of a relationship between symptom form and early temperament would result if it could be shown that children with specific symptom characteristics possessed idiosyncratic temperament patterns in their first year.

To test for such a relationship, the symptoms listed by the NYLS project [9] were organized into four general categories:

TYPE A: *Impositional*—symptoms representing excessive imposition of the child's own needs (or ways of acting or

Table 4

MEAN TEMPERAMENT SCORES ACROSS THE FIRST FIVE YEARS FOR TWO GROUPS OF MODERATE-TO-SEVERE CLINICAL CASES

GROUP 1 [a]	PERSISTENCE	NEGATIVE MOOD	WITHDRAWAL	ADAPTABILITY
Year 1	–.15	–.57	–.64	.58
Year 2	–.19	–.96	.01	.10
Year 3	.12	–.38	.11	.01
Year 4	.49	.22	.15	–.29
Year 5	.35	–.35	.19	.12
GROUP 2 [b]				
Year 1	.26	.26	.04	–.06
Year 2	.36	–.24	–.18	.18
Year 3	.72	.52	.34	–.46
Year 4	.63	.14	.13	–.90
Year 5	.15	–.38	.05	–.50

[a] Moderate-to-severe male cases in the lowest three quintiles on first-year summary temperament scores.
[b] Moderate-to-severe female cases in the top two intervals on the parental pathology scale.

understanding) onto the ongoing situation.

TYPE B: *Nonaccommodational*—symptoms representing a refusal to accommodate to change, instruction, or education; a negativistic, underadapting positon.

TYPE C: *Withdrawal*—symptoms representing a tendency to withdraw from situations, shut them out, or cut down on awareness of external or internal events.

TYPE D: *Overadapting*—symptoms representing a tendency to overadapt to most situations, allowing others to dictate directions, abdicating making preferences, and being generally overcompliant.

All symptoms that seemed to represent one of these defensive positions were coded accordingly, as were clinical cases containing these symptoms. A number of clinical cases received more than one symptom code, but this complication seemed merely a reflection of the variability of how children express their behavioral problems.

When first-year temperament scores for clinical cases with each symptom form were compared with clinical cases without such symptoms, trends in expectable directions emerged. For example, two-thirds of the clinical cases demonstrating TYPE A (*impositional*) symptoms were above the first-year mean on the *persistence* dimension, while only half of the clinical cases without such symptoms fell above the mean. This trend was particularly strong among girls' clinical cases, and among moderate-to-severe cases. Two-thirds of the children with TYPE A symptoms also fell above the mean in their first year on the *negative mood* dimension, but were undistinguished by any trends on the other two temperament factors.

Children with TYPE B symptoms characterized by limited adaptability to change, provided similar results. The greatest discrimination from clinical cases without such symptoms occurred on the *adaptability* cluster, where approximately 60% of the TYPE B children fell below the mean, as compared with about 30% of clinical cases without TYPE B symptoms. The majority of TYPE B cases were also above the mean on the *persistence* and *negative mood* clusters, but so were the clinical cases with no TYPE B symptoms.

TYPE C (*withdrawing*) cases, in contrast, were discriminated in the first year solely in terms of the *withdrawal* cluster. The anomaly here was that the results were the opposite of what one might expect: three-quarters of the TYPE C children were *below* the first-year mean on this dimension, while the majority of cases with no TYPE C symptoms were above the mean. A more expectable result emerged with respect to the *persistence* cluster, where the majority of TYPE C children were below the mean, while approximately three-quarters of cases without TYPE C symptoms were above the mean.

There were too few cases with TYPE D symptoms to allow any statistical analysis of this category.

Although the total number of clinical cases, when divided into such groups, does not allow statistically strong discriminations to develop, with the exception of TYPE C (*withdrawal*) clinical cases the trends are in expectable directions; they suggest that if a child becomes a clinical case, the nature of that child's symptoms is, in part at least, a function of individual temperament style, as revealed during the first twelve months of life.

SUMMARY AND IMPLICATIONS

In the first of this two-part report, it was suggested that the etiology of children's behavioral problems resembled metaphorically the origins of earthquakes, with children's temperament analogous to the fault lines and environmental events, particularly parenting styles, analagous to strain. That article suggested that certain factors of parenting, as revealed through the NYLS data, were related to changes in areas of children's temperament that in turn discriminated clinical from nonclinical cases.

The findings presented in this paper continue to support this geological analogy. With the focus on *prediction* of subsequent behavioral problems, first-year temperament scores were found to be predictive of mild cases of either sex. Prediction of moderate-to-severe cases, however, could not be achieved on the basis of temperament data alone, but could be achieved for girls' cases by resorting to a global parental pathology score. While moderate-to-severe male clinical cases were harder to predict, there was evidence that escalations in temperament accompanied their progress into behavior problems. In addition, in a retrospective analysis of first-year temperament profiles of those children who subsequently became clinical cases, the trends suggested a correspondence between the *form* of the children's symptoms and their temperament during their first twelve months.

The practical implications of these findings would seem again analagous to earthquake prediction. It seems insufficient for geological prognosticators to know only where the fault lines stand, and it appears equally insufficient for predictive clinical purposes to determine *only* the child's initial temperament. By the same token, measurement of parental responses to the child, in and of themselves, are not enough, just as measurements from randomly placed strain gauges will not suffice. However, if we are to anticipate and minimize the consequences of the mismatching of a child's temperament with certain styles of parenting responses, we need further research into how the two interact; the present study adds to the evidence that the parent-child dyad is the unit we must consider to be at risk.

PLANNING THE FUTURE OF A SEVERELY HANDICAPPED AUTISTIC CHILD

Katharine Sangree Stokes

How do parents of a severely handicapped child plan constructively and realistically for his future? What are the most pressing problems to be addressed, and what, in anticipation, can parents do about them? The urgency of these questions and the difficulties in finding answers has become a central concern to me, the mother of a nonverbal, 21-year-old autistic child, as well as to the many parents with whom I have had contact through my experiences in founding a school for severely impaired autistic adolescents.

Planning for our child's immediate future has been an integral part of our family's ongoing present during all the years of his childhood. Adequate and appropriate remedial services did not exist when he and we needed them. Together with other parents we have worked to find, to support, and to create the necessary educational and social opportunities. Now, despite years of struggle, it is clear that he, who will be socially dependent throughout his life, will further require that provisions be made for a sheltered living and working situation, for adequate financial support, and for a caring person to act as advocate for his needs. The discussion that follows is the fruit of years of thought, the kind that occupies parents in the long nights after their more immediate cares are set aside. This thought expresses itself in questions, not answers. Generally speaking, one does not know the answers.

The Problem

A 21-year-old is no longer a child in the chronological sense. Yet for parents one's children are always one's children in that the relationship continues, and with it the ultimate concern for the child's welfare. For the parent of a severely handicapped child, not only concern but responsibility continues throughout life. His problem remains our problem. Over time we have come to realize not only that this "has happened to us, but that the problem is severe, unrelenting, and will last a lifetime" (Sullivan, Note 1).

For the severely handicapped autistic person, education, broadly defined, continues to be the most useful intervention. There are basic skills that he needs in order to be an acceptable and, I hope, productive human being. For persons such as our son, whose opportunities for formal education during his childhood years were nonexistent or grossly inadequate, those basic skills are still to be learned and can be taught. They include self-help, behavior control, simple communication patterns both receptive and expressive, as well as the ability to occupy his time with some degree of independence. Provision for appropriate, intensive education must be continued past age 21 if he is to achieve these goals. Yet neither funding nor facilities exist to provide these experiences to a person who is chronologically an adult.

In addition to further education, our son will need a living situation

Planning for the Future of a Severely Handicapped Autistic Child, Katherine Sangree Stokes, *Journal of Autism and Childhool Schizophreniz,* Vol. 7, No. 3, © 1977 Plenum Publishing Company.

that is protective yet encourages increasingly independent as well as interdependent behaviors. Development of an interpersonal human being takes place in interaction with caring others. This he has had at home. If our son is to continue to grow in awareness of others, his future home must also include persons who can care for him as an individual.

Normally a 21-year-old is out of the parental home and on his own. Parents may choose to provide a few more years of financial support in order that this child complete his education. Even with this continued dependency parents have long since stopped having to "be there" supervising this child every hour of his day and night, to transport him to doctor or dentist, to buy his clothes, to decide when he needs a haircut, to teach him how to care for himself, to protect him from harm. Not so with a severely impaired autistic child. The normal process of decreasing caretaking by the parents and the increasing independence of the child takes place so slowly that it will never be completed. Understanding supervision will always be necessary to mediate those situations that are unpredictable, that present new problems, that require judgment. These handicapped people are no longer children, yet they continue to require the loving caretaking services that parents provided when they were younger.

This is no longer an appropriate task for us. My husband and I are now in our late 50s. Our autistic son is the youngest of four children; the other three are adults who have left our home to fashion their own futures. It is high time that we attend to our own needs and bring to a close those years of orientation to child care by providing some measure of assurance that our man-child can live his own life in dignity without us.

The Individual

Sam, our son, is an exceptionally handsome 6-foot-2-inch, 190-pound young man. At first glance he can "pass for normal," and part of learning to enjoy living with such a child is to be able to respond with compassionate humor to the baffled responses that he evokes, as well as to be understanding and helpful when people are frightened of him. Sam is a gentle, loving person who, in spite of his size and physical maturity, evokes affectionate response not only from his family but also from other persons with whom he comes in contact, persons such as his sister's friends, young children who enjoy playing with him, and adolescents who are hired to act as companions to him.

Nonverbal expressively, with comprehension hard to assess, Sam can follow simple verbal directions. As long as the request or suggestion fits into his expectations, he responds appropriately. But his confusion and his attempts to *do something* when instructions are not the usual ones suggest the degree of distress he must feel in a verbal world that he cannot share. Sam moves easily in those environments that are familiar and structured, his home and his school. His self-help skills are fair to good. He dresses himself completely and with an innate color sense. He is still learning to brush his teeth well enough to suit his dentist; shaving is new and hard to master. Independence in showering and in food preparation is hampered by his apparent inability to distinguish degrees of heat. Most difficult of all for us, his parents, and perhaps for him, is his inability to know what to do with himself in his unstructured free time. Aside from a retreat into stereotyped, world-shutting-out autistic behaviors, Sam is lost when there is "nothing to do." He shows that he wants something to do. He paces, he impatiently hums, and eventually he finds something irritating (to us) to do like dumping liquid soap down the sink—if he is left alone too long.

Sam the man, in spite of his body size, is emotionally like a small child. His jumping up and down with glee or excess spirits shakes the house. Bizarre behavior? Perhaps. But Sam's present childlike unrestrained delight, the eager vividness in his face at the sight of food or persons he likes is a quality we treasure, for it developed slowly from the withdrawal and misery of his earlier years. Today, even in the body of a man, Sam the emotional child is a lovely fey person, one who knows how to enjoy simple pleasures, who has a kind of unselfconsciousness and delight that is infectious and lovable.

His expressions of distress are equally unrestrained. Suddenly, without apparent antecedents he will be found weeping silently, inconsolably, or he may beat his head and bite his hands in what appears to be deep frustration or inturned anger. Although Sam uses self-destructive rather than outwardly aggressive behaviors to express his distress, the spectacle of an almost 200-pound man so unrestrained is frightening to the uninitiated. Sam still sucks his fingers, and we are working to eliminate that behavior. It is conspicuous and unseemly, and it makes us uncomfortable. But sometimes we wonder if those fingers are not a protection for him. For Sam's size and his normal appearance lead to expectations that he cannot begin to fulfill. Police assume that an adolescent is surly or arrogant when he does not respond to their verbal commands. Lost one day and searching for help, Sam looked into the windows of a stranger's house. He was reported as a "peeping Tom" and came close to being brutalized by the police. It was those fingers that assuaged the fear and anger sufficiently to suggest that rather than his being a dangerous person it might instead be he who needed help. This description of Sam is an attempt to show the kinds of behaviors and suggest the emotional needs that must be taken into account in planning for his future. *Sam is a child, in the body of a man, and I wonder if it is not better that the world he contacts know this as soon as possible.*

Developmental Needs

Sam's needs are not those of an adult; they are the needs of a growing person whose emotional and cognitive development has not progressed in the usual way. There is a lawful pattern of learning about the world that characterizes normal child development. If he is provided with an adequate social environment that is responsive to him as an individual, the normal nonhandicapped child progresses in an orderly way acquiring the behaviors and attitudes conducive to a normal adult existence. Severely handicapped autistic children do not follow this pattern. For whatever the reasons, their development is not only atypical but retarded or arrested at levels of early childhood. In order for development to continue, the environment must be able to meet the individual's needs as they exist at his particular developmental level. For Sam this means looking at his childlike qualities, identifying related needs, and attempting to provide an environment conducive to progressive growth.

This focus on childlike qualities and on meeting childlike emotional needs may sound like heresy to those who are struggling to help retarded persons become accepted as adult citizens in our society. At first glance my point of view may appear contrary to enlightened efforts to plan working and living environments on the principles of *development* and *normalization* (National Association for Retarded Citizens, 1973; Wolfensberger, 1972). These principles emphasize making available to retarded persons situations of living and working that are as similar as possible to those of the mainstream of society. But development and normalization are not necessarily the same thing. It is important to distinguish between developmental needs that may be atypical and normalized patterns of living.

The proponents of development and normalization rightly specify that the retarded person as well as the normal one needs provision not only for shelter and for reasonable safety but also for the right to take risks. These as well as opportunities for work and play, for companionship, and for sexual expression are necessary for continued growth and development as a human being. They imply an environment where physical, cognitive, social, and emotional needs are met. Provision of good physical care is relatively easy; to meet cognitive, social, and emotional needs is more complex.

What are the emotional needs of autistic persons such as Sam? In spite of his physical maturity and well-developed genitals, he is not a heterosexual, mature person. He has not developed and is not likely to develop the interpersonal skills that lead to adult sexual expression. Yet Sam needs other human beings who not only care about him but who enjoy sharing with him in reciprocally satisfying human contact. Sam does not need a sexual partner in the adult sense, but he needs someone to hug occasionally as well as someone to comfort him when he is troubled. As mentioned above, Sam can evoke this response from persons beyond his family circle; I believe it is related to his childlike qualities, and I do not want him to lose that asset. He needs the security of an environment simple enough and structured enough so that he knows how to meet its expectations. He also needs stimulation in the form of going places and doing things. He needs the ambience of an atmosphere where other people know how to enjoy themselves and can take pleasure in including him, at least on the periphery. These persons can provide for Sam not only role models but also experiences that he cannot yet provide for himself. Such an environment, shared with other more competent persons, can enable Sam to maintain his zest for life and to expand his options.

Residential Facilities

Planning adequately for the future of a severely handicapped autistic person involves looking more closely at his future home, at what needs to be provided in living and working environments designed for persons as handicapped as he. These will have to be sheltered situations shared with persons who can assume responsibility for his welfare.

Residential environments providing optimal opportunities for emotional and social development for persons such as Sam are rare to nonexistent. That the atmosphere of large state institutions is not conducive to such growth is well known. Leo Kanner, in follow-up studies of his autistic patients, notes that not one of the persons who were able to emerge from autism sufficiently to "function as adults in varying degrees of nonpsychotic activity . . . had at any time been subjected to sojourn in a state hospital or institution for the feeble-minded . . . that such an eventuality has invariably cut short any prospect for improvement" (Kanner, Rodrigues, & Ashenden, 1972) and that "state hospital admission was tantamount to a life sentence" (Kanner, 1971).

Parents who have reached the point where they must choose to place their child in such a facility may have difficulty in finding an institution that will accept him. Shall it be an institution for a child or for an adult, for the retarded or for the mentally ill? Facilities for children reject adults. Facilities for the mentally ill reject the retarded. These are agency distinctions that may have little relevance for a person such as Sam who is both an adult and a child, considered to be both retarded and mentally ill. It is common experience for parents to be told that their child is ineligible for one type of institution because of the other facets of his handicap. One factor influencing these rejections relates to assumptions of hopelessness concerning the retarded and the adult in contrast to the mentally ill child. Cure, a medical model, rather than constructive developmental change, an educational model, seems to be the criterion of success.

Awareness of the inadequacy of public institutions to provide an environment conducive to developmental change has led to federal support for deinstitutionalization and a movement toward establishing living situations in the community. The thrust to provide a more humane and normalized environment for retarded persons has led not only to enunciation of the principles of normalization and development but also to a growing effort to put the principles into practice. There is a lot of creative thinking and planning taking place. To my knowledge, however, the implications, much less the specifics of providing opportunities for continued emotional growth for retarded/autistic persons have not been explored.

In order to translate the principles of development and normalization into programs, it is important that we identify those factors that lead to continued human growth, rather than creating programs in reaction to the evils of the past and the present. I am concerned that the original inspired theories may have become slogans with prestige value such that superficial adherence to the appearance of normalization may be replacing thoughtful provision for a life style at whatever compromised level that would be emotionally satisfying to the severely handicapped residents. The principles are correct—development and normalization, but on whose terms? What is *normal* for an adult whose cognitive and emotional levels are in some ways similar to those of a 2-year-old but whose experiences (spanning 20 years) have been different from those of a small child? A living situation for an autistic person that provides as normal an environment as is possible must meet his developmental needs. Before they can be met, they must be understood. Yet identification of the emotional needs of a person with an adult body and childlike behaviors is a problem that has, to my knowledge, not been addressed.

Nowhere have we found more than a suggestive description of the *quality* of life for the resident himself (Baker, Seltzer, & Seltzer, 1974). Provision of "living experiences appropriate to the functioning level and learning needs of the individual" (National Association for Retarded Citizens, 1973, p. 8) should, but does not necessarily, imply appropriateness to the emotional level. In relation to the dehumanizing atmosphere in traditional residential facilities, there is a statement that "retarded individuals should be treated so as to promote emotional development. They cannot be treated as children throughout their lifetimes because they are then deprived of the opportunity to learn adult behaviors" (National Association for Retarded Citizens, 1973, p. 8). But in these dehumanizing institutions they are *not* treated as children. They are waited upon, considered to be incompetent, herded like cattle, denied the opportunity to do things for themselves. In contrast, normal children are allowed to explore, experiment, and make mistakes, while being protected from situations they are not yet able to master. If we really mean that retarded adults should be provided the opportunities to continue to develop, then we do not necessarily mean that they should immediately be learning "adult behaviors."

Far too often, normalization is defined in terms of the behaviors that normal adults consider to be adult behaviors; we would be most comfortable if the retarded adult behaved the same way. These may not necessarily be the kinds of behaviors that lead to cognitive and emotional growth. Instead, we may be talking about teaching the retarded or autistic person how to be inconspicuous, how to be socially inoffensive, how to behave in ways that will not make trouble for the adults who come in contact with him, who care for or supervise him.

Normalization implies, among other things, the provision of opportunities to assume responsibility for oneself. In order to develop independent functioning, autistic people need intensive educational intervention. They need close supervision, not to limit their freedom, nor to keep them dependent, but to help them to build the foundations of caring for others and for themselves, to help them discover that they as individuals can change their environments, that what they do has an impact on others, that they can make a difference. It is my view that in order to further development of autistic people one must combine the teaching of skills with the discovery of a way to foster the motivation to use those skills to affect the environment and the persons in it, motivation so singularly lacking in autistic people. This kind of supervision and intensive intervention requires that severely handicapped autistic people live in close contact with those who care for them.

Autistic people can contribute to the pleasure of others, especially if those others enjoy a caretaking role. In order to create the kind of environment where the emotional needs of the autistic-retarded person can be joyously met by the nonhandicapped, a residence must take into account the needs of the caretakers as well as those of the retarded residents. The problem then becomes one of meeting the needs of a group of persons whose individual contributions to their joint living situation are quite unequal. How can one define and clarify the satisfactions that autistic-retarded persons can provide for the nonretarded in order that meeting the needs of the autistic-retarded people can be and will remain a source of delight to the caretaking person? And how can this be done in a reasonably responsible, financially viable way? Bettelheim (1974) and Goldenberg (1971) touch upon these issues with populations who differ from ours in the behaviors they present. Baker et al. (1974) surveyed and evaluated a number of models of community residences, among them a sheltered village where retarded and nonretarded persons, within an atmosphere of religious dedication, apparently happily share each other's lives. Experience gained from establishing residential situations for retarded people in the community has helped to identify factors that relate to staff satisfaction or dissatisfaction. These include good living arrangements and provision for adequate privacy, congruence with career goals and opportunities for professional advancement, the availability of backup and resource persons, and of crisis intervention on a 24-hour basis. They also include opportunities for free time away from the job. Although all these factors are important, none of them addresses directly the contribution of the handicapped person to the contentment of the nonhandicapped person sharing the same living space. Nowhere have we seen this problem adequately dealt with.

Summary and Recommendations

Residential and work facilities expressly designed to meet the needs of severely handicapped autistic people are virtually nonexistent. That adequate services do not exist for persons who are mentally handicapped is not news. The thrust to deinstitutionalize retarded persons and the philosophy and techniques designed to help them move into the mainstream of society are geared to the vast numbers of moderately handicapped persons. The principle of *normalization* does not, in my view, consider with any sophistication the *developmental* needs of these handicapped people—certainly not of autistic people. These are yet to be identified, and this must take place before they can be incorporated into programs. In the rhetoric of planning agencies there will always be a small number of persons who "require institutionalization." It is convenient to ignore the evidence that institutions are equally damaging to severely handicapped autistic persons and that given the right environment they too can often continue to develop and become productive human beings.

To prevent long-term institutionalization for these people and the attendant loss of their humanity, social planning should include (1) provision for residential facilities with an interpersonal environment that fosters maturation; these will need to be sheltered situations that are shared with nonhandicapped persons; (2) provision of a network of sheltered situations where there is simple productive work to be done that is comprehensible and therefore satisfying to these people.

In order to enable social planners to effectively provide for autistic people, there will need to be research investigating (1) the developmental and, particularly, the emotional needs of severely handicapped autistic adults; (2) the meeting of these needs as they affect the person's ability to develop emotionally as well as cognitively; (3) identification of the factors that enable handicapped and nonhandicapped persons to share their lives with one another in a way that is growth producing for both groups (there are, apparently, a few residential situations that may meet this criterion. Communes having care of the handicapped person as their "product" is one possibility. That the sheltered village mentioned earlier may be another suggests that there could be value in an in-depth exploration into the relationship between the villagers, both handicapped and nonhandicapped. The essence of the successful sheltered village concept may be not that it is sheltered but that it promotes shared living); (4) the kinds of work situations that are satisfying as well as possible for these people. There needs to be creative problem solving that goes beyond the assembly line and sheltered workshop paradigms. This should include exploration into the kinds of activities that have *meaning* to autistic people and a development of the requisite skills. For example, could these people be productively used on farms where animal functions must be tended and food (which they understand) is produced? What about work teams with a mentally competent person (possibly one with a physical handicap) to structure the task, to supervise the workers, and to negotiate with the employer?

There also needs to be further research into the development and the dissemination of teaching methods appropriate to both children in schools and adults in work and living situations that can develop autistic people's motivation for independent work and play.

As I take our 6-foot-2-inch son out for a walk after supper because he is physically restless (there being no nearby recreation program that *uses* his enormous physical vitality, and if there were, he could not get there without my taking him), as I stay up beyond the hour I would like to go to bed because my adult child is not yet ready to settle down but cannot manage to make the decision to go to bed on his own when he is ready, I wonder how much longer we can continue our efforts to provide for our own needs in relation to him as well as how to continue to smooth the path for other parents who share similar problems.

Speech, Vision, or Hearing Disabled

Perhaps in the area of speech more than other areas of exceptionality, parents can do something to help the disability. Parents are often the most significant contributors to preventive measures and early intervention attempting to alleviate speech disabilities before they become firmly established. The attitudes and behaviors of parents, teachers and important others may in fact contribute to the maintenance of a speech disability. Counseling is most important in helping those involved with the child to learn about and accept the need for change. The professional helper must be cautious and carefully gauge the person's capacity for learning and acceptance. Parents need to discover who they are, what attitudes they hold, what expectations they have for their children, and what revisions are necessary. The goals of counseling should be to assist parents to identify their own needs, goals and fears, to provide information, and to help parents communicate with their child in a more productive way.

In learning to cope with the exceptional child who has a hearing loss, parents would benefit from early family counseling. Group work which involves parents who have learned to cope with their child's disability can be supportive, helpful, and informative. Accurate, early diagnosis is important to the child's language development.

Early intervention is also important in educating the visually disabled child. Parents can enhance early sensory, motor, language, and social skills development of the child. Parent groups provide counseling opportunities, information, resources, and support. Like all children, those who are exceptional because they cannot see or whose vision is limited still have the basic needs for acceptance, encouragement, and parents who have realistic expectations for their future.

Counseling Parents Of Stuttering Children

Eric K. Sander

Eric K. Sander (M.A., University of Iowa, 1959) is a graduate clinical assistant, Cleveland Hearing and Speech Center, Western Reserve University.

Grateful acknowledgment is made to Professor Wendell Johnson of the University of Iowa for his assistance with the preparation of this article and most particularly for the use of his file of recorded interviews with parents of stuttering children.

What is the clinician's role in the prevention or early treatment of stuttering? He cannot with clear conscience reassure parents that their stuttering child will 'outgrow' the problem.[1] Or, if in his mind no problem exists (in the child), it will probably not suffice simply to tell parents that they have 'nothing to worry about.'

The task of counseling parents of children thought to be stutterers needs to be outlined more thoroughly than has been done. Schuell (*25*), in a short article, formulated a series of three structured interviews which could be used as a basis for working with parents of stuttering children. Additional thoughts are offered in an article by Brown (*5*) and in the texts of Van Riper (*26*), Johnson (*19*), and Berry and Eisenson (2).

When parents cooperate in a counseling program with insight and determination, the outlook for the young stutterer is most favorable. Johnson (*15*) observed 46 stuttering children shortly after the onset of the difficulty. He reports, 'At the close of the study (the median period of observation was two years, four months), speech was judged to have improved in 85 per cent of the cases and to be "normal or nearly normal" in 72 per cent.' Johnson attributes the improvement to be largely the result of parent counseling. In a study of 69 stuttering children, Jameson (*14*) reports that 'normal or near normal speech' was acquired by 20 of 25 children who were referred within one year of the onset of stuttering but by only '44 per cent of those who first attended after more than one year had elapsed.' Continuing, she states that 'normal or near-normal speech was acquired by 82 per cent of the children who attended for advice before five years of age and by 37 per cent of those who began treatment over five years.'

That the adult stutterer faces at best a laborious, imposingly difficult process of recovery emphasizes the necessity for prompt preventive measures. Two distinct reasons for early counseling are stated by Jameson (*14*):

> 1. The speech of a young child with a stammer is not fully stabilized. His hesitations are usually repetitive and seldom accompanied by anxiety; consequently, when environmental pressure on his speech is reduced, he is more likely than an older child to regain normal speech.
>
> 2. The mother of a younger child is, as a rule, willing to accept advice on his management at home. When, however, an older child who has been stammering for some time attends for treatment, not only is his stammering more firmly

[1] In 1938 Bryngelson (*6*) hazarded the guess that 40 per cent of stuttering children could be expected to overcome their difficulty without the help of a clinician. More recently, Glasner and Rosenthal (*11*) reported that of a group of 149 first-grade children who at one time were thought by their parents to have 'stuttered,' 81, or over one-half, had stopped stuttering without the benefit of professional assistance.

Counseling Parents of Stuttering Children, Eric K. Sander, *Journal of Speech and Hearing Disorders*, Vol. 24, No. 3, © Journal of Speech and Hearing Research.

established, but if the mother has been in the habit of correcting it, she probably finds it difficult to change her attitude.

Examining the Child

In evaluating the fluency of a child's speech, his age should be considered. Davis's early study (*9*) established the general trend (with the exception of syllable repetitions alone) of a decrease in nonfluency with age. Observations by Metraux (*23*) from a study of the language development of 207 preschool children confirm and supplement the findings of Davis. Metraux found a marked decrease in repetitions among children after the age of four. Whereas repetition of words and phrases at 24 and 30 months is a compulsive sort of thing (the repetition may often be broken by introducing a new subject or object), at 42 months repetitions are more likely to be related to other persons and social situations, demands for attention, information or encouragement. After the age of six most children do not differ greatly in fluency from adults.

Johnson (*19*) reports data on the average number of nonfluencies for 42 young stutterers, ages two to eight, matched with 42 nonstutterers. The average child in the stuttering group prolonged or repeated parts of words approximately 10 times more frequently than the average of the nonstuttering group. On the other hand, no significant differences existed between the two groups in the average amount of revision and interjection. The problem of establishing criteria for 'stuttering' *vs* 'normal nonfluency' in a general or basic sense is spelled out in a study by Johnson and his associates (*17*), in which the data referred to here and similar data from 94 additional subjects are reported.

The speech clinician should arrange, if possible, to record the child's speech so that the instances and types of nonfluencies can be closely studied. Careful observation is needed to determine the presence of avoidance reactions distinctly related to the child's speaking efforts: grimaces, hand movements, elbow shrugging, lip compression or preformation, eye blinking, disturbed breathing, *etc.* Such observations are in order not so much to decide whether or not the child *is* a stutterer (the question is ill-phrased) but (*1*) to gain insight into the presence of any circular reactions by the child toward his own speech behavior and (*2*) to secure a clear perception of what the parents may be reacting to in the child's speech.

Brown (*5*) believes that the examiner 'should be as informal as possible' and careful not to exert 'too much pressure' on the child's speech. The beginning clinician is likely to evaluate the child's speech solely by conversing with him in a relaxed atmosphere. A more complete speech examination, however, might take into account the child's reactions to pressure, his performance under stress. By applying the same pressure devices used in desensitization therapy,[2] it may be possible to reproduce, as Berry and Eisenson (*2*) put it, 'in token if not in complete form, the type of behavior in the child's home or school environment to which he reacts unfavorably.'

The child's apprehension or sensitivity to his speech interruptions may determine whether he needs to be included in the therapy program. Much can be learned from the child himself if he is old enough to be interviewed. It might be interesting to ask him, 'Why are you here with your mother?' or 'Why did you come to see me?' The writer recalls one incident in which the child glibly answered, 'Because I stutter. I don't talk right.' The mother, who insisted that the child knew nothing of his difficulty, was openly nonplused.

Counseling Procedure

As with the physician who is able to cure pneumonia while helpless with the common cold, our direct therapeutic methods have been aimed primarily at the older stutterer. It is easy to become absorbed with the dramatic symptomatology of the adult stutterer and blinded to more profitable avenues of early treatment. Only re-

[2]The method of desensitization therapy, as originally outlined in Van Riper's text (*26*), aims to develop in the child a callous resistance to environmental fluency disruptors. The child is subjected to carefully controlled gradations of environmental pressure of the sort that may be precipitating his particular nonfluencies.

cently has adequate attention been focused upon problems associated with the onset and early treatment of stuttering.

When confronted with a young stutterer,[3] usually it will be necessary for the therapist to deal with the attitudes and behavior of the parents. Those aspects of parental behavior which adversely affect the child and influence his speech must be altered if he is to make a satisfactory adjustment. Lack of collaboration with parents of young stutterers is a shortcoming of many speech therapists. In the school situation, the family may not even be consulted. The young stutterer, however, cannot be disattached and adequately treated apart from his essential relationship with the parents.

A few words of general procedure seem in order before entering into a discussion of the counseling process. To begin with, the therapist must always determine whether the child's speech can rightly be considered disturbed. A careful examination of the child should not only precede the interviews, but is an absolute necessity if we are to guide the direction of the counseling sessions. It would seem both futile and unrealistic, for example, to attempt to convince a parent that her child's nonfluencies are perfectly natural if he is already reacting to his speech, struggling or displaying a habitually excessive degree of tension. If the child's speech is within normal limits, treatment justifiably concerns itself entirely with the parents, their attitudes and speech evaluations.

Brown (*5*) recommends that the examination of the child's speech be done in the presence of the parents and then repeated alone. He continues, 'The behavior of the parents during the child's nonfluencies should be observed, and the child's reactions to their behavior.' The parents may later be asked, 'Is this the sort of thing you're concerned about?' or 'Does he do more of this at home?' Letting parents listen to a recording of their child's speech and asking them to indicate those moments when he is 'stuttering' is often enlightening.

Parents are not likely to come to the speech pathologist with any degree of insight. The novice or over-anxious therapist must constantly remind himself to 'apply the brakes,' so to speak, never exceeding the parent's capacity for learning or acceptance. When parents are lacking in insight, seeking help but unprepared to acknowledge their role, it will often be desirable to have the child brought to the clinic initially, regardless of his speech, and somehow occupied. In this way, parents, waking to an unpleasant situation, are less likely to break subsequent appointments.

The counseling relationship should be structured. Schuell (*25*) suggests a series of at least four interviews with several follow-up conferences at three- to six-month intervals. More conferences may be necessary depending upon the complexity of the problem.

In some cases parent-education groups may be organized, but the limitations of such an approach should be recognized at the outset. Through intimate contact and awareness of the individual problems of parents, more effective counseling is usually accomplished. Clark and Snyder (7) describe the advantages of an informal group therapy program for parents of pre-adolescent stutterers in which a permissive atmosphere prevails and the therapist does a minimum of interpretation. They report, 'Each parent sees faults and shortcomings in the others, he feels less guilty about his own, and is therefore better able to admit them and cope with them.'

The need for bringing the father into active participation in the counseling program is emphasized by Clark and Snyder. A similar observation is made by Glauber (*12*), who reports that 'when the father did take a consistent and active interest in the stuttering child, the prognosis was invariably more favorable.' Clark and Snyder (7), Glauber (*12*) and Despert

[3]The problem of definition is crucial at this point. According to Johnson (*19*), a child, before being classified as a stutterer, should show unmistakable anxiety-tension reactions in relation to his speech nonfluencies and be definitely regarded as a stutterer by his parents, teachers, or other responsible persons. It is, of course, obvious that if parents regard the child as a stutterer they have a definite need for counseling regardless of the actualities of the child's speech.

(*10*) all paint a dominant mother and passive father picture as the typical accompaniment of stuttering. LaFollete (*22*) in this connection reports that the fathers of older stutterers when compared with a control group on the Allport Ascendance-Submission Test showed greater submissive tendencies. Yet the evidence does not warrant the generalizations of Clark and Snyder to the effect that stutterers lack well-defined masculine identification or that they are somehow the victims of a father-child disturbance.

Evaluating the Parents

Some speech therapists never get beyond the 'don't-label-him-a-stutterer' type of counseling. Often, after a period of calm observation, the nonfluencies subside and are recognized as a passing phase toward maturity. But most frequently the need arises for doing more than imparting *do's* and *don't's* or passing out pamphlets. The case history is an important tool of the counselor for discovering and evaluating the significance of causal and precipitating factors related to the stuttering from which productive insight is gained and beneficial modifications can be made in the home environment.

Parents of stutterers are often critical and almost always overeager about the way their child is speaking. It is difficult to pass off these attitudes as mere products of the end result. Considerable information regarding the parents, the child and the home situation needs to be obtained. It is assumed that the reader enters this discussion with some information on the essentials and techniques of effective interviewing. Johnson, Darley and Spriestersbach (*20*) offer some particularly valuable suggestions for case history interviewing of parents of stuttering children.

Simply telling the parents early in the counseling program how stuttering often develops is not nearly as effective as having them trace back, if possible, the onset and development of the problem in their own child. They should be given an opportunity to re-evaluate their thinking in concrete vivid terms related to the child's own history. When did they first focus attention on the child's speech? Just exactly what happened in the *beginning*? Under what conditions? How did it sound? Can the parents imitate it?

With older children the memories of parents are usually hazy. It may not pay to unearth the beginnings, to stir up unstirred guilt feelings. If the parents have not delayed in coming for advice, however, it is often possible to pinpoint the date of their first concern by associating other events with the onset. What parents observe in the beginning are usually simple, relatively effortless repetitions (*8*). They may insist that these repetitions are something the child had never done before, yet most probably he did (*4*). To be correct, then, the initial parental judgment of stuttering is probably coincident with the first attentive observations by the parent of the child's early nonfluencies. We might ask: Why were the parents so attentive? Did they have any reason to be concerned about the child? Was he ill? Did he have an accident? Are the parents inclined to worry generally about their children? Is there stuttering in the family background?

Whatever it was that the child did in the beginning, what did the parents do about it? How did they react to it? Darley (*8*) found that in 48 of 50 families, suggestions calculated to help the child 'overcome his stuttering' were made by one parent or both. The accounts of how parents react, their ways of thinking, are often interesting. They may have the vague notion that what they first noticed and called stuttering continued to occur, that the child constantly 'stuttered' from that point on.

What do parents believe is causing their child to stutter? In many cases this will not tell us a great deal about the child, but it will help us to evaluate and understand the parents and the way they have approached their child's problem. Parents are likely to externalize their problems, project their own anxieties to the child. Darley (*8*) reports, 'Only 16 of 100 parents attached importance to the parental role (not necessarily their own) in the development of the child's stuttering, and not even all of those 16 parents considered that role to be necessarily the primary causal factor.'

So blinded may parents be by a tenacious belief that their child's speech is somehow disordered that they are often unable even to describe what it is he is doing. Their expressed feelings are but verbal blindfolds; they tell us little about the child. 'He stutters.' 'He has difficulty.' 'He starts with the first word wrong.' 'He has good days and bad days.' It is generally a nondescriptive, evaluative language that parents use. They seem to have a particular need to become conscious of the distinction between 'fact' and inference, between description and evaluation.

An understanding of the parents would be incomplete without some idea of their standards of fluency. Bloodstein, Jaeger and Tureen (*3*) report that parents of young stutterers are more inclined to react to nonfluencies as stuttering than are parents of nonstutterers. What concepts do the parents have of normal speech? How do they want Johnnie to talk? How would Johnnie have to be talking before the parents could consider his speech as normal? Such information is not for the counselor's benefit alone; the point cannot be overstressed that these parents need to discover themselves, become aware of their excessively high standards of fluency, and revise them accordingly.

Counseling Program

By now we have given up the search for an unidimensional answer to that all too familiar question, 'What causes stuttering?' We need not fret over subtle dilemmas which have little practical consequence. Whether the child is, as Van Riper (*26*) suggests, being driven to 'the acquisition of adult forms of speech at too early an age,' or, as Johnson (*19*) expresses it, influenced by parents who 'have persuaded themselves that the child's speech is disordered,' is not of life or death importance. In either instance, parents must recognize the essential normality of early nonfluent speech, stop direct attempts at correction, eliminate or reduce apparent fluency disruptors, and give the child a position of love and security in the home. Even the psychoanalysts (*12*) share some common ground as far as treatment is concerned when they attribute stuttering to the maternal relationship and recognize that parents themselves must undergo treatment.

The general objectives of the counseling program thus seem clear. Following the framework suggested by Johnson (*19*), we might reduce our purposes to two basic aims:

1. Parents should be supplied with the information they need in order to appreciate the nature of normal childhood speech. They are helped by knowing the essential facts about normal speech development, especially as far as fluency is concerned. They are helped, too, by knowing about the more important conditions under which children—and adults for that matter—are more and less fluent in speech.

2. Parents should be led, so far as possible, to recognize their own insecurities, their excessive psychological need to have their child speak extremely well and perhaps to excel in other ways too, and, in general, their specific discontents and the reasons for them.

The order in which these two goals have been presented is important. An effective approach involves a *positive* stress, a realistic appraisal of the child's assets. Feelings and behavior deeply rooted in past beliefs are not easily modified. An accusing finger should never be pointed at the past mistakes of parents. It is far better to change the attitudes of parents through a consideration of what Johnnie is doing right, not what they have done wrong. 'They need to be encouraged to accept their child as he is, and to rejoice in his growth and the possibilities of his future,' as Johnson (*16*) has put it.

In order to appreciate fully the part they play in the development or prevention of stuttering, parents must first recognize the essential normality of early speech hesitations. A two-fold problem exists: (1) What sort of information should parents be given? (2) How should this information be presented? Much information relating to stuttering and nonfluent speech behavior is available in texts and research articles (*4,9,17,18,19,23*). Most parents are in want of such information and can usually benefit from it, provided the therapist is sufficiently sensitive to their needs and feelings and has established a warm and open relationship with them. The ingenious therapist must present the necessary information in such a manner that it will be accepted and acted upon by parents.

Nearly two decades ago Carl Rogers (*24*) wrote a few wise words on the limitations of a strict educational approach in dealing with the feelings or emotions of parents:

> To the beginner in clinical work, education of the parent would seem the answer to a great many of the problems which children present . . . . There would seem to be only one real risk to be considered in the use of such techniques. If a parent is given information which runs strongly counter to his own emotionally determined attitudes he will not only reject the information but may reject the worker as well. To this extent a direct educational approach may block further therapeutic effort, and this must be borne in mind in deciding upon treatment.

The futility of imparting on an intellectual level advice which the parents are not emotionally prepared to accept must be recognized. At no time should the parents be cornered or made to feel guilty because of something they have done. Unless diplomacy is used, the parent, once put on the defensive, will immediately be alienated. As Kanner (*21*) says, a mother 'may be thrown into a state of guilty anxiety without comprehending the basic origin of her panic. Nothing is gained even if she expresses verbal agreement. True and helpful insight can come only from within.' Our task is to get the parents implicated but not deeply disturbed, informed but not guilt-ridden.

The interview following the case history is usually devoted to a discussion outlining the development of speech, the normality of repetitions and perhaps a few beginning words concerning our present knowledge of how stuttering develops. Some questions might first be addressed to the parents. 'How many times do you think the average child at the age of two or three repeats (every hundred or every thousand words)?' 'Do you think normal children repeat at all?' After the therapist has secured an idea of what the parents think, they should be told basic information about early speech development. The following transcript, from an interview by Wendell Johnson, may be suggestive:

> There's been a lot of research done on your children and the way they talk and how speech develops. In children between the ages of two and five years, they *all* repeat. Repetition, in fact, begins with the birth cry. The birth cry is repeated over and over again. It has to be. During the first year, depending upon how you define a repetition and allowing for variations, it's pretty accurate to say that about half of all the infant's vocalizations are repetitions. A child doesn't say 'da.' He says 'da-da-da-da.' This is normal. This is utterly normal. This is essential. Without this you would have abnormality.
>
> Now there is no given Tuesday when the child stops it. He does this all his life. Between the ages of two and five years when children are learning to talk in words and sentences they all repeat—sounds, words, phrases. The average child at that age repeats a *s-s-sound* like that or or words like that *or-two or-two or-two* or more words like that. He does this—up to 100 times per 1000 words is within the norm, a little over 100. They all do it. The mean is from 35 to 50 depending on the type of testing situation. Now that's quite a bit, you see.

Berry and Eisenson (*2*) use a somewhat different approach:

> We ask parents to think about and tell us in what activities aside from speaking the child is likely to be repetitious. Parents, through such a procedure, are likely to become consciously impressed that their child, in common with most normal children, can beat a drum *ad nauseam*, can ride a tricycle *around and around and around*, can listen to the same records *over and over and over* again, and can enjoy listening to the same story told or read to them without alteration of word or syllable, time after time and day after day. Parents must be helped to realize the normality of repetition—that its presence in speech is not in and of itself to be evaluated as an abnormal phenomenon.

Often a mother will be found who hesitates a good deal more while speaking than does her child. In such cases, assuming the mother considers herself a nonstutterer, it may be particularly helpful, as Berry and Eisenson (*2*) phrase it, 'to have them turn a mirror and reflect on their own speech.'

Home Situation

Too much hurrying, stimulation and excitement is disrupting for the child and should be avoided whenever possible. Parents should eliminate family quarrels and conflicts in the presence of the child which contribute to an emotionally charged home environment; they need not, however, and should not, shelter the child in an overprotective fashion from all 'undesirable' influences. Gottlober (*13*) gives this exposition of how overprotection may follow the diagnosis of stuttering:

> It is quite common to have a parent report that the patient's blocking becomes more frequent when he suffers a disappointment or is punished. When things go smoothly days pass without a sign of hesitancy. The cause and effect become obvious and gradually the entire family is cudgeled into doing the little despot's bidding. No one wants to be responsible for making him 'stutter.'
>
> If an effort is made to understand and treat a child properly from the beginning, this type of behavior need never develop. By bending over backward later and giving him many times the original attention and sympathy he should have got originally, he is only being encouraged in his maladjustment.

Everyone enjoys being listened to. Parents can help a young stutterer by displaying an interest in his message rather than by registering pity for his difficulty. Speech situations will be less frustrating for the child if parents will refrain from interrupting him before he finishes his thoughts. Of course, if the child, lacking words, finds himself groping for a noun, parents may aid him in building a vocabulary.

Counseling implies more than prohibitions. It is necessary to bring about certain positive, constructive changes in the child's environment. Parents should plan to spend more time together with their child. Schuell (*25*) suggests some activities that might be initiated during the counseling program.

Beasley (*1*) comments:

> While one or the other parent may be with the children almost constantly, the time spent together more frequently involves a doing *for* them rather than a doing *with* them. . . . Often parents can see their way clear to working with the child on a task a teacher may have suggested, or they may spend long hours transporting the child for weekly lessons to a distant center, but they fail to realize the value of a similar amount of time spent with the child for enjoyment and relaxation.

By attracting the child's interest in some useful activity within his realm of achievement, parents can help him experience emotionally satisfying accomplishments. Success breeds self-confidence. Everything should be done at home to give the child successful speaking experiences. The talking he does should be both enjoyable and rewarding. In those situations when the child speaks with relative ease he should be encouraged to talk; when he appears to be unusually nonfluent, it is best not to stimulate him further, although he should never be discouraged.

The constructive aid of parents should be enlisted to discover conditions which exist in the home. Van Riper (*26*) has set forth a list of six everyday situations conducive to nonfluency. It might be useful to mimeograph information of this sort to aid parents in carrying out situational analysis assignments. An effective assignment consists of having parents observe for a week the situations in which their child appears overly hestitant; also, those situations in which he speaks quite fluently. These assignments serve a twofold function: (1) Probably most important, they help parents to separate fact from inference through careful observation. Parents, like all human beings, tend to respond to their own anxiety states. In a sense they are too observant; in another sense, not careful enough in their observations. (2) These assignments aid in the elimination of environmental pressures which disrupt the fluency of the child's speech. By recording these circumstances in detail, detrimental influences can be established and eliminated. Parents will do things differently as they come to recognize and correct their past mistakes.

Caution must always be exercised before upsetting the family situation. The fundamental task is to alter the parental conviction that a child is grossly peculiar if he displays some speech hesitations. The therapist cannot hope to eliminate all of the child's nonfluencies. But the parents can learn to reduce their criterion of what is normal.

Brown (*5*) suggests that parents cultivate an objective attitude by observing the repetitions in the speech of normal children outside the family.

It might be wise to have them actually tabulate the number of interruptions in their child's speech and in the speech of other children. Perhaps the therapist might arrange a visit with the parents to a preschool nursery. To have the concerned parents of a hesitant, yet normal speaking child observe a severe stutterer with pronounced anxiety-tension reactions would further impress upon them how stuttering in the apprehensive adult differs from the simple and relatively unconscious repetitions of all children.

Telling parents to avoid showing concern for the child's speech is not enough. As Johnson (*19*) says, 'They must not be concerned.' And this requires a basic re-evaluation of their attitudes. Quite often parents will insist that they have done nothing to show their concern for the child. But a beginning swimming student, concerned lest he drown, is not likely to float; so too, an anxious mother, deeply disturbed by her child's speech, will find it difficult, if not impossible, to keep a poker face. It should be explained to parents how their evaluations have a self-reflexive effect both upon themselves and upon the child.

It is a good idea to avail parents of literature on stuttering and general semantics to the extent that they can grasp and comprehend the information. Literature, well chosen, is a great help to the intelligent parent and will make subsequent interviews more meaningful by providing an effective basis for communication. Books and pamphlets should not be given out indiscriminately, however, without a consideration of aims and a prior review of their content with the parents.

Summary

Some suggestions, based in large part upon the research and counseling interviews of Professor Wendell Johnson, were outlined for counseling parents of children thought to be stutterers. Central to this discussion has been the suggestion that parents learn to describe the behavior of their children, particularly with respect to speech, apart from their own evaluative reactions. The speech clinician must impart to parents essential information on stuttering and early speech development. In order to make speech a pleasant and rewarding activity for the child, undesirable influences in the environment must be modified and positive changes introduced.

Parent Counseling By Speech Pathologists And Audiologists

Elizabeth J. Webster

Elizabeth J. Webster, Ph.D., is Associate Professor of Speech, University of Alabama, in the Children's Division of the Speech and Hearing Clinic.

In the course of their clinical work speech pathologists and audiologists must have frequent contacts with parents of children with communication disorders. These contacts are a vital part of the clinical role. How clinicians handle them makes a marked difference in the clinical contribution.

Clinicians refer to their work with parents by a variety of terms. For example, Rittenour (1964) distinguishes guidance as the information-giving, recommendation-making functions which help parents define and cope with the facts of their children's problems, and counseling as the process of helping parents "explore and alleviate their sense of helplessness, anxiousness, and self-condemnation." Some clinicians (Matis, 1961) subsume the guidance and counseling functions under the term *therapy*, while others (Bice, 1952; Campanelle, 1965) use *counseling* to refer to all the clinician's work with parents. In this paper *counseling* will be the general term used. Specific functions included under this heading will be outlined in some detail, since the functions a clinician serves are more basic than the label by which they are designated.

Contacts with parents vary in length. Clinicians may have only brief interviews with parents on a one-time basis, as in most diagnostic interviews. Or they may do long-term counseling; that is, they may have continuing, regularly scheduled meetings with individuals or with groups. Contacts with parents also vary in purpose. Clinicians serve such purposes as giving information, assisting parents in coping with issues which face them in light of this information, and helping them clarify their roles with their children. Because these contacts with parents are a vital part of the clinician's contribution, it is imperative that he be conscious both of the nature of his parent contacts and of his goals for each such contact.

The first purpose of this paper, then, is to outline a point of view regarding counseling with parents of children with communication disorders. Because a point of view emerges from the assumptions upon which it is based, some assumptions will be made explicit regarding: 1) parents of children with communication disorders, 2) ways in which counseling can benefit these parents, 3) tools for promoting communication, and 4) the role of the clinician as parent counselor.

The second purpose of this discussion is to suggest ways in which speech pathologists and audiologists can implement this point of view in a continuing series of counseling sessions with groups of parents. A brief assessment will be made of some of the differences between counseling with one person and counseling with persons in a group situation.

Parent Counseling by Speech Pathologists and Audiologists, Elizabeth J. Webster, *Journal of Speech and Hearing Disorders*, Vol. XXXI, No. 4, © Journal of Speech and Hearing Research.

PARENTS OF CHILDREN WITH COMMUNICATION DISORDERS

First it is assumed that whatever other problems these parents may have, they are caught in a vicious circle of breakdown in communication with their child. This assumption is based on the following premises: (1) Wherever there is a speech or hearing problem there is some degree of breakdown in communication. (2) This breakdown leads to difficulties in interpersonal relationships. (3) Difficulties in interpersonal relationships lead to further breakdown in communication.

The parent contributes to the child's problems and vice versa. This statement does not imply that parents are the cause of the child's difficulties with communication. There are numerous causative factors. As Wolpe (1957, p. 1016) states, "It is neither the parents nor the child who are responsible for the emergence of a problem . . . It is a two-way channel, and the parent is neither entitled to total credit nor to total blame for his child's behavior." In any case, whatever has caused the child's communication problem, it can be assumed that at the time clinicians see the child, that child and his parents are experiencing some degree of anxiety in their communication and thus in their relationships with each other.

Parents bring these difficulties with their child to visits with clinicians. When parents seek out speech pathologists and audiologists, they are aware that their child needs help. They may not be seeking help for themselves. Wolpe (1957, p. 1015) postulates that, ". . . anxiety has been mobilized in the parents to the degree that they seek help with the objective of getting the child's behavior so changed that the parental anxiety can be dissipated." Clinicians must recognize that many parents who contact them do not assume at the outset that they need help for themselves.

Many of these parents experience a great deal of guilt. They wonder what has caused their child's problem, how they have contributed to it, what they have done wrong. For example, one mother said with some bewilderment, "I guess I must be treating her wrong—the doctor says so—so does my mother—but I swear I don't know what I've done differently with her than with the other children." Parents also seem afraid that whatever it is they have done to their child, they cannot keep from doing, and so they will continue to "cause the child's problem."

It seems obvious that if parents are laboring with such feelings as guilt, fear, and bewilderment, they must also have defenses against these feelings. Thus it is assumed that they will confront the clinician with some defensive behavior. They may show hostility rather than reveal their anxiety, or appear overly aggressive when they are almost paralyzed by fear.

These parents are trying to cope with their problems in the best ways that they know. However, they can be helped to deal more creatively and productively with those problems. But it must be remembered that parents, not clinicians, do the rearing of the child. Clinicians can serve a vital role in helping parents to clarify issues in their child rearing; they can work to support parents' efforts to do the best that they can do. But to the extent that clinicians openly or subtly demand to take the lead in directing the child rearing, they do in fact devalue the parents and attempt to usurp parental rights.

Finally, it is assumed that parents have in them a drive toward greater health. It is important to help them to recognize this drive, and to permit them to realize their potential for growth. Parents with whom I have worked have had at least four basic motivations which they could be helped to utilize. These are termed basic motivations because they frequently are obscured by such forces as anxiety, guilt, and defensive behavior. The first basic motivation is the desire to do what is right for the child; the second, to understand and accept other human beings, including the child; the third, to communicate more effectively with the child; and the fourth, the desire for fulfillment for themselves as well as for their child.

The first three seem self-explanatory,

but perhaps a word of explanation is needed about the last one. Parents often say such things as, "I live only for the children," "If my child gets better, that's all it will take to make me happy," or "My family is all that matters to me." Often mothers seem to lose themselves in their children. However, the writer's experience is that whatever parents may say, they want to be recognized as unique and worthwhile human beings apart from their roles as parent, housekeeper, bread-winner. They have needs for their own self-growth and satisfaction. One mother illustrated this when she said, "I like it in this group that we use first names. Mostly out places I'm only 'Bryan's mother' or 'Mrs. _________', and here I feel like just me." Another mother, who had questioned her rigidity in making her children, aged seven and twelve, take daily naps, revealed some of her unique needs when she said, "I guess I'm so rigid about the . . . naps because you see this is the only time during the day I can be all by myself . . . my husband is gone and it's different to be alone in your own house, and maybe I'm funny, but I like it . . . and it's different than when he's there at night after the children go to bed." When asked what it meant to her to have time alone, she said, "I don't know that I can say . . . but like free of any worry . . . or to think your own thoughts . . . not to have to talk or answer questions . . . I don't know, it's just the only real freedom I feel all day." As this mother talked it seemed apparent that the nap for the children was not as crucial as was the feeling of freedom for her. Parents have needs for themselves, to be themselves. They can be helped to recognize, understand, and utilize these needs to their greater satisfaction.

WAYS IN WHICH COUNSELING CAN BENEFIT PARENTS

Experience has shown that counseling can help parents modify the vicious circle of poor communication with their child and establish, or re-establish, better communication. There are three important ways that participation in counseling can provide assistance.

First, it can help parents to verbalize frankly about issues in their relationships and forces which motivate them, such as their own needs, goals and fears. Perhaps this is the most important thing that counseling offers parents: it provides them with a situation in which the clinician is willing for them to be themselves, to disclose their own thoughts and feelings, and to speak of their needs, anxieties, fears, joys, and successes. As Beasley (1956) stated, "to the extent that parents themselves are granted acceptance and respect they will be more free to give this to their child . . . Since the problems of a child in language and speech originate and exist in an interpersonal setting, modifications of this environment may be highly important if change in speech is to take place . . . the speech therapist's knowledge and understanding of the parents can do much to bring this about." It is only as parents become aware of their own feelings and of issues in their relationships that they can clarify them. Only as they clarify their part in the relationship can they deal more creatively with their child. Their own openness in communication with an understanding clinician can lead them to communicate more openly with their children. Thus they can participate in creating a different interpersonal setting for communication with the child.

Second, counseling can provide parents with important information. They need facts, simply and honestly presented, about their child's specific disorder. They can begin to clarify issues only when they have this knowledge. This information also can alleviate, at least temporarily, their anxiety and guilt. However, just having facts is not enough. Parents also need help in organizing and assessing what the information means to them.

The third way that participation in counseling can help parents is to provide opportunities for them to experiment with tools for promoting better communication. Clinicians can introduce tools in the counseling situation and encourage their use. However, the professional person's role is that of introduction and experimentation with tools; he cannot make others accept his ideas.

TOOLS FOR PROMOTING COMMUNICATION

It is obvious that every aid the child acquires, be it a hearing aid, pharyngeal flap surgery, or more adequate articulation, also assists the parents. There also are some less obvious tools which parents can acquire to assist them in their communication with their children. Much time should be spent with parents on these more subtle aids, among which are: (1) attempting to understand the child's feelings and to verbalize this understanding to him; (2) trying to accept the child's feelings even when his behavior is unacceptable; (3) giving the child times with the parents when they can concentrate on communicating with him; (4) giving the child opportunities to communicate at times when he has a chance to feel success and satisfaction; and (5) attempting to communicate with the child on his level. Each of these tools will be discussed briefly here.

Attempting to Understand What the Child Feels and to Verbalize This Understanding. Routinely parents say they accept the idea that the verbalization of emotions is an important part of communication. Many, however, do not encourage the expression of emotions, or understand what they might do when the child expresses them. If parents are to communicate more fully with their child, they must acknowledge his emotional, nonrational side. They also must encourage him to verbalize about this. Further, when the parent attempts to put his understanding of what the child might be feeling into words for the child, he promotes better communication between them. In time this will help the child verbalize his feelings for himself. Parents can be helped to speak of their understanding simply and on the child's level. If the clinician is going to encourage the parent to try to verbalize what the child may be feeling, he must also help the parent to practice doing this in a simple and direct fashion.

Trying to Accept the Child's Feelings Even When His Behavior is Unacceptable. It is difficult to differentiate between behavioral symptoms and the emotions experienced by the child; for example, a child may fight when he feels hurt, isolated, or afraid. Parents need help in understanding the implications of this principle. They need many chances to discuss ways that they can limit behavior while still accepting and feeling compassion for the emotions which lead to the behavior.

Giving the Child Times with the Parents When They Can Concentrate on Communicating with Him. Often mothers think that they must devote every waking moment to their children; they cannot freely do this. Often, although they invest a great quantity of time with their children, they are distressed about the quality of the time. A mother expressed it as, "So much of what I say to him is 'don't', or 'you can't' . . . and I'm really not listening to him . . . and he knows my mind is on something else, he feels it . . . and that's bad for him and me both."

Parents can be encouraged to share with the child short periods of time which are the child's to use as he likes. Short times, freely given, can be more productive than longer times when the parent cannot really participate in the child's world. It is the quality rather than the quantity of time for communication between parent and child which makes a significant difference in the child's growth and development.

Giving the Child Opportunities to Communicate at Times When He Has a Chance to Feel Success and Satisfaction. Most parents can be helped quite easily to structure situations which are relatively free from pressure for the child in which he is free to communicate as he can. They can find much for which to give the child genuine praise. Perhaps a mother summed up this point when she reported, "His grandmother came this week-end, and Joe got quiet like always. . . . Only this time I didn't nag him to talk to her like I always do . . . and the more I tell him to talk, the less he talks . . . So, while Joe was watching TV, Mama (the grandmother) asked him what was on, and he told her and told her. My, how he talked! When I told him I thought he talked good to grandma . . . and I really meant it . . . he just said, 'Oh, Mama', but he grinned all over like he really liked it." If children learn from the reinforcement of successful experiences, certainly parents can do much by structuring situations in which the child has a chance to feel that he communicated successfully.

Attempting to Communicate with the Child on His Level. Wyatt (1962) has pointed out that adults help children overcome their communication difficulties by using speech closer to that which the child is using. Often parents seem to think this means they must talk baby-talk to their child. It does not. Parents can best understand the principle of corrective feedback by observing the clinician providing such feedback. Parents' observation of a clinician should be coupled with repeated opportunities to practice behaving in this way.

THE ATTITUDES AND ROLE OF THE COUNSELOR

The essential requisite for those who do counseling is positive regard and respect for the persons they counsel. The clinician must attempt to communicate his faith in the parents' ability to manage their lives productively and meaningfully. He must wholeheartedly attempt to provide a situation in which they feel free to recognize and disclose what is meaningful to them. He must permit them to express their feelings as well as their thoughts. Beasley (1956) says, "The (clinician) should listen to what people are saying—really listen—and attempt to understand the emotional import of the topics parents choose to raise, the problems they describe, the observations they make about their child, and the relationships among family members on which they comment." The clinician's attitudes and verbalizations should encourage the parents' attempts to discover and clarify their ideas and feelings.

The clinician introduces tools that may be helpful to parents. He also takes the lead in attempting to maintain a laboratory situation in which parents may test the use of such tools. Another requisite for the speech pathologist or audiologist who serves as counselor, then, must be broad knowledge of the content of his field. He must be skilled in his clinical area—able to convey facts and to answer questions completely and accurately.

The clinician will make educated decisions about which of parents' questions to answer directly and which ones to help parents explore for themselves. It is no justice to a parent to let him struggle with a question which the clinician's training equips him to answer. For example, direct questions such as, "Is my child's speech development delayed?" deserve a direct answer. The skilled professional person will willingly share his knowledge. He will also give the parent opportunities to talk about what the information means to him. On the other hand, the clinician should know that there are many questions for which there is no one valid answer because they are largely matters of opinion or preference. These are the questions which parents should discuss in order to find their own solutions. For example, the clinician can ask the parent his ideas on such questions as, "What should I do when my child plays with matches?" or "What should I say to him when I can't understand what he's telling me?" Parents will have to do what they can in these matters anyhow; so it seems illogical for the clinician to impose his solutions on them.

The clinician must realize that change takes place slowly. It can be neither forced nor hurried. Parents often verbalize insights long before they do anything about changing their behavior. For example, a mother suddenly realized, "... they say I should be more permissive, and maybe I should . . . (pause) . . . Y'know, I've just gotten the idea I'm too permissive—Why, I'm letting them walk all over me!" This insight did not lead to an immediate change in attitude or solution to the problem; however, it did seem an idea of potential importance to her. If the clinician's goals include helping parents to clarify issues for themselves, he must be patient with the process.

Finally, a word of caution about the content of counseling sessions seems in order. Because so much of parents' verbalization is problem-centered, it is easy to think this is all they want to discuss. Such a problem-centered approach overlooks important aspects of parents' worlds. They also have their joys, successes, humorous incidents, and prideful moments to relate. Parents need to be conscious also of the good that is in their lives. They can learn from this, too. If the clinician tries to remain parent-centered he will listen to what parents choose to talk about—the successes as well as the failures, the joys as well as the problems. He will be able to laugh with them even as he is able to view their suffering with compassion.

THE CLINICIAN'S ROLE IN GROUP COUNSELING

The group situation is similar to the two-person exchange in many ways. In both situations the clinician wants to respect individuals; he wants to understand not only what each person says but also what it means to him. In the multi-person situation this task is more complex because the counselor has to respond to more people. In both situations the clinician wants to introduce tools for their potential value to parents. The number of persons may make this more difficult, as some individuals wish to spend time on one fact, while others are ready to move on.

An advantage of the group situation is that parents often help each other to clarify issues. They offer support to each other. In short, they can serve to provide more than one counselor.

On the other hand, parents may conflict with each other in the group situation. The clinician must decide how he is going to handle these conflicts. He has at least these options: (1) he can ignore negative feelings between persons and go on as if they were not operative; (2) he can make these feelings the only issues which are explored in the counseling time; or (3) he can recognize and verbalize his understanding of the conflicts, and yet not devote the whole of the counseling time to them. The third option seems most desirable. When there are serious communication problems between parents and children, the majority of the counseling time should be used for raising and clarifying these issues. Thus, the effective clinician must hold the attitudes and respect the tools of psychotherapy, but group parent counseling must provide for discussion of issues other than difficulties between group members. Parents need the psychotherapeutic benefits of group membership. However, they also should learn about their child's specific communication disorder. They need help in assimilating the information the clinician has to offer them. They need chances to discuss what their child's problem means to them. Therefore, the clinician must provide a structure which permits parents to disagree with each other, but he must provide also for discussion of important content which is unique to these people.

If parents are to learn from each other, there must be group interaction. The clinician leads in developing a group climate which fosters both verbal interaction and the trust necessary to disclose thoughts and feelings. The clinician cannot provide for group interaction by lecturing. Neither does he encourage it by remaining the dominant member of the group. He must be willing to relinquish some of his authority. The clinician sets the example for the group by honoring the contributions of each parent. He often returns questions to them for discussion rather than attempting to give all the answers. Skill in handling questions makes a vast difference in how quickly group members talk with each other rather than just with the clinician. The clinician notices and reinforces group members' support of each other and their attempts to understand and clarify the statements of another.

Care must be taken not to overlook parents who find it difficult to talk in a group. The more quiet people must be helped not to feel isolated. The clinician can honor the ways that they do participate; for example, he can note a person nodding in agreement, or frowning as if puzzled about a point, and ask him to verbalize his thoughts. If he wants to help the quiet people talk more, he must let them do it as they feel they can. He must guard against putting them under so much pressure that he further diminishes their ability to verbalize. It may be helpful to the clinician to remember that problem-solving can also begin in silence.

The clinician must remain part of the discussion group. If he refuses to engage in discussion, to share himself, and to give examples, he separates himself from the group and is less useful. In group counseling as in work with individuals, the clinician maintains a position which is not scolding or preaching, neither is it laissez-faire. Rather, he is an open, warm, accepting participant.

CONCLUSION

The question sometimes arises, "Can't the speech pathologist or audiologist do damage to parents by attempting to counsel with them?" The answer depends in part on how one defines counseling. If counseling means the imposition of prescriptions without care for the person for whom they are prescribed, one may indeed do damage. The nonaccepting, noncompassionate clinician runs the risk of hurting parents; so does the one who focuses concern on the child to the exclusion of concern for the parents. The speech pathologist or audiologist who leaves to others the interpretation of the information his field has to offer may do parents great harm. The same can be said for the clinician with limited knowledge who gives faulty information.

On the other hand, it is virtually impossible for one person to damage another by listening to him, by trying to understand what the world looks like to him, by permitting him to express what is in him, and by honestly giving him the information he needs. In this view of counseling, the clinician serves as an accepting listener. He delays his judgment of parents and tries to accept them as they are and as they will become. Further, the clinician uses the tools and knowledge of his profession, as well as his clinical concern for parents. Whatever tools the clinician chooses to introduce, his goals should include helping parents increase their consciousness of their own attitudes, feelings, and behavior. As parents become more conscious of these factors, they can clarify issues in their communication with their children. Thus they can create a different interpersonal situation in which their children communicate.

Finally, for some parents clarification of issues leads to marked modifications of behavior; for others it does not. And the clinician cannot know with certainty which of these outcomes will prevail. If he demands sweeping or rapid changes, he will be doomed to frequent disappointment, just as he will be if he sees no improvement. These are sobering and humbling realities. At this stage of knowledge the clinician who counsels parents must have, or acquire, a tolerance for the ambiguous results of his counseling efforts.

Perhaps a prime requisite for the speech pathologist or audiologist counseling parents is respect for himself as a participant in a drama of which the final act has not been written, but in which his role may make a vital difference.

Procedures for Group Parent Counseling in Speech Pathology and Audiology

Elizabeth J. Webster
University of Alabama
University, Alabama

Much of the parent counseling done by speech pathologists and audiologists involves one clinician interacting with one set of parents for one or two conferences. This type of counseling occurs, for example, in diagnostic interviews where the speech pathologist or audiologist and the parents of a child with a communication disorder discuss the child's disorder, the results of speech and/or hearing testing, and the clinician's recommendations.

In addition to such individual contacts, many clinicians also are called upon to counsel groups of parents of children with communication disorders. Often this group work is done on a continuing or long-term basis; that is, a group of parents is seen for a specified number of sessions, perhaps regularly for the length of time that their children are enrolled for speech and/or hearing therapy.

Earlier (Webster, 1966), I discussed assumptions upon which both individual and group parent counseling may be organized and suggested tools which may be introduced to parents. I suggested that the clinician: (1) works to implement attitudes of respect and support for parents, (2) encourages and supports parents' attempts to verbalize and to clarify issues relating to communication with their children, (3) provides necessary information, and (4) is aware of his limitations in counseling.

My purpose here is to suggest how group discussion and role-playing can be utilized in working with groups of parents in the setting of a speech and hearing program, particularly with groups of parents seen for long-term counseling.

GROUP DISCUSSION

Informal discussion is the chief medium in group parent counseling. Such informal discussion is facilitated by holding parent meetings in a room with comfortable furniture and chairs arranged so that each person can see all other persons in the group.

The clinician implements his belief that the group exists to serve parents by asking them to bring topics for discussion and by encouraging them to verbalize their concerns and questions. The clinician serves as discussion leader who insures that each parent has a chance to speak and who encourages group members to listen and respond to the speaker. The clinician must remember that parents have varying skills in verbalization and must not require all to be equally sophisticated in discussion.

The clinician helps to build a positive group spirit by pointing out similarities in the concerns felt by different parents. Initially parents tend to think of the differences between them; but as McDonald (1962) pointed out, when the clinician gives parents the opportunity to discuss that which is important to them, they find much commonality in their concerns, fears, disappointments, and hopes. Further, when parents are encouraged to discuss topics they select, discussions usually move from being almost exclusively child-centered to being more parent-centered; that is, parents discuss their children less and discuss themselves more.

The clinician's leadership is not just laissez-faire leadership. He shares responsibility for bringing discussion topics to the group and introduces content that he considers important. The clinician is the only group member aware of some information that parents should know, and he should not assume that parents can discover and explore all of this content by themselves. For example, the mother of a child with a repaired cleft palate told a group that her son was to have pharyngeal flap surgery during the next school vacation, and she was worried about "what it is for and what it will do to him." The clinician realized the mother needed information, so he explained the procedure and its potential benefits. When he had finished, the mother said, "Good. I understand the reason for it, and some of the mystery is taken away." The point here is that a speech pathologist or audiologist shares the knowledge which he feels might be helpful to parents, whether or not they suggest such content for discussion.

It is the clinician's responsibility to introduce tools he thinks will help parents. In an earlier article I suggested introducing the following tools for promoting better parent-child communication: (1) listening to try to understand what the child thinks and feels; (2) trying to accept the child's thoughts and feelings while not necessarily accepting his behavior; (3) trying to verbalize understanding of the child's feelings; and (4) trying to verbalize to the child more on his level rather than on an adult level (Webster, 1966).

These tools can be discussed in a variety of ways. For example, in parent groups that I conduct, the tool of listening to try to understand is introduced early. I ask parents to try to understand the meanings of events to their children and to speculate about the feelings their children have in certain situations. Parents are asked to practice this way of listening to each other as they talk in the group and to try to verbalize their understanding of the meanings and feelings conveyed by other parents. Then parents are given the assignment of listening to and trying to understand a person outside of the group and of reporting their experience to the group. This reporting provides another possibility of free group discussion. For example, one mother reported,

> Sunday when people were visiting, Jim walked around saying, "I'm so big, I'm so big," over and over. I was about to holler at him to quit when I thought about how we were supposed to understand what somebody was feeling, so I tried to figure it out. I guess (he felt) good, and big, and maybe real proud to show off.

Another mother told the group,

> I ran into the grocery in a big hurry and ran into a woman I hadn't seen in months, and she started telling me her troubles with her son, and I got so interested listening to her (she reported some information the woman gave her and commented at length about the compassion she felt for the woman). It got me in trouble, though . . . my husband was so mad when I was late getting home.

Experience indicates that these listening assignments serve to promote discussion about such related topics as: times when parents really have listened to others, times they have refused to listen or have been too busy to do so, and about how they feel when people won't listen to them. Such practice exercises can serve the clinician's purposes of helping parents increase their group interaction and discussion, their awareness of the feelings of others, and their ability to verbalize such awareness.

However, it should be noted that the clinician who encourages parents to speculate about their children's emotions must not lead them to assume either (1) that their children experience the same emotions they do, or (2) that they can know positively what their children feel. Rather, the clinician helps parents to speculate about the emotional realms of children. He also supports the recognition by many parents that emotions are acceptable even though some of the resultant behaviors are unacceptable.

ROLEPLAYING

A second procedure for working with parent groups is roleplaying—that is, the acting out or demonstrating of situations. The clinician should point out to parents that he is asking them to participate in a demonstration process; he probably should not dwell on the label for the process, as it often symbolizes to people that they must be actors. The clinician's goals in roleplaying are to help parents gain understanding of behavior and to experiment with varied behavioral approaches to situations.

Roleplaying involves three steps: (1) the warm-up period, in which the leader helps the group delineate the situation to be acted out, assigns roles, and helps each person begin to create his role; (2) the actual acting out of the situation; and (3) discussion of the situation. This often is a circular process, in that new situations to be "roleplayed" may be suggested in the discussion.

Discussion is an integral part of roleplaying, used both in the initial warm-up period and in the final step of the procedure. However, roleplaying goes farther than discussion in that it requires bodily action. One value of roleplaying is that it provides for participation at the level of demonstration as well as at the level of discussion. As Wolpe states, "Unlike a discussion group, which often remains solely on an intellectual level, role enactment insures emotional participation in the very dramatic management of the scene. . . ." (1957, p. 1008). Another value is that roleplaying "is here and now, natural and spontaneous" (Corsini et al., 1961).

Although roleplaying has the advantage of encouraging emotional involvement, it also has limitations, and the clinician must use this procedure with caution and sensitivity. Many people are terrified by the thought of being asked to act out a role; this fear will probably prevent them from exploring ideas through the medium of roleplaying without a great deal of help from the clinician. Again, parents may feel anxious about revealing negative aspects of themselves. Another danger arises from the fact that roleplaying may reveal differences between people, and may induce feelings of separation in parents who disagree with the majority of the group. The clinician must be skillful enough to help parents cope with such feelings. Further, parents often assume that there are right and wrong ways to play roles. If the clinician also holds this assumption and insists that parents play a role in the "right" way, he puts tremendous pressure on them and probably defeats his purpose of helping them clarify their ideas and behaviors.

Perhaps the greatest danger in roleplaying is the opportunity it affords the clinician to manipulate parents. The clinician who uses this procedure must continue to re-examine his attitudes, for he cannot disguise his negative judgment of certain parents, his hostility toward others, or his demands that parents change. Such attitudes will show in what he asks a parent to do in the way of roleplaying. For example, if the clinician's bias is that a mother is to blame for her child's communication problem, he can easily manipulate the roleplayed scenes so that the mother shows up poorly.

It is imperative that before the clinician uses roleplaying he must have experienced the playing of roles himself, as it is through his own experience that he will understand the nature of roleplaying and its potential benefits and dangers. However, in professional practice the clinician usually should not participate in the actual playing of roles. Rather he should serve as director or leader, because when he is involved in the action he is less able to respond to the whole group and to see many sides of the situation in an unbiased manner.

Situations to be roleplayed often arise from parents' discussion. For example, the father of a deaf boy reported that he thought people often stared at his child and several other parents stated that this was a problem for them, too. The clinician suggested that this father show what his son did, asked another parent to be a person staring at the child, and asked a third person to play the father. The three roleplayed a situation in a grocery store. In the ensuing discussion parents stated what they thought each participant felt in the roleplayed situation, thus giving them an opportunity to clarify their impressions.

In addition to suggesting the roleplaying of situations which have been discussed, the clinician may suggest that parents roleplay situations which illustrate specific points. For example, the clinician can ask parents to explore the use of simple language patterns with children through the role-playing of situations in which they attempt to speak in a simplified fashion. The tool of listening to understand can be illustrated through role-playing a situation in which one person tries to listen to another. Through role-playing the clinician can help parents to experiment with such concepts of discipline as that of trying to provide freedom within limits. For example, in groups I conduct, parents are assigned to report on one time that they were able to set and maintain a rational limit, stating why they set the limit, how they explained it, and why they felt good about the incident. Some parents have reported verbally on their experience, while others have shown (i.e., roleplayed) what happened.

Corsini points out that roleplaying can be used by clinicians of various theoretical orientations (1966). He gives suggestions for ways of introducing and conducting roleplaying (Corsini et al., 1961).

The clinician must remember that all group members need not roleplay in order to benefit from the procedure. Often persons who have not participated in the action have contributed quite easily to the discussion, thus participating in a way which is comfortable for them. Further, many parents have reported that, although they were unable to participate either in the action or in the discussion, some of their ideas were clarified from watching others roleplay. Clinicians should respect and accept a parent's refusal to participate in roleplaying, and should consider it as reflecting that parent's need.

The judicious use of discussion and roleplaying, then, provides the speech pathologist or audiologist with procedures for helping parents explore and clarify both their ideas and their behaviors.

REFERENCES

CORSINI, R. J., *Roleplaying in Psychotherapy*. Chicago: Aldine (1966).

CORSINI, R. J., SHAW, M. E., and BLAKE, R. R., *Roleplaying in Business and Industry*. New York: The Free Press (1961).

GINOTT, H. G., *Between Parent and Child*. New York: MacMillan Co. (1965).

MCDONALD, E. T., *Understand Those Feelings*. Pittsburgh: Stanwix House (1962).

WEBSTER, ELIZABETH J., Parent counseling by speech pathologists and audiologists. *J. Speech Hearing Dis.*, **31**, 331-340 (1966).

WOLPE, ZELDA, Play therapy, psychodrama, and parent counseling. In L. Travis (Ed.), *Handbook of Speech Pathology*. New York: Appleton (1957).

A Hearing Impaired Child in the Family
The Parent's Perspective

Ellen B. Liversidge

Gregory M. Grana

Mr. Grana is a parent counselor at the Mama Lere Home Parent Teaching Program of the Bill Wilkerson Hearing and Speech Center, Nashville, Tenn. Mrs. Liversidge, the parent of a young hearing impaired daughter, Gray, lives in Burlington, Vt. Their descriptions of parent viewpoints toward the problems and challenges related to a child's deafness were given at the 1972 A. G. Bell Association National Convention as part of the session on "A Comprehensive Educational Program: Infant/Pre-Primary." The session was chaired by (Mrs.) Kathryn B. Horton, Chief of Language Development Programs at the Bill Wilkerson Center.

A Mother's Perspective

To discuss, from a mother's perspective, the implications of a child's hearing loss, I have taken a trip back in time to December 1967 when our experience with deafness first began. I have also thought back to the many fine conversations I have since had with other mothers of deaf children, and to all the things these mothers have shared with me and taught me.

I will begin by telling you our own story, as there is too much variation in individual reactions to generalize. I remember sitting in the hospital trying to think what spinal meningitis meant; all we could come up with at that frightening time was that it sounded horrifying and that there were epidemics at army camps. Once the fear of our daughter Gray's dying was over, I spent long hours in the hospital library morbidly reading about all the possible after-effects of meningitis and attempting to prepare myself for the worst. After Gray started to respond and sit up again, I noticed that, as I entered her room at the hospital, she didn't turn her head to the sound of my voice. I was filled with a sick feeling, for I had read of deafness as a possible result of meningitis.

Sharing my suspicions with the pediatrician, I was somewhat reassured when he told me children are often temporarily deafened by meningitis, and that the hearing would probably return gradually as she became stronger. Nothing changed after Gray came home, although we imagined that her hearing was slowly coming back. For a time we would sneak around behind her back and bang things to see if she would respond.

Finally the time came for an audiological assessment. When she was first diagnosed as having a severe sensorineural loss, I reacted with hostility and would not accept the verdict. When a well-meaning social worker asked me how I felt that day, I recall having said something nasty. Gray was then scheduled for a re-evaluation, and this time, before we went, I contacted an old friend of the family who was an audiologist and asked for his opinion. He told me that, in his experience, deafness as a result of meningitis was permanent in every case. I had a good cry by myself at

A Hearing Impaired Child in the Family: The Parent's Perspective, Ellen B. Liversidge and Gregory M. Grana, *Reprinted from Volta Review*, Vol. 75, March 1973, Official Journal of the Alexander Graham Bell Association for the Deaf, Inc.

home that night, then set about my task of convincing the rest of the family that it was true. This was difficult, particularly with one set of grandparents who were convinced that we should only rent hearing aids and "wait and see."

The trips in and out of Philadelphia with Gray for fittings and, later, for auditory training were taxing and exhausting. I wanted to know what to do and I read books voraciously; yet I consistently felt that what I was doing wasn't quite right or adequate. It was a long, bleak, and lonely winter. I am sure other mothers have experienced some of the feelings of apprehension that were mine. All the help seemed to center on Gray, and I experienced feelings of isolation and fatigue. I became very engrossed in "the problem"; yet much of me wanted it just to go away. I know of one mother who went back to school to learn about the problem – but also to escape it. Most mothers and fathers who are able to receive early comprehensive counseling and information can ease through this period fairly quickly and learn to channel their energies constructively.

acceptance and positive action

The point of positive action finally came for me the following summer when Gray changed therapists and we were fortunate to be involved in a program which combined the qualities of practical, natural language therapy, shoulders to cry on, good humor, and occasional home visits. Gray began to gather language, the hearing aids no longer seemed like mysterious, buzzing boxes, and we no longer thought that she looked rather unfamiliar with them on. We began to accept – and to help others accept – her hearing loss. We gradually learned what Gray could and could not hear, tried and discarded concepts of what "working with Gray" meant, and finally evolved a comfortable, natural approach. As Gray would tag along with us during the day, we would talk in simple and complete sentences about what was happening. The most formal "work" that was done involved sitting down to do puzzles and to read stories. Gray continued to blossom in her language development and personality, began to sleep better at night, and became *Gray – a child with a hearing loss* – rather than a puzzling enigma: a deaf child.

sharing ideas and experiences

Of great therapeutic value at this early stage was the time I spent with another mother of a deaf child. She had been through these early emotional and medical experiences and could offer support and advice from a personal yet more objective vantage point. Most mothers want to know everything that they can right away; yet, it takes time to assimilate all the information. The need to share the often painful experiences and feelings is very strong. It can be encouraging and comforting, for example, to know that another mother eventually overcame her sensitivity toward her child's hearing aids being stared at in the supermarket.

From the outset it is very important to consider the whole family constellation – father, mother, deaf child, and siblings – when mapping counseling and educational plans. Fathers are too often overlooked and, in a sense, shut out from the learning and decision-making processes. They are too seldom given the opportunity or encouragement to become involved, and their wives are often their only source of information. This can place a tremendous burden on the wife and decrease the possibilities for husband and wife to share in the often frustrating, sometimes joyous process of raising a deaf child. This problem is being recognized now in many places throughout the country. In Vermont, where we now live, every effort is being made to include fathers and to enable them to interact with each other as well as with their wives and professionals. Most respond eagerly to this inclusion. The parent orientation sessions often help the husband and wife learn to interact and communicate with each other more successfully in matters concerning the hearing impaired child.

The need for information and emotional support is great from the very beginning. First questions range from the guilt-ridden "How did this happen to us – to our child?" to queries about audiograms, hearing aids, and the future. I was very fortunate in these early days to have not only another mother to share feelings with, but also an audiologist who took pains to teach me much about hearing and deafness, lessons and personal letters from the John Tracy Clinic, and correspondence with the Volta Bureau. Yet, as I look back, I can see that a cohesive, comprehensive educational program for the whole family would have been of even greater benefit to all of us.

I have heard many mothers say that their early information was very misleading and incomplete. This was expressed also in George Fellendorf's paper, "The Inseparable Twins – Early Diagnosis and Parent Counseling." In more than 80% of the families he surveyed, the parents or grandparents first suspected that something was wrong with the child and then took him to a doctor for diagnosis. Only 9% of the responses indicated that it was the medical doctor who first suspected a problem. The advice given by doctors varied: "Just wait." "Take his tonsils out and he'll be okay." "Don't do anything – he'll talk when he's ready." One of my friends was told simply that "boys talk late," even after her son had had meningitis. Another who had suffered rubella early in the fourth month of pregnancy had been told by her obstetrician that there was no danger after the first trimester. She was bitter for a time, for she had not looked for any complications and had thus lost valuable time for amplification and language development. It might seem strange that the task of educating others and pressing for a favorable, receptive environment for deaf children should fall, to a great extent, to us as parents. Yet we are the ones who understand the problem most intimately and who have the greatest emotional commitment.

reaching a turning point

There seems to be a turning point for mothers when they have overcome the initial heartache and confusion, when they understand deafness and language in terms of their own child, and when they feel competent and knowledgeable in working with, loving, and managing their child. Progress toward this point is gradual, yet it is a nice level of sophistication to reach. There are continuing needs – to trade experiences with other parents, to pinpoint evolving requirements for the child, to reassess the child's amplification needs, and to re-evaluate educational placement and goals. Having reached this turning point, many mothers are of immeasurable value in counseling others who are still in the early stages of coping and learning. Some mothers have enough energy left over to devote time to the organizational aspects of their parents' group, to push for favorable legislation in their states, or to contribute knowledge toward informing the public. These are often therapeutic activities – filling a need to spread to others what has been learned and to prepare a more accepting and understanding climate for future parents and deaf children.

One very positive outgrowth of having gained perspective on a child's deafness and the scope of his handicap is the dawning of awareness of the child's uniqueness and specialness. Nowhere have I seen this more eloquently expressed than in Paul West's book, *Words for a Deaf Daughter*, in which Mr. West learns to explore and share his daughter's special, rather surreal world. To his daughter Mandy, who is autistic as well as deaf, he says:

> Tasting-testing with you, I have found new ways into the world. You discover what you discover because you have lost what you've lost; or, rather, you recover what men have lost precisely because they neglect to use something which you never even had and therefore could not "lose." I tag along on your voyages of exploration, and together we sneak into the randomness, the arbitrariness, of the universe as distinct from its patterns. . . . You have taught us the virtue of play for play's sake, and, as it were, have commandeered our senses, so that we hoard impressions and bits of offbeat information on your behalf, longing to tell you and hoping that, one day, we will.*

With my own daughter, I am constantly impressed, and renewed, by her sense of color and form, her appreciation of the smallest bug or flower, her love of collecting rocks and sticks and bringing them all into the house as treasures. I am moved by her earnest questions about how much others can hear – one night while lying in bed without her hearing aids, she asked me if I could hear her from the next room, from upstairs, from the kitchen. Her growing awareness and matter-of-fact acceptance of her hearing loss provide all the courage a parent could ever need. When another child asks Gray about her hearing aids, she explains in simple, unaffected terms that she can't hear very well without them. Her boisterous, unique nature is a gift to those who know and love her. Other mothers have shared with me similar thoughts about their own children – their lack of guile, their ability to love the smallest thing in nature, the special joy their presence can bring to a family. For a mother, it is a fulfilling experience to have this kind of appreciation for one's deaf child. None of us as mothers would have chosen to be the parent of a deaf child – it can be exhausting both emotionally and physically; yet, because of our children, our lives are far richer and more exciting than any of us might have imagined possible.

**Words for a Deaf Daughter*, Paul West. New York: Harper & Row, 1970.

A Father's Perspective

In its efforts to prepare parents to work effectively with a hearing impaired child, the Bill Wilkerson Hearing and Speech Center recognizes and emphasizes the importance of the father's role. More and more, fathers have impressed us with their concern and sense of responsibility toward meeting the immediate and future needs of their children.* They have said: "I need to know there is something I can do and to know what to do." "We brought the child into the world, and we must do all we can." "We owe the best care to the child." "A man will try anything to help his child." One grandfather who drives for two hours each month to attend the Saturday workshops for fathers reflected this attitude when he said:

> I think my two grandchildren are something special because they are going to have to make a life for themselves. Not having had any experience with the deaf, I hardly know just what to do to help them. I want them to know I love them, although I have 13 other grandchildren to love; so I can't be too partial to them. I do try to teach them more about different things than I would a child who can hear. It is something we have to live with.

---

*My comments are representative of the experiences of 12 families over a year's time. Supporting these findings are the teaching staff's six years of contact with numerous other families.

The fathers realize that while they may previously have operated on one set of life plans, they must now prepare to shift to new ones. Their first comments in a parent education session are often: "Tell us what to do and we'll do it." "Knowing what to do is half the struggle." It is not surprising, then, that the fathers in our parent education program chose as their first priorities "information on ways to aid our children" and opportunities to "share problems and ways to meet them." Eager to begin, they immediately requested a schedule for appointments with a teacher to demonstrate under the instructor's guidance their individual ways of talking to their children.

Fathers also ask to be taught how to aid mothers in working with the child. Often a father will admit that he is at a complete loss as to what to do, especially when his wife feels a large measure of guilt or responsibility for the condition of the child and any lack of progress. Fathers seek ways to develop and strengthen the coordination of the roles of both parents in supporting and encouraging the child. One man said: "I feel guilty when I can't be at home very much during the week to help. And when my little girl is sick, I know that it's especially difficult for my wife." Another asked, "How can I help my wife cope with her everyday life at home?" When that question was discussed during a father's workshop, the group suggested:

1) plan time for your wife to do for herself as she wishes;

2) plan time as a couple, without the children;

3) check out your own feelings before entering home after work, and try to be aware of what your wife's day has been like – then let each other know how you feel before dealing with important matters;

4) give your wife an opportunity to report to you not only her learnings from individual sessions with the child, but her feelings as well.

looking toward the future

While they concentrate heavily on the present, fathers also have a strong future orientation. If they have never before had contact with deaf persons, they have little experience on which to base long-range plans. After learning of a child's deafness, a father may ask himself, "What kind of schooling will it take?" "Where?" "I guess we'll have to move!" "I wonder what work I can find to do there." Looking toward the future, fathers may counsel each other to "set your goals high." But later in their meetings they will wonder aloud, "Will she be happy?" "Will he have normal children of his own?" "Will he be able to earn a living?" This last question sent sparks flying at one parent session when a significant portion of the discussion dealt with a father's experience with the door-to-door "panhandling" sales of a deaf adult. Reminiscent of a scene in Joanne Greenberg's book, *In This Sign,** the fathers demonstrated irritation and resentment toward deaf persons who present an unproductive image. While the fathers thought society's views of, and vocational aid to, the handicapped had improved, they nevertheless expressed an attitude that there is "no excuse for this sort of thing."

Some fathers are concerned with hiding their worries from the world and from their wives. Society's image of the strong and silent male takes its toll. Fathers may reason: "Well, you know, women take things harder than men." "Someone's got to be the stronger of the two." "If I showed any sympathy, any weakness, we'd lose ground." And their wives in turn may observe: "He keeps things to himself." "He doesn't show his feelings." "He's a lot more tender inside than he lets on." In a fathers' discussion group, as these men watch others wrestle with similar struggles,

******In This Sign*, Joanne Greenberg. Holt, Rinehart & Winston, 1970.**

they abandon the pretense that there are really no problems and that they've never been bewildered and confused.

working with the hearing impaired child

Many fathers' concerns center on child management. While they may be embarrassed by questions and stares at the child's hearing aids, they may be even more upset by a child's temper tantrums. "I cannot allow my child's handicap to influence discipline," said one father, "but what do you do when you try not to be overprotective and then get that guilty feeling that you've been too hard on your child, who may not have understood?" Much time in the parent sessions has been spent discovering methods to encourage appropriate behavior. These included: 1) Be alert to behavior which is desirable and which you would like to have repeated. Immediately encourage the child with attention, praise (in words smiles, hugs, pats on the back) or other kinds of responses or consequences perceived by the child as pleasing. 2) Remember there are some behaviors which at first do not occur in full-blown, complete form. Recognize the small, sequential steps and demonstrate them for your child. Encourage him to try and keep trying until he masters each step. Be satisfied to help him learn these small steps without punishing mistakes. Repeat the method over a period of time until the child has learned the whole.

Fathers also wonder what explanations should be offered to their other children and to friends of their children, when and how much to tell their own friends or an inquisitive stranger, and what to say to relatives who continue to deny the child's hearing impairment. In sharing their efforts at explanation, the fathers made these suggestions: 1) Children can understand that ears can be "broken" and that "boxes and wires" help to fix them. 2) Brief and to-the-point statements outlining the diagnosis, treatment, and prognosis, have been found to be more comfortable and appropriate than those which leave the door open to misunderstandings on the part of strangers, friends, or even relatives who may wish to remove the hurt by denial.

In later sessions, with words filled with frustration, the fathers will share their experiences of repeated attempts to explain that the child will not talk immediately upon receiving hearing aids and that progress will be slow. "It's never easy," said one father, "for people to understand that you're not just turning up the volume. They have to picture my 3-year-old as a new-born."

While all the fathers watch carefully for progress, their degrees of expectation vary. One father will ask, "Do you think he will learn to talk?" Another will state, "I've no doubt that my daughter is going to talk." In many subtle and not so subtle ways they challenge, "What and who is responsible for progress?" Early in the program, a father who was not a very active participant compared his child with another who had made more progress. He turned to his wife and asked, "What are you doing wrong?" Later, he came to understand that other factors were involved. Where progress is so closely monitored, patience has become the fathers' watchword.

challenging assumptions to promote interaction and cooperation

These concerns have encouraged us at the Bill Wilkerson Center to emphasize the contributions of the father in our parent program. Thus, instead of reiterating that "fathers really oughta wanna," we have been trying to determine what creates the discrepancy between the actual and desired involvement of the fathers. Contributing to this discrepancy, we feel, are three questionable assumptions, which deserve to be challenged:

1) fathers are primarily providers and are not everyday interactors with children younger than 3 years old;

2) fathers will not be able to supply much helpful information about children;

3) fathers will be able to obtain all the information they need from mothers.

ASSUMPTION NO. 1

In the past, society has been reluctant to ascribe to fathers those functions which women have, by interest, time, and nature, been considered better able to provide. Questioning this assumption, however, one father strongly declared, "I want to be trained just as well as my wife." In regard to time spent with the child, another father commented, "My concentrated work with my daughter during the week and on the weekend can make it more 50-50 rather than 80-20 between my wife and myself." If a program acknowledges this assumption and serves to educate only the mothers, the fathers withdraw. "Honey, you know how to do it better." "I really don't know how." "As my wife learns more, I am not able to relate effectively to my daughter." Apparently, where society and society's institutions, including parent programs, emphasize the role of mothers almost exclusively, fathers may take a step back and let things be, quickly learning not to try where they are not made to feel wanted. Yes, there is a difference between saying a person is "welcome anytime" and inviting him to an occasion planned specifically with him in mind.

ASSUMPTION NO. 2

Educators are learning to rely more and more on parents' descriptions of the child and his interaction with his environment. However, they need to know what *both* parents know. Why is it, then, that when a couple is interviewed about their young child, the mother is more often encouraged to answer by the interviewer's eye contact with her or by his turning or facing in her direction? Is it assumed that "mother knows best"? In such small but significant ways in the very beginning, a father may soon learn non-involvement. It may be a professional concern not to embarrass him with questions that he may not be able to answer; yet the mother is only one-half of the two participant-observers in the home. A heavy reliance on information from mothers who work outside the home also carries a great risk. And, in many instances, fathers have been known to be the first to suspect or identify a loss of hearing, to note developmental delays in other areas, and to monitor closely the child's progress.

ASSUMPTION NO. 3

This assumption may be rooted in a concern not to demand time away from the typical "breadwinner's" job, especially for those families of low income. However, when programs and methods of intervention are designed almost solely with the mother in mind, her additional burden of educating the father may prove unbearable. It is difficult for some mothers to shift to the "teacher" role with their husbands. Also, there may be few opportunities for lengthy and uninterrupted conversation between mother and father. Even when time is available, difficulties in communication between parents often arise under stress, blocking the transfer of information and discouraging the mother's own application. When fathers have been asked for information which was originally given to mothers, the results have been disappointing. Also, fathers who do not participate on a firsthand basis lack the opportunity and experience to develop necessary skills for working with the child. Secondhand information and experiences do lose in translation. Fathers press mothers, "Is that really the way I'm supposed to do it?" And many debriefing sessions at home conclude with, "Well, I just wish you had been there!" Fathers say: "I guess it's necessary for my wife to go alone at times when I can't get away, but I'd rather know firsthand." "I learn better by coming here." "I find it helpful to talk to other fathers who understand." And mothers have said: "It wouldn't be the same without my husband in the program." "I can't do it alone." "You just have to work together as husband and wife!" Still, some of these same mothers may know or feel that the father holds them primarily responsible for the child's learning.

It is not certain where the questioning of these assumptions will lead. Surely, however, in a day in which life styles of couples are changing, to say "parents" must mean "father" too. An uneducated or untrained parent is an intervention obstacle which at best neutralizes the efforts of the other parent or at worst destroys by discouragement. Where both parents are informed and skilled, intervention is strengthened by mutual understanding and support.

We're learning to plan with both parents in mind. The individual sessions with the child are attended by mother and/or father. Parent meetings are for *both* mother and father, and there is a father's monthly workshop on Saturday. If there is one definite thing that these sessions have taught us, it is that we have not yet arrived at our final objective – the fathers are still educating us to find ways to meet their needs.

Early Childhood Services for Visually Impaired Children: A Model Program

ABSTRACT: A program of services for young visually impaired children and their parents, including diagnosis and intervention strategies, was established with a three-year grant under Title III of the Elementary and Secondary Education Act in the Montgomery County (Maryland) Public Schools. The program includes a full spectrum of educational services for the children and counseling and training for the parents. Based upon independent validation by the U.S. Office of Education, the project is now a fully-funded part of the vision services provided by the school system and serves as a national demonstration site. Project materials, including assessment booklets, intervention manuals, and a social services document, are currently being field tested in various parts of the United States.

ROSEMARY O'BRIEN

Ms. O'Brien is project director and supervisor, Vision Services, Montgomery County (Maryland) Public Schools.

Origin

A program for young visually impaired children and their parents, funded under Title III of the Elementary and Secondary Education Act for a three-year period beginning in 1971, was implemented as a part of the vision services program of the Montgomery County (Maryland) Public Schools. Any child, from birth to school readiness or eight years of age, is admitted if his vision is judged to be sufficently impaired that it (with best correction) may interfere with his successful functioning in school or in his environment. We believe, and the literature supports this belief, that it is extremely important that visually impaired children be given ample time to grow in a richly stimulating and supportive setting until they are developmentally ready for a meaningful and successful school experience. The focus of this early intervention program is to provide a diagnostic and prescriptive program of sensory stimulation and basic experiential readiness. The program includes motor, language, tactual, and basic concept development; utilization of remaining vision; and nurturance of a healthy self-concept by early training in daily living skills, orientation and mobility, and body awareness.

Philosophy

There is sufficient evidence to indicate that the theoretical "compensation" for vision loss does not usually occur automatically. Optimum use of very low degrees of remaining vision and of the additional modalities of hearing, touch, smell, and taste, so vital to the visually impaired child, must be encouraged and trained from infancy on so that each child will reach a level of maximum utilization. Initial diagnostic assessment provides baseline information from which individual developmental levels can be determined and prescriptive program objectives identified. Final assessment determines appropriate referral to existing programs.

Levels of Services

☐ The Early Childhood Program of Services for Visually Impaired Children is divided into three component groups: 1) a parent-infant group; 2) services to children enrolled in private special schools and in day-nursery programs; and 3) the Learning Center program. While these services differ considerably, the primary focus of each remains the same, namely, the child himself, with support to the parents and siblings. In addition, attention is given to the interaction (or lack of interaction) between the child and the members of the family.

Parent-infant intervention

Intervention includes the development of an early, parent-guided program of sensory, motor, language, and social development for the child. Equally important is a counseling, information, and support program for the parents to aid them in their own emotional growth and attitudinal development following the diagnosis of blindness or severe visual impairment. The training of parents in early child development, demonstration home teaching, and parent counseling are provided for the parents and their children from birth to about two-and-a-half or three years of age. These services are provided by a trained teacher of the visually impaired, the program social worker, and the project director.

Counseling

It is essential that assistance to parents include counseling in accepting their child and his impairment, in recognizing his abilities and assets, and in developing realistic expectations for him. It is also important that a feeling of self-confidence in the parents be supported by assurances that they are doing a good job and by the provision of information about early child development, behavior management techniques, and the resources and services available to them. The itinerant vision teacher and the project social worker visit the home on a regular basis, one determined by the readiness of both the parents and the child to profit from these services.

Other programs

Consultative support and demonstration teaching is provided to teachers in private special schools and in day-nursery schools which enroll young visually impaired children, such as the Center for the Handicapped, Maryland Association for Retarded Children, the Headstart program, a Montessori school, and the preschool program run by the Lions Club. There are, in addition, the two classes that meet daily in the Learning Center setting at a public elementary school. Here there is the important advantage of the constant presence of "normal" models, children who do not have identified physical impairments. Children without additional impairments who could profit from a group experience and beginning readiness activities are phased into this group at two-and-a-half to three years of age. Several fully sighted, less mature children from the regular kindergarten are usually included in those activities from which they can profit. This is in keeping with the philosophy of the vision program that visually impaired children should not be isolated if it can be avoided.

Learning Center classes

Instruction

☐ Diagnostic assessment and prescriptive program planning are utilized in order to individualize instruction. While all children participate in an enriching early childhood program under the direction of an early childhood specialist, one-to-one and small group instruction is provided by itinerant vision teachers. Two specialists trained in the education of blind and partially seeing children share these responsibilities in addition to home teaching for parents and infants and itinerant teaching for children who have moved from the Learning Center into kindergarten or first grade in their neighborhood schools.

Integration

A developmental approach is utilized to train sensory, motor, language, tactual, and basic concept development. Skills of daily living, orientation, body image, and spatial awareness are included as needed in each child's program. Individual readiness for higher cognitive development is monitored and intervention provided. As these children with visual impairments mature and become ready for larger group kindergarten experiences, they join those classes in the school on a limited schedule. This facilitates full integration and a more positive early adjustment to the mainstream the following year.

Language development

A small class of multiply handicapped visually impaired children, three to eight years of age, participate in an experience-oriented program conducted by a language development specialist. This is best described as a total immersion approach to language. Every experience is a language experience, including all levels of skill development, body image, self-care, etc. In addition to the stated criteria for all visually impaired children enrolled in the Learning Center, children in this group must have, as measured by audiological examination, enough hearing to develop language. The language development teacher functions as a full member of the protect team by providing assessment and training for children in the pre-kindergarten group who suffer from speech and language problems or delays.

Services for Parents

☐ During the first two-and-a-half to three years of a child's life, both he and his parents are pupils in the (often) trial-and-error school of parenting and developing positive affective relationships. Following the trauma of diagnosed severe visual impairment or blindness, it is essential that professional intervention in the form of counseling, education, and information be made available to the family. It is the duty of the project staff to define an educational program for both parent and child which allows flexibility for utilization of other interdisciplinary specialists. These may include the school medical advisor, physical therapist, psychologist, or others.

Goals for parents

Specific goals for parents include: 1) development of competence and confidence in caring for their visually impaired child; 2) acceptance of the handicap, including an understanding of the specific eye condition and its implications for efficient functioning and learning; 3) participation in parent discussion and training groups and in broader school activities; 4) development of an understanding of various techniques and approaches to child management, e.g., communication skills based on Parent Effectiveness Training (P.E.T.); 5) realistic and loving acceptance of the child; and 6) formulation of realistic goals for the child. Study groups for parents are held one morning each week and many include observation and discussion of the Learning Center program, courses in various behavior management techniques, or lectures and demonstrations by volunteers and invited consultants.

Parent training

A basic premise underlying the parent training program is that many approaches to behavior management should be taught in order to develop a repertoire of useful skills. In these classes with other mothers from the Learning Center and from the regular school population, the focus is on skill development. Parents are encouraged to discuss their experiences and to practice the application of skills learned to resolve problems and conflicts. An important advantage in including mothers from the regular school population is the growing realization by Learning Center mothers that their children share most behavior patterns and problems in common with other children who have no physical impairment. This is a valuable device for teaching early acceptance of the fact that all problems cannot be attributed to vision loss.

Determination of services

Intervention in each case, including the specific instructional program, the schedule of home visits, and the amount and kind of parent participation and counseling is dependent upon: 1) the child's functional use of any residual vision; 2) his orientation to and interaction with his parents and his environment; 3) his social development; 4) his need for further assessment; and 5) parent readiness for contact with services.

Project Validation

☐ In April 1974, as the project neared completion of its third year of operation under Title III, it was referred by Maryland State Department Title III officials to the U.S. Office of Education for validation. A team of out-of-state validators subsequently judged this project innovative, exemplary, and worthy of national dissemination. In addition to the validation of the stated objectives, the project received high ratings for its approach to early intervention for both parents and children, parent training in various methods of behavior management and other social services, implementation of an intensive diagnostic and prescriptive program in the Early Childhood Learning Center, provision of a total language experience program for multiply handicapped blind children, and provision of appropriate assistance to nonpublic schools which enroll children with visual impairments.

Awards

In July 1974, the project received an Educational Pacesetter Award from the National Advisory Council on Supplementary Centers and Services. Mrs. Inez C. Eddings, chairman, presented the award because of the project's success in areas relating to innovativeness, pupil achievement, cost effectiveness, and program administration. This was followed in December 1974, by an Excellence in Education Award from the National Association of State Advisory Council Chairmen. In making the award, Mr. Rosco Shields, Jr., chairman, described the project as a nationally significant innovation which holds the promise of revolutionizing patterns of contemporary American education.

Effects of validation

As a result of the validation team report and of the documented success of the project, the Montgomery County Board of Education assumed full funding of all staff and services on July 1, 1974. This action phased this model program into the mainstream of education in the public school system. Services for visually impaired children (K-12) have been offered in Montgomery County since 1954. Another effect of the validation report was the decision of the Maryland ESEA, Title III State Advisory Council to provide a fourth year of funding to establish the project as a national demonstration site. This was done to field test the instructional approaches utilized in the program and to provide on-site training for interested professionals.

Field Testing

☐ Since so little is available in the literature for assessment and intervention below age three, project staff has worked diligently to identify, define, and develop assessment measures and objectives appropriate for early developmental levels. Our goal was implementation of a valid early childhood education program with defined intervention for special needs. Efforts were made to review, refine, and compile assessment measures in order to develop or adapt any instrument(s) that would be comprehensive and that would not exclude a handicapped child, especially one with a visual impairment. The second step was an ongoing review by staff of all available curriculum materials and suggested approaches to intervention. Until recently, little was available below kindergarten level. Except for certain areas, e.g., language stimulation and motor development, little intervention has been found for ages birth to four years. As a result, applicable materials and approaches were compiled and at least one suggested lesson plan or intervention was written by staff for each objective when nothing useful was available.

Booklets and manuals

It was never part of the project plan to field test or publish any materials and this suggestion was met with some consternation by the project director and staff. Defined objectives included in somewhat voluminous curriculum binders had been selected or developed for application to our small population and to individual needs within it. The position of the Title III committee that future attempts to replicate this model of services should not be hampered by staff having to go through the same difficult early steps to define the program was a reasonable one. With all possible speed, two assessment booklets (birth to three years and three years to school readiness) and matching intervention manuals were prepared. The assessment format for objectives provides a diagnostic checklist to identify appropriate intervention which is presented in detail in the intervention manuals. An additional social services document including objectives, rationale, suggested activities, and assessment strategies was prepared for use at sites participating in the field testing.

Testing Sites

☐ Because of funding realities, it was necessary to plan within a one-year time-frame for completion of the fourth year objectives. This was noted as an unrealistic constraint from the outset. Currently, project materials have been presented to teachers and administrators for field testing in Allegheny County and Philadelphia, Pennsylvania; DeKalb County, Georgia; San Diego, San Jose, and San Francisco, California; and at the Utah School for the Blind in Ogden. They are also being used throughout Texas by the Texas Commission for the Blind, by the University of Texas at Austin in its Early Childhood Centers, by the Texas model Early Childhood Project in Galveston, and by special classes and centers for the handicapped in Dallas, Houston, and San Antonio.

Returns

Because the incidence of severe vision impairment is low (especially those identified in the preschool years), it has been necessary to include many sites. The minimum number of children needed for the validation study is at least 100 with visual impairments, 100 with multiple impairments, and 200 without impairments. It is hoped that returns will exceed these minimum numbers. Post-assessment booklets will be returned in June 1975 and, upon completion of the statistical analyses, a final report will be prepared. Needed revisions and refinements, including suggestions from teachers involved in the field testing, will be made and the documents will be prepared for publication and distribution in 1975-76.

Conclusion

☐ The prospect of compiling and assimilating ideas, including the expertise of some of the nation's finest teachers in the field from coast to coast, is an exciting and tremendous prospect. Whatever the finished document may be, however, it must be remembered that there is no "cookbook" approach to meaningful intervention with parents and children. In every instance the instructional strategy suggested is always and only *one* way of working toward an objective. While creative and dedicated teachers do not have time for curriculum development during a busy school year, they will ultimately use any curriculum manual as a resource or perhaps a beginning. If this final document serves that purpose in any setting, its goal will be realized.

For the future

The Montgomery County Title III Early Childhood staff anticipates an ongoing, fluid approach to meeting the needs of young visually impaired children and their parents. It has been gratifying to have this model of services identified by many as appropriate for all young children. If it provides direction and assistance for educators and parents in other school systems to meet the needs of young children with visual or other impairments, it will have been a job worth doing. (Because Montgomery County has an excellent preschool program for hearing impaired children, specific intervention for this population is not included, i.e., signing and speech reading.)

Piaget's Theory and the Visually Handicapped Learner

Rose-Marie Swallow, ED.D.

Dr. Swallow is associate professor of education at California State University in Los Angeles.

Abstract: *Research based on the writings of Piaget indicates that the cognitive functioning of the visually impaired child is slower to develop than that of his sighted counterpart. In addition, there may be a developmental gap between the operative and figurative aspects of his thought as well as difficulties in image formation. The author reviews current literature and presents basic educational tenets based upon interpretations of Piaget's work and research findings. She emphasizes the blind child's need of direct physical experiences with concrete objects and verbal interaction with both adults and members of his peer group to learn about the world around him.*

The works of Jean Piaget and his collaborators offer to Special Education a frame of reference for understanding the behavioral manifestations of cognitive functioning. Studies of thinking help us to recognize the intellectual potential of visually handicapped children and to analyze the structures and processes of preoperational and operational thought. (An operation is defined as "an action capable of occurring internally and of which, according to Piaget, the essential characteristic is reversibility" [Inhelder, 1966, p. 302].) Thus we hope to be able to differentiate more easily between intellectual potential and certain deficiencies in symbolic imagery. Piagetian research on the blind child seems to indicate that the blind child suffers a developmental lag: that is, a slowdown in the speed of development through the different stages. Likewise, a developmental gap may exist between the operative and figurative aspects of thought. Knowledge of these developmental lags and cognitive gaps as well as the visually handicapped child's difficulties in image formation may lead us to a better understanding of the specific deficiencies in symbolic reasoning apparent in many blind children. This atypical developmental pattern may, however, be normal development for this group of exceptional children.

The visually handicapped child, and particularly the child who is totally blind, has special needs as he progresses through cognitive stages of intellectual development. The objectives of this paper are, therefore, to review current literature in relationship to Piaget and the visually handicapped child and to deduce basic educational tenets based upon interpretations of Piaget's writings and research findings. This exercise should broaden our approach to and awareness of the kinds of curricula needed to help the cognitive development of visually handicapped learners.

PIAGETIAN LITERATURE Although there is a vast literature on the writings of Piaget, he himself has been relatively unconcerned with pedagogical issues. What we have witnessed under the rubric of education has been a proliferation of books on how to develop a cognitive curriculum—in the main a set of lesson plans that are essentially the experiments Piaget has employed to test the products of the process. Most contain the classic balls of clay for conservation, graduated sticks or straws for seriation, circles and squares varied in color and size for classification, and a set of poker chips for one-to-one correspondence. I myself possess a whole shelf of booklets containing the same learning activities.

As a special educator, I have adapted and, when necessary, modified these or similar sets of so-called "learning tasks" for the visually handicapped child. However, I have also questioned the extent to which these tasks are learning activities. Do they not actually serve to determine whether or not the child already has the operation? When the child can spontaneously sort blue and yellow (or smooth and rough), large and small, the circles and squares by color (or texture), shape and size, we know that he can classify specific objects according to three variables. And what about the child who cannot perform the task? Are we only to keep repeating the same or similar activities? Are we only to keep presenting simpler sequential tasks? Do our programs result in teaching specific skills with little or no relationship to cognitive development? We must avoid a curriculum based upon training isolated product skills with limited operational knowledge of the processes of cognitive development.

Piaget has not been directly involved in clinical experimentation with visually handicapped children. Rather, a group of researchers has investigated—sometimes very poorly—the cognitive development of blind and partially seeing children. The first problem that occurs to a few of them, usually those possessing limited knowledge both of Piaget and of the visually impaired child, is what to do about residual vision. (Comparatively few visually handicapped children are totally blind.) One solution has been to blindfold the children with remaining vision. However, this is not a valid testing method in that it is asking subjects to perform the tasks without a sense with which they normally operate. On the other hand, the data analysis must in some way account for the degree of remaining vision. A second

Piaget's Theory and the Visually Handicapped Learner, Rose-Marie Swallow, *The New Outlook for the Blind*, September 1976,

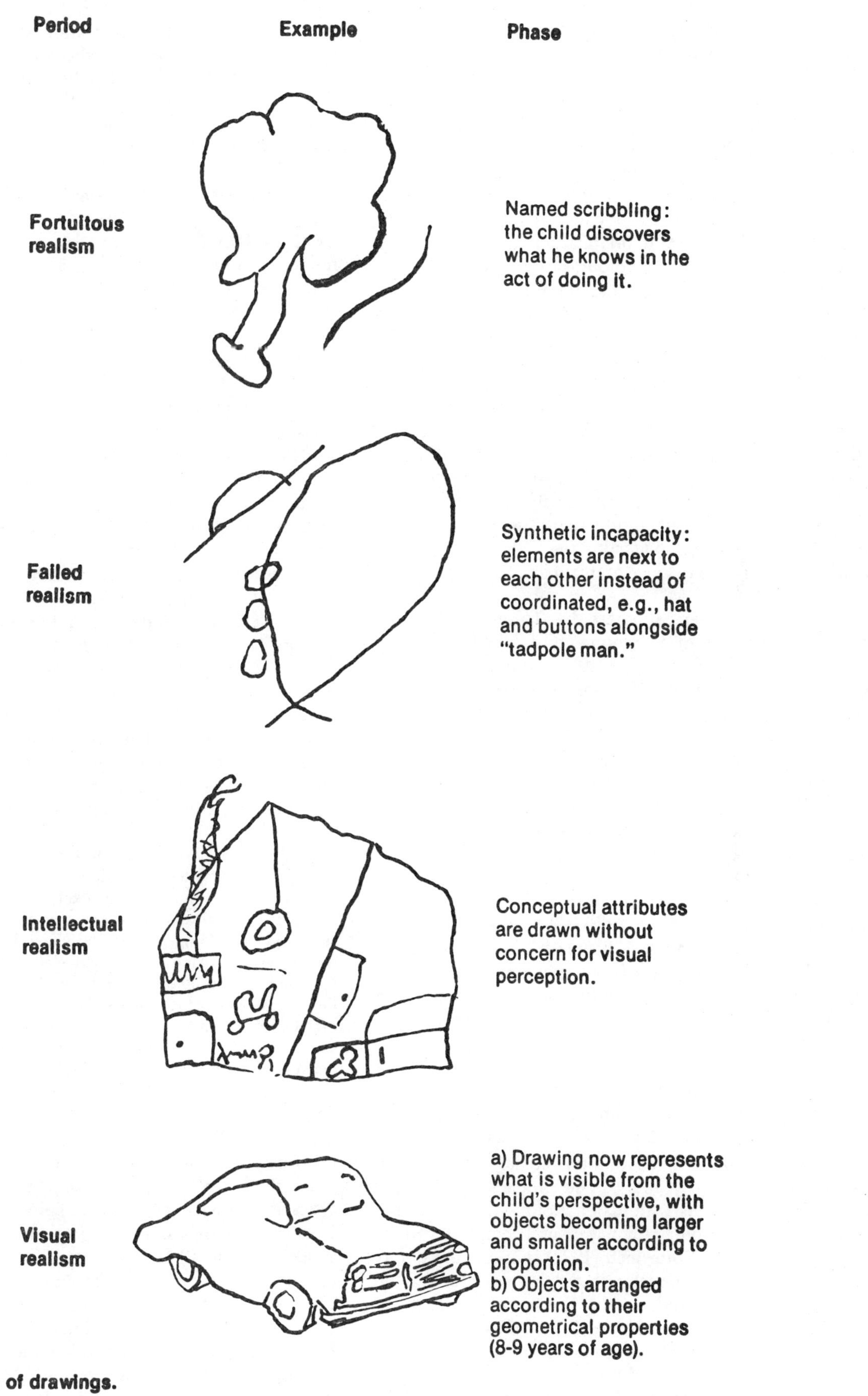

Figure 1. Evolution of drawings.

pitfall in research with the blind is to compare them with a "matched" group of sighted subjects who are sometimes blindfolded. Given our present knowledge concerning the figurative aspects of cognitive functioning, how can we claim that these comparisons are valid?

RESEARCH RESULTS Research results generally indicate that the blind child displays some developmental lag or symbolic gap. Often the recommendations for education to remedy these gaps offer little more than was known when Valentin Hüay began his first school for the blind in Paris in 1784. Thus even today much of the research utilizing Piagetian tasks offers little useful information to the classroom teacher. Education must develop its own methods and strategies based upon relevant research findings concerning cognitive development and sound psychological principles of learning.

Miller (1969) studied 26 visually impaired youngsters, ages six to ten, on conservation tasks using balls of clay and beakers of water. After blindfolding every subject "to control the amount of visual impairment," he found that an increase in the ability to conserve was a function of age although partially sighted subjects performed significantly better than the totally blind. His findings support the proposition that visual intactness is an important determinant in the development of reasoning, suggesting the ". . . importance of visual interaction with the environment as a factor in conservation" (p. 104).

Similar findings were reported by Tobin (1972), who explored the problem of developmental lag in 189 visually handicapped children, ages five to 17, using two balls of clay. Among the 117 subjects who were classified as conservers the following responses resulted: a) Plus/Minus (e.g., None added or taken away) 29 percent, b) Reversability (e.g., "They were the same before") 52 percent, c) Co-ordination of Relations (e.g., "The sausage is longer but thinner") 8 percent, d) Shape (e.g., "It has only been changed in shape") 8 percent, e) Identical Action (e.g., "The ball would be the same if rolled out") 3 percent, f) Weight (e.g., "It would still weigh the same") 1 percent. "The youngest subject giving an explanation in categories (c) to (f) inclusive, was seven years, ten months" (Tobin, 1972, p. 196). In another study, Cromer (1973) found no significant differences between blind and sighted conservers in the use of dimension reasons (c) to (f). However, 93 percent of the non-conservers (blind and sighted) used dimensions to support their erroneous prelogical reasoning. All mentioned only one dimension ("because it's high," "because it's thin," etc.). Language used by the blind did not differ from that used by the sighted in these conservation tasks. Cromer also found that changes in cognition often preceded changes in language.

Tobin (1972) asks how developmental lag relates to restrictions in the visually handicapped child's learning experiences and interactions with his environment and whether differences are traceable to the nature and complexity of the stimulation received. Gottesman (1973) supports the theory that the same developmental patterns that exist for sighted children exist for the blind, but that the rate of development is slower for blind children. Hatwell (1966) observed two- to three-year differences in performance of conservation of mass tasks between groups of blind and sighted children.

For methodological reasons Cromer (1973) was not satisfied with Hatwell's original research. His own research revealed no differences among his 36 five- to nine-year-olds (blind, sighted, and sighted but blindfolded) regarding the age of attainment of conservation although the manner by which the blind children processed the environment differed from the blindfolded sighted children. He did suggest that ". . . the achievement of full conservation might be delayed for the blind due to impoverished perceptual schemes" (p. 249).

STAGES OF COGNITIVE DEVELOPMENT At this stage of the argument, certain clarifications may sharpen our interpretations of research findings. Basically, the mental development of the child appears to consist of four stages: sensorimotor (0–24 months), preoperational (2–7 years), concrete operations (7–11 years), and formal operations (11 years and upward). Each of these stages extends the one preceding it, reconstructs it on a new level, and finally surpasses it (Piaget & Inhelder, 1969). The order of succession is characterized by thinking patterns that can be observed. Each stage has distinct characteristics of thinking. The problem is to understand the underlying mechanism.

Maturation

According to Piaget, four general factors are associated with mental development: 1) maturation, 2) learning, 3) social education, and 4) equilibration (Inhelder & Piaget, 1964). Maturation is concerned with growth, particularly physical growth and the maturation of the central nervous system. It plays a role throughout mental development and is dependent upon action and experience: certain behaviors therefore depend upon the functioning of specific structures. For example, the coordination of vision and grasping occurs at approximately four and one-half months. The blind infant does not coordinate the actions of sound and grasping until approximately six months later, at around 10 to 11 months of age (Fraiberg, Smith, & Adelson, 1969).

> Typically, for the first six months the blind infant tends to maintain his hands tightly fisted at shoulder height in the neonatal posture, a position in which they are least likely to encounter each other or to find objects. Typically too, there is no finger play at midline. The sustained mutual fingering normally found in the sighted baby at 16 weeks requires vision for its practice and pleasurable repetition. In the absence of vision as an "organizer" for midline engagement of the hands, and without help from the parents, the totally blind infant's hands may not unite at midline at all, and the maturational sequence that leads to coordinate use of the hands and reciprocity between the hands can be impeded (p. 134).

Learning

Learning, the second factor of mental development, is essentially the role of experience, of concepts derived from the actions performed upon objects. Piaget theorizes two types of learning experiences: 1) physical experience, which consists of acting upon objects in order to abstract their properties, and 2) logical-mathematical experience, which consists of acting upon objects in order to learn the resulting actions. "Logical-mathematical concepts presuppose a set of operations that are abstracted not from the objects perceived but from the actions performed on these objects, which is by no means the same" (Piaget & Inhelder, 1969, p. 49). Learning, both physical and logical-mathematical, can be seriously

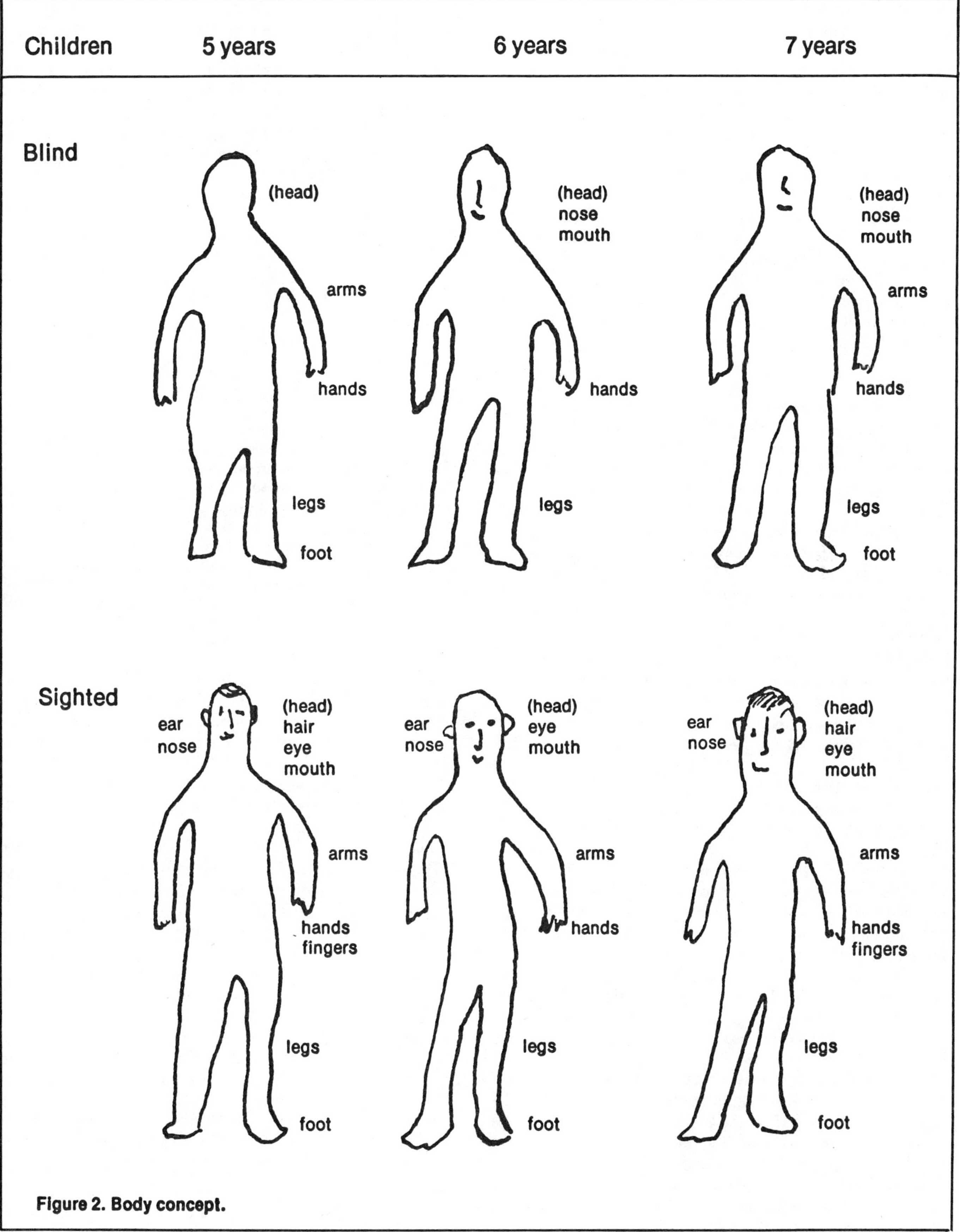

Figure 2. Body concept.

NOTE: This figure is based upon spontaneous priority responses: that is, those body parts which were mentioned by 50 percent or more of the children within each of the six groups (blind 5, 6, and 7 years and sighted 5, 6 and 7 years). In all groups the head was given as the lead so it is included in parentheses and is not to be considered a priority response.

delayed if there is no intervention early in the blind child's sensorimotor period.

Studies (Fraiberg *et al*, 1966, 1969) have shown that an appropriately stimulated blind baby will at five months of age grasp objects upon contact, make fleeting pursuit movements, and explore a table surface. On the other hand, a normal blind baby who has been grossly deprived of early tactile stimulation and grasping experiences has hands that are weak and awkward and fingers that are not useful for tactile exploration.

Hands need to be developed and fingers extended in order to support the body in crawling. There is a marked delay in creeping and independent walking in totally blind infants. Fraiberg, *et al*, (1969), point out that this delay is due to the absence of the external stimuli for reaching usually provided by vision. When a child begins to reach out on the stimuli of sound cues alone, he will propel himself forward. He must develop the concept of object permanence before he will reach out.

With the absence of vision there is also no incentive for the baby to sustain an elevated head position. Both head control and trunk control are prerequisite to locomotion. A child who is not physically mature will be delayed in locomotion and grasping and therefore will lack the number of experiences needed for development of physical knowledge (knowing the properties of objects) and logical-mathematical knowledge (knowing the functions and means of objects). Is it any wonder that the normal blind learner may demonstrate a lag in cognitive development?

SOCIAL EDUCATION The third developmental factor, social education (which includes language), involves both social interaction and social transmission. From the very beginning the blind infant is more dependent than his sighted counterpart upon the mother figure for stimulation and social contact. It has been demonstrated with sighted infants that the development of object permanence is influenced by the quality of mother-child interaction (Bell, 1970). If this is true, then the blind infant may be further handicapped if the mother figure is not involved in the infant stimulation program.

Social transmission depends upon the ability of the child to operate effectively during social contact. A blind child enrolled in an educational program requires active integration and participation in all activities within the classroom and on the school yard. "Social action is ineffective without an active assimilation by the child, which presupposes operatory structures" (Piaget & Inhelder, 1969, p. 166).

It should also be noted here that visual loss affects imitative learning of facial expressions and gestural movements. Blind individuals show less facial expressiveness and fewer gestural patterns. This may affect sighted persons in their responsiveness to blind individuals within a given social situation. It will also affect the blind person's ability to judge the impact and understanding of his remarks upon the listener.

Maturation, learning, and social education constantly interact in the development of thought and cognition. "In the development of the child, there is no preestablished plan, but a gradual evolution in which each innovation is dependent upon the previous one" (Piaget & Inhelder, 1969, p. 157).

Equilibration

The fourth factor of mental development, equilibration, is the key to understanding the cumulative effects of the preceding three concepts. Equilibration, a self-regulatory mechanism of mental development, results from a series of compensations on the part of the learner as he responds to external stimuli. The resulting adjustment is based upon previous learning in a kind of loop-back system and upon anticipatory affective factors, e.g., motivation and values. These two aspects, the affective and the cognitive, are inseparable within the concept of equilibration, which clearly depends upon previous maturation, learning, and social education.

Beth Stephens and Katherine Simpkins (1974) in their study, *The Reasoning, Moral Judgment, and Moral Conduct of the Congenitally Blind*, give us an excellent example of how equilibration involves maturation, experience, and social interaction.

> In stories involving falsehoods, the subject was to consider intention versus consequence in determining the gravity of the fabrication. One such moral judgment assessment involved stories of two boys. In the first story the boy intentionally gave wrong directions to a man, but, despite the misinformation, the man did not get lost. In the comparison story, a boy who had just moved to town gave a man what he thought were correct directions, but they were incorrect and the man got lost. The blind subjects generally decided the second situation was more serious, regardless of the positive intentions of the boy. Although responses of blind subjects indicated some consideration of intention versus consequence, the exceedingly traumatic interpretation the blind subjects gave to being lost probably influenced the final response.

The difference in responses between the blind and sighted students to this particular situation can be more easily understood when one considers the interactional effects of maturation, experience, and social learning: First, it is a monumental task for the congenitally blind child to become oriented to and mobile in his environment. Second, based upon his experiences, the fear and hopelessness of being lost is quite traumatic. And third, when a blind child seeks help, the basis of this act must be trust. Now we can perhaps understand how the affective and cognitive aspects of equilibration are inseparable and result in any given behavior based upon feedback and anticipation. (It should be stressed that "moral judgment" is actually a social dimension transmitted through and modified by generation after generation of a sighted society.)

The results of Stephens and Simpkins (1974) study indicate that the differences between the blind and sighted people on measures of moral judgment and conduct are relatively inconsequential compared with deficiencies in logical reasoning. They conclude that classification and class inclusion tasks are particularly difficult for blind children.

> Thus these blind subjects of average IQ did not achieve concrete level operational thought with the facility, dispatch, or completion that might have been assumed by their performance on the Wechsler Scales. Review of development over the 12-year period, CA 6-18, indicates that although improvement in concrete reasoning did proceed (albeit dilatorily) in most instances, logical thought which involved spatial orientation and mental imagery represented an area of continuing inability. Moreover, tasks involving formal or abstract thought generally were not attained by subjects who were 18, and were incomprehensible for younger subjects (p. 56).

These findings and conclusions do not altogether agree with Higgins (1973), who suggests that the condition of total congenital blindness alone is not sufficient to produce a delay in the formation of the intellectual structures underlying classification, and that deficiencies in classification skills appear to be figurative (perceptual) and symbolic rather than to be operational in origin.

SYMBOLIC REPRESENTATIONS If there are qualitative and quantitative differences in the thinking of the blind child, how can this be explained? The answer may lie partially in the role of the symbolic function and language. Piaget writes of five interrelated behaviors which give rise to symbolic representation. These five behaviors appear in increasingly complex order: 1) deferred imitation, 2) symbolic play, 3) drawing or graphic images, 4) mental images, and 5) language.

An example of early deferred imitation occurs when the infant waves his hand in some immature manner, perhaps by opening and closing his fingers in imitation of grandma's "bye-bye." Even at the sensorimotor level of imitation, the significance of vision is apparent. Although the child may continue to open and close his hands after grandma has departed, this is considered practice (exercise play).

Deferred imitation also occurs when the human model is absent. The child evokes the images and imitates the gestural, postural, or movement behavior: he has observed some behavior and after a while, recreates that behavior without the presence of the model. This constitutes the beginning of symbolic reasoning. The role of vision as a unifier for observation cannot be minimized. One cannot imitate at any level what has not been observed. One imitates what one has experienced.

Piaget's next level is symbolic play: the game of pretend-

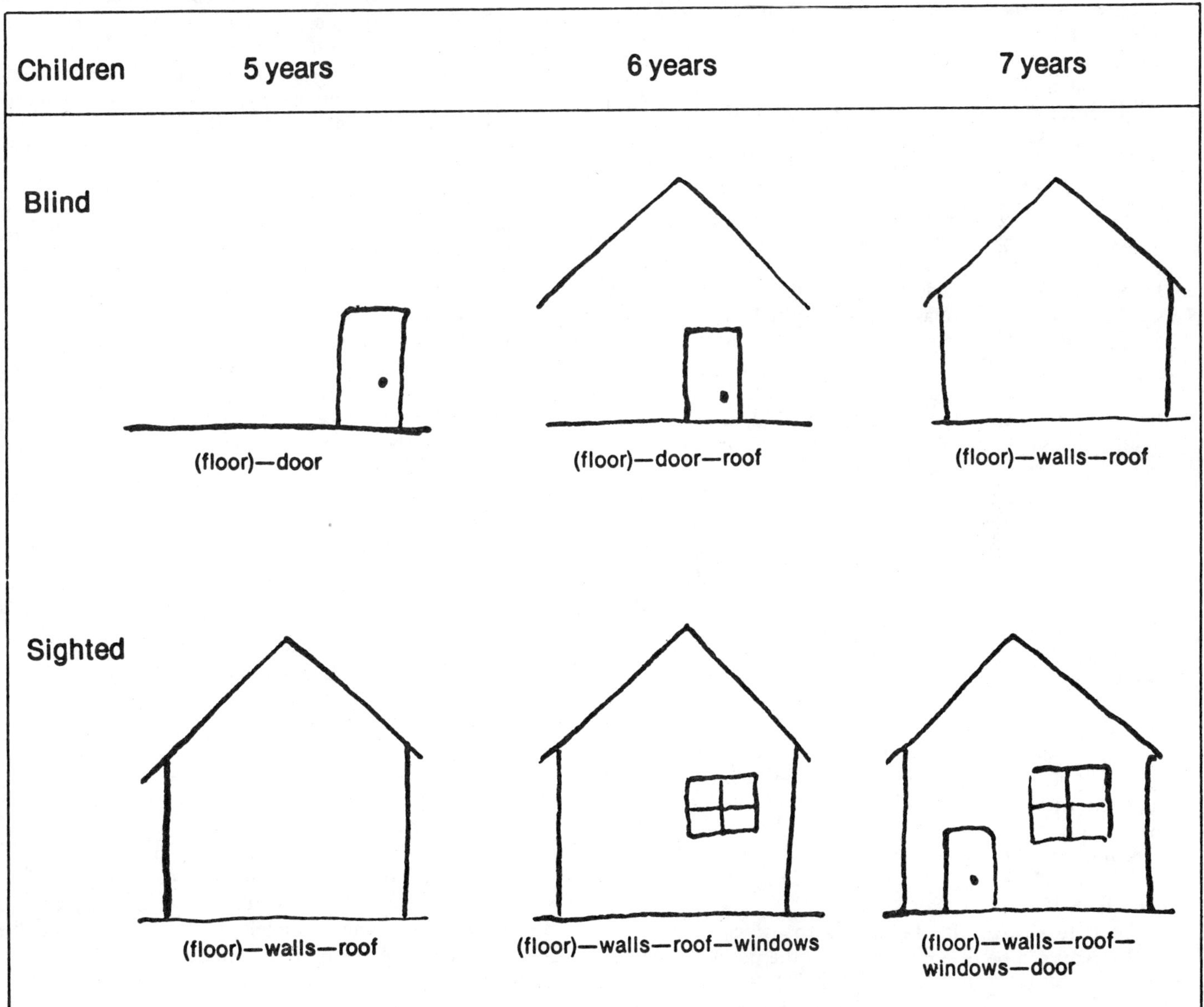

Figure 3. House (outer structure) concept.

NOTE: This figure is based upon priority responses: that is, those items which were mentioned by 50 percent or more of the children within each age group (blind 5, 6, and 7 years and sighted 5, 6, and 7 years). In all groups the floor was given in the lead question and it is included in parentheses and is not to be considered as a priority response.

ing. The child may pretend to be asleep; he may get out a mixing bowl, wooden spoon, and cupcake pan and pretend to make cupcakes; or a group of children may build an airport with construction blocks.

Categories of Play

Piaget and Inhelder (1969) outlined three main categories of play and a fourth which becomes a transition between symbolic play and adult crafts: a) *exercise play*, a primitive form of play which has its beginnings in the sensorimotor period consists of repeating activities for the pleasure of it: waving "bye-bye;" b) *symbolic play*, the preschooler's way of adapting to the adult world, is "make-believe" play, in which the objects are symbols for something else about which the child is thinking; c) *games with rules* (marbles, hopscotch, etc.), are transmitted socially from child to child and thus increase in importance with the enlargement of the child's social life; d) finally, out of symbolic play develop *games of construction*, which are initially imbued with play symbolism but tend later to constitute genuine adaptations (mechanical constructions, etc.) or solutions to problems and intelligent creations (p. 59).

Play bridges the gap between concrete experiences and abstract thought. Symbolic play is the means by which the child adapts to the adult world. Piaget believes that it is indispensable to the child's affective and intellectual equilibrium. The visually handicapped child with reduced visual input, fewer opportunities to observe adults, and fewer encounters with others is severely limited in the variety of living experiences which form the basis of play. "The symbolism of play . . . may even fulfill the function of what for an adult would be internal language" (Piaget & Inhelder, 1969, p. 60).

Symbolic play or make-believe games ". . . imply representation of an absent object" (Piaget, 1962, p. 111). Play is both imitative and imaginative. In the main the blind preschooler is not cognitively ready for many play activities. What this should say to the teacher is that the child needs an increase in direct daily living experiences, working alongside the active adult. He needs to be directly involved in all opportunities for learning and should only infrequently be without direct, active social contact. Also, he should not use his bedroom as his center of operation: bedrooms are generally private worlds which lack adequate social stimulation.

Drawing

Piaget states that drawing is an intermediate step between play and mental images and rarely occurs before two or two and one-half years of age. The drawings of a young child are essentially realistic in nature because the child begins by drawing what he knows about an object. The periods in the evolution of drawings are shown in Figure 1 (Piaget & Inhelder, 1969).

Definite changes in the child's spatial conceptual development can be observed between the periods of "intellectual realism" and "visual realism." Intellectual realism shows no awareness of perspective or metrical relationships, but it does show topological relationships such as proximity, separation, and order. These relationships are primitive in that they are internal to a particular figure; they do not express the relationships among figures in a more complex field. It is not until the period of "visual realism," after the age of seven or eight, that projective spatial reasonings are followed by Euclidian relationships. The child can project a straight line and also understand elementary perspective, e.g., the chimney is no longer tilted because the roof is on a slant. He can now project himself to another viewpoint and is no longer egocentric in his perspective. At nine to 10 the child can draw an object from a perspective other than that at which he views it.

Coordination of Perspective

In a study by Dr. Poulsen and myself (1973) coordination of perspectives reflected more than any other task the spatial conceptual deficits in low-vision adolescents. The students' abilities to conceptualize projective space was the focus. They were shown mountains both on a concrete model and graphically illustrated—hidden behind or in front of each other—in a set of nine pictures. Those subjects with low visual efficiency (not necessarily the greatest visual loss) performed most poorly on this task. Low visual efficiency may have more to do with poor graphic imagery than development of visual perception per se. The low vision and partially seeing students continually oscillated between egocentric and decentered thought. The demands for spatial reasoning were beyond their cognitive abilities. Only two of the 10 subjects mastered the concrete operation involving bi-dimensional projective space. There was clearly a deficit in symbolic imagery at this level.

Mental Images

Mental images are relatively late in developing and appear also as internalized imitations. Perceptions and images are classified under the figurative aspects of cognitive functioning as opposed to the operative aspects (actions and operations). At the preoperational level, reproductive images are limited to perceptual imitation and are static in nature, evoking what has been perceived previously. "Reproductive images may include static configuration, movement (change in position), and transformation (change in form), for these three kinds of realities occur constantly in the perceptual experience of the subject" (Piaget & Inhelder, 1969, p. 71). Static, kinetic, and transformational images therefore represent what is actually occurring in the child's environment. Kinetic and transformational images are possible only after the period of concrete operations. When blindness occurs before the age of six, visual imagery is believed to atrophy. Before the period of concrete operations, the image is static and cannot give rise to operatory structures. "After the age of seven or eight, the image becomes *anticipatory* and so better able to serve as a basis for the operations" (Piaget & Inhelder, 1969, p. 79).

Interestingly enough, the reproductive image level is where we may again assume that there are catastrophic effects upon the cognitive development of the blind child due to experiential deprivation. This may be more detrimental than the loss of ability to perceive the environment.

In a comparative study (Kephart, Kephart, & Schwarz, 1974, p. 442) of blind (N = 49) and sighted (N = 37) children, the Kephart Scale was used as a means for assessing the personal and environmental awareness of blind children between the ages of five and seven years enrolled in residential centers. (Note: Brekke, Williams, & Tait (1974) concluded that there are important differences between blind children who have been institutionalized and those living at home in the area of conservation: their results favor home placement.) The spontaneous responses of the blind and sighted to the body image (verbal construction) game revealed that, in constructing an imaginary friend, the blind subjects mentioned fewer body parts at each age level. The chart is based upon those body parts mentioned by 50 percent or more of the children. In all situations the head was given as the lead response. The authors wonder why the fingers and ears were not mentioned, considering their importance in receiving tactile and auditory information.

Similar responses were also given to the "House Concept." "The outer structure of the house (walls and roof) is mentioned by the sighted children at all age levels. The blind children, on the other hand, began at age five by mentioning the door and at age six the door and roof. By age seven, the blind children had omitted the door as a priority response, and walls and roof became the preferred response. The sighted group, in contrast, by age seven had completed the physical structure of the house" (pp. 424–425).

Probably the most revealing and alarming information from the study is that at all ages the blind children centered their attention on their own bedrooms, whereas the sighted children equally divided their attention between the bedroom and kitchen. (This crucial point was previously alluded to in the need for direct experiences in the development of symbolic play and social interaction.) The restrictive environmental information of the blind was apparent across all age categories, with the sighted children giving two descriptive responses to every one offered by the blind.

ROLE OF LANGUAGE Finally, the role of language appears in the development of the symbolic function. Language is slowly acquired and is based upon imitation. Piaget believes that language does not constitute the source of logic but rather is structured by it. The roots of logic have their beginnings in the general coordination of actions. For this reason we find that blind children, lacking in the abundance of experiences necessary for the development of operational structures, appear deficient in logical operations. Friedman and Pasnak (1973) state that "... blind and sighted children are approximately equivalent in classification and seriation at 8 years of age; thereafter the blind begin to fall behind, especially on verbal tasks.... The lack of vision impairs performance on verbal tasks as well as manipulative tasks when these tasks involve conceptual abilities" (p. 61).

Research studies with the blind using the Wechsler Intelligence Scale for Children (WISC) indicate that on Vocabulary, Similarities, and Comprehension subtests the blind had the lowest scores (Gilbert & Rubin, 1965; Hopkins & McGuire, 1966; and Tillman, 1967a). "The blind tend to approach abstract conceptualization problems from a concrete and functional level and consequently lag behind the sighted child" (Tillman, 1967b, p. 112).

These depressed mean scores may be due to classificatory cognitive delays. Classification skills are closely related to language functioning on the WISC. Stephens and Simpkins (1974), by means of factoring, found in their blind subjects (N = 75, ages 6–18 years) Similarities loading with combinatory logic and Comprehension loading with hierarchical classification. The authors noted that the operational processes of their blind subjects drew heavily upon a verbal component (Verbal WISC plus Piagetian tasks) and appeared to be compensatory in nature.

"Verbalisms" (i.e., giving an acceptable definition of a word, but not accurately identifying the real object) in the blind have been frequently noted over the years. Harley (1963) found that verbalism was significantly related to lack of experience; the children with the least experience were highest in verbalisms. "It was found that a girl who played trumpet in the school orchestra was not familiar with a trombone. Several children who had extensive auditory experiences with violins could not tactually identify a violin. It seems that it cannot be assumed, as with sighted children, of comparable characteristics, that blind children have a familiarity with the items about them which they mention in their speech" (Harley, 1963, p. 53). And blind children have no visual means of verification of auditory input except for "hands on" tactual experiences.

CONCLUSION The need for direct, concrete experiences for blind children is of paramount importance. Direct physical experiences with the real object, total sensory and conceptual involvement with concrete objects, appropriate verbal interaction with other children and adults will help to give blind children a knowledge of the realities around them.

The blind child is at a serious disadvantage in experiencing things and situations in their totality, let alone abstracting the physical and logical-mathematical knowledge necessary for cognitive development. If a teacher systematically incorporates levels of representation and levels of operation into content areas, the child will develop cognitively according to his potential operational rate. The task for the teacher is not easy. Learning must be continuously monitored, planned, and sequenced. The total classroom environment must fulfill the individual needs and requirements of each child—feeding into the child the necessary content in order that he may develop intellectually.

This important role of the teacher has not received the necessary emphasis in many preservice and inservice training programs. Although most teacher training institutions agree theoretically upon the competencies needed by the teacher, they do not consistently evaluate skills, methods, and techniques required to achieve their goals. Despite the fact that everyone verbalized the need for direct experiences in conceptual development, there seems to be an excessive use of models (a poor substitute for direct experience). Most institutions have a comprehensive viewpoint of education, but in practice spend an inordinate amount of time developing academic skills. A cognitively oriented environment should attend to the means of an education: that is, cognitive growth along with the acquisition of academic skills. Activities to promote cognitive development should occur naturally and easily in programs based upon the following Piagetian tenets: 1) cognitive development is a gradual, evolving process dependent upon social, emotional, and physical growth and cannot be understood in isolation; 2) individual differences and patterns of growth influence functioning but are also affected by the sequence, variety, and quality of symbolic experiences; 3) knowledge of reality must be discovered and constructed through the activities of the child at his cognitive structural level; 4) activities promoting spontaneous exploration, either physical or intellectual, occur at all levels (at the same time, the role of verbal mediation in problem solving tasks should not be minimized); 5) a cognitively oriented curriculum continuously develops and reinforces spatial-temporal and logical-mathematical reasoning; 6) generative learning rests upon the child's spontaneity and creativity, whereas factual learning comes through practice, repetition, and memórization. Therefore, teachers must develop their curriculums and structure their classrooms wisely.

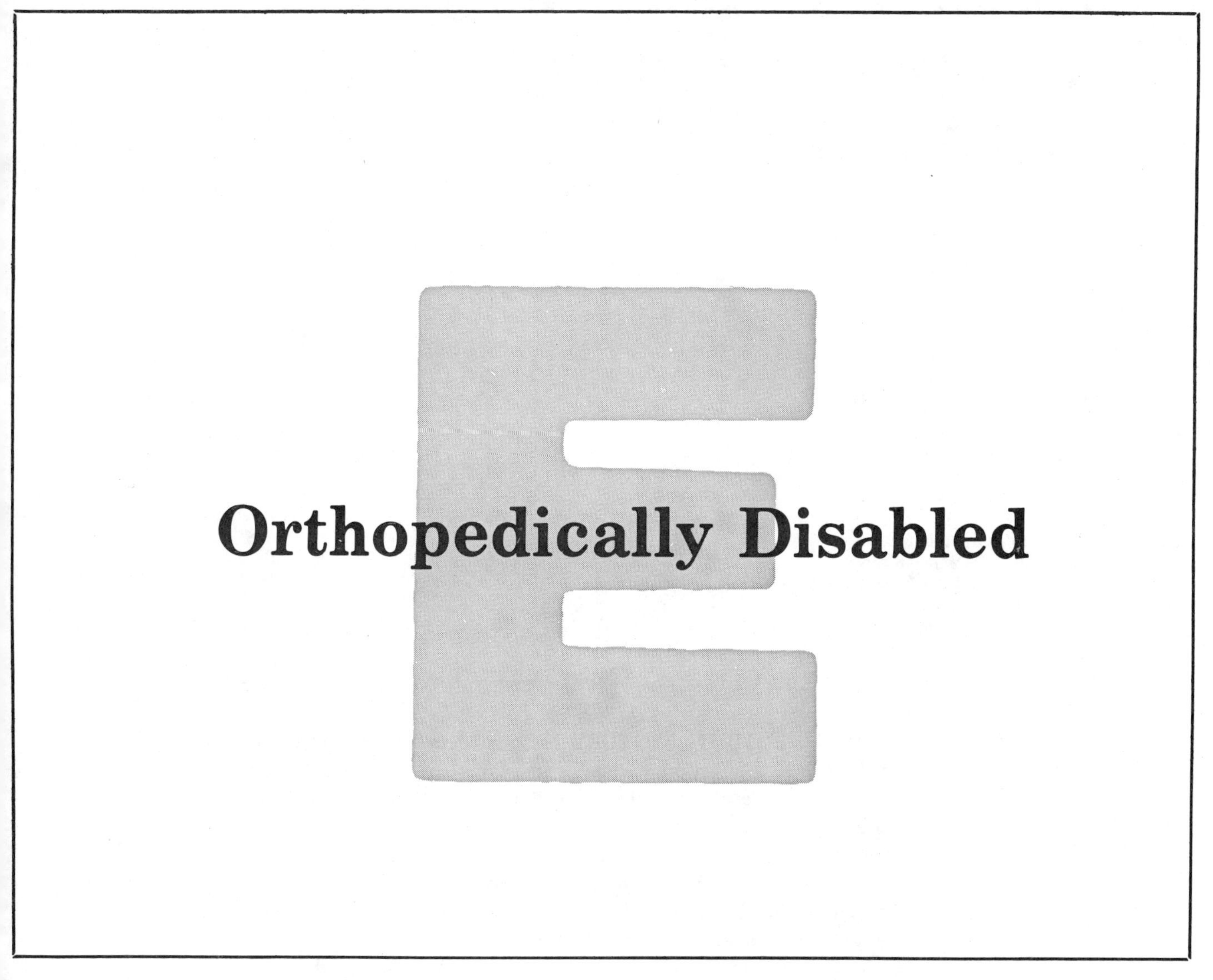

Orthopedically Disabled

In the family of a handicapped child, everyone is affected. Since children often help parents determine their own worth, parents suffer because they view themselves as failures. Both parents may suffer under the strain of simultaneously rejecting and overprotecting the child. Once the child's dependence is seen as final and made routine, parents may be suspicious of any treatment program. Parents, operating out of love, often feel guilty in an attempt to take responsibility, thus seeking the magical power to prevent a reoccurrence or a spreading of the disease or handicap to other family members. The mother suffers depression, anger, and a lower sense of maternal competence. The father, often called upon to be the family's Rock of Gibraltar, may experience a personality change which results in an overly neat, compulsive, neurotic-like constriction of his personality. The orthopedically handicapped child suffers, perhaps not least from living in a society which sees "cripples" as overly sensitive, self-pitying, and lacking in self-confidence. Even siblings suffer, since parents seem too casual in their acceptance of non-handicapped children; lack of time spent with them is seen as rejection, and siblings may have a poorer state of mental health than their handicapped siblings.

With the orthopedically handicapped, attitudes and anxieties are social components of physical disability and are frequently contagious. Behavior is partially physical, partially socially determined. Helping professionals must fight through parent's defense mechanisms such as: the child is normal, lazy, or, although physically disabled, mentally brilliant. Counselors must correct unrealistic success fantasies or fatalistic failure attitudes and must separate out behavior in the child which is physically determined and limited as to change from socially determined dependencies which are amenable to change. Since the disease is partially social, the entire family must be included in treatment; realistic, positive attitudes are as important for parents as for the handicapped child in working toward the goal of achieving the degree of independence possible commensurate with the disability.

Physical Disability in Children And Family Adjustment

Thomas E. Jordan, Ph.D.

Dr. Jordan is professor of education at Southern Illinois University, Carbondale. His background includes, on the elementary school level, the teaching and psychological evaluation of handicapped children. On the college level, he has had several years' experience in preparing personnel in educational psychology, special education, and rehabilitation; in clinical psychology; and in research on the behavioral aspects of disability in school children.

THE TWENTIETH CENTURY has been described as the century in which a large proportion of mankind has been freed from material want. People today believe that happiness in the conventional sense is an attainable goal rather than a fortuitous accident in a lifetime of hard work and deprivation. The deliberate protection of our rights to "life, liberty, and the pursuit of happiness" extends from childhood through adulthood. It is of course clear that expectations of happiness are generally sound. Most young people make the transition from adolescent happiness to marital happiness without too much difficulty. This is a matter of probabilities and can be predicted on the basis of personal maturity and adjustment. Young persons establishing their families will be successful for determinate reasons arising partially from their backgrounds of experience and the nature of their concept of family living.

Several things may seriously affect the extent to which a couple successfully establish a home. Their personal qualities and their personal expectations are important factors. A third matter beyond their control, but of particular interest in this context, is the set of realities presented by the birth of children.

In most cases the reality and the expectations coincide; occasionally they do not and a family attempts to cope with a child whose deficiencies are unexpected. The impact of such an event is partially determined, as is the success of the marriage, by the personal resources of the couple who married and established the family.

This paper will consider the effect that disability in a child can have on the life adjustment of families with handicapped children. It will attempt to describe the events and to understand their implications. The organization of these remarks will have a structure I would like to make clear. The concept of development is valuable in understanding

Physical Disability in Children and Family Adjustment, Thomas E. Jordan, *Rehabilitation Literature*, Vol. 24, No. 11, Reprinted with Permission for Rehabilitation Literature.

the impact of disabled persons on their families. Development means the following things:

1) An event, like a person, has a present, but it also has a past from which it emerges and a future whose form is partially determinate.
2) A family, like a person, has a cycle of growth, and it too emerges from a past state and changes as its members age or mature.

Into this life cycle there may be introduced concepts whose value is to illuminate a facet, or conceivably several aspects, of problems. Some concepts help us understand processes—happenings—and others help us understand people. Further, some processes are helpful at one stage but not at another. In a few cases concepts at one stage in the existence of a family may help predict subsequent events. Obviously, this last idea is important since it would help us anticipate problems and make plans.

We may begin by considering, say, a child with cerebral palsy. The selection of one with this condition is deliberate. Cerebral palsy is in many ways a model disease. It incorporates just about every possible type and degree of disability. It offers limited but not illusory possibilities of progress. It produces every conceivable reaction because of the endless combinations of symptoms and corresponding reactions. It calls on just about every discipline in the development of a therapeutic regimen.

The Crisis at Birth

The birth of a child is an occasion of stress for the entire family. The expectant mother has experienced increasing discomfort and the father and children have realized that further adjustments in family living are probable. Attention shifts from the several members of the family to the mother and from her to the child. A certain degree of stress is normal, and the delivery becomes a source of stress reduction; possibly family attention will eventually be refocused—diffused—in an approximation of the previous pattern. Put another way, the birth of the baby is the object of attention, but it seems probable others will get their previous share of family attention. This means father as well as the children!

The end of pregnancy sometimes can bring the delivery of a child with visible signs of neurological damage, accidental or developmental. In this case, rather than the delivery signaling the end of a tolerable degree of anxiety, it marks the transition to a period of sustained indecision and heightened anxiety.

This atmosphere of crisis is not unique to cerebral palsy, of course; it applies to other conditions such as mongolism, spina bifida, and other obvious errors of prenatal growth. (The matter of "visibility" is a separate issue to be considered later.) So, in that sense, specific disease entities lose their singularity, although the topic we are considering is properly formulated as family reactions to the class of events we call congenital anomalies.

The anxiety that families radiate during the crisis surrounding the birth of a child with obvious defects arises from several sources. First, there is the general lowering of the threshold for tolerating problems, due to fatigue and upset of family routine. This is normal and subsides within several days in usual circumstances. However, the birth of the sick infant generates more anxiety. Parents expect that a typical baby will be a perfect baby, a child without blemish—an expectation to which exceptions are common and inevitable. There is shock, as a consequence of birth of a defective infant, and there is a natural tendency to look for a reason. A feeling of personal responsibility for the child's condition is a common reaction, as is one of attaching blame to the other parent. The mother may feel responsible in a vague way and have feelings of inadequacy that feed on imaginary failings while pregnant. Zuk[26] and Boles[2] have called attention to the mediating role that a mother's values play. If she has certain religious convictions, she may feel more anxious as a consequence. On the other hand, religious values may depersonalize guilt and responsibility, leading to an ill-defined anxiety. The gap between expectations of perfection and the reality may lead literally to flight. One such mother is known to have gathered her clothes and, within a matter of hours after delivery, vanished into the night, abandoning her ill-formed baby to whatever care fate might provide.

The reactions of fathers are also diverse. Fathers seem to have a more ready mechanism at their disposal: simply putting the entire matter in the wife's lap is all too common. In such cases the basis is laid for an entire pattern of subsequent behavior—largely built around avoiding responsibility.

The Early Years

The early years of life for families with cerebral palsied children are not smooth. Feeding commonly is a problem, and fragility raises many health problems. A delicate child is a source of worry, and health problems that are thrown off routinely by other children are only slowly emerged from by young children with cerebral palsy. (A recent study indicates that the cerebral palsied have a death rate considerably higher than is found in the general population.[20]) Colds become more than nuisances, they become sieges of debility that last for weeks. They become occasions for serious nursing, and energy normally allotted to other members of the family is diverted into the care of the sick child. The secondary consequences of the period of sickness are feelings of neglect in other children and a disturbance of the normal household routines. Brothers and sisters may become hard to handle, and the father may feel neglected, creating discord. As with all such family crises the reactive process is circular or spiral in nature, and the situation becomes more aggravated until relieved by the return to good health of the child.

Emerging Symptoms

It is entirely too simplified to view the delivery of an unfinished child as an immediate matter of heightened anxiety and subsequent reactions. In many cases, as we know, congenital disabilities are invisible. Cerebral palsy may not be apparent unless the infant is moving. Medical personnel can detect neuromotor difficulties of a gross sort in infants. But to parents, particularly young parents having their first child, all babies wiggle in a useless random sort of way, and disturbances of tonus are not perceptible. In such cases an invisible disease that they have been told their baby has becomes a mysterious source of worry. What is the "it" that is apparent to nurses and physicians? Will it be outgrown? How about a vaccine as in the case of poliomyelitis? Is it *really* true there is something wrong? This is anxiety but of a different sort. It is anxiety in the face of the unknown. It is anxiety that comes and goes as motor symptoms dissolve into peaceful sleep, only to appear when the child wakens.

Since cerebral palsy is not always recognized at birth, it does not follow that all mothers of the cerebral palsied are overwhelmed from the time they leave the hospital. The anxiety that we find in many—but not all—parents of the cerebral palsied arises a year or so after the child is born. Recognizing a nonvisible disease may not be easy, particularly if a child meets all the expectations parents hold for babies. Inexperienced parents may believe most infants have feeding difficulties and that theirs is no exception. They may only later come to realize their child is not demonstrating the kind of motor activity expected during the first year.

Normally the Moro reflex is gone by the end of the first three months of life, as is the tonic neck reflex. The persistence of these primitive responses is abnormal and is highly indicative of delayed neuromotor development. Not every parent is aware of this, and we consider it normal for them to be oblivious to clinically important signs. A less obscure matter is head control, which babies usually attain by the time they are three months old. This is an overt type of behavior that may be recognized by an alert parent. Such a parent is probably well informed and consults Dr. Spock's book conscientiously and frequently. Here then is an element of importance in understanding why parents react differently to the rates at which infants develop. Well-educated, alert mothers are more likely to perceive that there are norms of attainment to which children usually conform. Also, an experienced parent, one with older children, is more likely to perceive and then assess the rate at which a youngster is growing than will a new parent. (This is not restricted to parents of handicapped children; there is the example of the mother with a boy with an IQ close to 200. She thought that all boys talked in sentences at 12 months!) In such matters ignorance is bliss for a limited period of time; it begins to give way to doubt and anxiety as youngsters fail to reach developmental levels at the usual time.

Dependence

There is another factor in parental reaction to physical disability not apparent immediately that is a concomitant to delays in motor development. Infants are not bundles of reflexes, they are complex little people with personalities that are distinct at an early age. From infancy children are social creatures and they exhibit patterns of social behavior. Bathing a baby is a happy time, giving pleasure to mothers—and to fathers. As we say so often, they are so helpless and so lovable. In fact: they are helpless; they depend on us for their food, for the love that makes them grow, and for the care that protects them. Their very dependence on us is satisfying and helps us toward maturity as we help them.

The total physical and psychological dependence of infancy is normal, and it is to be expected. In the case of physically handicapped children, however, the normal stage of serious dependence may mask an abnormal degree of dependence. The pattern of interaction of mother and child in matters of feeding and care is typically one of early serious dependence, which normally gives way to a lessened degree of dependence as a child attempts self-care and self-feeding. Parents of children who are cerebral palsied may for a time not realize that dependence that is normal and delightful at one age is inappropriate later. This is a kind of problem that ticks away and evolves into anxiety only with the passage of time. The neuromotor problem exists but without concern or worry in parents. Parental anxiety slowly emerges as a child at 15 months shows little willingness to walk, to feed himself, or to grasp toys. A child at two years may fail to progress socially, to make spontaneous moves towards independence. In this case parental reactions may be due to social rather than neuromotor problems. Obviously, parental reactions on social grounds alone occur in children whose physical limitations are not extreme.

At this point friends and relatives are inclined to advise that children will "grow out of it." Of course this does not happen, since it would require a doubling of the developmental quotient in many cases to allow a child to catch up. Such alterations in the rate of maturation are not common, and parents may now realize that "something"—vague and unspecified—is wrong.

The School Years

Let us pursue the development cycle a little further. Starting school is an experience for more than just children. Parents tend to prize this step because of the achievement potential their children represent. A child's succeeding in kindergarten, our values tell us, will open the door to success in elementary school. This in turn may lead to high school success and college. Fantasy about our children's success is normal, and we all realize the crucial role that education plays. Today's technological revolution seems to make school success a corollary of economic and social success. Failure at the bottom rung of the educational ladder consequently produces parental concerns. These are likely to be more naked reactions when children have physical disabilities. It seems that visible defects in children make parental perception less distorted, as Zuk has pointed out.[25] We may expect, therefore, that a child's reaching school age is important and can precipitate family reactions.

In line with this general desire of parents that their child make the progress expected of most children, you may recall the change for the good in family attitudes that occurred in parents of trainable children about 10 years ago when schools and classes for them were opened. These parents felt better because their children were doing what other children were doing—going to school. For the purposes of this discussion it really does not matter that the schools sometimes were not very good or that the children made little academic progress; the point is that the children engaged in an activity expected of children during the middle childhood years. A reduction of anxiety in the parents was understandable since their own needs relating to their children were now being met.

Adolescence

Adolescence is a period of stress in families with nonhandicapped children. It follows that to parents of physically handicapped children adolescence is a period of stress producing a variety of responses. The form the responses of families take depends largely on what is perceived in the handicapped adolescent.

In some adolescents with physical handicaps problems may arise where before none existed to a serious extent. For example, handicapped adolescents may produce anxiety in their parents by engaging in fantasies with worrisome content. A boy or a girl may entertain unrealistic vocational goals, dreaming of becoming a member of a profession. In some cases adolescents may entertain ambitions whose lack of a realistic base is obvious to parents, but not to the children. To some extent we—society that is—may be responsible. There is an unfortunate tendency to offer as models the superman who has triumphed over all obstacles, enticing the handicapped adolescent into unprofitable fantasy. As we know, all too often a person's predictable failure to become outstanding, indeed even adequate, produces its own reaction, further complicating the self-concept of the adolescent with whom the family must cope.

The need for self-acceptance of one's physical appearance can make problems for the family of an adolescent. Physically disabled adolescents find the discrepancy between their appearance and that of other boys and girls distressing. Added to the normal discomfort of adolescence, which is partially neurotic, is a reality-centered discomfort. This arises as the young person recognizes the failure to be normal in appearance.

A little later this sense of personal devaluation may give way to problems arising from the conventional expectation of earning a living and raising a family. Many handicapped persons, of course, do earn a living, but many do not. Probably only a minority marry, which is particularly true of the cerebral palsied.

The Ecology of Disability

Now, it might seem that this catalog of human ills and limitations inevitably produces intense family maladjustment. In many cases this is so. Certainly much of the research bears this out. Farber's studies[6–10] and those of Klebanoff,[15] Boles,[2] Holt[11, 12] and Schonell[21, 22] demonstrate this. On the other hand, family reactions to disability are sometimes excellent. Excellence, in this context, has several connotations. An excellent reaction may be no reaction; when disability is mild a family may find its routines altered only slightly and its expectations barely modified. Excellence may be attributed to realistic and therapeutically oriented attitudes toward a child with serious limitations. In some families such attitudes exist, and the result is that team efforts at rehabilitation are successful, within the neurological limits of the child. In such situations positive attitudes do not usually arise spontaneously but are the result of deliberate attempts to create them. Excellent attitudes are as much a therapeutic goal for parents as speech or mobility for children. This means that treatment for physically disabled children includes the attempt to assist their families. Failure to consider this is the consequence of a limited and inadequate concept of disease. Current concepts of disease recognize that it is ecological—that it affects the diseased person directly and also produces a secondary effect on other people. This effect is as real when a person is cerebral palsied as it is when a person has an infectious disease. Attitudes and anxieties are social components of physical disability and are as contagious as microbes. Unfortunately, bad attitudes are usually more difficult to eradicate and feelings of guilt and worry may be suppressed, only to appear as irritation and petulance among members of the family.

Need for Research

Let us now consider disability and its impact on family life as a challenge to our ingenuity. The object is not to consider tricks of "researchmanship" but to try to identify aspects of the problem that may be profitably explored.

Review of Research

A brief review of pertinent research seems in order. First, there have been the sociological studies on retardation by Bernard Farber of the University of Illinois.[6-10] These have been classic studies in which theory and concepts were applied to the families of retarded children and the situations that arise. Saenger[18, 19] has given a picture of mental disability and the scope of adjustments brought about, using slightly less technical concepts. Equally helpful have been the pictures of family adjustment to a variety of conditions in children by Davis,[4] Little,[16] Denhoff and Holden,[5] Stein and Longenecker,[23] Westlund and Palumbo,[24] and Farber.[9] Zuk has given a personal, or subjective, dimension to the problem by looking as a clinician at family reactions.[25, 26] Jordan[13] applied the Parent Attitude Research Instrument to mothers of retarded children and found an interesting relationship to aspects of child growth. In a further study[13] a similar pattern of values was identified in mothers of cerebral palsied children. Collins[3] has found Catholic mothers of cerebral palsied children more introverted and depressed than non-Catholic mothers. Both groups were more introverted than a control group of mothers. Much of this literature has been reviewed elsewhere by Jordan.[14]

After we have noted these contributions there are few left to consider. This is because the concept of disability as a family issue is not particularly old. There are many unraised questions, of course, and the answers to some are undoubtedly being sought by conscientious investigators at this moment. Saucier at McGill University is conducting research on the familial consequences of chronic illness in children, using a socioanthropological model of family structure.

Problems of Application of Research

All of this research is fine, but physical disability produces problems at the level of application. What does the conscientious worker say and do to help a family? How much is possible? Who should do what, and how, to help a family cope with a moderately involved cerebral palsied child? The answers are too often locked in the private thinking of experienced workers. Clearly more exchange of information is needed to capitalize on what we know informally. I should like to suggest some modes of inquiry into this problem area.

Suggested Problems for Research

An ideal approach would be to take a chronically ill child, study his family, cure him, and study the family during the process. I wonder if we do not have a paradigm for studying pieces of this problem: We might analyze the self-concept and psychodynamics of obese children. They experience much of the doubt and self-rejection that really sick children experience. Obesity is often a condition that yields to diet. Without a doubt this condition is a useful paradigm, and it can help us understand child and family relationships over a period of time.

The pattern of adjustment or maladjustment—depending on the condition—is slow to emerge in some families. In others it is rapid. There are some conditions in children that produce family reactions quickly, instantaneously in some cases. This kind of problem can yield to serious study. Accidents involving fire or lye burns can produce swift crises in families. In such situations families respond differently.

Research may be profitably directed to family patterns of reaction that have a slow rather than swift onset. Attention should be paid to the patterns of reaction that emerge in children who are moderately ill for a long time but that shift eventually as the child enters the terminal phase of illness. Leukemia is an example, and its slow but merciless development produces a pattern of reaction in the family that might offer an opportunity for profitable study.

All patterns of reactions to disability present fundamental questions. Are patterns of reaction disease-specific? By this we mean, is there a pattern of family adjustment or style of reaction specific to a given disease. Looking at the matter in another way, we may ask if patterns of adjustment and reaction are consistent for visible disabilities. Do parents or brothers and sisters of mongoloid children react in a determinate response to the visibility of mongolism? Are such parents more reality oriented at the same level of functioning than, for example, parents of children with metabolic forms of mental retardation?

There are the standard questions concerning ecological variables. Do rich and poor, white and colored, well and poorly educated families develop consistent patterns of adjustment to a given disease?

How a child's physical disability affects different persons can be measured by noting discrete events in their lives. Using this approach we can identify a series of incidents: minor arguments between members of a family, nerves frayed by the task of coping with a physically dependent child who is heavy and hard to manage, an incautious comment creating a storm. The set of events may conclude in the tragedy of family disintegration. This approach is fragmentary, however, and it usually consists of anecdotal materials that rarely do more than arouse one's sympathy even when they occur in a long and comprehensive list.

A more productive approach is needed if families are to be helped. We need to establish dimensions of reaction so that our analysis will be more than a catalog of human predicaments and dilemmas.

A useful dimension is integrity of family patterns; that is, we identify expected patterns of neighborhood and community activity and patterns of interaction within the extended family circle. Deviation from the expected patterns, a simple hypothesis of discrepancy, becomes an indicant of family response to physical disability in one of its members.

A theoretical issue of considerable interest may be noted at this point. Families react to the reality we as outsiders perceive, but they also react to what they think they see; that is, there is a *phenomenal* reality to which a family reacts. Frequently, there is a discrepancy between the reality, in the disease sense, and the formulation of that reality, its phenomenal nature. This discrepancy between what a disease is and what it seems to be is a major dimension of disease of all types. Over 25 years ago we had our first and practically only piece of work on what disease means to afflicted children.[1] It is important for us to understand how the pivotal person in the family—the sick child—perceives his own condition. It may be that this is a key to the reactions of other members of the family and as a testable problem can be applied to virtually every form of handicap in children and adults.

Complementary to the issue of families and their goals is that of parents and siblings and their individual goals. The goals may be formulated as successive social roles usually entered into. Girls normally progress from marginal family responsibilities to full responsibilities when they establish their own homes. In some families this normal evolution of responsibility may be speeded up as siblings share the heavy burden imposed by another child. The girls also may not establish their own homes at all, a consequence of choice or of necessity as would-be suitors perceive the presence of a chronically ill brother or sister. Parents also experience change in role. They were not parents when they married, nor will they normally remain so, in the nurturing sense, once the youngest child has left home. When there is a member of the household who is physically dependent, the "youngest" child (meaning the handicapped person) never does leave home. Parents do not continue role change; they do not evolve into grandparents but, rather, remain parents of a young child for the rest of their days. Evolution of personal roles within the family circle is an index of progress toward family goals; it becomes, therefore, a measure of adaptation to the presence of a physically handicapped person.

A vital subproblem here, of theoretical and practical importance, is the repertoire of role constructs that relatives of handicapped persons use to order their personal lives. Both role constructs and semantic differential technics could be used to advantage to shed light on the personal dimensions of response of relatives to the problem.

Another class of questions may also be raised. Many of us who have worked with handicapped children and their families have noted the circularity of adjustments to children's traits and the determinate effect a family has on many of those traits. For example, a family reacts not to the number of damaged cells in the system of a brain-injured child, but to the behavior projected from the neurological substratum. Fortunately or unfortunately the skills a child projects are partially determined by the values and attitudes the family exhibits. The circularity emerges as those very attitudes emerge as a reaction to perceived child traits. Obviously, the disability state in many cases, for example, organically caused retardation, cannot change, but family patterns of reaction can change. By designating the family unit as an object of our assistance through counseling, we insure the probability of our own efforts reaching their potential level of effectiveness. A family assisted to react and adjust will at least be less likely to hinder rehabilitation and, if experience is not too cautionary, to assist actively at times. Family participation in the rehabilitation process becomes a research topic of importance since it is a vital element.

An obvious subject for research is the process of socialization in handicapped children. Since we know little of the socialization process in nonhandicapped children we have little knowledge on which to presume. It may seem strange, but it is true. The amount of useful information on how normal children grow is very small. The amount of information on how handicapped children grow is even smaller. We need to know if growth potentials in infancy are always met. We should ask at what point mothers of handicapped children treat their youngsters differently and if it is always necessary. Mothers probably train many children to be handicapped—in the personality sense. How can we minimize a process until we know what it is? Let us hope to see more work on the basic processes of socialization of children, handicapped children in particular.[17]

Roles of the Disciplines

We must consider which professional disciplines can give new insights on family reactions. To a surprising extent much of our knowledge of family reactions to disability has come from psychologists and sociologists, but comparatively little of a fundamental sort has come from social workers. Because of their heavy work load they have failed to report what they know, which is unfortunate in view of the strategic nature of their contacts with families. The social caseworker, if an alert observer, can reach useful conclusions after sustained contact with families in difficulty. Social workers generally adopt a frame of reference in their work that decreases the probability of mere repetition in their family contacts. Using concepts of change and growth they try to move families in positive directions and are sensitive to changes in family integration. Perhaps more than some other professional personnel social workers can give breadth and vitality to current concepts of families and their problems. In a complementary fashion psychologists can contribute to the study of the problems. Assisting both social workers and rehabilitation counselors, psychologists can design studies that will produce realistic conclusions. These, in turn, can lead to more productive and strategic intervention in the process of family reaction to the presence of a physically disabled child.

In conclusion it may be observed that we are slowly turning our attention to nonmedical aspects of physical disability. As we apply our energies to the family aspects of physical disability in children we contribute in a fuller way to the understanding of human behavior. We begin to see that the behavior of handicapped persons is explained partially by disease processes and partially by social factors. When all aspects of disability are considered we may well conclude that the challenges to our professional ingenuity posed by psychological and social factors are at least as important as those produced by medical considerations.

List of References

1. Beverly, B. I. The Effect of Illness upon Emotional Development. *J. Pediat.* May, 1936. 8:5:533-543.

2. Boles, G. Personality Factors in Mothers of Cerebral Palsied Children. *Genet. Psych. Monographs.* 1959. 59:159-218.

3. Collins, H. A. *Religious Values and Adjustment in Mothers of Cerebral Palsied Children.* Unpublished paper, 1963.

4. Davis, F. *Polio in the Family; A Study in Crises and Family Process.* Unpublished dissertation, University of Chicago, 1958.

5. Denhoff, E., and Holden, R. H. Family Influence on Successful School Adjustment of Cerebral Palsied Children. *Exceptional Children.* Oct., 1954. 21:1:5-7.

6. Farber, B. Effects of a Severely Mentally Retarded Child on the Family, p. 227-246, in: Trapp, E. P., and Himelstein, P. *(eds.) Readings on the Exceptional Child.* New York: Appleton-Century-Crofts, 1962.

7. Farber, B. *Effects of a Severely Retarded Child on Family Integration.* Lafayette, Ind.: Child Development Publications, 1959. *(Monographs of the Society for Research in Child Development.* Ser. no. 71, 1959. 24:2)

8. Farber, B. Family Organization and Crises: Maintenance of Integration in Families with a Severely Mentally Retarded Child. Lafayette, Ind.: Child Development Publications, 1960. *(Monographs of the Society for Research in Child Development.* Ser. no. 75, 1960. 25:1)

9. Farber, B. Interaction with Retarded Siblings and Life Goals of Children. *Marriage and Family Living.* Feb., 1963. 25:1:96-98.

10. Farber, B. Perceptions of Crisis and Related Variables in the Impact of a Retarded Child on the Mother. *J. Health and Human Behavior.* Summer, 1960. 1:2:108-118.

11. Holt, K. S. The Home Care of Severely Retarded Children. *Pediat.* Oct., 1958. 22:4 (Pt. I): 744-755.

12. Holt, K. S. *The Impact of Mentally Retarded Children upon Their Families.* Unpublished dissertation, Sheffield Univ., 1957.

13. Jordan, T. E. *The Mentally Retarded.* Columbus, Ohio: Merrill Books, 1961.

14. Jordan, T. E. Research on the Handicapped Child and the Family. *Merrill-Palmer Quart.* 1962. 8:4:243-260.

15. Klebanoff, L. B. Parental Attitudes of Mothers of Schizophrenic, Brain-injured and Retarded, and Normal Children. *Am. J. Orthopsychiatry.* July, 1959. 29:3:445-454. (Part of a doctoral dissertation in clinical psychology, Boston University Graduate School, 1957)

16. Little, S. A Note on an Investigation of the Emotional Complications of Cerebral Palsy. *Nervous Child.* Apr., 1949. 8:2:181-182.

17. McKinney, J. P., and Keele, T. Effects of Increased Mothering on the Behavior of Severely Retarded Boys. *Am. J. Mental Deficiency.* Jan., 1963. 67:4:556-562.

18. Saenger, G. *The Adjustment of Severely Retarded Adults in the Community.* Albany, N.Y.: New York State Interdepartmental Health Resources Board, 1957.

19. Saenger, G. *Factors Influencing the Institutionalization of Mentally Retarded Individuals in New York City.* Albany, N.Y.: New York State Interdepartmental Health Resources Board, 1960.

20. Schlesinger, E. R., Allaway, N. C., and Peltin, S. Survivorship in Cerebral Palsy. *Am. J. Public Health.* Mar., 1959. 49:3:343-349.

21. Schonell, F. J., and Rorke, M. A Second Survey of the Effects of a Subnormal Child on the Family Unit. *Am. J. Mental Deficiency.* Mar., 1960. 64:5:862-868.

22. Schonell, F. J., and Watts, B. H. A First Survey of the Effects of a Subnormal Child on the Family Unit. *Am. J. Mental Deficiency.* July, 1956. 61:1:210-219.

23. Stein, J. F., and Longenecker, E. D. Patterns of Mothering Affecting Handicapped Children in Residential Treatment. *Am. J. Mental Deficiency.* Mar., 1962. 66:5:749-758.

24. Westlund, N., and Palumbo, A. Z. Parental Rejection of Crippled Children. *Am. J. Orthopsychiatry.* Apr., 1946. 16:271-281.

25. Zuk, G. H. Autistic Distortions in Parents of Retarded Children. *J. Consulting Psych.* Apr., 1959. 23:2:171-176.

26. Zuk, G. H. The Religious Factor and the Role of Guilt in Parental Acceptance of the Retarded Child. *Am. J. Mental Deficiency.* July, 1959. 64:1:139-147.

The Guilt Reactions of Children with Severe Physical Disease

Richard A. Gardner

The author studied 23 parents to test the hypothesis that psychological processes other than the classical process might explain the inappropriate guilt reaction of parents of severely ill children. Some of the parents did suffer guilt for reasons described by the classical process—i.e., it was related to unconscious hostility toward the child—but the guilt of some of the others is more readily explained by the alternative hypothesis that it represents an attempt at control of the uncontrollable. In some parents neither mechanism seemed to be operative.

THE AUTHOR HAS OBSERVED that most parents of children with severe diseases such as leukemia, cystic fibrosis, cerebral palsy, and brain injury exhibit at one time or another an inappropriate guilt reaction concerning their child's illness. Typical comments include: "It's my fault he got measles encephalitis. I shouldn't have sent him to camp." "We had sexual relations during the last month of my pregnancy. Maybe that did it." "God punished me for not going to church."

Freudian psychoanalytic theory(2) holds that this inappropriate guilt reaction is related to unconscious hostility against the stricken child and that the illness represents the magic fulfillment of these unconscious hostile wishes, therefore the guilt. Freud's theory of a constant association between repressed hostility and guilt has become so deeply ingrained that many psychiatrists do not consider exaggerated or inappropriate guilt to stem from any other cause. The fact that one can almost always ferret out some hostility toward the person over whose misfortune the patient feels guilty has further served to strengthen this connection.

So ubiquitous is this guilt reaction that the author wondered whether in some of these parents other processes might be operative. If the classical hypothesis were the only one, then one would have to assume that most parents are secretly so hostile that they wish their child to have suffered the catastrophic illness. One plausible alternative is that the guilt might be an attempt to gain some control over this calamity, for personal control is strongly implied in the idea: "It's my fault." When guilt is used in this way, not only is the individual convinced that he had the power to prevent the illness, but also implied is his ability to avert its recurrence in the sick child as well as its appearance in siblings and possibly even in the parent himself. Such inappropriate guilt may stem, then, not from hostility but from love and affection, from the desire to see the illness undone and/or prevent it in the future.

A study of these parents was carried out in an attempt to determine the psychodynamics of this guilt reaction. Although the study was structured specifically to compare the likelihood of the classical explanation with the author's alternative, it did allow for the possibility that neither was an appropriate explanation and that other mechanisms might be present.

Freudian psychoanalytic theory holds that these guilt-ridden parents suffer from at least one of three psychopathological processes.

Dr. Gardner is instructor in child psychiatry, College of Physicians & Surgeons, Columbia University, and is on the faculty, William A. White Psychoanalytic Institute, New York, N. Y. His address is 54 Forest Rd., Tenafly, N. J. 07670.

This paper was the recipient in 1967 of the Gralnick Foundation Award, given to a recent psychoanalytic graduate for an original contribution to the field.

The author wishes to thank Dr. Norton Garber for his valuable assistance to the study while he was a senior medical student at New York University College of Medicine.

The Guilt Reaction of Parents of Children with Severe Physical Disease, Richard A. Gardner, *American Journal of Psychiatry*, Vol. 126, No. 5, Reprinted with the Permission of Richard A. Creshett, M.D.,

The first hypothesis holds that the parents harbor an excessive amount of unconscious hostility toward the stricken child and that the illness represents the magic fulfillment of these unconscious hostile wishes. The guilt, then, is appropriate to this hostility, and it is postulated that were these parents not so hostile to their children, they would not feel so guilty. In summary, the essential elements in process 1 are:

1. Excessive hostility
2. Normal inhibition of hostility
3. Magic thinking

The second classical hypothesis maintains that the parents' hostility against the child is not excessive but that the superego is unduly intolerant of even the normal degree of hostility that any parent at times feels toward a child. Here, too, the illness is regarded as the magic fulfillment of the parents' hostile feelings. Accordingly, the guilt is related to a conscience that is overly critical of even normal hostile feelings that occasionally arise in the healthiest parent-child relationship.

The essential elements in process 2 are:

1. Normal degree of occasional hostility
2. Excessive guilt over normal hostility
3. Magic thinking

The third Freudian hypothesis is a combination of the first two processes.The individual is inordinately hostile and feels excessively guilty. The guilt is greater than what might be appropriate even to the exaggerated hostility because the parent feels responsible for the illness, which he regards as the magic fulfillment of his hostile impulses. The essential elements in process 3 are:

1. Excessive hostility
2. Excessive guilt over hostility
3. Magic thinking

If the author's hypothesis were valid, process 4, comprising the following elements, would be operant:

1. Normal degree of occasional hostility
2. Normal inhibition of hostility
3. Magic thinking

With this theoretical construct in mind, the study was conducted as follows: Parents of severely ill children at the inpatient and outpatient departments of the Babies Hospital, Columbia-Presbyterian Medical Center, New York City, were told that a study was being conducted to learn more about the reactions of parents in their situation so that doctors would be in a better position to counsel them. They were advised that participation would entail five to six hours of interviewing and testing; in addition, they were told that the examiner would be available to assist them in handling their reactions to the child's illness.

Thirty parents were approached, and 23 participated in the study to its completion. The inquiry was divided into four sections.

The Study

Section 1

The primary purpose of this section was to determine if the inappropriate guilt reaction was present. It was originally decided to place parents exhibiting the guilt reaction in the experimental group and those without it in the control group. However, some parents, although not blaming themselves, did blame others (e.g., the doctor). Therefore two experimental groups were formed: group A for those who blamed themselves and group B for those who blamed someone else. The control group, group C, exhibited no need to blame anyone.

Although it was recognized that there might be different parental reaction patterns to each illness, the guilt reaction focused upon did not appear to be related to the nature of the disease, and therefore the parents were not grouped according to the child's disorder.[1]

The interview was structured and the questions were asked so as to provide the greatest likelihood that the parents would describe the guilt reaction de novo. Other background information was obtained so that the parents would not realize that the primary focus of the interview was the guilt reaction. Questions posed early in the interview were designed to elicit general reactions to the child's illness; during this period the guilt reaction was sometimes described. Later questions made more specific reference to the guilt and blame reactions, and if they were present, further details were elicited to ensure that the parent was being placed in the proper group—either experimental (A or B) or control (C).

Section 2

A scale consisting of three sections was devised which attempted to specifically

[1] For the reader's interest, the children of the 23 parents studied suffered from the following illnesses: cerebral palsy, 7; leukemia, 3; hemophilia, 2; chronic glomerulonephritis, 2; congenital esophageal atresia, 1; multiple systemic congenital anomalies, 1; chronic asthma, 1; nephrotic syndrome, 1; craniosynostosis, 1; cystic fibrosis, 1; pontine glioma, 1; intra-atrial septal defect, 1; and chronic peritonitis, 1.

evaluate in an objective way the relative degree of both loving and hostile feelings that the parents felt toward the child. A parent whose feelings of affection markedly predominated over those of hostility (some of which is expected even in the most loving parent) would obtain a high score. The parent whose hostile feelings predominated over the loving feelings (some of which also exists even in the most hostile parent) would obtain a low score. Each parent's score was expected to fall at some point on a continuum between marked affection and marked hostility on the Affection-Hostility scale.

Section 2A

This section was devised to evaluate the parents' scores on the Affection-Hostility scale for material *in conscious awareness.* Mothers were given 33 questions and fathers 21.[2] The questions were in part derived from Levy's criteria for the determination of maternal feeling through observations and questions(9, 10, 11, 12), but additions and elaborations were made by the author. Typical questions for the mothers included: "When you were a child, what were your feelings about playing with dolls?" "When you were a teen-ager, what were your feelings about helping care for younger children and/or babysitting?" "Before you were married, how many children did you hope to have?"—"Why that number?" "Do you have any pictures of your children?"—"May I see them?" "What kind of feelings do you have when you see a new baby?" "Are you the kind of woman who likes to cuddle new babies?"

Of the 33 questions posed to the mothers, 21 were appropriate to the fathers as well, providing a separate conscious Affection-Hostility scale for each sex. Face validity only is claimed for these criteria. Since the author's criteria have incorporated many of Levy's, his scale cannot be compared with mine to establish content validity. Since no other scales measuring maternal affection are known to the author, content validity of his criteria will have to await future work.

Instead of using Levy's somewhat vague 1 to 5 scoring system, a more rigorous system of +1, 0, and −1 was utilized in an attempt to make the data more meaningful. A question was scored by +1 if the answer definitely indicated warm, loving feelings toward children, −1 if the reply revealed hostility, and 0 if the question was not appropriate or the answer gave no clear-cut information in either direction. The mothers' scores could range from −33 to +33 and those of the fathers from −21 to +21. An attempt to establish reliability was made by having the other examiner independently score a response, and then disagreements were discussed for possible resolution. If differences could not be resolved, a 0 score was given. No claim is made that this represents true statistical reliability, but it was an attempt in this direction.

Sections 2B and 2C evaluated *unconscious factors* operant in determining the parents' position on the Affection Hostility scale.

Section 2B

The parents were presented with a series of 12 pictures, each selected because it tended to elicit data about intrafamilial relationships. Seven were chosen from popular magazines and five from the Thematic Apperception Test (TAT)(14) (cards 1, 2, 7GF, 13B, and 19). The parents were told: "This is a test of imagination, one form of intelligence. While looking at the picture, try to make up as dramatic a story as you can. It is part of a test of creative ability. So let your imagination have its own way as in a myth or fantasy. Give it free rein." Scoring was done according to the same criteria employed in section 2A. Scores could range from −12 to +12.

Section 2C

The parents were presented with a series of 35 short phrases for sentence completion designed to elicit a response involving children. Some of the questions were taken from the Miale-Holsopple Sentence Completion Method(7). Miale-Holsopple items 1, 6, 8, 16, 30, 40, 58, 70, and 73 were utilized. Other items were designed by the author, e.g., "The sick kitten. . . . ," "Boys and girls. . . . ," "Mothers often. . . . ," "Kids are. . . . " and "The lame animal. . . ."

The parents were instructed:

> This is a test to see how rapidly you can make up an end to these uncompleted sentences. Although it is hard, try to tell me the very first thought that comes into your mind, as rapidly as you can. Most people give some responses that are embarrassing, difficult to say or seem silly, but try to be as honest as you can. Most people take less than a second to respond. I will measure your speed with a stopwatch. See how fast you can do this. It is one measure of

[2] Space does not permit the complete inclusion of these as well as subsequent scales to be described in this article. However, all questionnaires with guidelines for scoring are available from the author.

intelligence.

Then, one or two trials were made with nontest items such as "Bread and. . . . ," and "The tree. . . ."

Scoring was done on the +1, 0, and −1 basis as in sections 2A and 2B. The score of 0 was given for all responses begun after three seconds. Scores could range from −35 to +35.

Scoring in sections 2B and 2C was based on each examiner's interpretation, and an attempt at reliability and the minimization of bias was made by independent scoring by each examiner; an attempt at resolution of differences was made, and a score of 0 was assigned if such agreement could not be obtained.

The total score on the Affection-Hostility Scale was determined by adding the totals of sections 2A, 2B, and 2C. It could vary from −80 to +80.

Section 3

The only scale the author learned of that purported to test hostility inhibition was that of Siegel(16). His scale is derived from questions on the Minnesota Multiphasic Personality Inventory (MMPI), and he claims validity via its correlation with a scale of authoritarianism. I not only questioned this assumption but the face validity of some of Siegel's items as well.

Accordingly, a Hostility-Inhibition scale of 28 true-false questions was designed by the author. Its purpose was to specifically evaluate the degree of inhibition in the conscious awareness of and the expression of hostility. As with the items in Siegel's scale, some were taken from the MMPI(6), but others were designed by the author. Twenty-five MMPI questions were utilized: numbers 26, 30, 75, 82, 91, 96, 105, 150, 162, 195, 201, 225, 232, 277, 282, 316, 368, 382, 426, 438, 443, 502, 503, 509, and 536. The author devised three questions: "A pacifistic approach has enabled me to avoid many arguments and conflicts." "Once a week or oftener something happens that gets me angry." "I make it a rule to avoid discussing religion or politics because it most often leads to differences of opinion and even arguments." Face validity only is claimed for these questions.

The questions were presented on a mimeographed form that included directions requesting the parent to mark each statement as true or false as it most closely applied to himself. After the parent had written his answers, the test was reviewed to ensure that all questions had been understood and answered appropriately.[3]

Scores could range from −28 to +28, with −28 representing ideally healthy, free, and appropriate handling of hostility and +28 a pathologic degree of inhibition of hostility.

Section 4

The author could find no scale for evaluating magic thinking. Accordingly, a scale was designed to ascertain the degree to which the parent utilized magic thinking processes to control events generally not considered controllable. Questions concerned beliefs in such subjects as faith healing, the power of prayer, fortune-tellers, horoscopes, superstitions, Christian Science, and predicting the future. Face validity only is claimed for these items. An attempt to achieve reliability was obtained by independent scoring and matching as described above. Fourteen questions were asked in an open-ended manner, similar to section 1. Responses were scored +1, 0, or −1 depending upon the degree of magic thinking implied in the response. The score could range from −14 to +14, with −14 representing relative freedom from magic thinking and +14 a marked degree of utilization of magic thinking.

Table 1 summarizes the scores to be expected of parents in group A, i.e., parents exhibiting the inappropriate guilt reaction if the psychodynamics of their guilt were to be explained by each of the four postulated psychodynamic formulations.

Results

Of the 23 parents who completed the study, ten were placed in group A (inappropriate guilt reaction), three in group B (blame reaction), and ten in the control group, group C. The results are tabulated in table 2.

In discussing the data, I will confine myself to groups A and C since group B consisted of only three parents.

The ten parents in group A had a significantly lower average score on the

[3] It was surprising that many parents did not understand a question, yet marked it true or false just to place an answer in a box, or if they did understand it, placed their answer in a box inappropriate to their intended response. The verbal review was necessary to be sure that the most accurate data were being used.

TABLE 1
Anticipated Results for Each of the Four Psychodynamic Formulations

PROCESS	SECTION 2 (AFFECTION-HOSTILITY SCALE)	SECTION 3 (HOSTILITY-INHIBITION SCALE)	SECTION 4 (MAGIC THINKING SCALE)
1 (Classical)	Low	Normal or low	High
2 (Classical)	Normal or high	High	High
3 (Classical)	Low	High	High
4 (Author's)	Normal or high	Normal or low	High

Affection-Hostility scale (+4.1) than the ten control parents (+14.6), suggesting that the guilt group on the whole harbored more hostility toward children than the parents without the guilt reaction. The difference between these two groups was significant at the 0.05 level on the Sum of the Ranks Test. Groups A and C showed similar averages on the Hostility-Inhibition scale (section 3) and Magic Thinking scale (section 4).

More important than average figures are individual scores that, on analysis, are more meaningful in establishing the presence or absence of any of the four postulated psychodynamic formulations. The scores of each of the ten parents in group A were studied to determine if they fell into any of the patterns outlined in table 1. Before this could be done, normal ranges had to be delineated for each of the sections in the group C data. This was done by listing the results of each section in group C in numerical order and ascertaining a natural cutoff point for the few highest and few lowest figures. Such cutoff points usually delineated the middle two-thirds as the normal range. The results of these determinations are shown in table 3.

These criteria were then used to decide whether a section score in a group A parent was in the high, low, or average range and thereby to determine whether a score pattern fit into any of the four processes of psychodynamic formulations. To facilitate this, the specific high, low, and normal ranges were substituted for the categories outlined in table 1. The results are shown in table 4.

Of the ten parents in group A, five did not obtain scores that would place them in any of the four categories. Of the other five (see table 5), two had scores suggesting that their guilt could be explained on the basis of classical psychodynamics, and three by the alternative hypothesis suggested by the author.

These three parents had the highest section 2 scores of the ten parents in group A, i.e., they rated highest in parental affection. One of the three obtained a score of +32, which was eight points higher than the highest control group score in section 2. This would lend further evidence to the author's view that the guilty reaction can arise out of affection and devotion and not necessarily hostility. No attempt is made to explain the psychodynamics of the remaining five parents.

To translate this into perhaps more meaningful clinical terms, the protocol of two parents who demonstrated psychodynamic processes 1 and 4 will be summarized.

Case 1. C. K., a 53-year-old Jewish housewife, was the most striking example of process 1: She exhibited a high level of hostility, normal inhibition of hostility, and a high degree of magic thinking. Her 14-year-old daughter had cystic fibrosis. The symptoms had been present since infancy, but a definite diagnosis was not made until she was 11. In the more than three years since learning the diagnosis, Mrs. K. suffered with feelings of guilt. The guilt centered around ideas that she had not done enough for the child when she was younger and that she might have made mistakes during the girl's upbringing but did not know exactly what these were. Other guilty preoccupations were with biblical quotations in which God punished people for their sins through their children. These obsessions were associated with anorexia and insomnia. On numerous occasions she had mentioned these feelings to physicians and had been told "not to think that way."

Mrs. K.'s score on section 2 (Affection-Hostility) was −3, placing her lower than any member of the control group (range +1 to +20) and eighth among the ten parents in her own group A(guilt) group.

As a child, Mrs. K. had not enjoyed playing with dolls or helping her mother with housework. She never enjoyed baby-sitting or caring for younger siblings. She did not breast-feed her child. Typical responses in section 2B included: "The children looked intently at the apples, but the mother doesn't like the way the apples look, they're rotten or something, so she doesn't buy them." To TAT card number 1 she responded: "He'll never be a musician. He's just not cut out for it. He thinks you'll get somewhere by just sitting there and staring."

This parent's magic thinking exhibited itself in a deep involvement with the rituals of orthodox Judaism, continuous use of prayers, belief in miracles, faith healing, and mental telepathy, and marked adherence to common

TABLE 2
Results of the Study

PARENT	SECTION 2a	2b	2c	2(TOTAL)	3	4
				GROUP A		
RA	(+ 3	– 2	+ 5)	+ 6	– 10	+ 2
AM	(+ 13	– 7	– 7)	– 1	+ 5	0
MM	(0	– 4	– 2)	– 6	+ 1	0
MC	(+ 9	– 5	+ 3)	+ 7	– 28	– 12
MMc	(+ 4	– 9	0)	– 5	– 10	– 1
CK	(4	– 4	+ 5)	– 3	+ 4	+ 1
AF	(+ 18	0	+ 3)	+ 21	– 4	+ 4
JB	(– 21	– 4	+ 3)	– 22	– 11	– 1
ES	(+ 25	+ 1	+ 6)	+ 32	– 4	+ 3
EM	(+ 9	– 2	+ 5)	+ 12	+ 1	+ 1
Range				– 22 to + 32	– 28 to + 5	– 12 to + 4
Average				+ 4.1*	– 5.6	– 0.6
				GROUP B		
WH	(+ 11	– 8	+ 1)	+ 4	– 4	+ 6
SK	(– 2	+ 2	+ 8)	+ 8	– 22	+ 10
TF	(+ 8	– 9	+ 6)	+ 5	+ 1	+ 1
Range				+ 4 to + 8	– 22 to + 1	+ 1 to + 10
Average				+ 5.7	– 8.3	+ 5.7
				GROUP C		
EM	(+ 9	– 1	– 5)	+ 3	+ 9	0
AG	(+ 13	+ 6	+ 10)	+ 29	– 3	+ 3
CM	(+ 1	– 2	+ 2)	+ 1	+ 9	– 4
SB	(+ 16	+ 3	+ 5)	+ 24	– 10	– 2
RL	(+ 19	– 2	+ 2)	+ 19	– 3	– 11
MS	(+ 3	– 4	+ 3)	+ 2	+ 5	+ 6
BB	(+ 12	+ 1	+ 3)	+ 16	– 12	+ 2
MH	(+ 22	– 1	– 1)	+ 20	– 9	+ 2
PH	(+ 14	– 4	+ 5)	+ 15	– 10	– 2
GG	(+ 13	+ 3	+ 1)	+ 17	– 10	– 7
Range				+ 1 to + 29	– 12 to + 9	– 11 to + 6
Average				+ 14.6*	– 3.4	– 1.3

* Differences between groups A and C significant at the 0.05 level (Sum of the Ranks Test).

TABLE 3
High, Low, and Normal Ranges from the Analysis of Group C Data

RANGE	SECTION 2 (AFFECTION-HOSTILITY SCALE)	3 (HOSTILITY-INHIBITION SCALE)	4 (MAGIC THINKING SCALE)
High	+ 21 or above	+ 6 or above	+ 1 or above
Normal	+ 10 through + 20	– 9 through + 5	– 2 through 0
Low	+ 9 or below	– 10 or below	– 3 or below

TABLE 4
Anticipated Scores for Each of the Four Psychodynamic Formulations (Tables 1 and 3 Combined)

PROCESS	SECTION 2 (AFFECTION-HOSTILITY SCALE)	SECTION 3 (HOSTILITY-INHIBITION SCALE)	SECTION 4 (MAGIC THINKING SCALE)
1	Low (+ 9 or below)	Normal (− 9 through + 5) or low (− 10 or below)	High (+ 1 or above)
2	Normal (+ 10 through + 20) or high (+ 21 or above)	High (+ 6 or above)	High (+ 1 or above)
3	Low (+ 9 or below)	High (+ 6 or above)	High (+ 1 or above)
4	Normal (+ 10 through + 20) or high (+ 21 or above)	Normal (− 9 through + 5) or low (− 10 or below)	High (+ 1 or above)

TABLE 5
Group A Patients Whose Scores Fell into One of the Four Psychodynamic Patterns

PARENT	SECTION 2	SECTION 3	SECTION 4	PROCESS
AR	+ 6	− 10	+ 2	1*
CK	− 3	+ 4	+ 1	1*
AF	+ 21	− 4	+ 4	4**
ES	+ 32	− 4	+ 3	4**
EM	+ 12	+ 1	+ 1	4**

*Classical hypothesis
**Author's hypothesis

superstitions.

Clinically, Mrs. K. was observed to be an angry woman whose hostility to her daughter could not be overtly expressed. Guilt over her daughter's illness was probably related to her unconscious hostility toward the child. This anger, she probably felt, was magically realized in her daughter's illness.

Case 2. E. S., the parent whose scores most confirmed the author's hypothesis, showed the highest maternal feelings of the 23 parents in the study. She also manifested normal inhibition of hostility and an abnormally high degree of magic thinking. She was a 41-year-old Catholic housewife whose eight-year-old son had an intra-atrial septal defect that had been known to the family for six years. During this period the mother was intermittently obsessed with the idea that the cardiac defect was caused by the baby's having fallen off the bed when she was lax in watching him one day when he was about one year old. Numerous reassurances by physicians that this could not have been the cause did not assuage her guilt. In addition, she felt that because she was a divorced Catholic, God was punishing her by making this child of her second, "sinful" marriage a defective one.

During her childhood she had enjoyed caring for her younger brothers and liked playing with dolls. As a teen-ager she frequently baby-sat for her nieces and nephews and asked to do so without pay. Prior to marriage she planned on having four to six children. At the time of the study she did indeed have six children, whose pictures she proudly displayed to the examiner. During interviews she would caress and soothe her child, and she smiled with pride when the examiner made a complimentary comment about the boy. Of the 33 questions in section 2A she scored 26 pluses, six zeros, and one minus. Her only negative response was that she had wanted a boy during her pregnancy and had only chosen a boy's name.

In section 2B some typical responses were: "They'll buy apples from the lady and go home and make pies and enjoy themselves." "The teen-age children are entertaining their friends, dancing is going on. Upstairs there's either a son or daughter in college studying." For one picture, she was the only one of the 23 parents who described the main female figure as being pregnant. Of the ten parents in group A, Mrs. S. achieved the highest score in this section.

She also scored higher than any other parent in section 2C and was third highest of the 23 parents in the total study.

Her score in section 3 revealed a normal degree of inhibition of hostility.

The score of +3 in section 4 indicates a greater than average amount of magic thinking. She was sure that God directly helps each doctor do his work; she prays frequently, believes in miracles, clairvoyance, and fortune-tellers, and has many superstitions.

This mother well demonstrates that parents with high scores on the Affection-Hostility scale can nevertheless exhibit the prolonged inappropriate guilt reaction, and she supports this author's thesis that predominantly loving, not hateful, feelings toward the child can be a significant factor in the psychodynamics of this guilt reaction.

The clinician should be aware of this possibility when working with parents who exhibit an inappropriate guilt reaction to their child's illness. To assume that only the Freudian formulation is correct may lead to a false interpretation of the situation and can serve to unnecessarily increase the parent's burden. Dredging up every shred of even normal hostility to explain the guilt reaction along classical lines may only increase the guilt and cause humiliation. Moreover, telling such guilty parents that the situation is not their fault is usually of little clinical value. Whether the guilt is due to unconscious hostility, the need to control the uncontrollable, and/or related to other mechanisms suggested by this study, it is an essential mechanism that can best be resolved through its understanding and analysis.

It has been the author's experience that those parents whose guilt arises from the need to gain control over the uncontrollable can be helped by encouraging participation in the child's treatment program. Feelings of impotency and helplessness are thereby reduced and the resultant need for magic power diminished. The author has had considerable experience with such recommendations for the parents of minimally brain-injured children(3) and has found that encouragement of parental participation in the child's education, drug management, and psychotherapy have been useful in alleviating this guilt.

It has been my intent in this study to demonstrate that it is *possible* to explain the inappropriate parental guilt reaction along lines that do not require a problem concerning hostility to be present. Although statistically proven validity and reliability are not claimed, and the number of patients in this study is small, the data strongly suggest that the psychodynamics of only two patients out of ten appear to fall into the classical pattern; the other eight follow other mechanisms, one of which relates to the excessive need to control the uncontrollable. If I have been successful in demonstrating that other mechanisms do exist and that one of these can be related to an exaggerated need to control, I will have accomplished my aim.

Discussion

This study presents an attempt at clinical confirmation of the author's thesis that guilt can be utilized as a defense mechanism in the handling of existential anxiety. The term "existential," as used here, refers *only* to its dictionary meaning, viz., that which pertains to existence. Existential anxieties arise in man by virtue of his existence in the world. They include anxieties over death and harm from one's fellow man as well as from the overpowering forces of nature. Man experiences these anxieties because of his relative impotence in controlling such forces. The term does *not* refer to its more specific use by the so-called "existentialists," although there is certainly some overlap between their and my use of the term.

Although most defense mechanisms and neurotic symptoms are considered devices to ward off, protect against, and handle anxiety, guilt is not usually included(1, 15). The use of guilt as an alleviator of existential anxiety has occasionally been described. Kierkegaard(8) described a type of guilt that he equated with responsibility. He felt that the concept of fate leaves man impotent to change his environment, but with guilt and its implication of personal responsibility, the individual commands a certain degree of control over his milieu.

May(13) refers to Kierkegaard, and in discussing this type of guilt he mentions chronically ill tuberculosis patients who became panicky when reassured by well-meaning friends that the disease was due to accidental infection by the tubercle bacillus.

> If the disease were an accident, how could they be certain it would not occur again and again? If, on the other hand, the patient feels that his own pattern of life was at fault . . . he feels more guilt, to be sure, but at the same time he sees more hopefully what conditions need to be corrected in order to overcome the disease.

Such references are rare, and in general psychoanalysts have not given this mechanism the attention it deserves.

The author holds that a fuller appreciation of this guilt mechanism lends greater understanding to a variety of psychological processes. In another work(5) I have elaborated upon its utilization in the formation of certain symptoms of involutional depression and schizophrenia and have demonstrated how this concept contributes to a better understanding of such phenomena as the origin of religious belief, original sin, scapegoatism, and prejudice. Elsewhere(4) I have shown how this concept of guilt lends greater understanding to the biblical Book of Job.

REFERENCES

1. Freud, A.: The Ego and the Mechanisms of Defense, trans. by C. M. Baines. London: Hogarth Press, 1937.
2. Freud, S.: Civilization and Its Discontents (1930). London: Hogarth Press, 1951.
3. Gardner, R. A.: Psychogenic Problems of Brain Injured Children and Their Parents, J. Amer. Acad. Child Psychiat. 7:471-491, 1968.

4. Gardner, R. A.: Guilt, Job and J. B., Medical Opinion and Review 5(2):146-155, 1969.
5. Gardner, R. A.: The Utilization of Guilt As a Defense Mechanism Against Anxiety, Psychoanal. Rev., in press.
6. Hathaway, S. R., and McKinley, T. C.: The Minnesota Multiphasic Personality Inventory, Revised. Minneapolis, Minn.: University of Minnesota, 1968.
7. Holsopple, J. Q., and Miale, F.: Sentence Completion—A Projective Method for the Study of Personality. Springfield, Ill.: Charles C Thomas, 1954.
8. Kierkegaard, S.: The Concept of Dread (1844), trans. by Wetter Louvie. Princeton, N. J.: Princeton University Press, 1944.
9. Levy, D. M.: Problems in Determining Maternal Attitudes Toward Newborn Infants, Psychiatry 15:273-286, 1952.
10. Levy, D. M.: Maternal Feelings Toward the Newborn, presented at the World Federation for Mental Health, Berlin, Germany, August 13, 1956 (unpublished).
11. Levy, D. M.: Behavioral Analysis. Springfield, Ill.: Charles C Thomas, 1958.
12. Levy, D. M.: "A Method of Analyzing Clinical Observations of Relational Behavior," in Hoch, P. H., and Zubin, J., eds.: Current Approaches to Psychoanalysis. New York: Grune & Stratton, 1960.
13. May, R.: The Meaning of Anxiety. New York: Ronald Press Co., 1950.
14. Murray, H. A.: Thematic Apperception Test. Cambridge, Mass.: Harvard University Press, 1943.
15. Noyes, A. P., and Kolb, L. C.: Modern Clinical Psychiatry. Philadelphia: W. B. Saunders Co., 1963.
16. Siegel, S. M.: The Relationship of Hostility to Authoritarianism, J. Abnorm. Soc. Psychol. 52:368-372, 1956.

Gifted and Talented

Counseling parents of gifted and talented children is uniquely challenging in that support systems for such parents are not readily apparent. It seems characteristically human to sympathize with another's sorrow, but to share in another's joy, it has been said, requires the attributes of an angel; few of us realize our angelic attributes.

Counselors can help parents of gifted and talented children realize that the child is a person with basic needs to develop emotionally, socially, physically as well as intellectually.

Parents can realize and accept their feelings of conflict or inadequacy. Then they will be able to share in the identification and development of the special abilities possessed by their child. As in all areas of educating exceptional children, parents are the first and most important teachers.

PARENT PERSPECTIVE

Anonymous

A MOTHER AND FATHER OF A GIFTED CHILD FIND THE HELPING PROFESSIONS HELPLESS

Somewhere, somehow, someone must have solved a problem like this before. Four of our six children are gifted.

You would think with all the gifted children around, plenty of answers would exist for any little old problem they might have. Instead we seem to be up against a reinforced stone wall, no matter what direction we turn.

Our priest tells us to pray and that time is a great healer. The physician—their pediatrician, says all the children, including the one we are now concerned about are healthy, so what have we to complain about?

The psychologist went over the boy with a fine tooth comb. He says he used all the tools at his command—projective techniques, objective tests, subjective counseling, individual tests and group achievement tests. Everything came out beautifully. The child tests out gifted intellectually, and is highly creative. All the achievement test scores in reading, arithmetic, spelling and social studies are more than two years above the boy's grade placement. He will soon be ten and is going into the fifth grade. None of the Mental Health Inventory scores revealed anything which needed a second look. All of them were well above average, both socially and emotionally.

The school principal we were looking to as our last resort, but with the greatest hope. He has been, to our great disappointment, the least helpful. His response to our plight was less than worthless. He did not think we deserved any sympathy at all, and as for ideas we drew a blank with him there, as well. After we told him our story, all he had to say was he wished problems like ours, were the only ones he had.

How do you like that for understanding and responsiveness? Coming from a gifted person, who is a professional Educator, and also the parent of gifted children, his answer sure wasn't worth much.

Of course it is comforting to be told that if the child does not seem to be full of acute problems, as we fear, he really isn't. That regardless of what seems to be happening to him, what matters is not what is actually happening, so much, as the fact that as far as he is concerned, these problems are not bugging him as much as they are bothering his parents.

Here is what is on our minds. We instinctively feel he is suffering some kind of miseries, otherwise he would never be biting his nails to the bone. Yes maybe he will outgrow this problem. Furthermore, if all were completely well with him—would he still be bedwetting, when he is almost ten years of age?

Parent Perspective: A Mother and Father of a Gifted Child Find the Helping Professions Helpless, (Anonymous), *The Gifted Child Quarterly,* Vol. 18, No. 2, Summer 1974, © The National Association for Gifted Children.

We think we know what the trouble is. It all had to do with his brother who is thirteen. In every way this child is neater . . . to use the popular term . . . besides he really is neater in appearance and all his habits. He is better organized, and tries more to please other children and adults. Younger brother is less well coordinated, his hair never looks as if it has been combed, even immediately after he puts the comb down. His clothes always manage to hang lopsidedly on him, and look as if he slept in them, though they may be brand new. To top all this big brother's talents are indeed of a higher order both intellectually and artistically, where we are told the younger boy—the one with the problems—also has good talent. However how can he follow an act—like the one which precedes him—that of his older and better brother?

Our questions really are two. First has anyone ever heard of a child whose test scores showed him doing well – emotionally, when facts seemed to contradict test evidence? Secondly what kinds of things can parents do to help a younger child who though gifted follows on the heels of an older child who is even more gifted and talented, in the very same areas as that of the younger brother?

Any and all help will be ever so appreciated . . . We are in any case so happy to learn organizations exist, which try to help gifted children.

The above facts reached the Editor in the form of a letter. It was further unique in that it was signed by both parents. Most of our mail when from parents either comes from the mother or father.

Detecting Creativity: Some Practical Approaches

Lewis E. Walkup

Is it possible to tell whether a person is creative before we have seen him in action, grappling with a concrete problem? Can we do this during an interview? . . .

At first glance, anyone who is familiar with the literature on creativity might think that these questions have been pretty thoroughly answered, or at least that answers were being found. Certainly the psychologist can call on a wide selection of scientific tests that have been devised to measure various aspects of creativity. No one claims that these instruments are perfect, but they are always being refined, and new ones invented.

Very good; but I am not a psychologist. Rather, I am an applied scientist who has just finished a career in technical research where the exercise of creativity is just as important to my team of men as the forward pass is to a football team. The question of how to tell a creative person has therefore been a very important one in my working life, and I have had to answer it without the resources of the psychological laboratory.

How many businesses, industries, or research institutes have a hiring process sophisticated enough to include a battery of creativity tests? How many would be equipped to interpret the results if they did have the tests? And if they measured a person's general creative ability, how could his prospective employers know whether that ability would express itself in the specific ways they needed? It is rather ironic that the pure scientist, whose interest in creativity is powerful but not urgent, should have plenty of tests for it, while the applied scientist whose economic lifeblood is creativity in his associates has to fall back on common sense.

Still, if we are looking for creativity in others, we ought to be willing to use a little ourselves. In my work I have had to create ways to recognize creativity, to teach and cultivate it, and to establish a climate where it would thrive, all on a very practical level. The following are some suggestions for practical tests of creativity which can be used in the hiring process. Many more could be worked out, and I can recom-

---

*Readers' comments concerning ways to detect creativity without the assistance of scientific testing tools are invited.

mend this as a very interesting creative challenge for management.

As has been reported elsewhere, one of the best ways to ascertain the creativeness of an individual is simply to ask him if he is creative. Most people have a pretty good estimate of their own creative ability. Furthermore, most men are quite honest about this point, especially if they realize that it will do them no good to get a job under false pretenses which will surely be found out later. (Of course, the person being interviewed may not use your terms when he thinks about himself, and you may have to explain what you mean by "creativity," or give examples of the kind of thinking you are after.)

But this test should not be relied on completely, because it might throw out valuable people who have not recognized their own creative potential. For this reason one must go further in the search for signs of actual or latent creativity.

One very simple and practical test for creative ability is to find out how many patents the individual has, or how many articles he has written that contributed uniquely to an art. Simple reviews or reports of specific experiments should not be counted in such an evaluation.

Even if he has no concrete results to show yet, the applicant may be of a creative habit of mind. It is a challenge to the interviewer to find out how the person thinks, and what his approach to a problem is likely to be. One method is to ask him to recall some of the experiments he has performed, either in training or in his professional work, that impressed him as being particularly beautiful in some way. If he rises to this challenge he may reveal a love of intellectual activity and a preference for problems over rote learning. Remember that creative persons enjoy talking about the parts of a subject they *do not* know, while others prefer to talk about what they *do* know.

While you are trying to get to know the subject's thinking processes, you might attempt to learn how much he *visualizes* when he thinks about a problem. Creative individuals, at least in the fields of science and technology, apparently almost always have the gift of mentally reproducing, and using in their thinking processes, visual images and other sensory equivalents of the real phenomena they are working on. Such sensory equivalents can be enormously complex and sophisticated, and sometimes appear to have almost the intensity of hallucinations. This power may be a valid criterion of creative ability. (The subject has been developed in greater detail in *Perceptual and Motor Skills*, 1965, *21*, 35-41 and the *Journal of Creative Behavior*, 1969, *3*, 122-127.)

What are you really after, however, is a feeling for the subject's basic mental orientation. Individual differences may not be a popular subject at present, but people do differ widely in the sorts of activities they *like* to perform and consider proper and interesting uses of their time and effort. We have all met individuals who are strongly oriented toward physical activity. They will work all day at physical labor, come home and play softball until dark, grab a bite to eat, and then go bowling. For them, physical activity is the essence of life. Others feel the same way about emotional activity. However, potentially creative people are likely to have a strong intellectual orientation.

The word "intellectual" has been so much used and misused recently that I had better define my own use. What is meant here by intellectual activity is a thought process in which the thinker adds something unique and personal to the material that is being processed by the brain. This kind of thinking is quite different from the simple storage and retrieval of information which, coupled with the expression of emotional likes and dislikes, makes up most of what the average person does with his mind. For example, if a subject is asked to discuss some current issue, he is very likely to produce a warmed-over version of what was said in last week's *Time* magazine. This is not intellectual activity under our definition. On the other hand, if the subject presents some new and unique way of looking at the issue, intellectual activity is taking place.

You can quickly tell whether the subject enjoys this sort of thinking. The point is important; the presence *and liking* of intellectual activity in our sense may not be proof that the person is creative, but he must have this attribute to be very productive in creating. The reason is simple: if his creativity is to be more than an occasional accident, he will have to do an enormous amount of highly complex thinking, and he simply will not do it unless he actually enjoys it. Of course, this principle is not unique to creativity — no one is likely to develop proficiency in any activity, from basketball to playing the violin, unless he really likes it.

This testing approach has the practical advantage that it is easy to apply in an ordinary conversation on almost any topic. Sometimes the results can be very striking. I remember pressing one candidate to talk about a problem of current interest, only to find that he kept quoting authorities on the subject and simply would not, or could not, tell what he himself thought, even though the topic did not require the insights of experts to be discussed intelligently. Clearly, there is a vast difference between the kind of thinking we are looking for, and the kind which can earn high IQ scores without creativity. The interview procedure can bring out this difference very clearly.

A variation of this sort of interview-testing is useful for finding out whether the applicant is creative in his particular field of work. It consists of presenting him with a relatively simple problem in his branch of technology but one which he is not likely to have met specifically or to have read about in the past; the interviewer can tell when the problem is new to a subject just by his reactions to it. (Incidentally, it is a very good exercise in creativity for the interviewer to find new problems for this purpose.) The subject should understand that you are not looking for a specific "right answer" to your question, but possible approaches which might be used to solve it.

A good illustration of this type of problem is one which has often been used on physics graduates. The subject is asked how he would go about measuring the velocity of a rifle projectile over the first, say, 15 feet of its travel out the the muzzle of a gun, to an accuracy of 0.1 per cent. Any graduate in physics is familiar with a number of physical phenomena that could be used to put together a device for making this measurement; not all, by any means, can use what they know when the information has to be applied in an unfamiliar context.

It is interesting to observe how different types of people think aloud about this problem. Surprisingly, many simply refuse to tackle the question at all. When pressed, they end up saying that if they were faced with this problem in real life, their only course would be to search the literature and find out how it was solved in the past. Their minds freeze on this as the only possible course of action, and they are unable even to begin thinking of others.

Other applicants make a few feeble attempts such as suggesting the use of a stop watch, presumably because this is the only way they have seen velocities measured. Some remember doing an experiment in high school or college in which they used a ballistic pendulum to measure the velocity of projectiles, but most of them are vague about how this approach worked and cannot arrive at any idea about the possible accuracy of the method. And yet all of them are reasonably familiar with means that could be used — decade counters, for instance, that work so rapidly that they could count thousands of pulses during the flight of the projectile over 15 feet. They also know — or would know if they were reminded of it — that the projectile could be used to make or break electrical connections at two points along the range.

When given this sort of problem, the creative subject always starts out venturing some kind of solution, probably several, even though many of them are ridiculous. As he progresses in his thinking his ideas become less ridiculous, and such applicants usually come up with four or five ideas that are reasonably practical, even though the details have not been worked out. Characteristically, such people leave the interview promising to think further about the problem and to invent more solutions.

This problem-setting technique brings out a well-known characteristic of creative people: they are intellectually adventurous, and willing to attempt solutions even though the first attempts are far from the mark. Thus they produce a variety of possible answers before narrowing them down to the most promising. As Alex Osborn put it:

> It is almost axiomatic that quantity breeds quality in ideation. Logic and mathematics are on the side of the truth that the more ideas we produce, the more likely we are to think up some that are good. Likewise it is true that the best ideas seldom come first.[1]

The non-creative person is unable to use this principle that "quantity breeds quality." He may be as intelligent as the creative person according to formal tests, but he becomes hypnotized by the first idea he has and can see no farther;

---

[1] *Applied Imagination*, 3rd rev. ed. (Scribners, 1963), p. 131.

or he may be so concerned with being "right" that he will not take the risks which the creative person enjoys.

There is an old saying that "it takes a thief to catch a thief." In one more version of the interview test, we can use a person we already know to be creative to recognize creativity in our subject. In planning such an interview, one instructs the known-creative person to talk with the subject about his own problems, his embryonic inventions, his aspirations, and especially about the road blocks that are keeping him from solving some interesting problems. In such interviews, the new man is given plenty of time to advance his own ideas, to ask questions, and to think out loud on his own. If you can't pry the two men apart after 30 minutes, you can be pretty sure that you have found another creative person. But if the conversation dies out after a few minutes and your known-creative interviewer returns the subject to you before his time is up, you may be pretty sure that the new man is not very creative, no matter what other strong points he may have. This is one of the most reliable ways to detect latent creativity.

It must be pointed out that in such interviews it is not knowledge of the field that makes for rapport between the two people; it is the *kind* of thinking they do. The man under examination need not necessarily know very much about the interviewer's field, although there must be some common areas of technology between them, as there certainly would be if the new man were an applicant for a job in the interviewer's area. Of course, if this technique of interviewing were to be applied to more general cases, interviewers would have to be chosen for some overlapping of knowledge and experience with the subject's.

As I have already said, these methods were developed in practical situations to fill very practical needs, and as such they do work. They are not intended as bases for quantitative tests, though numerical scales could probably be used for convenience in rating applicants on any of the factors. Many more tests of this kind are possible; doubtless any reader of this *Journal* who has coped with the problem of recognizing potential creativity in job applicants has his own favorite methods. It would be interesting to hear from some of these people.

Parents as Identifiers of Giftedness, Ignored But Accurate

Thomas E. Ciha, Ruth Harris, Charlotte Hoffman
Rockford, Illinois, Public Schools
Meredith W. Potter, Associate Professor of Mathematics,
Rockford College

ABSTRACT

A stratified sample of 465 kindergartners enrolled in Rockford Public Schools, were administered the Slossen Intelligence Test and two performance subtests of the Wechsler Intelligence Scale for Children. Children who scored 132 and above on the SIT were identified as gifted for purposes of the study. The WISC performance scores were scaled and an I.Q. equivalency assigned according to the normed technique developed by Massey. Students who were not identified as gifted on the SIT but who achieved a WISC equivalence score of 120 or above were called "hidden potential." Parents were administered a questionnaire asking them if their child was gifted according to stated criteria. Teachers were asked to identify gifted students in their classrooms. The parents nominated a total of 276 (39 gifted, 36 hidden potentials, and 201 non-gifted by either criterion). They correctly nominated 39 of the total 58 for an effective of nomination of 76%. The kindergarten teachers nominated a total of 54 students (13 gifted, 7 hidden potentials, and 34 non-gifted). They had an effectiveness of nomination of 22%. Effectiveness within geographical and social and economic stratifications is discussed. This study indicates that at the kindergarten level, parents are more able than teachers to assess their children's abilities. However, the commonly-held belief that parents tend to over-estimate their own child's ability cannot be denied by this study.

In Rockford we stress the following approaches:

1. *Acceleration* wherein the bright child is allowed to progress through required subject at his own pace;
2. *Enrichment programs* that utilize special activities to allow children who have completed routine assignments to work with a variety of projects that delve further into topics being covered in the classroom, and
3. *Differential education* for gifted, based on the concept that the bright child, who is already competent in the skills being taught, should be provided with challenging activities that he would not ordinarily be exposed to in the traditional school program.

If we can assume parent-identification has validity, and so begin to incorporate activities to spark the intellect of our bright youngsters, offering alternatives and tolerating behaviors that allow and encourage academic precocity and 'creative positive' abilities, even through their performance during the kindergarten years, gifted youngsters will confirm this identification of exceptional intellectual potential. Teachers *and* parents, however, must be trained not only in what behaviors to observe, but in what behaviors to encourage. Working together, administrators, curriculum specialists, teachers, and the school psychologist can effect the changes needed to provide challenging programs

Parents as Indentifiers of Giftedness, Ignored but Accurate, Thomas E. Ciha, Ruth Harris, Charlotte Hoffman, and Meredith W. Potter, *The Gifted Child Quarterly,* Vol. 18, No. 3, 1974, © The National Association for Gifted Children.

for bright and highly gifted youngsters.

The researchers conclude that parents can be utilized as an immediate gross screening device to identify those children who might benefit from immediate gifted programming.

IMPLICATIONS

Perhaps the most significant aspect of this study is obvious that it is often overlooked: Parents do know about their own children. Teachers should listen to parents, assess differences in children, and program accordingly. Teachers do not absorb the techniques of individualized teaching, cross-grade grouping, team teaching, student-teacher decision-making, and interest-center grouping (to mention just a few). Class room experience must be augmented by a program of rigorous inservice teacher training.

The Illinois program does not support special teachers for gifted youngsters, but concentrates instead on creating teacher awareness of special abilities and provides inservice training to assist teachers in adapting instructional programs to meet the needs these differences create. Kindergarten teachers, traditionally charged with implementing a general curriculum and with supplying remedial measures when so indicated, may feel both inadequate and apprehensive when confronted with a child who enters school with skills far beyond those planned for the kindergarten class. The building principal and the school psychologist can schedule special sessions with the kindergarten teacher to help provide appropriate programming according to indicated needs. The results of this study would evaluate that these sessions together with parent conferences, would help to create an awareness of the vast differences in four and five year olds and would open the way for several programming alternative.

EFFECTIVENESS OF PARENT IDENTIFICATION OF GIFTED CHILDREN AT THE KINDERGARTEN LEVEL

It is important to discover the potentially academically talented student early if that talent is to be maximized. Unfortunately, the accepted and valid means of identification of intellectual giftedness has traditionally been general academic performance and individual psychological evaluation. The academic performance criterion usually precludes early intervention, and intensive individual psychological evaluation is prohibitive economically. This causes many school districts to utilize less accepted and perhaps less valid criteria such as standarized test scores and teacher nomination. Neither of these methods can be accomplished at the onset of the kindergarten year. Additionally, standardized tests repeatedly miss the under-achieving child, the non-reader, and the child evaluated on a "bad day."

Although widely used, teacher nomination has been shown by a number of research studies to exclude more than half of the qualified children from gifted programs. In a study by Pegnato and Birch in 1959 teachers identified fewer than 50 percent of gifted seventh thru ninth graders as measured by an IQ of 136 on the Stanford-Binet. Cornish in 1968 investigated teacher identification of a sample of sixth graders and found teachers correctly identified only 31%.

Acting upon the hypothesis that the percentage decreased continually into the lower grades, Jacobs conducted a study in 1972 with 12 kindergarten teachers. He found that these teachers nominated only 4.3% of the children identified as fifted by his study criterion, a full scale WPPSI IQ of 125 and above. In marked contrast, however, this same study revealed that 61% of the children identified as gifted had been so nominated by their parents.

The present study investigated whether parents of kindergarten children were more effective identifiers of giftedness than the teachers, and whether parents might be used as a gross screening device to identify the very young gifted child at the beginning of his schooling.

METHOD

Of the 3027 kindergarten children in Rockford Public Schools a stratified sample of 465 (approximately 15%) was selected. The population of Rockford is divided by natural geographic boundaries into four distinct quadrants. The northeast quadrant is predominately white upward mobile and socio-economically as well as educationally advantaged. The southeast quadrant is an older stable residential area in addition to being partially industrialized. There is a large middle class white population, a Swedish community as well as a factory worker transient white low socio-economic group. The northwest quadrant is cross-cultural consisting of the city's most prestigious families, a young white apartment dwelling population, and a middle class black population. Several of the schools in this quadrant are in compliance with the state guidelines for integration. Several schools in this quadrant, however, have high minority populations and the southwest quadrant has high minority enrollment with children in this quadrant culturally disadvantaged. The stratified sample selected not only represented the four geographic quadrants in their respective numerical ratios but additionally reflected minority, socio-economic, and Title I funded school children. Once these criteria had been met, whole kindergarten classes were isolated to facilitate the testing procedure and to insure that children attending morning versus afternoon classes, children that walked and children who were bussed were chosen in proper proportions. Only those classes were deemed eligible in which no student had been previously exposed to the study instruments. Finally 30 schools comprising 14 kindergarten classrooms were selected by a RANDU random number generator on the IBM 1130 computer.

Rockford College undergraduate students were trained to administer the Slosson Intelligence Test (SIT) and two subtests of the Weschsler Intelligence Scale for Children (WISC), picture arrangement and block design. Each kindergarten child in the sample was administered the individual psychoeducational battery of the SIT and WISC subtests. Fifty-eight children were located who had an SIT score of 132 or above. These 58 children were considered to be gifted for the purpose of this study. Thirty-six additional children were isolated whose WISC scaled scores exceeded 120 but who SIT scores fell below 132. The WISC performance scores were scaled and an IQ equivalency assigned according to the normed technique developed by Massey.[1] These children were deemed "hidden gifted" (HP) for purposes of this study.

A questionnaire, listing some generally accepted characteristics of intellectually gifted children, was sent home by the individual schools to the parents of each child in the sample.[2] The parents were asked to indicate whether or not they believed their child to be gifted. Where necessary, help in reading the form was provided to the parents by school personnel. The 14 teachers of the selected classes were asked to nominate those children in their classes who might be intellectually gifted.[3] Neither parents nor teachers had access to the test data. The parents of 276 children thought their child might be gifted. This group of 276 consisted of 237 non-gifted children (SIT IQ: range=74-131; M=107.3). Of these children 36 had WISC subtest scores that qualified them as HPs. The teachers nominated a total of 54 students who might be gifted. This group of 54 consisted of 41 average ability children (SIT IT: range=88-131; M=112.4) and 13 children with SIQ 132 and above. Of the 41 children misidentified by their teachers 7 qualified as HPs.

---

[1]Massey, James O. Supplementary WISC TEST PROFILE, Palo Alto, Calif. Consulting Psychologist Press, Inc. 1968.
[2]Questionnaire is available from authors upon request.
[3]Questionnaire is available from authors upon request.

RESULTS

The parents nominated a total of 276 (39 gifted, 36 HPs, and 201 non-gifted by either criterion) children as possibly gifted. They correctly nominated 39 of the total 58 for an effective of nomination of 67%. The kindergarten teachers nominated a total of 54 students (13 gifted, 7 HPs, and 34 non-gifted). They had an effectiveness of nomination of 22%. Of the 41 students of average ability identified as possibly gifted by their teachers, only 7 were found to be HPs, and of these 7, only 3 had not previously been isolated by their parents. Of additional interest is an analysis of the identification by quadrants. In the upper-middle class white NE quadrant the teachers identified as gifted only 1 of the 18 qualified students for an effectiveness of nomination of 5.5%. Parents nominated 11 of the 18 qualified students for a 61% effectiveness. In the lower middle-class white SE quadrant teachers missed 19 of the 24 qualifying students for an effectiveness of 21%, whereas parents correctly identified 18 of the 24 children for a 75% effectiveness of nomination. Only in the cross-cultural, well integrated NW quadrant did the teachers and parents each nominate about half of the gifted students. In the high minority SW quadrant where 4 children were identified as gifted, the parents nominated all 4 children whereas the teachers picked only 2 of them.

DISCUSSION

In as much as most studies on gifted programming stess the need for early implementation, an effective means of identifying potentially academically gifted kindergartners is vitally important. Although a majority of studies report that teacher nomination is frequently utilized as an economy measure, this study reaffirms earlier reports that correct identification by teachers at the kindergarten level is below 25%. This study indicated that at the kindergarten level parents are more able than teachers to assess their children's abilities. However, the commonly-held belief that parents tend to over-estimate their own child's ability cannot be denied by this study. Nevertheless, parents can be utilized as an immediate gross screening device to identify those children who might best benefit from immediate gifted programming. The low correlation (r=.37) between the performance subtests of the WISC and the SIT would tend to affirm that the two tests are in fact measuring different attributes. The fact that parents nominated 36 of the 53 children identified as HPs would suggest that much more thorough investigation of the non-verbal five-year-old is needed, and that until better inexpensive identification instruments are developed parental opinion of a child's academic potential is a source of useful information and a more effective means of screening at the kindergarten level than teacher nomination.

REFERENCES

Cornish, R. L. "Parents; teachers', and pupils' perception of the gifted child's ability, *"Gifted Child Quarterly,* 1968, 12 14-17.

Pegnato, C., and Birch, J. W., "Locating gifted children in junior high schools: a comparison of methods." *Exceptional Children,* 1959, 25, 300-304.

Jacobs, Jon, "Effectiveness of Teacher and Parent Identification of Gifted Children as a Function of School Level, *"Psychology in the Schools,* 1971, 8, 140-142.

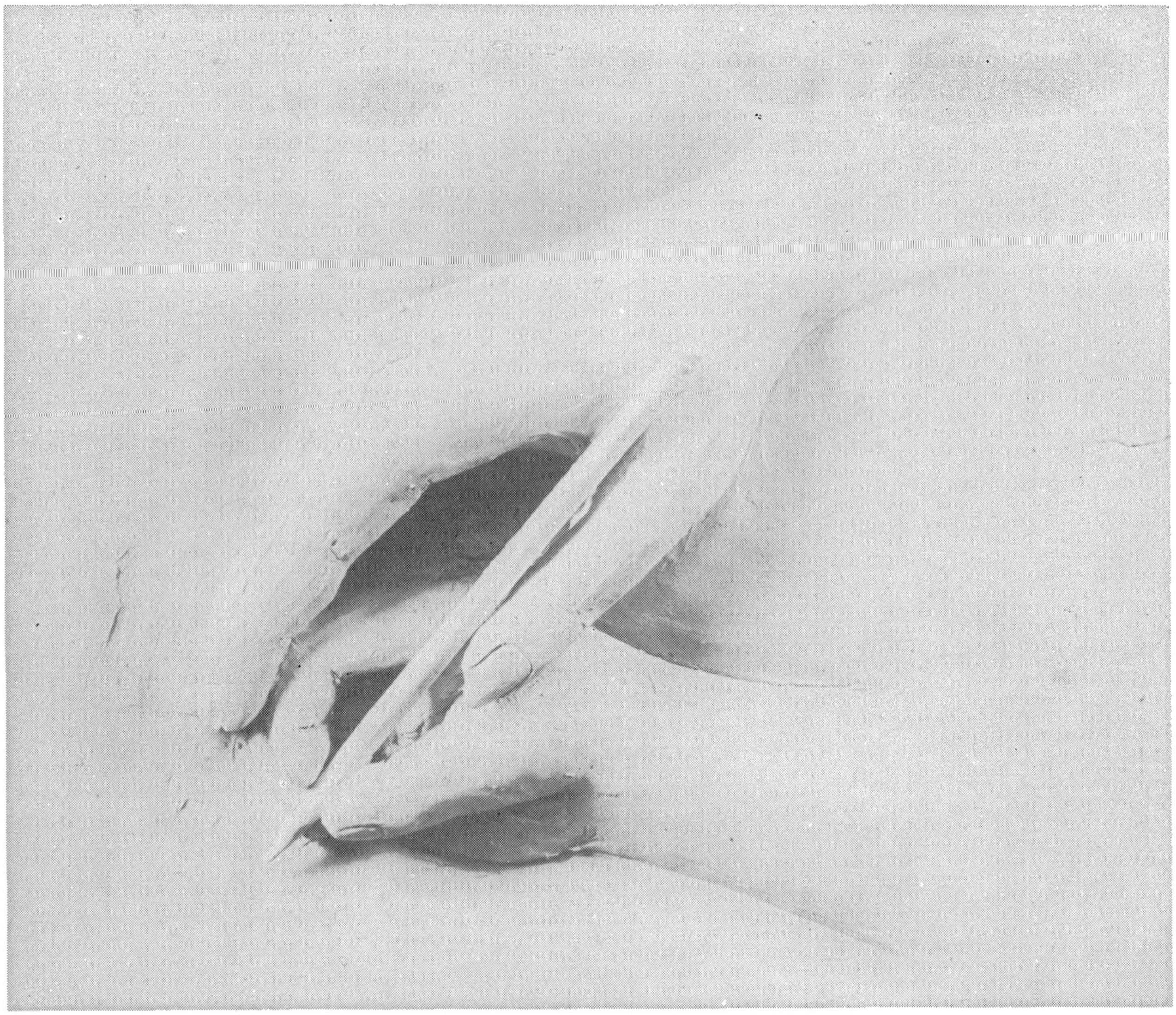

STAFF

Publisher	John Quirk
Editor	Dona Chiappe
Editorial Ass't.	Carol Carr
Permissions Editor	Audrey Weber
Director of Production	Richard Pawlikowski
Director of Design	Donald Burns
Customer Service	Cindy Finocchio
Sales Service	Diane Hubbard
Administration	Linda Calano

Cover Design Donald Burns
Cover Photo Richard Pawlikowski

Appendix: Agencies and Services for Exceptional Children

Alexander Graham Bell Association for the Deaf, Inc.
Volta Bureau for the Deaf
3417 Volta Place, NW
Washington, D.C. 20007

American Academy of Pediatrics
1801 Hinman Avenue
Evanston, Illinois 60204

American Association for Gifted Children
15 Gramercy Park
New York, N.Y. 10003

American Association on Mental Deficiency
5201 Connecticut Avenue, NW
Washington, D.C. 20015

American Association of Psychiatric Clinics for Children
250 West 57th Street
New York, N.Y.

American Bar Association
Commission on the Mentally Disabled
1800 M Street, NW
Washington, D.C. 20036

American Foundation for the Blind
15 W. 16th Street
New York, N.Y. 10011

American Medical Association
535 N. Dearborn Street
Chicago, Illinois 60610

American Speech and Hearing Association
9030 Old Georgetown Road
Washington, D.C. 20014

Association for the Aid of Crippled Children
345 E. 46th Street
New York, N.Y. 10017

Association for Children with Learning Disabilities
2200 Brownsville Road
Pittsburgh, Pennsylvania 15210

Association for Education of the Visually Handicapped
1604 Spruce Street
Philadelphia, Pennsylvania 19103

Association for the Help of Retarded Children
200 Park Avenue, South
New York, N.Y.

Association for the Visually Handicapped
1839 Frankfort Avenue
Louisville, Kentucky 40206

Center on Human Policy
Division of Special Education and Rehabilitation
Syracuse University
Syracuse, New York 13210

Child Fund
275 Windsor Street
Hartford, Connecticut 06120

Children's Defense Fund
1520 New Hampshire Avenue NW
Washington, D.C. 20036

Closer Look
National Information Center for the Handicapped
1201 Sixteenth Street NW
Washington, D.C. 20036

Clifford W. Beers Guidance Clinic
432 Temple Street
New Haven, Connecticut 06510

Child Study Center
Yale University
333 Cedar Street
New Haven, Connecticut 06520

Child Welfare League of America, Inc.
44 East 23rd Street
New York, N.Y. 10010

Children's Bureau
United States Department of Health, Education and Welfare
Washington, D.C.

Council for Exceptional Children
1411 Jefferson Davis Highway
Arlington, Virginia 22202

Epilepsy Foundation of America
1828 "L" Street NW
Washington, D.C. 20036

Gifted Child Society, Inc.
59 Glen Gray Road
Oakland, New Jersey 07436

Institute for the Study of Mental Retardation and Related Disabilities
130 South First
University of Michigan
Ann Arbor, Michigan 48108

International Association for the Scientific Study of Mental Deficiency
Ellen Horn, AAMD
5201 Connecticut Avenue NW
Washington, D.C. 20015

International League of Societies for the Mentally Handicapped
Rue Forestiere 12
Brussels, Belgium

Joseph P. Kennedy, Jr. Foundation
1701 K Street NW
Washington, D.C. 20006

League for Emotionally Disturbed Children
171 Madison Avenue
New York, N.Y.

Muscular Dystrophy Associations of America
1790 Broadway
New York, N.Y. 10019

National Aid to the Visually Handicapped
3201 Balboa Street
San Francisco, California 94121

National Association of Coordinators of State Programs for the Mentally Retarded
2001 Jefferson Davis Highway
Arlington, Virginai 22202

National Association of Hearing and Speech Agencies
919 18th Street NW
Washington, D.C. 20006

National Association for Creative Children and Adults
8080 Springvalley Drive
Cincinnati, Ohio 45236
(Mrs. Ann F. Isaacs, Executive Director)

National Association for Retarded Children
420 Lexington Avenue
New York, N.Y.

National Association for Retarded Citizens
2709 Avenue E East
Arlington, Texas 76010

National Children's Rehabilitation Center
P.O. Box 1260
Leesburg, Virginia

National Association for the Visually Handicapped
3201 Balboa Street
San Francisco, California 94121

National Association of the Deaf
814 Thayer Avenue
Silver Spring, Maryland 20910

National Cystic Fibrosis Foundation
3379 Peachtree Road NE
Atlanta, Georgia 30326

National Easter Seal Society for Crippled Children and Adults
2023 W. Ogden Avenue
Chicago, Illinois 60612

National Federation of the Blind
218 Randolph Hotel
Des Moines, Iowa 50309

National Paraplegia Foundation
333 N. Michigan Avenue
Chicago, Illinois 60601

National Society for Autistic Children
621 Central Avenue
Albany, N.Y. 12206

National Society for Prevention of Blindness, Inc.
79 Madison Avenue
New York, N.Y. 10016

Orton Society, Inc.
8415 Bellona Lane
Baltimore, Maryland 21204

President's Committee on Mental Retardation
Regional Office Building #3
7th and D Streets SW
Room 2614
Washington, D.C. 20201

United Cerebral Palsy Associations
66 E 34th Street
New York, N.Y. 10016

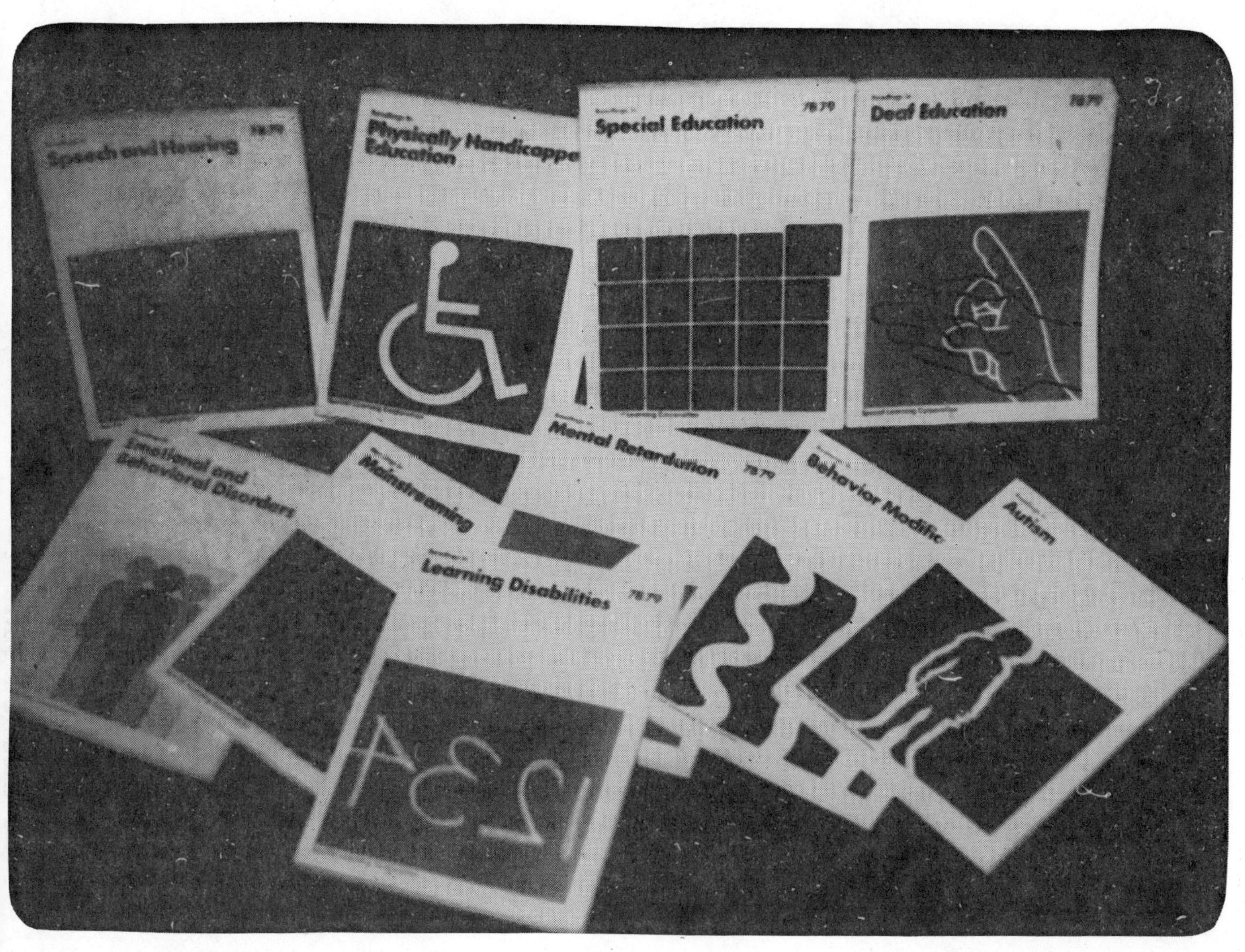

SPECIAL LEARNING CORPORATION
42 Boston Post Rd.
Guilford, Conn. 06437

SPECIAL LEARNING CORPORATION

COMMENTS PLEASE:

Does this book fit your course of study?

Why? (Why not?)

Is this book useable for other courses of study? Please list.

What other areas would you like us to publish in using this format?

What type of exceptional child are you interested in learning more about?

Would you use this as a basic text?

How many students are enrolled in these course areas?

_____ Special Education _____ Mental Retardation _____ Psychology _____ Emotional Disorders
_____ Exceptional Children _____ Learning Disabilities Other _____

Do you want to be sent a copy of our elementary student materials catalog?

Do you want a copy of our college catalog?

Would you like a copy of our next edition? ☐ yes ☐ no

Are you a ☐ student or an ☐ instructor?

Your name _____ school _____

Term used _____ Date _____

address _____

city _____ state _____ zip _____

telephone number _____

C/P

CUT HERE ● SEAL AND MAIL